THE **MONEY** ADVISER

THE MONEY ADVISER

THE CANADIAN GUIDE TO
SUCCESSFUL FINANCIAL PLANNING

BRUCE COHEN

WITH ALYSSA DIAMOND

Published in 1999 by
Stoddart Publishing Co. Limited
34 Lesmill Road
Toronto, Canada
M3B 2T6
Tel. (416) 445-3333
Fax. (416) 445-5967

This special edition, produced for *Reader's Digest*, contains revisions
made by the author for the publisher's second revised paperback edition,
published in Canada in 1999.

ISBN 0-7737-3187-3

Jacket design: Bill Douglas @ The Bang

Printed and bound in Canada

Table 29.1, "Value-Averaging Spreadsheet," is reprinted by
permission of International Publishing Corp., Chicago.

Contents

Preface

ON JUNE 7, 1988, THE FINANCIAL POST printed my first personal finance column and I began getting paid to write about what had been a hobby for years. As a *Post* staffer, I earned a decent living, was able to help a lot of people, and — most importantly — got access to many of the country's top financial experts. I learned something new every day. In early 1997 I became Senior Writer for Dynamic Mutual Funds, a large investment company, where I continued to learn from top-notch financial advisers and money managers.

Now, I'm semi-retired, working on my own as I see fit and enjoying the benefits of all the financial planning I've done for myself.

This book is a compilation of a lot of the things knowledgeable people have taught me — and a few I've figured out myself. It makes no attempt to set out three, five or ten easy steps that will make you rich. I don't believe that's possible. Instead, I just explain how financial stuff works so you can set your own strategies, recognize your own opportunities and make your own decisions. In personal finance, there are no one-size-fits-all solutions once you go beyond the basics. There is, however, a set of concepts that underlie the whole shebang.

Virtually all financial books have a high MEGO factor. That stands for "My Eyes Glaze Over." My challenge was to be accurate and reasonably detailed yet still readable. Each chapter was "test-driven" by at least two experts and at least two "normal" people.

Special thanks go to Christopher Gobeil, who checked the entire manuscript for accuracy. Chris is a Montreal-based Registered Financial Planner and Chartered Accountant with experience in both Quebec and the common law provinces. Gerry Rosenberg, a Toronto financial planner, also waded through the whole draft.

Other experts who read specific chapters include Wendy Hannam, Robert Lo Presti, David Jarvis, Bob Barney, Jim Rogers, Ian Markham and Steven Kelman. Many, many others provided information.

Thanks also go to *The Financial Post*, which gave me use of its library and permission to reprint articles.

Alyssa Diamond helped with research and editing. She also provided much-needed counsel and encouragement when the going got tough.

Utmost gratitude goes to Mary-Anne Mackett, who also slogged through the whole manuscript and its revisions. Mary-Anne provided lawyerly insights and was a key non-financial test driver for the financial explanations. She believed in the project and made sure I did too.

Please appreciate that this is a general reference for the general public. You must use your own judgement and/or obtain professional advice to determine if the information is appropriate for your own situation.

Legal and technical details reflect the legislative and financial environments as of mid-1998. Tax laws and regulations change often. I suggest confirming significant details with a professional adviser or Revenue Canada.

The Money Adviser was first published in 1994. This is my fourth revision. Before I wrote this book, I did not fully appreciate the dynamic nature of the financial services industry. I guarantee that by the time you have read this there will be many new products and services available. While I've tried to keep the book current, the main thrust is to explain basic concepts that seldom change. Understand that all new products and services are based on those ideas. If you understand the basics, you should be able to assess new developments as they occur.

This edition includes, for the first time, reference to a few Internet sites. The Net is an amazing, useful source of information. I have added only a few sites. They are not necessarily the best-known sites, but they are particularly useful. I did not try to provide a full list of addresses because there is a site for almost every financial company, association and government agency around. To find information on other organizations, simply key the name into a search engine such as Alta Vista or Yahoo, both of which have Canadian sites.

This book has just one purpose: to give you more understanding and confidence as a saver, investor and consumer. I hope you find it readable and useful.

Bruce Cohen
Toronto

Financial Planning: Why Bother?

MOST PEOPLE DO LITTLE OR NO FINANCIAL planning. They don't budget. They probably have life insurance, but don't really know if it's enough or too much. They may think about investing, but don't really set aside the money. If they have RRSPs at all, they tend to view the plans mainly as tax breaks. And credit makes living oh so easy.

These people horrify financial advisers. Yet they put food on the table and clothes on their backs. They raise kids, buy cars, take holidays, eventually pay off homes and ultimately retire.

So why bother about financial planning?

While most non-planners do get by, they make a trade-off. Without realizing it, they choose to take time and effort that could be spent enjoying life, and spend it instead on worrying. Worrying about expenses they can't afford . . . about mortgage rates at the next renewal . . . about credit cards that never get paid off. They worry about how hard they work in unsatisfying jobs. And they worry about losing those jobs because they can't do without the money.

Financial planning is about relieving that anxiety and avoiding stress. Instead of spending a lot of time worrying, you spend a bit of it deciding where you want to go and working out how to get there, anticipating the occasional detour.

Financial planning should not mean busting your head too much over problems such as budgeting, taxes, insurance and mortgages. The point is not to become an accountant, math whiz, stock jockey or penny pincher. Rather, it's to find out how to balance your means with today's lifestyle and tomorrow's goals. That doesn't require a lot of time, heavy-duty arithmetic, get-rich-quick schemes, tax games or a heap of sophisticated knowledge. All you need are a few basic principles — and common sense.

You can do a lot on your own. There are times when you will need professional advice, but even then you'll get more value — and feel better about your decisions — if you understand the concepts and lingo.

Financial planning is not about becoming rich. It's about directing your spending and your saving to those areas that provide the most satisfaction. Wealth by itself is rarely an answer. The sad reality is that without planning, lifestyle expectations and expenses can easily rise faster than income. At every level. Many financial advisers have no trouble citing examples of clients with six- and seven-figure incomes who are over their heads in debt. Even some lottery winners are now destitute.

Conversely, there are many people with modest incomes who are rolling in dough. Some live in plush homes, drive luxurious cars and take exotic vacations. They can stretch their dollars because they have defined — and live within — their means, because they're prepared for pitfalls, and because they can take advantage of opportunities. These people are financially comfortable.

In brief, the financial planning process is about:

1. Setting goals: Where do you want to go?

2. Compiling a net worth statement: Where are you now?

3. Developing a plan: How do you get from here to there?

4. Implementing that plan — and measuring your progress from time to time.

The elements of a financial plan are:

1. Cash flow and debt management: Can you comfortably handle your day-to-day expenses?

2. Adequate emergency fund and insurance: Are you prepared for periodic setbacks?

3. Taxation: Are you keeping as much as you can — prudently?

4. Effective saving/investing: Are you putting away enough and earning enough — considering your goals and tolerance for risk?

5. Estate planning: Have you prepared for the orderly distribution of your wealth to those you care about?

Why bother about financial planning? To feel in control of your life. To enjoy what you have. To look forward to the future. That's what this book is all about. Nothing more, nothing less.

2

Financial Goal-Setting

GOALS ARE THE FOUNDATION OF YOUR financial plan. They are critical in deciding how much to spend and how much to save, where to live, where to work, and so on.

This chapter describes the first part of a three-part process. Here, you decide where you want to go. The next chapter will help you determine where you are now. Chapter 5 then deals with the key element in getting from where you are to where you want to be — actually managing your cash flow.

Buried in chapter 1's sermon was a key notion: Financial planning is not about becoming rich. It's about directing your spending and your saving to those areas that provide the most satisfaction. What are those areas? What's most important to you now? Where do you see yourself in five years? Ten years? Twenty years?

Written goals are important because they help you stay focused and let you measure your progress.

Want to identify your *key* goals? Try this exercise from Calgary chartered accountant Laurie Glans. Get your spouse and some paper, pens, highlighters and a timer. Set the timer for five minutes. Without talking or pausing to think, each of you should answer this in writing: *What do I want to have/be/do when I grow up?* Write for the full time. When time runs out, take a new sheet and for five more minutes answer this: *What do I want to have/be/do now?* Next, spend three minutes on each paper highlighting the goals that came out. Mark short- and long-termers in different colors. Trade papers with your spouse and agree on six goals, three short-term and three long. Re-do each as a clear statement. Edit it after a week. Then review it every six or 12 months.

Don't be afraid to dream. With a bit of direction and discipline, you'll be amazed at what you can achieve. Don't be afraid to fantasize. If you want a BMW, say so. A lot of impressive cars are driven by people with unimpressive balance sheets.

Don't be afraid to be stodgy. If you don't want to be in debt, make that a goal.

If you're married, you and your spouse should each draft a set of goals. Then comes the compromising. One partner wants the BMW. The other wants to pay off the house as quickly as possible. Better a bit of haggling now than family feuds later.

Make your goal statements as precise as possible. Here are some examples:

- I want to have my credit cards paid off in one year.

- I want to be able to take two years off to care for my children full-time.

- I want a larger house for the family.

- I want to retire at 55 with an indexed annual income of $45,000 in today's money.

- My net worth should be at least $1 million when I am 50.

- When I am 50 and my net worth equals $1 million, I will buy a BMW.

Here are some generic goals. They'll be covered in more detail later in this book. This list is based on a modular system outlined by financial writer Richard Birch. I've expanded his list and used my own ranking. Feel free to do your own juggling; in financial planning, few things are gospel.

1. Buy adequate insurance.

2. Pay off consumer debts, especially costly credit cards. As each loan is cleared, use the payments saved to fund other goals.

3. Buy a home or set up an alternative investment fund.

4. Start making RRSP contributions as soon as possible and put in your maximum each year. This serves two functions — on top of providing a handy tax break. First, it creates a last-resort emergency fund for major disasters such as prolonged job loss. Second, as you'll see later in this book, time is your most powerful ally in funding a comfortable retirement.

5. Save for your children's education. A new federal grant makes Registered Education Savings Plans more attractive than ever.

6. Pay down your mortgage. Lump-sum prepayments are powerful money-savers.

7. Build an emergency fund to cover setbacks such as car and home repairs. Many financial planners put this item near the top of the list, maybe in third position. I would rather use the money to get ahead of the mortgage amortization if the lender is flexible about juggling payments. Mortgage paydowns yield much higher returns than bank or money market fund deposits. If disaster strikes and you're ahead of the amortization, your lender may allow you to cut or skip payments until you're back to where you'd have been had there been no prepayments. In effect, you've provided yourself with a form of emergency cash flow.

8. Invest for long-term security.

9. Invest for gain. Since your major commitments have already been covered, this is where you can really build wealth. Unfortunately, without planning most people won't reach this point.

How much savings are required to meet a goal? Say you want to accumulate $5,000 in five years and you can earn 5% a year after tax. Turn to appendix A-5 at the end of this book. Find the number — or "factor" — at the intersection of the five-year row and the 5% column. It's 5.5256. Divide your $5,000 goal by that. The result — $904.88 — is the sum you need to sock away at the end of each year.

If you can make your first deposit now, use the factor from appendix A-6 — 5.8019.

I can almost guarantee you will revise your goals as your life twists and turns. Don't worry. The idea is not to be glued to a piece of paper, but rather to have a focus and some priorities. These help you direct your spending and saving to those areas that provide the most satisfaction.

So, do you really want that BMW?

3

Snapshots of Your Finances

HOW MUCH ARE YOU WORTH? STOP laughing. You are probably worth more than you think, unless you've done a fairly recent "net worth statement."

Net worth is your true wealth — the difference between the assets you own and the debts you owe. Say you have a $200,000 house with a $150,000 mortgage. You don't own a $200,000 house; you own a $50,000 house surrounded by a borrowed $150,000 house.

Last chapter, you looked at where you want to go — your goals. The net worth statement shows where you are now.

If you've ever filled out a bank loan application, you prepared a net worth statement. We'll go a tad further to meet three objectives:

1. Calculate net worth. That's usually very interesting.

2. Compile a decent set of records. That's usually very boring.

3. Compile a quick-reference showing where all the cash is stashed and when investments come due. That's usually very handy.

Your net worth statement is a snapshot of your financial position on a particular day. It's often based on December 31 data, prepared and updated in late January or early February as year-end statements arrive. Of course, you can do yours July 1. Or maybe on your birthday. Just pick a convenient date and keep it consistent to measure your progress.

Compiling your net worth is often a treasure hunt. You have to search out bankbooks, RRSP certificates, loan agreements and all kinds of other mouldy papers. Get a bunch of file folders before you start. As each document surfaces, stick it in an appropriately marked folder to cover objective 2, the record-keeping function. You don't need a complex filing system. Keep it simple so it's easy to maintain, but detailed enough so it's easy to find things. Remember that in the event of death or injury, some-one else will have to go through your records. Here's a sample filing system:

- **Key Data.** This folder should be the most accessible. It holds summary lists of the basic information you or a stand-in would need if an emergency happens. For example: legal information such as your birth date, social insurance number and passport number; financial account numbers; the amounts and timing of automatic bank deposits and withdrawals; phone numbers of important people.

- **Auto.** Your car insurance policy, registration documents, service records and all the newspaper articles on smart maintenance you clip but ignore.

- **Employment.** Your resumé, job evaluations, letters of commendation (or condemnation). Maybe add a companion file called Employment Future, for clippings and notes.

- **Family.** A catch-all file for stuff like that address list of relatives you never write to, the clumsy but endearing self-portrait your child did in kinder-garten, and the will of the bachelor millionaire uncle who just happens to be your favorite relative.

- **Financial — Bank.** Bankbooks and statements, account agreements, etc. You might tape one safe deposit box key to this folder so you know it won't get lost.

- **Financial — Brokers.** Account statements and agreements.

- **Financial — Credit Cards.** Keep account agreements and the booklets that list all the wonderful features of your cards. Each month I take all the flimsy little charge slips listed on my bill, staple them to the statement and file the whole thing. Several times that archive has put money back in my pocket by quickly letting me correct billing errors, return unneeded items or make warranty claims.

- **Financial — Employer Benefits.** Odds are your employer has spent a lot of money trying to explain your fringe benefits. Odds are you've never read the booklet, and may have even tossed it. Maybe you're one of those people who always buys holiday medical insurance, unaware that your employer's plan already covers you. Read your booklet and keep it handy for reference. Yearly pension statements could also go here, or with other retirement documents.

- **Financial — Flyer Points.** Human brains were not designed to hold all the rules, limits and bonuses of these programs. Folders were. Also, keep account statements; airlines do make mistakes.

- **Financial — Income.** One folder for each breadwinner. If you file your pay stubs you can do an early estimate of your tax position. You're also covered if your employer fouls up your tax slip in February.

- **Financial — Investments.** I find it helpful to have one folder for each investment. A handy place for prospectuses, account statements, reports and clippings.

- **Financial — Life/Health Insurance.** Policies for individually owned life and disability coverage. By the way, your Key Data file should list *all* your insurance, including the freebie coverage from your credit cards.

- **Financial — Loans.** Loan agreements. When you clear a loan, you get proof of final payment. Keep such statements for at least five years or until the property is sold.

- **Financial — RRSP.** Just like Financial — Investments.

- **Financial — Tax Receipts.** A set of folders — or envelopes within one folder — that correspond to the lines you complete on your return. One for T4s from work, another for RRSP contribution receipts, a third for charitable donation slips, etc. That sounds unwieldy, but it's an easy way to file slips as they arrive. How many times have you searched for a wayward flimsy?

- **Financial — Tax Returns.** If you photocopy your annual return and receipts, you'll have a nice uniform set of papers that's easy to file. Stash the actual receipts in a secondary storage box. Keep returns at least six years.

  Here's an alternative. Instead of keeping separate files for receipts and returns, set up one folder for each tax year. Stick all receipts in it. After sorting them and doing your return, file the full set back in the one folder.

- **House — General.** Your home insurance policy, a copy of your deed or mortgage, condo papers, etc.

- **House — Utility & Tax Bills.** Current-year statements. If you can write them off as a business expense, store the bills with your tax records for at least six years.

- **Legal Citizenship, Birth & Death.** Passports and birth/death certificates for immediate family members.

- **Legal — Wills, Etc.** Copies of wills and powers of attorney for you and your companion. Marriage certificates too. Also, wills and power of attorney for mom and dad or any others for whom you're responsible.

- **Medical.** Tax receipts would go in the tax files. This is for eyeglass prescriptions, vaccination records, etc.

The good news is that once you do all this work, you should find it very easy to file and find your papers. The bad news is that a snoop or crook would also find it easy. Consider the case of the nosy nanny. This Ontario woman combed through her employer's files, got bank account and PIN numbers, and made off with a fair bit of cash. Keep your files locked.

Now let's get to the net worth statement. The tables in this chapter provide two samples, a fairly basic one and a far more detailed version. Use one or the other. Or combine elements.

Table 3.1 is the basic sample for a couple named Tom and Kim. I've made separate columns for each spouse and one for joint assets. While it's easier to lump everything together, this way you can make sure the right person owns the right stuff. For example, if one spouse is in a much lower tax bracket, he or she should hold any fully taxed interest-bearing investments. We'll discuss this and other tax-saving techniques later in the book.

Normally, assets come first, arranged by liquidity. Liquidity is how easily you can get at the cash.

Then come liabilities — your debts. Often they're divided into short-term loans due within one year, and long-term loans. I've taken a different approach to highlight the business and investment loans with tax-deductible interest.

The summary in the third section subtracts the liabilities from the assets to determine the net worth — the difference between what you own and what you owe.

Table 3.2 is the more detailed version of the same net worth statement. By itemizing maturity dates and account numbers, this one document shows where everything is. This quick reference is the third objective set out for this chapter. Keep a copy in your Key Data folder.

I've divided the holdings into three broad categories — regular monetary assets, retirement assets and personal assets. Sub-categories are ranked by liquidity and then, for reference, comes a detailed list of each one's components.

The following sub-categories will probably meet your needs for regular monetary assets. If not, tinker.

1. **Cash and near-cash.** This money is available almost instantly. Show each savings and chequing account along with brokerage account cash balances,

money market funds, cashable term deposits, Canada Savings Bonds and any life insurance cash-surrender value. For that cash-surrender value, consult your policy or agent.

2. **Investments.** This money is readily available, but you could face a capital loss if you sell at the wrong time. Show stocks, bonds and mutual funds that hold them. My sample mutual funds are grouped by type. Show the current market value, readily available from newspaper tables.

   Your GICs, if any, are probably locked in, but listing them by maturity date may show that some money will be freed up sooner than you think. Don't forget to add on interest accrued since the last compounding date. To calculate accrued growth on strip bonds, see chapter 6 and table 25.2 in chapter 25.

3. **Accounts receivable.** List major money owed you by family or friends. If you're paid on a two-week lag, you might include that, but don't get carried away. Also include big cheques heading your way, perhaps a tax refund or an insurance claim.

4. **Illiquid investments.** Show investment real estate, tax shelters and active business investments. There is value, but what are the odds of selling at a good price when you need the money?

My sub-categories for retirement assets are cash, fixed-income and equities because that's the major mix for RRSPs.

1. **Cash.** Money market funds and low-yield liquid savings accounts.

2. **Fixed-income.** Listing GICs and bonds by maturity lets you see when money is coming up for renewal. Include interest accrued since the last compounding date. Also include bond mutual funds.

3. **Equities.** These include stocks as well as mutual funds that invest primarily in stocks. Show the current market values.

My sample also includes an entry for employer's pension plan, because that information is readily available for my mythical person. If you are in a "defined-benefit" pension plan, the numbers on your annual statement might make no sense. Feel free to ignore illiquid entries like pensions, but be consistent from year to year.

The third broad asset category — personal assets — can be a pain.

Theoretically, it includes your house, cottage, car, furniture, artwork and pots and pans (even the dirty ones). That's because those things have value (even the dented ones).

But that value is hard to gauge. Also, our homes account for so much of our wealth that real estate market ups and downs can unfairly distort year-over-year measurement, even though we have no plans to sell.

If you have a mortgage, include your home — at its original cost so you can show your equity as an asset and the mortgage as a liability. After the mortgage is paid off, consider dropping the home from the statement on grounds that any proceeds on sale would likely be put into another home. If you want to keep the home on the statement, decide whether to carry it at original or current value. Be consistent from year to year. For reference, record your decision and rationale in a list of notes attached to the statement.

I also ignore my home furnishings since it's doubtful I could — or would — sell them for anything more than pocket change. You might feel otherwise.

I did include a car, since it's easy to value and a car loan represents a significant liability. There are guides to used car values; ask your banker or librarian. Or, do straight-line depreciation over the vehicle's expected life. If your two-year-old car will last three more years, value it at 60% of the purchase price now and knock off another 20% in each of the next three years.

That's it for assets. Next come liabilities.

Separate tax-deductible and non-deductible loans. Within each group, divide your loans into short-term and long-term debt. Short-term normally includes credit card balances, personal lines of credit and loans due within one year.

Show the interest rate on each. In the comments section, show the creditor and account number. Maybe a phone number too.

After listing your liabilities, subtract total debt from total assets to get — voilà — your net worth. But you're not done yet. Prolong the fun with a bit of analysis. Consider:

- Do you have too many bank and brokerage accounts? Too many individual investments? Too many loans? What can you consolidate to make life easier?

- Are cash and near-cash holdings sufficient or overloaded? Depending on how secure your income is, it's a good idea to have three to six months' expenses socked away in fairly safe liquid holdings.

- Do your investments match your objectives? Are they too stodgy? Are they properly diversified? Look for problem areas. For example, do all your RRSP deposits mature in the same year? Is your portfolio tax-effective with interest-bearing investments inside your RRSP and equities outside? (Do you know what I'm talking about? If not, don't worry; later chapters will go into detail.)

- Ignoring your mortgage, is there too much debt? Ideally, consumer debt — credit card balances, car loan, etc. — should be no more than 20% of your annual take-home pay.

  There is also a rule-of-thumb that compares short-term assets like cash, money market funds and Canada Savings Bonds to short-term debt. Those assets should total 1.5 to two times the total short-term debt.

  Is there lazy money sitting in cash and near-cash holdings that can be used to pay down loans? You're better off paying down a 17% credit card balance than earning 4% or so on a fully taxed Canada Savings Bond.

  Can your loans be consolidated at a lower rate? Are there unsecured loans? Are there assets that can be used to secure them in order to get a lower rate?

Keep your net worth statements in a folder or binder. Calculate the percentage change from year to year. Are you at least matching inflation? Can you do better by saving more, investing better or reducing debt? Most importantly, do you see yourself gaining more control over your money? Are you moving toward your goals?

TABLE 3.1: Basic Net Worth Statement

Net Worth at 1-Jan-94

Assets	Current Value			
	Joint	Tom	Kim	Total
Cash & Near-Cash:				
– Chequing account	1,770			1,770
– Brokerage cash balance				
– Money market fund	9,254			9,254
– Short-term deposits/savings bonds	4,090			4,090
– Life insurance cash value		17,836		17,836
*** Subtotal	15,114	17,836		32,950
Investments:				
– Stocks & equity mutual fund		41,329	3,497	44,826
– Term deposits, bonds & bond funds	6,127		5,826	11,953
*** Subtotal	6,127	41,329	9,323	56,779
Accounts Receivable:	1,213			1,213
Illiquid investments:		8,000		8,000
Retirement Assets:				
– RRSPs		91,468	27,694	119,163
– Employer pension credits			62,492	62,492
*** Subtotal		91,468	90,186	181,654
Personal Assets:				
– Home (purchase cost)	342,500			342,500
– Art			16,000	16,000
– Vehicles	27,887			27,887
*** Subtotal	370,387		16,000	386,387
**** Total Assets	392,841	158,633	115,509	666,983
Liabilities:				
Business & investment loans:		5,000		5,000
Non-deductible loans:				
– Home mortgage	182,963			182,963
– Car loan	11,236			11,236
– Credit cards	1,232			1,232
**** Total Liabilities	195,431	5,000		200,431
Summary:				
Total assets	392,841	158,633	115,509	666,983
Total liabilities	(195,431)	(5,000)		(200,431)
***** Net Worth	197,410	153,633	115,509	466,552

TABLE 3.2: Detailed Net Worth Statement
Net Worth at 1-Jan-94

Regular Monetary Assets	Current Value				
	Joint	Tom	Kim	Total	Acct # & Contact/Remarks
Cash & Near-Cash					
ABC Bank chequing account	1,770			1,770	212-12345 R. Smith 555-9999
DEF Brokerage cash balance					313-67890 555-0000
GHI Money Market Fund	9,254			9,254	DEF Brokerage 555-0000
JKL Trust cashable deposit 1-Nov-94	4,090			4,090	123456-902 J. Cash 555-1111
Life insurance cash value		17,836		17,836	UL-33390-876 R. Baker 555-7777
* Total Cash & Near-Cash	15,114	17,836		32,950	
Investments					
Equities – Mutual Funds:					
– MNO International		7,383		7,383	PAC: 8883321 555-2222
– PQR US Fund			3,497	3,497	PAC: 32-9806 1-800-555-2222
– STU American Growth		7,845		7,845	
– VWX Canadian Equity		10,000		10,000	Unless specified otherwise,
– YZZ Canadian Special		10,000		10,000	assets are in DEF Brokerage
Equities – Common & Preferred Shares:					Joint: 33460
– Widget Co.		5,219		5,219	Tom: 33461
– Supreme Money Loser		882		882	Kim: 33462
					Call 555-6666 I. Jones
***Subtotal		41,329	3,497	44,826	
Bonds & term deposits:					
– AAA International Bond Fund			5,826	5,826	
– BBB Trust GIC 9.25% 6-Jun-95	6,127			6,127	
***Subtotal	6,127		5,826	11,953	
* Total Investments	6,127	41,329	9,323	56,779	
Accounts Receivable					
Dental insurance claim	1,213			1,213	M. Dale 555-3333
* Total Accounts Receivable	1,213			1,213	
Illiquid Investments					
ABC Fund limited partnership #1		8,000		8,000	32987-J I. Jones 555-6666
* Total Illiquid Investments		8,000		8,000	
*** Total Regular Monetary Assets	22,454	67,165	9,323	98,942	
RRSP — Cash & Near-Cash					
Cash balance		16		16	Unless specified otherwise,
Earn A Lot Money Market Fund		5,000		5,000	assets are in DEF Brokerage
					Tom: RRSP 33462-S
Total RRSP Cash & Near-Cash		5,016		5,016	Kim: RRSP 33986-S
RRSP — Fixed Income					
Mutual funds:					
– Yield A Lot Bond Fund		17,769		17,769	
– YAL World Bond Fund		12,712		12,712	
– Sleep Tight Mortgage Fund		11,392		11,392	
		41,873		41,873	

TABLE 3.2 CONTINUED

Retirement Assets		Joint	Current Value Tom	Kim	Total	Acct # & Contact/Remarks
GICs & strip bonds:						
— GIC ABC Trust 01-Mar-94 10.875%				4,844	4,844	62-87543 $ Shop 555-7777
— GIC XYZ Trust 23-Mar-95 10.625%				3,215	3,215	11-623659 $ Shop 555-7777
— GovtQue $20,000 28-Dec-2001 11.355%			7,764	6,287	14,051	
— GovtCan $18,750 01-Mar-2006 10.398%			5,197	5,197	10,394	
— QuHydro $55,000 15-Feb-2008 10.999%			11,595		11,595	
— OnHydro $40,250 27-May-2009 10.567%			7,892		7,892	
— OnHydro $50,625 15-Apr-2011 9.773%			9,358		9,358	
			41,806	19,543	61,349	
Total RRSP Fixed Income			83,679	19,543	103,222	
RRSP — Equities						
Mutual funds:						
— UUU Premium Balanced			2,773	8,151	10,924	
Total RRSP Equities			2,773	8,151	10,924	
** Total RRSP			91,468	27,694	119,162	
** Employer Pension Credits				62,492	62,492	M. Dale 555-3333
*** Total Retirement Assets			91,468	90,186	181,654	

Personal Assets						
Home (purchase cost)	342,500				342,500	
Art				16,000	16,000	
Car (10-year depreciation)	18,650				18,650	
Boat (10-year depreciation)	9,237				9,237	
Total Personal Assets	370,387			16,000	386,387	
**** Total Assets	392,841		158,633	115,509	666,983	

Liabilities						
Business & investment loans:						
— DEF Brokerage margin		5,000			5,000	
		5,000			5,000	
Non-deductible loans:						
— Home mortgage 1-Jun-94 9.25%	182,963				182,963	554268 ABC Bank (J. Dyer) 555-9999
— Car loan 3-Sep-96 11.25%	11,236				11,236	539011-P RQT Trust 555-2345
— Credit cards	1,232				1,232	Visa/MasterCard: see Key Data file
	195,431				195,431	
Total Liabilities	195,431	5,000			200,431	
SUMMARY:						
Total Assets	392,841	158,633	115,509		666,983	
Total Liabilities	(195,431)	(5,000)			(200,431)	
*****NET WORTH	197,410	153,633	115,509		466,552	

4

The B-Word: Budgeting

CHAPTER 3 COVERED NET WORTH — WHERE you stand today. Chapter 2 dealt with goals — where you want to go. This chapter will focus on how to get from here to there.

It's about "cash flow management." That's a fancy term used by financial planners who are afraid clients will turn off and drop out when they hear the B-word — budgeting.

Sugar-coat it all you want, but there is no way the average person can meet his or her goals without setting some priorities and managing inflow and outgo. With a budget, you set parameters for how much to spend in given areas. That enables you to take control.

But that doesn't mean you have to watch every penny or spend hours on bookkeeping.

More importantly, it doesn't mean you have to deny yourself the things you want. Budgeting should be a positive, not a negative, exercise. A good budget says, "Yes, you can have what you really want — because at some point you sat down and objectively fit it into your game plan."

It also works wonders for relationships. In a good budget, the two partners earmark how much of the money can be spent on their favorite pursuits. Then, each one spends while the other shuts up. One big upfront battle over the plan instead of never-ending skirmishes.

Many budgets are begun at the start of each year, then are quickly abandoned. Here are some reasons why:

- They're based on a negative view. You don't have to give up all the good things in life. A good budget will free up money for what you really want by controlling unimportant spending.

- They're too tight.

- There are no written rules on which accounts cover what. That creates confusion and frustration.

- Lots of time goes into data collection, but not analysis. The exercise becomes meaningless.

- No rewards are built in. Budgeting works best if surplus funds provide a treat every so often.

- You get bogged down in too many accounts, especially when using printed forms. Almost every budget worksheet has separate accounts for mortgage payments, heating, hydro and telephone. Why? If you're over budget in one of these items, can you really cut back? The same goes for gasoline, auto insurance and licence fees.

If you suspect there's a problem area, set up a precise account. Otherwise, use general categories. The idea is not to pinch every penny, but to ensure you're living within your means and that most of your spending is truly meaningful.

Pay Yourself First

MANY PEOPLE have trouble saving money because they go about it backwards. They plan to save whatever is left at the end of each month. But typically there's hardly anything left.

The answer is the "pay yourself first" concept, a long time financial-planning tool. Decide to save a set percentage each month and have that automatically deducted from your pay or your bank account.

This plan is extremely effective because we tend to spend our take-home pay. You will face some adjustment in the first few months, but most people doing PYF find they quickly get used to it. Track spending for a while, and you will probably find you lose a lot through "leakage." Leakage consists of relatively small amounts spent on fairly meaningless cash purchases: junk food at work, a dash to the convenience store because you went to the supermarket last week without bothering to do up a shopping list, etc. Believe it or not, those expenses mount up. When you have less money on hand, you instinctively become more selective.

Have your PYF deposit placed directly in a money market fund for later distribution, or to a designated investment account.

Monthly investment plans are an ideal way to make RRSP contributions. PYF is also a good way to save up vacation or Christmas money. A friend in Montreal buys Canada Savings Bonds and Quebec Savings Bonds through payroll deduction. The CSBs bought in the fall are paid off by the following November, just in time to fund holiday gifts and a winter vacation. The QSBs run from spring to spring, and she uses them for her summer holiday.

For long-term savings, many advisers suggest starting with 10% of take-home pay and moving to 10% of gross. A 10% PYF plan is the core strategy of *The Wealthy Barber*, the incredibly popular personal finance book by David Chilton. David feels there's little point in budgeting for "wants" like CD players or vacations because personal wants quickly become "needs" and get purchased whether you have the money or not.

He feels just putting 10% of pay into an international mutual fund with a solid long-term record will do the job for most people. But understand that this 10% fund is in addition to making a maximum RRSP contribution. That may sound like a lot of money to set aside. It is — up to about 20% of pay, assuming you use one year's RRSP tax refund for the following year's contribution. But the PYF concept makes it quite doable. Within a few months, you won't miss the money.

By the way, your PYF plan can — and should — include clearing existing debt. As you'll later see, that "investment" provides an excellent risk-free, tax-free return. That is, if you use the money to become debt-free, not to clear your cards for a new spending spree.

Sample Systems

WHILE EACH person's financial situation is different, here are two budget systems that might do the job.

The first is for the very reluctant or the very busy. It's used by two friends of mine. Their big concerns are funding current-year vacations, investing in RRSPs and paying down their mortgage. They've set monthly targets for those areas. They have one problem spot — restaurant meals. So they've budgeted that expense. That's it. As long as they meet those targets, they don't care where the rest of their money goes.

To simplify bookkeeping, they rely heavily on a credit card that breaks the monthly statement into categories. They check that no category goes too far out of line, but they don't micro-manage individual spending. Since they always pay the full credit card bill on time, they pay no interest. The card issuer does their bookkeeping for free, and they get flyer points for each charge.

The second sample system is a more conventional one that posts each expense to an account. You will probably want to add or delete some accounts, but this list should get you started:

- **Groceries and entertainment.** By combining these items, you avoid having to decide how to post the cost of entertaining at home or dashing out after work because you don't feel like cooking. These expenses are also quite variable; if one month you go over, you can easily cut back during the next. If you have pets, put their food in this account. They're family members too.

- **Personal.** One account for each family member. This is an allowance. While the individual should not have to account for the money, there should be basic rules on what it will cover. For example, does lunch at work come out of this account or the grocery fund? If you have children, here's a good place to track daycare expenses. As the kids grow older, the daycare money can be shifted into allowances and other child-rearing costs.

- **Clothing.** This works just like the personal account.

- **House.** Use two subaccounts. Fixed Expenses covers all recurring items over which you have little or no control — rent or mortgage, taxes, utilities, insurance and maybe cleaning. Maintenance and Furnishings covers spending you can control — from kitchen dinnerware to sunroom plants. Special projects such as renovations or major repairs might merit their own subaccounts.

- **Car.** If you get too many parking tickets, track that expense in the interest of behavior modification. A maintenance subaccount might be useful if your car is getting old and you're debating whether to replace it. Otherwise, lump together all related expenses. Would you start walking if your gas bill ran over budget?

- **Savings.** Use subaccounts for your emergency fund, RRSP contributions and special concerns such as your child's education.

- **Vacation.** A true necessity. Setting aside a certain amount each month will build a fund to finance well-planned trips or last-minute getaways.

- **Gifts.** A major expense for many families, especially at Christmas. Set aside a bit each month. Include charitable giving; planning donations helps you maximize use of the charity tax credit.

- **Medical.** Even if you're in excellent health, budget a token amount. Include the pets, too. If unspent money piles up after a few months, shift it to another account.

- **Miscellaneous.** Postage stamps, lottery tickets, etc. Budget a token amount each month.

- **Adjustments.** The handiest account. Say you're $20 off when reconciling income and expenses. Why spend hours looking for the error?

- **Income.** One for each working person, plus one for other sources such as bank interest.

   If you're not living on investment income, don't track it — just let those accounts grow. Why track that stuff for tax purposes? Computers at your financial institution or brokerage already do the job to spit out receipts at tax time. The exception would be if your investment income is high enough to require installment tax payments and the optional bills you get from Revenue Canada don't fit your current circumstances.

   Why not track just take-home pay? That's all the money you have to work with. Many financial advisers encourage people to record their gross income and all deductions so they can estimate their income tax before year-end. But many pay stubs already provide year-to-date totals. If they don't, why not just stick the pay stubs in the income folder I mentioned last chapter and tally them only when the need arises?

That's the framework. Once you set your accounts, estimate your take-home pay and divide it up, as shown in table 4.1 at the end of this chapter. If this is your first go at budgeting, you might want to project just three months instead of a full year.

Every month does not have to balance. Maybe your annual car insurance bill will produce a bulge. To handle that situation, overestimate car spending in the preceding months to build a surplus. Aim for balancing the budget at least once during the year — perhaps at the six-month mark — but still watch each month-end position to make sure you don't go too far astray.

So now you know how much you can spend this month. Let's tackle the hardest part — bookkeeping.

Compulsive spenders are often advised to record every expense, at least for a while. But most people really aren't spendaholics, and few things undermine a budget more quickly than the tedium of tracking every penny. Try this:

1. Set aside one time each week for budgeting.

2. Put a folder called "Post to Budget" in a convenient place. During the week, just shove bills and charge slips into that folder — don't deal with them until budget time. If you receive a cheque, deposit it immediately and stick the stub or a scribbled note into the folder.

3. Set up a ledger. See table 4.2. Better yet, there is now reasonably priced commercially produced software, such as Quicken and Microsoft Money, that make budgeting and tracking pretty easy. Update the ledger weekly, at budget time.

4. To simplify your posting:

- Identify those accounts where you tend to pay cash — for example, Groceries and Entertainment, Personal, maybe Miscellaneous.

    Say you've budgeted $700 for this month's Groceries and Entertainment. At the start of the month put some cash in the G&E envelope, perhaps $300. Record that $300 as one ledger entry. Then spend it. Don't itemize that spending unless there's a problem. As the envelope runs low, top it up and post that amount.

    Say that at the supermarket you use grocery cash to buy an $8 book, a "personal" expense. When you get home, shift $8 from the Personal envelope to the G&E envelope. Or stick a note in the G&E envelope that says "Personal owes G&E $8" and settle the accounts when you top up the envelopes.

- Use your credit card whenever possible — as long as you pay on time to avoid interest. When signing the charge slip at the store, note the expense account on your copy of the flimsy. At home, stick the slip in the Post to Budget folder. At your weekly budget time, record the expense in your ledger and put the charge slip in another folder or envelope called "Charge Slips Posted But Not Paid. I'll discuss that folder later, in the chapter on credit cards.

- Say your phone bill arrives on Monday and your budget time is Sunday. Just stick the bill in the Post to Budget folder. On Sunday, write the cheque and record it in your ledger. Save all bookkeeping for that one time.

Using a computer lets you keep a running tally of what's been spent and what's available. If you don't have a computer, consider doing that tally weekly or every two weeks for problem accounts.

At the end of each month, compare reality to your plan. The month-end analysis form in table 4.3 can help. The first data column shows what you planned to spend for each account. The second shows what you actually spent. The third subtracts column 2 from column 1, producing a variance. The fourth column is copied from your original plan for the following month. The fifth column adds columns 3 and 4. That way, you automatically adjust for any surplus or deficit.

Examine column 5. Are there any accounts with big surpluses? Maybe you've budgeted $500 a month for vacations, but don't plan to go away until later in the year. Why not segregate that money by moving it to a 30-day term deposit? Next month, add another $500 and roll all the money into a new deposit. Better yet, consider using one money market fund account to park all surplus cash. It's liquid, but pays a decent yield.

Maybe one account has built up a surplus because you were way off in estimating spending. There are probably accounts with deficits. Shift the surplus money to cover those shortfalls. Document what you've done by writing notes on the form, and review your explanations when you revise your budget plan. If you're new at budgeting, revise your plan every three months. Over time, you'll probably find yearly revisions are enough. Remember, though, that a budget is only a guide and should be able to be changed at any time.

What if all the accounts show deep deficits? You're in trouble. Immediately revise your plan for the upcoming months so each shortfall is gradually covered. Be realistic. You still have to eat. And no matter how committed you are, you will still need some money for discretionary spending like entertainment. Remember that budgets get abandoned when they're made too tight.

For an added incentive or thrill, use graph paper to chart your monthly income and total spending, one line for each. If you now spend more than you earn, you'll be able to see your progress as you gain better control of your money. If you earn more than you spend, use the chart to measure your progress toward financial security.

TABLE 4.1: Sample Budget Plan — Childless Couple

Account	Jan	Feb	Mar	Apr	May	Jun	Jul	Aug	Sep	Oct	Nov	Dec	Total	% of Income
Groc/Ent	500	500	500	500	500	500	500	500	500	500	500	500	6,000	8.3
Personal — 1	200	200	200	300	200	200	300	200	200	200	200	200	2,600	3.6
Personal — 2	150	150	150	150	150	150	150	150	150	150	150	150	1,800	2.5
Clothing — 1	50	50	50	50	50	50	50	50	50	50	50	50	600	0.8
Clothing — 2	200	200	200	200	200	200	200	200	200	200	200	200	2,400	3.3
Home — Fixed	1,650	1,650	1,650	1,650	1,650	1,650	1,650	1,650	1,650	1,650	1,650	1,650	19,800	27.4
Home — M&F	200	200	200	200	200	200	200	200	200	200	200	200	2,400	3.3
Car	800	800	800	800	900	800	800	800	1,700	800	800	800	10,600	14.7
Sav — RRSPs	1,100	1,100	1,100	1,100	1,100	1,100	1,100	1,100	1,100	1,100	1,100	1,100	13,200	18.3
Sav — Invest	450	450	450	450	450	450	450	450	450	450	450	450	5,400	7.5
Vacation	500	500	500	500	500	500	500	500	500	500	500	500	6,000	8.3
Gifts	50	50	50	50	50	50	50	50	50	50	50	50	600	0.8
Medical	25	25	25	25	25	25	25	25	25	25	25	25	300	0.4
Misc	25	25	25	25	25	25	25	25	25	25	25	25	300	0.4
	0	0	0	0	0	0	0	0	0	0	0	0	0	0.0
	0	0	0	0	0	0	0	0	0	0	0	0	0	0.0
	0	0	0	0	0	0	0	0	0	0	0	0	0	0.0
Expenses	(5,900)	(5,900)	(5,900)	(6,000)	(6,000)	(5,900)	(6,000)	(5,900)	(6,800)	(5,900)	(5,900)	(5,900)	(72,000)	99.8
Income — 1	3,000	3,000	3,000	4,500	3,000	3,000	3,000	3,100	4,675	3,100	3,100	3,958	40,433	56.0
Income — 2	2,400	2,400	2,400	3,600	2,400	2,400	2,400	2,400	3,700	2,500	2,500	2,500	31,600	43.8
Other	10	10	10	10	10	10	10	10	10	10	10	10	120	0.2
Ttl Income	5,410	5,410	5,410	8,110	5,410	5,410	5,410	5,510	8,385	5,610	5,610	6,468	72,153	100.0
Ttl Expense	(5,900)	(5,900)	(5,900)	(6,000)	(6,000)	(5,900)	(6,000)	(5,900)	(6,800)	(5,900)	(5,900)	(5,900)	(72,000)	99.8
	(490)	(490)	(490)	2,110	(590)	(490)	(590)	(390)	1,585	(290)	(290)	568	153	0.2
Year-to-date	(490)	(980)	(1,470)	640	50	(440)	(1,030)	(1,420)	165	(125)	(415)	153		

TABLE 4.2: Budget Ledger

This ledger was produced on a computer spreadsheet. There are several commercial software packages that do the same job and cost only about $50. If you don't have a computer, you can set up this format on a wide ledger book from an office supply store.

1994 Budget Ledger			Plan:	500	200	150	50	200	1,650	200	800	1,100	450	500	3,000	2,400	10		528.16	250.28
			Spent:	229	127	75	5C	213	1,174		21	1,100	45)	500	1,499	1,207	0			
			Cheque — Avbl.	271	73	75	5C	(13)	476	200	779	0	0	0	1,501	1,193	10			
			Book MMF:									1,000		500					O/S	Credit
Date	Amount	Balance		Groc/Ent	Pers—1	Pers—2	Cloth—1	Cloth—2	H—M&F	H—Fixed	Car	Sav—RRSP	Sav—Inv	Vac	Inc—1	Inc—2	Other	Adjust	Cheques	Card
Jan 1 Balances forward		3,744.06																	0.00	539.37
2 Paid mortgage	1,174.30	2,569.76							1,174.30										0.00	0.00
3 RRSP & mutual fund debits	1,550.00	1,019.76										1,100.00	450.00						0.00	0.00
4 Got paid!	2,705.71	3,725.47													1,498.52	1,207.19			0.00	0.00
5 Start-of-month cash	425.00	3,300.47		250.00	100.00	75.00													0.00	0.00
6 Bought a jacket on credit card	212.53	3,300.47					212.53												0.00	212.53
7 Used grocery cash to buy gas for car	0.00	3,300.47			(21.00)						21.00								0.00	0.00
8 Bought squash balls. Paid by cheque	26.54	3,273.93			26.54														26.54	0.00
9 Paid credit card bill	501.62	2,772.31																	501.62	(501.62)
10 Moved unneeded vacation money to money market fund (MMF)	500.00	2,272.31												500.00					0.00	0.00

Income and expenses are posted in the week they occur. But look at the Jan 6 entry. It's a $212.53 credit charge. It was posted to the Clothing expense account but not deducted from the chequing account balance. That's because it won't really be paid until the bill is due. At the far right, there is a column for tracking credit card charges. On Jan 9 the monthly credit card bill was paid. The amount due — $501.62 — was deducted from the chequing account balance and also from the unpaid credit card column.

The Jan 7 entry did not affect the chequing account balance either. It was just a cash swap between accounts. The Grocery account was credited with a $21 reversal because $21 of cash was spent on gasoline, not food. A $21 expense was posted to the Car account.

On Jan 8 a $26.54 cheque was written. It was posted to the Personal column and also to a column at the far right that tracks outstanding cheques. That column makes it easy to balance the chequebook.

The last entry requires some explanation that will seem complex. But it's not. Each month this couple socks away some money for vacation. They also run surpluses in some accounts and want to isolate that money to cover shortfalls in later months. Some people open a separate bank account for each stockpile. You might find it easier to use just one money market fund account as a parking spot. It will also pay more than savings accounts. Use a money fund at the institution where you bank so you can transfer cash between that and your chequing account.

But how do you keep track of which money market fund cash is for each expense account? Just duplicate this ledger. As was done here, show the $500 Jan 10 transfer as a budget expense. Then, in the money market fund ledger, enter $500 in the Vacation account. Say that next month you spend $700 for a spur-of-the-moment airline ticket. That's $200 more than the amount budgeted each month. No problem. Transfer in $200 from the money fund's Vacation account. Record that as $200 in the money market fund ledger and the budget ledger to show it's a reversal. Your budget plan says you can spend $500. In reality, you've spent $700 minus $200 from the money fund stash. So even with a last-minute getaway, you're still on track. For convenience, the MMF line in the ledger's top section shows how much money from each account has been parked in the money market fund.

Those well-versed in spreadsheets will find they can easily automate much of the posting and bank statement reconciliation.

MONEY MARKET FUND LEDGER						
Date	Amount	Balance	Groc/Ent	Pers—1	Sav—Inv	Vac
Jan 1 Balance forward	1,000.00	1,000.00	↑	↑	1,000.00	↑
Jan 10 From chequing	500.00	1,500.00	↑	↑	↑	500.00

TABLE 4.3: Month-end Budget Analysis Form

Add the variance from the current month to the next month's planned amount. A surplus will increase next month's allotment. A deficit will reduce it. You thus stay on track for the year.

Month Just Ended				Next Month	
Account	Planned	Actual	Variance	Plan	Revised
Groc/Ent	500	337	163	500	663
Personal — 1	200	200	0	200	200
Personal — 2	150	150	0	150	150
Clothing — 1	50	0	50	50	100
Clothing — 2	200	457	(257)	200	(57)
Home — Fixed	1,650	1,521	129	1,650	1,779
Home — M&f	200	24	176	200	376
Car	800	842	(42)	800	758
Sav — RRSPs	1,100	1,100	0	1,100	1,100
Sav — Invest	450	450	0	450	450
Vacation	500	500	0	500	500
Gifts	50	15	35	50	85
Medical	25	0	25	25	50
Misc	25	5	20	25	45
	0	0	0	0	0
	0	0	0	0	0
	0	0	0	0	0
Expenses	(5,900)	(5,601)	299	(5,900)	(6,199)
Income — 1	3,000	2,997	(3)	3,000	3,003
Income — 2	2,400	2,415	15	2,400	2,385
Other	10	3	(7)	10	17
	(490)	(186)	304	(490)	(794)

Next month you can spend $794 more than you take in. As indicated in table 4.1, you already planned to be over by $490. The other $304 is the surplus left over from January.

5

Cash Cushions

WHY DOES YOUR CAR HAVE A SPARE TIRE, A jack and a lug wrench? Not to prevent a flat, but to minimize its impact. Every so often you will get a flat. But if you're prepared, it'll be easy to get going again.

Every so often you will face a financial crunch. It's unavoidable. But a bit of preparation can minimize the impact and get you moving again toward your goals.

This chapter is about your financial safety net, which has three main components:

- A cash cushion to cover unexpected expenses and temporary needs.

- Life and disability insurance to replace your income. Car and home insurance to repair or replace your property.

- A will and a power of attorney to ensure your wishes are carried out when you can't act for yourself.

This chapter will deal in detail with the cash cushion. The other components have their own chapters later in the book.

A cash cushion ensures you'll have money when you really need it. Without one, you're forced to borrow — often through credit cards at high rates of interest. Every dollar you spend on interest is one dollar you can't spend on something more meaningful.

According to a common rule-of-thumb, your cash cushion should equal three to six months' take-home pay or expenses. But fit the cushion to your circumstances. How much you set aside should depend on your risk of facing a financial crunch. Consider:

- How secure is your income? The greater your security, the less need there is for a large emergency fund.

- What are your odds of encountering a financial emergency? Clearly, somebody driving a 10-year-old rustbucket has to be prepared for break-downs. So does an overweight chain-smoker who has a heart condition and works in a stressful job.

- How many people depend on you? Can you depend on family members or others?

- How much flex is there in your lifestyle? If the fridge conks out, can you easily cut other spending to pay the repair bill?

Maybe one month's income is enough. Maybe you need far more. As Toronto's go-go real estate market peaked in the late '80s, some accountants advised high-flying real estate agents to sock away a year's worth of expenses. That turned out to be excellent advice, since the market soon plunged and house sales stayed flat for about five years.

Cash does not necessarily mean money in the bank earning almost no interest but, rather, money you can access when required. It's highly unlikely you'll need several thousand dollars with no notice at all. Here's how you might stash $10,000, balancing concerns about accessibility, security and return.

- Most financial institutions waive transaction fees if you maintain a $1,000 minimum balance. So park $1,000 in your chequing-savings account. If that saves you $5 a month, it's the same as earning 10-12% in fully-taxed interest. Let's hope you'll never need that cash. But if you do, your only cost will be the transaction fees paid until the account is replenished.

- Add $500 to your basic chequing-savings account balance just to cover short-term blips. This — and the rest of your immediately accessible cash cushion — also serves as an opportunity fund. Maybe there's a store going out of business and you can reap dramatic savings on some items you had planned to buy later in the year. Buy now, and pay back the fund with the money you would normally be setting aside for the scheduled purchase.

- Put $3,500 into a money market fund, Canada Savings Bonds or short-term deposits. To compete with CSBs, several banks and trust companies offer one-year term deposits that can be fully or partially cashed early without penalty. They pay a bit more than CSBs and offer greater flexibility. Some are offered only during the annual CSB sales drive in October.

- If you have a flexible mortgage, consider using the remaining $5,000 to reduce it while continuing your previously set payments. Say you have 20 years left in your amortization — or payback — schedule and you now owe $100,000 at 6.5% with monthly payments of $740.50. A $5,000 prepayment will push you 22 months ahead on the payback schedule, saving you nearly $12,000 over the life of the mortgage. By saving you 6.5% interest, that $5,000 effectively earns 6.5% a year tax-free.

What if there's a financial emergency? Raise that issue with your lender *before* making the prepayment. You will likely find you can reduce or skip payments until that 22-month cushion is used up and you're back to the original payback schedule. In other words, you could free up as much as $740.50 each month for 22 months.

Here's an alternative for those who can handle greater risk. Instead of maintaining a $10,000 cushion, keep it at $5,000 and invest the rest for greater gains, perhaps through equity or bond mutual funds.

As part of this plan, set up a line of credit with your bank, trust company or credit union. The line of credit is a preapproved loan limit you can tap in full or part whenever you want. It doesn't cost anything until you use it. If a cash crunch overwhelms your basic $5,000 cushion, judiciously tap the line of credit until or unless you can redeem mutual fund units without losing money.

This route can be quite risky if you live close to the edge. In the worst case, you could have mutual fund units worth much less than you paid, mounting line of credit interest costs, and no income with which to service that debt.

Some advisers suggest minimizing your emergency fund in order to maximize your RRSP contributions. The idea is that RRSP money can be withdrawn if you really need it. If that's your only way to make a maximum RRSP contribution, consider it. But understand that once withdrawn, RRSP money can't be put back. You will be robbing the future to fund current needs, and the long-term tax-sheltered growth you sacrifice could make this the most expensive source of money you will ever have.

6

Any Interest in Compounding?

MOST PERSONAL FINANCE BOOKS SIDESTEP math. That's too bad, because just a few basic concepts open up a whole bunch of doors in the financial world.

The next few pages will show how compound growth can work for and against you. You'll see why $1 million may not be anywhere near as much as you think. You'll see how one 9% loan costs more than another, how to calculate the annual return on a mutual fund or other investment, and how financial institutions can artificially boost the advertised yields on their GICs.

Understanding compounding is one of the keys to understanding financial planning. As a former math klutz, I can assure you that mastering this stuff will make your future financial decision-making a whole lot easier.

Calculator ready? Let's go.

Here's compounding in its most familiar form: You put $1,000 into a two-year bank deposit at 5% compounded annually. After one year the bank owes you $50 interest. They add that to your principal, and for the second year you then have $1,050 earning 5%. Interest for that year totals $52.50. The deposit then matures and you're paid a total of $1,102.50.

Picture an inverted pyramid. The amount just grows and grows and grows. What would $1,000 be worth after 20 years of 10% compounding? $6,727.50. After 30 years? $17,449.40. While the timespan increased by 50%, the total accumulation rose by more than 250%. After 40 years, your initial $1,000 will be worth $45,259.26. And on and on.

Here are two easy ways to estimate future growth:

- **Rule of 72.** Divide 72 by your growth rate. That's roughly how long it will take your money to double. At 10%, about 7.2 years.

- **Rule of 113.** Divide 113 by your growth rate to see how long it will take your money to triple. At 10%, about 11.3 years.

Want a more precise calculation? Here are three ways:

- **Tables.** Appendix A-1 at the end of this book is a compound growth table. Say you're 14 years from retirement. If you invest $1,000 today compounding at 8% annually, how much will you have on the big-R day? Go to the row for year 14. Read across to the 8% column. Multiply the factor there — 2.9372 — by $1,000 to get the answer: $2,937.

   What if you earned 9% — just one percentage point more? Using the 9% factor — 3.3417 — you'll see your investment will grow to $3,342. That one percentage point difference produces nearly 14% more money. Always remember that compounding is exponential; over time the growth snowballs.

- **Business calculators.** Sold for as little as $25, these are programmed to do such calculations. Let's go back to the example above. Key in 1,000 and press the PV button for "present value." Key 9 and press the I button for "interest." Key 14 and press the N button for "time." Press COMP for "compute" and then FV for "future value." The screen should show something like 3,341.73.

- **Computer spreadsheet or scientific calculator.** The compound growth formula is PV*((1+1)^N). The above example would be 1,000*((1.09)^14).

   With a scientific calculator — the kind with lots of buttons that lots of kids get for school — first enter 1.09. Then press the 2nd F key for "second function." Then press the y-to-the-x key, enter 14 and press the = key. The screen should show 3.34173. Multiply that by 1,000 to get 3,341.73.

Compounding and Inflation

MOST PEOPLE associate compounding with making money. But it also works against you through inflation. Many believe inflation is dead because it's now just 1 to 2%. Say that in retirement you want $40,000 per year in today's money. How much will that really be in 20 years at 2% inflation? In appendix A-1, take the 2% factor in the 20-year row and multiply that by 40,000. That comes to $59,436. So, is inflation dead?

   If an item costs one dollar today, at 2% inflation, how long will it take that price to double? The rule of 72 tells us it would take about

36 years — well within your life span.

Appendix A-2 tells us how much a future dollar will buy in today's money. Many people dream of having $1 million in 20 years, while others think that $1 million won't be worth much then at all. See for yourself. Say inflation averages 3%. Go to the 20-year row, take the factor in the 3% column — 0.5537 — and multiply it by 1 million. Your $1 million will be worth $553,700 in today's money. Sort of puts a damper on some of the financial advertising you see, though it's still more than pocket money.

Frequency of Compounding

SO FAR WE'VE dealt only with annual compounding. But amounts might compound daily, weekly, monthly, semi-annually, etc.

The more frequent the compounding, the greater the growth rate. That's because at each compounding point, the interest to date is added to the principal and the cycle starts anew.

The formula for annualizing a rate that compounds more often is:

$$\left[1 + \frac{\text{Stated rate}}{\text{Frequency}} \right]^{\text{Frequency}} - 1$$

What's the annual equivalent of 6% compounding semi-annually? Using a business or scientific calculator, divide 0.06 by 2 to get 0.03. Add 1 and raise that to the power of 2 to get 1.0609. Subtract 1, and your annual equivalent is 6.09%. For daily compounding, use 365 as the frequency. This formula and a variation were used for the tables in appendix A-3 and appendix A-4.

Appendix A-3 could apply if you're offered a strip bond that yields 6% as above. Strip yields are based on semi-annual compounding. So 6% compounding semi-annually is the same as 6.09% compounded annually.

Appendix A-4 could apply if you're a retiree and you see that a monthly pay GIC yields 5%. In the "monthly" column in appendix A-4, find the closest rate to that; it's 5.008%. Read to the left, and you'll see that this equates to about 5.125% on an annual-pay deposit.

Many people believe earning 12% a year is the same as 1% a month. Go back to appendix A-4 and find the compound monthly rate that produces 12% annually. It's 11.387. Divide that by 12. If you earn 0.949% a month, you'll total 12% for the year.

The compounding frequency is also why a 9% car loan costs more than a 9% mortgage and a 9% interest charge by Revenue Canada costs still more.

Huh?

Standard mortgages compound semi-annually. So a 9% mortgage really costs 9.20% if you annualize the rate. Car and other consumer loans typically compound monthly. So their 9% rate is really 9.38% when annualized. Revenue Canada's interest rates compound daily, so its 9% is really 9.42% per year. Ready for a surprise? Credit cards like Visa and MasterCard don't compound the interest they bill you. 16% is 16%. Charge cards do compound — usually monthly.

Investment Returns

MANY INVESTORS have no idea of how their investments have done on an annual basis. Say you invested $1,000 seven years ago and now have $2,947. What's the average annual compound growth rate? Here's the formula:

$$\left[\frac{\text{Current value}}{\text{Original value}} \right]^{\left(\frac{1}{\text{time}} \right)} - 1$$

Using a business or scientific calculator, divide 1 by the amount of time — seven years. Store the answer — 0.14286 — in memory. Now divide the current value of $2,947 by the original value of $1,000 to get 2,947. Hit the 2nd F key and then the y-to-the-x one. Press the memory recall key to retrieve the 0.14286. Hit the = key to get 1.16696. Subtract 1 and your answer is 16.696% a year.

This exercise may seem academic, but it's not. Take the five-year escalator GICs that were introduced during RRSP season in early 1993. Each year the interest rate changes. Once you calculate the total maturity value, you can use this formula to calculate the blended yield — the true annual rate at which your money's growing, and one far lower than the final-year rate played up in the advertising.

Every so often, a small financial institution or deposit broker will hype advertised returns on regular RRSP GICs. Instead of using the above formula — the recognized standard — they calculate the so-called "average yield." Say you deposit $1,000 for five years at 5%. You end up with $1,276.28 — $1,000 of principal and $276.28 of interest. Using the formula above, that works out to 5% a year compounding annually. But if marketers want to hype the rate, they'll divide the total interest — $276.28 — by 5, since the money is on deposit five years. The result — $55.26 — represents the average annual earnings. It's also 5.5% of the $1,000 principal, so they claim the deposit pays 5.5%.

To make sure consumers can compare apples to apples, the U.S. Congress passed two laws requiring loan and deposit advertising to cite standard annualized rates based on the recognized compound interest formula. Those are the annualized percentage rate (APR) and annualized percentage yield (APY) you see on their ads. Our federal and provincial governments are now implementing an APR rule for consumer loans — but slowly.

Here's another, little-known use for this formula. Many people with self-directed RRSPs buy strip bonds. Those bonds pay the investor a set amount when they mature, but the bonds can be sold early for a market value that varies as interest rates rise and fall. Do you hold or sell?

Suppose that two years ago you paid $15,448 for a strip that will mature at $55,000 after 16.5 years. That represented annual growth of about 8%. After two years at 8%, you would expect the bond and its accrued growth to be worth about $18,019. But your broker tells you that because of the workings of the bond market, that strip could now fetch about $20,000 if you sell it early. So you're ahead by about $2,000.

Divide 1 by the time remaining — 14.5 years. That's 0.06897. Store it in memory. Divide the $55,000 maturity value by the current $20,000 market value to get 2.75. Use the y-to-the-x function to raise 2.75 by the 0.06897 you stored. The screen should show 1.07226. Subtract 1 and you'll see that because the bond's value has gotten ahead of itself, the best you'll do between today and maturity is about 7.2% a year. In other words, $20,000 growing at 7.2% will be worth about $55,000 in 14.5 years.

Is there another investment that's likely to do better than 8.9%? Although you may be trading a guaranteed yield for an uncertain one, you may feel the potential extra gain is worth the risk.

Series of Payments

ANOTHER COMMON compounding application: What will your RRSP be worth 20 years from now if it grows at 10%? Appendix A-1 lets you calculate the future value of one deposit, but what if you contribute $1,000 every year? You could do 20 compound growth calculations, or you could enter the wonderful world of annuities.

Many people think annuities are just retirement products. Wrongo! An annuity is a mathematical concept — a series of payments. Your monthly car lease payments constitute an annuity for the leasing company.

In this case, you'll have 20 annual RRSP deposits, starting one year from now. Instead of doing 20 calculations, use the factors in appendix A-5. The 20-year factor at 10% is 57.2750. Multiply that by the $1,000 deposited each year. Your RRSP will grow to $57,275.

That's if you wait a year to start contributing. If you contribute now and follow up at this time every year, you have an "annuity due." That's a start-of-the-year series. See appendix A-6. The 20-year factor there is 63.0025. That's 10% higher than the previous one, because each 10% deposit goes to work a year sooner. So your total accumulation is $63,002. Shifting each contribution forward by one year boosts your retirement pot by 10%. Easy, and risk-free. That's why so many financial advisers urge people to make RRSP contributions early in the year, not during the 60-day grace period the following January and February.

That's also why it pays to understand compound math. Now don't you feel like a better person?

7

Deep in the Heart of Taxes

THINK YOU PAY A LOT OF TAX? YOU'RE RIGHT. Taxes are the average family's largest yearly expense, according to Statistics Canada. Every year the Fraser Institute, a Vancouver economic think tank, calculates "Tax Freedom Day." That's the day by which the average Canadian has earned enough to pay all taxes for the year. Not just income tax, but sales taxes and user charges such as licence plate fees. That day usually falls about midway through the year. In other words, governments claim about half your earnings.

There's little you can do to ease the bite from consumption taxes like the GST or user fees. But some basic income tax planning can save hundreds or thousands of dollars.

The income tax rules are amazingly complex and change often, but nearly all planning opportunities rest on a few basic concepts.

Marginal Versus Effective Tax Rates

THREE LITTLE words that mean so much: marginal tax rate. Understanding this concept helps you determine how much of your earnings go to government. That knowledge then aids in a wide range of lifestyle career and investment decisions.

You really have two tax rates:

- The "marginal tax rate" is, technically, the tax rate on your top dollar of income. It's often referred to as your "tax rate" or "tax bracket."

- The "effective tax rate" is the percentage of income that's paid out in federal and provincial tax. It's also called your "average tax rate."

Many people believe these rates are the same. They are not. Canada has a "progressive" tax system. Ottawa and the provinces have established ranges so that higher amounts of income are taxed at higher rates. The 1998 ranges are shown in appendix B-1 at the end of this book.

Suppose you are in the 50% tax bracket. That means your top slice of income is taxed at 50%. Lower slices are taxed at lower rates. If you earn less than $100,000, you'll probably find your effective, or average, tax rate is 20-40%.

Here are four ways to use that information:

- Say you make $40,000 a year and are debating whether to give up your job to care for your kids. If your effective tax rate is 30%, knock that much off your salary. So, you'd really be giving up only $28,000. Subtract the cost of commuting and other work-related expenses plus the after-tax cost of daycare. Full-time work may not pay.

- After reaching the top marginal rate for salary, you'll keep no more than 50 cents from each additional dollar you earn from your job. Realizing that, you can make an informed decision on whether it's worthwhile to put in less time at work and more time with your family or in leisure pursuits.

- You're offered a new job. It pays $5,000 a year more, but requires dressier clothes and an additional hour in daily commuting. If your marginal rate for salary is 50%, the higher paycheque yields only $2,500 after tax. That's about $48 a week. Is that worth five extra hours of weekly commuting and the increased wardrobe cost? Probably not, unless the new job is more satisfying or offers better career prospects.

- Revenue Canada tells you that you can put $5,000 into your RRSP. That seems like a lot of money, but part of it is really an interest-free loan from government. That's because RRSP contributions are tax-deductible. Say you earn $5,000 a month and your marginal tax rate is 50%. Should you put one month's salary in an RRSP? If you don't, 50% of that money will be gone — taken by government as income tax. If you do, government will let you invest the full amount. So your upfront tax saving equals 50% of $5,000, or $2,500.

   Maybe. Let's get nitpicky. Remember that your income is distributed among several tax brackets. Say you are $2,000 over the threshold for the 50% bracket. The top $2,000 of your $5,000 RRSP contribution would generate a 50% tax saving worth $1,000. The other $3,000 would fall one bracket down. If the rate there is 45%, that part of your tax saving would

be worth $1,350. So the total tax saved would really be $2,350. That's
one reason many people are disappointed when their RRSP contributions
don't produce the tax refunds they were expecting.

Tax Rates on Investments

IF YOU'RE not confused yet, let's up the ante. Grab your calculator and
follow along.

You really have several marginal tax rates. That's because some forms
of investment income are taxed more heavily than others. The marginal
rate for each form of income is shown in appendix B-1.

Interest

Interest is fully taxed. If a GIC pays $100 of interest and the applicable
marginal rate is 50%, you'll lose $50 in tax and keep $50.

Capital Gains

Capital gains get off more lightly. Only 75% of the gain is taxed. If you
have a $100 capital gain and your overall marginal rate is 50%, you'll
lose $37.50 in tax and keep $62.50.

That tax break over interest reflects the increased risk of investing in
stocks, real estate and other property without guaranteed returns. The
capital gains marginal rates in appendix B-1 reflect that lower tax bite.

Suppose your marginal rates are 50% on interest and 35% on capital
gains. You have $1,000 to invest. A 5% GIC would pay $25 after tax.
Thanks to the lower tax rate on capital gains, your $1,000 needs only
about 3.8% appreciation to produce the same after-tax return.

How did I get 3.8%? You want a $25 gain after tax. Our example's
marginal rate for capital gains was 35%. That means you'll keep 65% of
the pre-tax gain. Divide 25 by 65 to get 0.3846. Multiply that by 10 to
get 3.8%.

If you sell a stock or other property for less than you paid, you have
a "capital loss." For investments like stocks, that loss can be used to
offset any capital gains in the current year or the three prior years. If you
don't have enough gains to use up your loss this year, you can carry the
loss forward for use in any future year. Other rules govern losses on
personal-use property, "listed" personal property like stamp or coin
collections, and shares in private corporations. Consult Revenue
Canada's capital gains tax guide or a tax adviser.

Capital gains investors used to get a special break — a lifetime exemption that allowed them to make up to $100,000 tax-free. That was killed in 1994 but it can still save you tax if you had unrealized gains in place on Feb. 22, 1994, and filed special exemption forms with Revenue Canada by April 30, 1997.

The most likely beneficiaries are mutual fund investors who "crystal-lized" their paper gains by reporting them on a special form with their 1994 tax returns. The tax-free gain reported for each fund was credited to a pool — one pool per fund. Technically, the pool is called an "exempt capital gains balance."

As the fund makes capital gains distributions, you can tap those pool credits to make the payouts tax-free. The pool credits apply only to distributions of capital gains, not interest or dividends. And one fund's pool cannot offset the tax bite on another fund's distributions even if both funds are run by the same fund group.

What if you sell your fund units before using up the pool? The unused credits can be applied against the taxable capital gain if you redeem at a profit. They simply vanish if you redeem at a loss. Do you think you might reinvest in that fund before 2005? If so, keep a minimal stake now. That way, your unused pool will remain intact to save you tax after you buy more units later.

Pool credits left after 2004 can't be used to make distributions tax-free. Instead, they'll be added to the holding's "adjusted cost base" for deter-mining the eventual capital gain or loss when the units are finally sold.

Investments such as common shares, collectibles such as art, and real estate such as a family cottage are treated differently than mutual funds. There is no ECGB pool to tap year by year.

Instead, the exemption claim sets a 'crystallization' value for each investment. That amount becomes the new cost base for the taxable cap-ital gain or the capital loss when the holding is finally sold.

This might seem academic since the deadline for claiming the exemp-tion is long gone, but you should be aware of it in case you're helping an older person, perhaps an elderly parent who was wise enough to take advantage of the exemption when it was still available.

Say John's common shares, bought for $20,000, were worth $60,000 on Feb. 22, 1994, and he had $25,000 of capital gains exemption avail-able. John set his crystallization value at $45,000 — just enough to use up his limit. In Revenue Canada's eyes, John sold the shares and imme-diately rebought them at the crystallized value of $45,000.

If John later sells the shares for $80,000, the taxable capital gain will be $35,000, based on his new $45,000 cost. Had he not made his election, the taxable gain would be $60,000 based on his original $20,000 ACB.

The crystallization rules for real estate such as a cottage are similar to those for John's common shares but require an extra step to exclude appreciation starting March 1, 1992, when Ottawa began phasing out the capital gains exemption for real estate.

Dividends

Dividends from Canadian corporations carry the lowest tax bite. If you have a $100 dividend and your overall marginal rate is 50%, you'll lose just $33.33 in tax and keep $66.67.

That's because of the "dividend tax credit." The dividend tax credit recognizes that corporations already face tax on profits before distributing them to shareholders as dividends. This credit does not apply to foreign corporations. Their dividends are fully taxed.

Many savers — especially retirees — learned about the dividend tax credit in 1992 after interest rates on GICs and bonds fell from 10%+ to levels not seen since the 1950s. Relying on interest-bearing deposits meant a dramatic drop in their spendable income.

But at that time, some decent stocks paid 7% or more in dividends eligible for the dividend tax credit. Thanks to that credit, a 7.75% dividend yields about the same after-tax return as a 10% GIC. In general, multiply the "dividend yield" by 1.3. To get the dividend yield, divide the total dividend paid on the stock over one year by the price you would pay for one share. Include your brokerage fee in that cost. Brokerage fees are ignored when dividend yields are quoted in newspaper stock tables and by brokers. You should include them, however, since they do increase your upfront cost.

The marginal rates for dividends shown in appendix B-1 already reflect the dividend tax credit.

Your Break-Even Point

HERE'S HOW to determine what investment return you need to break even after tax and inflation:

$$\frac{\text{Inflation rate}}{1 - \text{Marginal tax rate in investment}} = \text{Break-even rate}$$

Say inflation is 2% and you want to invest in a safe interest-bearing investment like a Canada Savings Bond. The precise marginal rate for interest income in your tax bracket can be found in appendix B-1, but let's assume it's 50%. Subtract 0.50 from 1 to get 0.50. Divide that into

0.02 to get 0.04, or 4%. If the CSB pays less than 4%, you'll be losing money on an after-tax, after-inflation basis. Frustrating.

Deductions and Credits

UNION/PROFESSIONAL dues, child-care expenses, RRSP contributions and a number of other payments generate tax "deductions." Canada/Quebec Pension Plan contributions, tuition fees, medical expenses, charitable donations and a number of other payments generate tax "credits."

What's the difference?

The higher your tax rate, the more valuable a deduction becomes. That's because it takes a chunk off the top of your earnings and makes it tax-free by deducting it from the income on which your tax is based. If you earn $50,000 and have a $5,000 deduction, your taxable income falls to $45,000.

The value of a deduction is thus determined by your marginal tax rate. If your marginal rate is 40%, a $1,000 RRSP contribution will save you $400 in tax. If your marginal rate is 50%, a $1,000 RRSP contribution will save you $500.

Tax credits are aimed at making the system more fair. Medical expenses used to be tax-deductible. That meant a $100 expense could generate about $50 in tax savings for a high-income person but only about $25 for a low-bracket taxpayer. As tax credits, medical expenses now generate about the same relief, no matter what your tax bracket.

While a tax deduction reduces your taxable income, a tax credit directly reduces the tax you owe. So a $1 tax credit is worth $1.

Really?

Not quite. Most credits reduce your federal tax before surtaxes and provincial taxes are calculated. Thus, they reduce the base for those surtaxes and provincial taxes. That means a $1 federal tax credit really saves you $1.50 or more in federal and provincial tax.

You may have noticed the term "non-refundable tax credit" on your tax return. These credits lose their value if you have so many deductions or so little income that you owe no tax. In the following cases, they can be transferred to others if they are not needed to reduce the owner's tax bill to zero:

- The pension and age tax credits can be shifted from one spouse to another.

- The disability tax credit can be transferred to any supporting person. This credit is worth more than $1,000 in tax savings, but many people miss it because they don't consider themselves disabled. Check the rules in the

T1 general tax guide. For more information, see a Revenue Canada pamphlet called Tax Information for People with Disabilities.

- The education and tuition credits can be transferred to the student's spouse, parents — including in-laws — or grandparents.

Alternative Minimum Tax

THE ALTERNATIVE minimum tax was implemented in 1986 to ensure that even with tons of deductions, those earning more than $40,000 still pay at least 25% tax.

Most people with employment income need not worry about it, but the AMT is a potential trap for those who invest in limited partnership tax shelters or reap enormous capital gains.

If you fall into either of those categories, get Revenue Canada's AMT worksheet. You will recalculate your taxable income, adding back tax shelter claims and/or the untaxed 25% of your capital gains and a few other special items.

Then you calculate the tax due and pay whichever is higher — your original tax computation or the AMT one.

If AMT has to be paid because of a sharp spike in income, you can reclaim part or all of it as a tax credit over the next seven years, assuming you don't face AMT again.

AMT used to be a trap for people who left jobs with large RRSP-eligible severance payments and those who made large pension or RRSP contributions to catch up for prior years. But the 1998 federal budget excluded those payments from the AMT rules. If you had to pay AMT because of a severance payment from as far back as 1994, contact Revenue Canada to see if you're due a refund.

The Value of Tax Deferral

WHY PAY today the tax bill you can put off till tomorrow?

Deferral is a fundamental concept in tax planning. Always pay income tax when it's due. Otherwise, you face stiff interest charges and even penalties. But there are ways to delay the day of reckoning.

Deferral provides two benefits. Let's examine them by looking at the most common — and easiest — deferral opportunity, an RRSP contribution.

First, when you defer tax you effectively get a free loan, since money that would have gone to the tax collector stays in your hands, at least for a while.

Suppose you're in the 50% tax bracket and your RRSP contribution limit this year is $10,000. If you don't make an RRSP contribution, you'll have to pay $5,000 of tax. If you do make the $10,000 contribution, Revenue Canada will put aside your $5,000 tax bill for as long as the money sits in your plan. So you get an interest-free $5,000 investment loan for 10, 20, 30 or 40 years. Or even longer.

As if that's not enough, Revenue Canada will also defer tax on your RRSP's annual earnings.

The second benefit of tax deferral comes at the day of reckoning. With good planning — or luck — the deferred tax bill will become payable in a year when you're in a lower tax bracket. Let's roll forward to retirement time. You're no longer in the 50% tax bracket. Your marginal rate is now 27%. Remember that $10,000 RRSP contribution back in 1998? Well, now you withdraw that money. But instead of having to pay $5,000 of tax, your new marginal rate means you'll owe just $2,700.

Capital gains investing is another form of tax deferral. Your stock, mutual fund units or investment real estate will, we hope, grow in value each year. But that appreciation is taxed only when the investment is sold. So, a patient investor can reap years of tax-sheltered compound growth.

"Universal" life insurance policies offer tax deferral too. Each year you can put a set amount into a "side fund," where it earns compound interest. But no tax is due until the money is withdrawn.

Annuities also offer tax deferral. Again, the capital earns compound interest, but no tax is due until you receive payments.

People starting a business used to benefit from tax deferral by setting a business year-end early in the year, often January 31, instead of using the normal December 31 calendar year-end. But the 1995 federal budget killed that break for new entrepreneurs. Those already using fiscal year-ends were given 10 years to phase in calendar year reporting.

Why It's Not Good to Get a Tax Refund

WITH TAX deferral, the government gives you an interest-free loan. When you get a tax refund, that means you've paid too much tax and, effectively, given government an interest-free loan.

RRSP contributions, tax shelter losses and certain other expenses generate tax deductions. Normally, however, you still pay that tax — through source deductions by your employer — before getting it back after filing your return the following year. So, in some cases, governments can get free use of your money for up to 17 months. Maybe more.

There may be a way to get your money back sooner. The Income Tax Act allows Revenue Canada to reduce the tax withheld from paycheques in cases of "undue hardship." But officials bend that rule if your tax account has been kept in good order and you can prove you have legitimate deductions for the current year. Revenue Canada is really just passing up money it would have had to return anyway.

Simply call the source deductions section of your district taxation office. Some offices have unofficial forms you can fill out. Others just ask for a letter. Attach copies of your documentation and provide the name, address and phone number of your employer's payroll officer.

Processing takes about eight weeks. If your request is approved, your employer will be authorized to deduct less tax from your pay, spreading the deduction amount over your paycheques for the rest of the year. Suppose you are entitled to a $3,000 refund because you contributed $8,000 to your RRSP. If there are 15 paycheques left in the year, each one's take-home amount will be increased by $200.

Remember that by boosting your cash flow now, you're giving up a tax refund down the road. Don't fritter away this extra cash flow; put it to use in debt reduction, investment or some other way that will help you meet the goals you set out earlier.

Income-Splitting

SUPPOSE YOU make a lot more money than your spouse. That puts you in a much higher tax bracket. Wouldn't it be wonderful if you could simply invest money in his or her name so its earnings will attract little or no tax?

That's the essence of "income-splitting," where you shift money to a spouse, a child or some other person. It is a wonderful idea, but Ottawa has already thought about it and imposed "attribution rules" that sharply limit its use. These rules "attribute" back to you any tax due. There are rules for spouses, children and others. We'll go over them briefly and then look at some planning opportunities.

Spouses

If you give your spouse money for investment, Revenue Canada will tax you on the interest, dividends or capital gains. Say you transfer some shares to your spouse in exchange for other property. Attribution rules will apply unless you receive fair market value. Be careful about transferring losers. Under a special rule, you would not be able to claim a capital loss, though the amount of the loss can be added to your spouse's acquisition cost for tax purposes.

There is, however, a bit of a loophole called "second generation income." Say you give your spouse $10,000 for the purchase of a compounding 5% GIC. Each year you are taxable on the first generation income — the $500 of interest earned by the $10,000 of capital. But all compound interest — the second generation income — belongs to your spouse without attribution.

If you lend your spouse money for investment, the attribution rules will apply unless you charge interest. You must base the interest rate on either a commercial rate or the "prescribed rate" Revenue Canada sets every three months. You can pick whichever is less. At today's low interest rates, this can be a very interesting ploy. Your spouse must pay the interest within 30 days of each year-end. You must report it on your return like any other interest income.

Attribution rules do not apply to income from an active business. Thus, you can give or lend money to an entrepreneurial spouse. Note that it must be a true business; you can't just give your spouse money to buy a limited partnership tax shelter. Also, these arrangements can be tricky, so you should get professional advice.

Minor Children

Here's a common situation. Mom and dad buy a GIC or Canada Savings Bond and put it in baby's name, figuring that means they won't have to pay tax on the interest themselves.

That ain't necessarily so.

The spousal attribution rules above also apply to children under 18. That includes grandchildren, great-grandchildren, nieces and nephews. But there are two exceptions:

- There is no attribution on capital gains. Instead of buying a GIC, suppose mom and dad took their spare $1,000 and opened an account for their child in an equity-based mutual fund. If the account is set up properly, the capital gains will be taxable in the child's hands, whether in the form of a yearly distribution from the fund or redemption of units. The attribution rules would apply to first-generation dividends or interest distributed by the fund.

- If you give your spouse investment money, the attribution rules apply to all future earnings. For gifts to a child — as opposed to loans — attribution stops at the end of the year the child turns 18 and becomes an adult.

Adult Children and Other Family Members

The attribution rules extend to income-splitting investment loans for children over 18, in-laws and grandparents. But that applies only if you lend — not give — them the money. This does not affect mortgage or consumer loans. Mom and dad can still help their kids by granting them a no- or low-rate deal.

Planning Opportunities

Some of the following strategies require professional advice. Several are discussed more fully in later chapters. All require careful documentation. Each person in the arrangement should have a separate bank account. Money flows into that account and then into higher-yielding investments.

For minor children, you can open a bank, brokerage or mutual fund account "in trust." Tax rules require clear separation between the adult who provides the money and the one who controls it as trustee. Also, the provider cannot reclaim the money, and the child gets full control on reaching the age of majority. Some institutions require a formal trust drafted by a lawyer.

Remember that once your child earns more than a certain amount — currently about $6,500 — he or she may have to file a tax return and pay tax. Also, you could lose full use of tax credits for your spouse or child. Use last year's tax return for a trial run.

- **Family expenses.** Say a couple both have income but there is a wide gap. Each partner should deposit their income into a separate bank account. Then, have the higher-taxed spouse pay all family expenses, while the lower taxed invests his or her full income.

  Say the lower-taxed spouse owes tax when the yearly return is due. As with family expenses, the higher-taxed one can pay that bill, so the first spouse's investment fund remains intact.

- **Gifts and inheritances.** The same as above. Say a woman who earns far less than her husband receives money from her parents. She should invest that in her own name so future earnings get taxed at her lower rate.

  Many people have relatives outside Canada. There is no attribution on money from a person who is not a Canadian resident for tax purposes. Say your parents, who live overseas, send your new-born $10,000. That belongs to the child and should be kept separate from money you provide.

- **Child tax benefit.** The "baby bonus" can be invested in your child's name without attribution. It's a great way to save for university.

- **Registered education savings plan.** RESPs are another way to save for your child's education. Investments grow tax-free until withdrawn, when the earnings are taxed in the student's hands and the capital comes out tax-free.

- **Child's allowance.** Yet another way to build a university or college fund. If your child has a part-time or summer job, make a deal. The child invests all take-home pay and you provide an equivalent amount to cover the kid's expenses now.

- **Spousal RRSP.** This is usually a long-term strategy aimed at saving future tax by enabling two people to balance their retirement incomes. It can also work in the short term if one spouse is planning to stop work in a few years.

- **C/QPP splitting.** You can have up to half your Canada or Quebec Pension Plan payments made to your spouse if you're both at least 60. The maximum split is determined by a formula. Contact your local federal Income Security Programs office or QPP.

- **Self-employed.** The self-employed can pay spouses and children reasonable salaries for bona fide services they perform in the business. As with income-splitting, the recipients become eligible for unemployment insurance, Canada/Quebec Pension Plan and RRSP contributions.

    Owners of incorporated businesses have more leeway. They should consult their professional advisers about dividend payments and estate freezing.

Sideline Business

HOBBIES OFTEN turn into sideline businesses. If the business is genuine — meaning there's "reasonable expectation of profit" in a few years — you can deduct expenses from the business income. And you can deduct a loss from your regular income. But you must be able to show your business is genuine.

Artists and writers have often had run-ins with Revenue Canada. So tax officials produced special interpretation bulletins for them — IT-504R and 525. Part-time farms — another big source of conflict — are covered by IT-322R.

Moving Expense Deduction

EXPENSES RELATED to moving can be a gold mine for those moving at least 40 kilometres closer to a new job.

Along with obvious transportation costs, you can write off the real estate commission on the home you sold and the legal fees and land transfer tax on the home bought at the new location. Revenue Canada has a pamphlet called Are You Moving? It lists the eligible expenses.

The move does not have to occur in the year you change jobs, just within a "reasonable" period. A 1989 court ruling allowed a taxpayer named Beyette to claim moving expenses five years after his new job began. He showed he intended to move earlier, but delayed that for financial and health reasons.

Students can deduct expenses for moving to take a summer job. The return to school is deductible only against taxable scholarships, fellowships, research grants or similar awards.

Equivalent-to-Married Tax Credit

THIS TAX credit is most often mentioned in regard to single mothers, but it has far broader applications.

It applies to women and men who are single, separated, divorced or widowed and who support a relative living with them. The EMTC lets you claim that dependent under the credit that would have been available for a spouse. It can generate more than $1,300 in tax savings.

Medical Expense Credits

THE AREA of medical expenses definitely requires planning. Here are some tips:

- To generate any tax savings, the medical expenses must be above 3% of net income or a certain dollar amount set every year. In 1998, that amount was $1,614. But one spouse can claim expenses for all family members. This claim should be made by the spouse with the lower income. The lower the income, the lower the 3% threshold.

- You can claim expenses for any 12-month period ending in the year. If you had unusable expenses last year, try to schedule this year's discretionary medical spending within 12 months of your previous spending. For example, you might find that your medical expense year runs from last June 15 to this June 15.

- The credits are based on when expenses are paid, not when the service is performed. Will your child need braces next year? It might be worthwhile to pay for them now.

- Make sure you claim all eligible expenses. They are listed in Revenue Canada Interpretation Bulletin IT-519.

Many people don't realize they can claim the cost of private — not provincially run — medical, drug and dental insurance. That includes out-of-Canada medical coverage for your sunbelt vacation as well as money deducted from your pay for employer-sponsored health plans. Increasingly, employer plans are imposing or boosting deductibles. Those unreimbursed payments qualify for the credit.

Charitable Donation Tax Credit

HERE'S ANOTHER area where planning pays off. You get a 17% federal tax credit for the first $200 of donations and 29% for everything over that. Clearly, you should maximize the amount over $200. Some tips:

- One spouse can claim the other's donations.

- Do you plan to make donations early next year? Shift them forward to this December to boost this year's total contributions. That's especially worthwhile if you are already over the $200 level. Each new dollar will qualify for the maximum credit and you'll get your tax break one year early.

- Combine several years' donations. You can save tax receipts for up to five years. Say you normally contribute $150 a year. You'll never qualify for the higher credit if you claim your donation each year. If instead you claim every other year, your charity will be in the same position but $100 of your donations will qualify for the 29% credit. If you combine five years of receipts, $550 will qualify.

- Donations qualify for tax credits only if the charity is registered with Revenue Canada and you get an official receipt. Many charities won't issue receipts for donations of less than $10; the processing is too expensive for them. So, should you pass up the Salvation Army bell-ringer on the coldest day of the year? No. You could write a cheque for $10 or more, attach a note requesting a receipt and drop that in his or her kettle.

- You can get tax credits by donating valuable art and other cultural property to museums. But there are special, complex rules. Get professional advice. You can also claim credits for donations to American charities like PBS TV if you have U.S.-source income.

- Would you like to leave money to a charity when you die? It's often better to give the charity a life insurance policy now. The charity will end up with more money, and you will get tax credits you can use while still alive. Again, there are certain rules. See Revenue Canada interpretation bulletin IT-244R3. Most life insurance agents are well versed in this area.

- The 1997 federal budget granted a special tax break for people who donate publicly traded securities, such as stocks and bonds, that have grown in value. They face tax on just 37.5% of their capital gain. That's half the normal tax hit. The move was aimed at encouraging large gifts. Between the special break and the charitable credit, Ottawa says tax relief will typically cover about 64% of those contributions.

The Easiest Way to Save Tax

'TIS BETTER to save than to earn. Money you earn is taxed. Money you save is not.

This seemingly simple concept can be a very powerful tool. It applies the marginal tax rate concept to the value of do-it-yourself projects and careful shopping.

Instead of putting in more time at work earning fully taxed dollars, would you be better off putting in more time at home? That's a personal decision based on career demands and prospects, but you can do some quantifiable analysis.

Earlier, I made the point that once you reach a certain income level, the time spent earning $1 leaves no more than 50 cents in your pocket after tax. But if you save $1 by doing a household job yourself or buying an item on sale, that investment of time leaves 100 cents in your pocket.

Suppose the planks on your deck need replacing — an easy one-day job for you and the kids. Do you spend a Saturday fixing up the deck or putting in more time at work? Suppose that extra work time is worth $300, while a carpenter's labor would run just $200. Use this formula to take a closer look:

$$\frac{\text{Carpenter's fee}}{1 - \text{Your marginal tax rate}} = \text{Real cost}$$

Say your marginal rate for salary is 45%. One minus 0.45 equals 0.55. Divide $200 — the carpenter's labor — by 0.55 and you find you must earn $363.64 in pre-tax dollars to be able to pay the carpenter $200.

If the carpenter wants only $150, this formula gives you the ideal rationale for not doing the job yourself — especially if you hate to hammer.

The same principle applies to shopping. You want a stereo. Should you "invest" four hours checking prices to save $50? As above, your marginal tax rate is 45%. Divide $50 by 0.55 to get $90.91. So saving $50 is the same as earning $91.Whether that's worth four hours depends on the value of your time and how much you enjoy shopping.

You can also reap high returns with little or no time cost. When grocery shopping, do you stock up on loss-leader items? They're the products sold below cost to entice you into the store. Maybe a $1.50 can of frozen orange juice is priced at 90 cents. You buy 12, a two-month supply. Your $10.80 purchase is worth $18. Divide your $7.20 of savings by your $10.80 cost and you'll find you've made nearly 67% on your money. That's tax-free and risk-free, assuming OJ isn't always on sale and your freezer doesn't conk out.

This routine won't make you a millionaire, but consider Statistics Canada's finding that the average family spends about $6,000 a year on groceries — their third-highest annual expense after taxes and shelter. Saving just 10% overall is worth $600. For someone earning $45,000, that's the same as a pre-tax salary bonus of $1,034 or 2.3%. Remember your goals from chapter 2? Why not earmark this freed-up money for one or more of them?

Fleeing the Taxman

MANY PEOPLE believe they can save tons of tax by moving themselves, or at least their money, outside of Canada. Legally, that's harder than you think. Get professional advice.

If you are moving, be aware that Revenue Canada may still consider you a Canadian resident for tax purposes. Call them for Interpretation Bulletin IT-221R2 and/or their plain English guide on emigration. If you do get non-resident status, you may face onerous departure tax on your investments, especially if you own an incorporated business.

If sending only money outside of Canada, be aware that you're still taxable on worldwide income from passive investments. And, as of April 30, 1999, you may face stiff penalties if you hold more than $100,000 in foreign accounts and don't give Revenue Canada the details.

8

Basic Banking

THE 1980s BROUGHT A REVOLUTION TO Canadian banking. After getting burned on billion-dollar loans to foreign governments and high-flying financiers, bankers concluded they could do as well, if not better, by just serving ordinary people, especially current retirees and baby boomers heading for the "serious saving" part of the life cycle.

Institutions began reverting to their more traditional roles as financial retailers. We've since seen an explosion of convenient personal services along with new or sharply higher fees for just about everything.

Where to Go

BANK? TRUST company? Credit union? Does it matter? It does, if you have special needs such as business banking or estate management. But if you just want a place to park your money, one institution is as good as the next — assuming you feel comfortable with the deposit insurance rules explained in the next chapter.

Don't overlook credit unions. Run on a non-profit community-oriented basis, they are often more friendly, flexible and innovative than the big institutions. Daily interest accounts and biweekly mortgages are just two of the now-common services they pioneered. Many believe credit unions are tied only to certain employers or specific religious or ethnic groups. Not so. Some extend membership to anyone who lives in the area.

Residents of Ontario and Alberta can also bank at provincial government savings offices.

For the rest of this chapter, I'll refer to all financial institutions as banks. Use these criteria to select one:

- **Convenience.** Is the branch close to your home or office? Are there automatic bank machines (ABMs) in the places you go? Even with automatic banking, odds are you will have to visit the branch at some point. If you choose a bank near home, it should have evening or Saturday hours.

  Smaller trust companies may pay higher interest rates than chartered banks. But go for convenience, not rates — at least on your chequing-savings account. Wise money managers don't leave much money in those accounts, so there isn't much interest earned. And whatever interest there is gets fully taxed. In other words, a slightly higher deposit rate may be worth only a few bucks a year. Go for convenience.

- **Size.** At smaller neighbourhood branches the staff can get to know you. They are then more motivated to correct errors quickly, waive minor fees and use their discretionary power to offer better deals.

  When I bought my first home, I had a fair bit of U.S. money. My branch manager had authority to improve the exchange rate by a certain amount, but he called the bank's currency desk and got me an even better deal. The difference paid for a dryer.

- **Reputation.** The branch's, not the institution's. Institutions are so large it's easy to find bad — and good   stories about each one. Service at branches varies widely. If your friends or co-workers like a particular branch, you probably will too. Be aware, though, that managers and staff can change frequently.

- **An edge.** Banking products are generally the same, but one decisive policy or use of technology might be enough to snare your business. I moved to a bank that had a money market fund with a low minimum balance requirement and no-fee transfers through a 24-hour phone line. I park cash in the money fund and switch it to my chequing account as needed. (Money funds pay much higher rates than deposit accounts, but be cautious. Make sure you won't be hit with transfer or withdrawal fees. You could be dunned up to 2% for redemptions that occur within 90 days of deposit.)

  Don't open an inferior account just because an institution offers an attractive mortgage, car loan or credit card. You can bank at one place and borrow from another. Banks are stores. One should get all your business only if it deserves it.

  Some people prefer to have separate saving and lending institutions. If they're together and your credit card or other loan is in arrears, the standard agreements let the bank tap your savings-chequing accounts without consulting you.

Maybe you like an institution's mutual funds and want a monthly investment plan. The fund has nothing to do with the bank's normal deposit accounts. It can easily draw money from another institution.

Obviously, each bank wants all your business. The more business you do at one, the more clout you have there as a customer. The bank may well cut the interest rate on a loan if you bring in other business. That's called "relationship selling" or "cross selling" and it's OK. But the bank cannot make you bring in other business in order to get a loan. That's called "tied selling" and it's a definite no-no.

- **Fees.** Check the minimum balance required for no-fee chequing and withdrawals. Fees on less commonly used services probably aren't that important; if one institution wins on one fee, odds are the competitor wins on another. The federal government offers an Internet calculator that shows what your banking activity would cost at major institutions. It's at http://strategis.ic.gc.ca/oca.

  Don't be influenced by the offer of a free set of personalized cheques or 50% off the first year's safe deposit box rental. Pick a bank for the long term. When you apply for credit, one consideration is your stability. One test of that is how long you've banked with the same institution.

Setting up an Account

WHEN IT comes to savings and chequing accounts, banking products are remarkably similar. No matter how they're gussied up with fancy names, these accounts fall into three categories: savings, chequing or combination.

Pure savings accounts allow no chequing. Interest may be calculated and paid just twice a year. Expect two or so free withdrawals each month. After that, you'll likely be charged $1 or more. Logically, these accounts should pay higher interest rates, but that's not always the case. Pure chequing accounts let you write cheques, but they pay no interest.

Combination accounts — which are now far more prevalent — offer chequing and pay interest on savings, usually daily and usually at tiered rates. With tiering, higher interest rates are paid on balances at higher levels.

Here are some points to check:

- What are the withdrawal fees? They can really mount up. That's why you should find out the minimum balance for no-fee withdrawals and park that much in the account. Keep that money in mind as part of your emergency cushion, but don't record it in your chequebook. That way, you're less likely to accidentally fall below the no-fee threshold.

- Is there is an administration fee if the balance falls below a certain level?

- How is the interest calculated? Look for an account that calculates interest on the daily closing balance. Even if a pure savings account offers a higher rate, the interest may be based on either the minimum or average balance over a monthly or semi-annual period.

- If interest rates are tiered, does the highest applicable rate apply to all your money or just the portion in that tier? Very few institutions pay the highest rate on all money. The top tier rates may look attractive but apply only on balances over the $60,000 deposit insurance limit. Those rates can also change daily and are probably still less than what you could get on treasury bills, money market funds or short-term deposits.
  Is there a no-interest zone? Your first $1,000 might not earn anything.

- When is interest credited? That's usually monthly, but a pure savings account may do it only every six months.

A bank won't open an account unless you provide your social insurance number. It's required by federal law.

A joint account can be set up so that withdrawals can be made either by all owners or by specified people only. It's convenient in that either spouse can tap it. It's risky if your marriage is on the rocks, since either spouse can drain it. Some couples keep one joint account for common expenses and individual ones for their own money.

When opening a joint account, you will have to indicate if there is "right of survivorship." That means the account automatically passes to the other owners when one dies. Otherwise, the money can be tied up until the estate is settled.

Combination and savings account agreements contain a curious clause allowing the institution to demand either seven or 30 days' notice of any withdrawal. That prevents a 1930s-style run. I once closed an account because I was unhappy with the bank. I demanded thousands of dollars in cash so they couldn't get in a final kick by charging me for a draft. It was a busy time at the tiny branch. Lo and behold, they invoked the seven-day rule. Don't play games with bankers.

Service Plans

LOTS OF people pay a flat monthly fee for a package of services. I don't know why. The list of services looks long, but I know only a few people who use enough of them to justify shelling out $100–$150 a year or more. Go through the list and price the services you want. If the service plan includes a discount on loans, make sure the institution's loan rates and terms are competitive.

Maybe the plan's fee is discounted if you keep a high balance. Compare the discount savings to the additional after-tax interest you would earn by putting the money in a higher-yielding vehicle.

Several people told me they have service plans so they can buy traveller's cheques without commission. How often do you need traveller's cheques? What's the value of saving a 1% commission? Can you get commission-free ones through your auto club, credit card, foreign exchange dealer or other financial institution? If you need foreign currency traveller's cheques, how competitive is your bank's exchange rate?

Service plans can pay off if you're a "senior." The starting age may be as low as 55. Institutions love older people and grant them pretty good discounts. Those younger should consider skipping the service plan and just maintaining the minimum balance required to avoid transaction fees.

Chequing

ALWAYS CARRY a cheque in your wallet. Your local merchant might have a stack of "counter cheques," but your bank will charge a stiff fee to process one. Counter cheques must be handled manually since they do not have your account number encoded in magnetic ink.

If you pay transaction fees, enter them in your chequebook register at least weekly so you don't inadvertently bounce any cheques.

If chequebook entries are in pencil, it's easier to correct mistakes. I know several accountants who record only the dollar amounts for their cheques. Cents are rounded up or down. That reduces the risk of error and makes it easier to balance the account. So they say.

Once a cheque is endorsed, anyone can cash it. If you want to sign it before going to the bank, or if you use an automatic bank machine, include your account number in the endorsement along with a statement that it is "for deposit only."

"Overdraft protection" is really just an expensive line of credit. The bank guarantees it will honor your cheques. Some banks charge $1 or more each month as a standby fee. Others charge only if there's an overdraft. That's just for the guarantee; it does not include the incredibly steep interest you'll pile up until the cheque is covered. Ask how long the bank will take to tell you you're in the red. That might be 30 days after the end of the month in which the overdraft occurred. Meanwhile, the interest meter keeps ticking. A friend of mine is a retired banker. He calls overdraft interest rates "unconscionable."

Don't bounce cheques. If it's in your nature to bounce them occasionally, bank at a credit union or trust company where the staff will call you before rejecting the cheque. There are such places.

Balance your account at least once a month. The standard agreement gives you just 30 days to notify the bank of any errors. After that, you may face a search fee. That time limit does not apply when the bank accidentally puts too much in your account (of course) or if it clears a cheque that was forged or signed by an unauthorized person.

Automatic Bank Machines

I BEGAN using ABMs more than 25 years ago when they were introduced in Washington, D.C. I was probably among the first clients there. I loved the convenience then, and I love it now.

As with every banking service, understand the fees. Is there a "session fee" for using the machine? Does that replace fees for each transaction, or is it an add-on?

Transactions may cost less at ABMs than at branch counters. Utility bill payments — which cost $1 or so each at the counter — may be free. Pay those bills a few days early to ensure the machine is emptied and your payment is processed by the due date. Your creditor recognizes the processing date, not the one on your ABM receipt. Similarly, your deposit or foreign exchange transaction may be registered on the processing date, not when it actually occurred. Be aware that foreign exchange transactions may carry a surcharge.

Cash machines can be addictive. If you pay transaction fees, limit withdrawals to once or twice a month. The fees you save will easily off-set the fully taxed interest you give up. If you don't pay fees, keep cash in your account and hit the machine as needed.

When selecting a financial institution, pick one with a convenient machine network. All Canadian ABMs are linked through networks, but there's a fee each time you use a machine from another institution. Those charges are normally not covered by your institution's no-fee service, though some small institutions absorb that cost instead of maintaining their own networks.

What if the machine goofs and you realize it at the time? Report it right away. If the ABM is not at a branch and has no phone, call the customer service line, listed in your phone book, as quickly as you can. ABMs are cleared regularly, and bank employees balance the transaction logs against the cash.

Your bank machine card won't work unless your "personal identification number" is keyed in. Never, ever, tell anyone your PIN. Even bank employees and police are not authorized to see it. Never write your PIN on your bank card, even in disguised fashion. The agreement you sign requires you to keep that number apart from the card and strictly confidential.

That's especially important now that most bank machine cards double as "debit cards," which work just like cash at more than 300,000 retailers. After the card is run through a terminal and the PIN is keyed in, the full amount due is automatically transferred from your account to the store's. Imagine how easily a crook could empty your account.

If you can't remember the PIN that was issued, your branch probably has a machine that lets you change it. Don't use an obvious one like your address, birthdate or phone number.

Say your PIN is 8374. If you must write it down, don't disguise it as a phone number by just sticking three digits in front. Make the thief's life harder by adding a familiar number. For example, add your daughter's birth month — June — to the second digit. So the "phone number" becomes xxx-8974.

Many people believe they're on the hook for no more than $50 if a crook uses their bank card. That's U.S. law and applies only if the loss is reported immediately. In Canada, your card is governed by the agreement you sign. It likely says you're responsible for all transactions up to the time you report the card's loss. Banks routinely waive that clause to avoid hassles, but they don't have to.

Worried about getting robbed at a bank machine? A U.S. survey found most ABM crimes occurred between 7 pm and midnight. Avoid machines in isolated spots and areas where a bandit can pop into a car and speed away. Avoid those hidden by shrubbery. Don't let anyone lurk just behind you; he or she may be trying to see you key your PIN. Don't dawdle at the machine to count your money.

So Many Accounts

THERE ARE more savings accounts than Canadians. You probably have a couple. Why not consolidate? Maybe have one account for routine expenses and another — better yet, a higher-yielding money market fund — for medium-term savings.

Consolidation can mean higher interest rates, less work in keeping track and less risk of losing your account.

Losing a bank account?

Yup. Every June, in the Canada Gazette, the federal government publishes a list of dormant bank accounts — those that haven't been touched for at least nine years. That list — in small print with one account per line — runs several hundred pages. Every year I recognize at least one name.

Most entries are for fairly small amounts, but it's easy to spot accounts worth $50,000 or more. I suspect those people died and left no record.

After ten years of dormancy — that's six months after the list is published — the accounts are turned over to the Bank of Canada. Those worth less than $500 are held for 20 years from the last transaction date and then given to the government. The rest are held indefinitely, waiting to be claimed. The central bank holds more than one million dormant accounts going back as far as 1908. The total value is more than $130 million.

Bank of Canada staff will do a free records search for you. Write to Unclaimed Balances Services; Bank of Canada; 234 Sparks St.; Ottawa, Ont. K1A 0G9. Include the full name of the person for whom you're checking, his or her past addresses and year of death if applicable.

If you are due money, you must go to the original bank branch and prove you're the owner. The bank may charge a search fee, especially if it has to comb through years of musty records to find the original documentation. There may not even be any records past ten years, so you would never be able to complete your claim.

The Bank of Canada registry only covers chartered banks. There is no reporting requirement for dormant account at trust companies, credit unions, life insurers and other financial companies.

9

Under the Covers: Deposit Insurance

YOUR MONEY MAY BE MORE — OR LESS — protected than you think.

Banks and Trust Companies

THE FEDERAL government's Canada Deposit Insurance Corp. protects your savings up to $60,000. Right? Not necessarily.

CDIC insures deposits at banks, trust companies and loan companies across Canada. Those chartered in Quebec are covered by the Quebec Deposit Insurance Board. One institution might be covered by both systems. Deposits at branches in Quebec may fall under QDIB. Those made elsewhere fall under CDIC. Fortunately, CDIC and QDIB have the same rules and work together in honoring claims. From now on, I'll refer just to CDIC.

To qualify, a deposit must be payable in Canadian dollars, bear interest and be due in five years or less. That includes most savings and chequing accounts, term deposits, GICs, loan company debentures, money orders, drafts and certified cheques. But it rules out foreign currency deposits such as the U.S. dollar chequing accounts many people have, as well as money market and other mutual funds sold by CDIC members. People constantly ask about coverage for mutual funds sold by banks and trusts. We'll look at that a bit later in this chapter.

CDIC coverage is limited to the oft-quoted $60,000, but that is "per person per member institution." Let's examine those three elements; you might be surprised.

The $60,000 limit covers principal plus accrued, or unpaid, interest. Thus, if you put $60,000 into a five-year RRSP deposit two years ago, all the interest you've earned is at risk. See table 9.1 at the end of this chapter.

Next, the concept of the "person." That's a legal person, not a human one. Take the case of a married couple, John and Mary, both 65. They deal with one institution.

- John gets total coverage of $60,000 for all regular deposits in his name — perhaps a chequing-savings account and a term deposit.

- Mary gets the same coverage for regular deposits in her name.

- Their joint accounts and deposits are treated as a separate person. That's another $60,000 of coverage.

- John's RRSP is another person and gets $60,000 of coverage — but only for insurable deposits. Maybe John has a series of RRSP GICs at one bank. They all fall under the one $60,000 limit.

- The same goes for Mary's RRSP.

- John also has a Registered Retirement Income Fund. That's yet another person, subject to another $60,000 of coverage.

- Mary has a RRIF too.

- John has an account set up in trust for their grandson. Deposits made in trust for another person qualify for $60,000 of coverage.

- Mary has a trust account for their granddaughter. Yet another $60,000 of insurance.

So this one couple qualifies for as much as $540,000 of CDIC insurance at just one institution. Spreading their money over two institutions — perhaps a bank and a trust company — would double their protection. That might even be possible without leaving their favorite bank's counter. Let's examine the concept of the "member institution." CDIC has more than 100 of them. Each one pays premiums to the corporation, based on its total insured deposits.

For a variety of legal and business reasons, the big banks and the major trust companies hold multiple CDIC memberships. For example, Royal Bank of Canada holds a membership. So does Royal Bank Mortgage Corp. and Royal Trust, which is owned by Royal Bank. They may take deposits over the same counter, but are separate entities to CDIC. Dividing money between them brings multiple coverage.

You might find, however, that the parent and its subsidiary don't offer the same range of products. For example, a chartered bank might offer term deposits of one year or less, while the mortgage subsidiary handles all GICs.

Dividing money among several branches of the same institution does not increase your CDIC protection. In CDIC's eyes, all your deposits at all the branches are totalled.

What happens when one institution absorbs another? Say you have $30,000 in each of two banks that merge. Under a grandfathering provision in the CDIC rules, your deposits will retain their separate coverage until maturity. But any new deposits would not be covered because your existing money adds up to the $60,000 CDIC maximum. To be protected, you would have to go elsewhere or book a deposit through one of the bank's subsidiaries that has its own CDIC membership.

If an institution fails, CDIC contacts the depositors and automatically processes their cheques. You do not have to file a claim. Payout can take four to eight weeks. No interest is earned during that processing period. RRSPs and RRIFs are normally sold to other institutions. The new institutions are not required to honor the previous interest rate commitments, but they generally do. Thus, the only change for the client is a new account number.

People who buy GICs for self-directed RRSPs and RRIFs should be aware of two wrinkles.

First, always check if the GIC is CDIC-insured. Some brokers buy "jumbo GICs" from institutions and divide them among retail clients. Those certificates pay higher rates because they lack CDIC protection.

Second, certificates held in self-directed plans are not individually registered as RRSPs or RRIFs. To the issuing institution, they're normal GICs. If the institution fails, those certificates will not be included when its RRSP/RRIF portfolio is sold to another institution. Your self-directed plan is paid off for the certificates covered by CDIC, and you will have to reinvest the money, perhaps at lower rates.

If you want to make sure that a deposit is covered by CDIC, just ask your institution or call CDIC's information line at 1-800-461-2342. New rules implemented in 1998 require every branch of each institution to have a CDIC-approved list of insurable deposits. Though I said this before, it bears repeating: mutual funds sold by banks are not CDIC-insured, even money market funds.

CDIC coverage may be in for major change. A series of failures among small banks and trust companies in the '70s and '80s left the fund with a major shortfall. That was covered by loans from the federal government and a steep increase in premiums for members, but the experience strengthened the view of CDIC's biggest members that the system needs reform. The federal government set up a special committee to consider a wide range of proposals aimed at either reducing coverage across the board or imposing some cost when people choose to deal with riskier institutions. Those ideas were not accepted, but may come up again in the future. Any changes in the CDIC rules would get prominent media coverage.

Other deposit insurance plans would also reduce their coverage if the CDIC limit is cut.

Credit Unions

DEPOSIT PROTECTION for credit unions varies widely from province to province. Depending on where you live, coverage may be guaranteed by the provincial government or only by the provincial credit union system. For details on coverage in your province, contact your credit union or Credit Union Stabilization Funds of Canada; 275 Bank St.; Suite 400; Ottawa, Ont. K2P 2L6. Phone (613) 238-6747.

Life Insurance Companies

LIFE INSURANCE companies are not covered by any government deposit insurance. Instead, in 1988 they created their own industry-run fund, the Canadian Life and Health Insurance Compensation Corp. CompCorp coverage depends on the type of account:

- Class A includes life insurance policies, RRSP and RRIF deposits, and segregated funds, which are a lot like mutual funds. If the insurer fails, coverage limits per person per member company are $200,000 for life insurance protection; $60,000 for RRSPs, RRIFs and Registered Pension Plans; and $60,000 for non-registered accounts.

- Class B includes life annuities and disability insurance policies, with no option for a lump-sum cash withdrawal. The coverage limit is $2,000 per month.

- Class C includes health insurance and has a $60,000 limit.

The 1994 collapse of Confederation Life Insurance Co. showed that CompCorp's $200,000 coverage limit for life insurance and $2,000 monthly limit on annuity payments are not high enough for many people. But CompCorp officials stress that these limits are not all you would get if your insurer goes under. In past cases, policyholders ended up with 90–100% of their coverage once CompCorp and the failed company's liquidators made arrangements with other insurers. Still, those arrangements can take several years and there is no guarantee that future replacement will run that high.

One way to protect yourself is to deal with insurers that have top ratings from the independent rating services cited in chapter 14. Be aware, though, that ratings can change. Confed Life had a top rating just three years before it failed. Another way is to divide your business among several large diversified insurers so each contract is fully covered by CompCorp. That will likely cost a bit more but you'll buy peace of mind. That's particularly important when individuals or their employers buy annuities to fund retirement or long-term disability.

For more information, contact the Canadian Life and Health Insurance Association Information Centre; Suite 1700; 1 Queen St. East; Toronto, Ont. M5C 2X9. Phone (416) 777-2344 in Toronto, 1-800-268-8099 from elsewhere.

Brokerage Accounts

YOU ARE covered by the Canadian Investor Protection Fund if your brokerage account is at a firm registered with any of the five self-regulating capital market bodies. They are the Investment Dealers Association of Canada and the Montreal, Toronto, Alberta and Vancouver Stock Exchanges.

The CIPF covers "general accounts" for up to $500,000. The cash component is, however, limited to $60,000.

"Separate accounts" fall under another $500,000 limit. They include RRSPs, RRIFs and trust accounts.

The CIPF was created by the brokerage industry in 1990 after the collapse of Osler Inc. wiped out the 20-year-old National Contingency Fund. CIPF is industry funded. Note that it only covers missing stocks and cash lost through fraud, negligence or the collapse of a member firm. It does not repay you if you lose money on a bad investment.

For more information, ask your broker for the CIPF brochure, visit the CIPF's web site at http://www.tcn.net/~fcpe or call them at (416) 866-8366.

A few brokerage firms have private insurance that supplements CIPF.

Mutual Funds

THERE IS no deposit insurance for mutual funds, but you are protected if a mutual fund company goes under.

When you deposit money at a bank, trust company or credit union, that cash becomes part of its assets. But that doesn't happen with mutual funds. The stocks, bonds and any other fund assets are owned by the unitholders, not by the fund's manager or distributor. Under securities regulations, those assets must be held in a custodian bank or trust company and be kept separate from the assets of the manager and distributor.

If a fund company goes out of business, another will take over its clients and their pooled assets.

There is also some protection against fraudulent or negligent salespeople. The Canadian Investor Protection Fund covers you if you buy fund units through a member investment dealer and that company can't replace your holding. Nova Scotia, Quebec, Ontario and British Columbia have provincial contingency funds that cover clients of independent mutual fund dealers to certain limits.

There are, however, no performance guarantees. If the fund's holdings fall in value, you lose money. Returns can't be guaranteed. Even money market fund units — which are normally fixed in price — suffered a bit in September 1992 when an unprecedented one-day spike in short-term interest rates reduced the value of their treasury bills and other short-term paper. Those who redeemed at that time lost some money. Those who held on were unaffected once the market readjusted.

TABLE 9.1: **Keeping Within the Limit**

This table shows the maximum deposit you can make and still keep both principal and accrued interest within the $60,000 deposit insurance limit. While CDIC insurance is limited to five years, the CompCorp life insurance deposit plan covers longer terms.

Term (yrs)	8.0%	7.5%	7.0%	6.5%	6.0%	5.5%	5.0%
			Interest rate on deposit				
			Interest compounds annually				
1	55,556	55,814	56,075	56,338	56,604	56,872	57,143
2	51,440	51,920	52,406	52,900	53,400	53,907	54,422
3	47,630	48,298	48,978	49,671	50,377	51,097	51,830
4	44,102	44,928	45,774	46,639	47,526	48,433	49,362
5	40,835	41,794	42,779	43,793	44,835	45,908	47,012
7	35,009	36,165	37,365	38,610	39,903	41,246	42,641
10	27,792	29,112	30,501	31,964	33,504	35,126	36,835
			Interest compounds semi-annually				
1	55,473	55,741	56,011	56,282	56,556	56,831	57,109
2	51,288	51,784	52,287	52,795	53,309	53,830	54,357
3	47,419	48,109	48,810	49,523	50,249	50,987	51,738
4	43,841	44,694	45,565	46,455	47,365	48,294	49,245
5	40,534	41,521	42,535	43,576	44,646	45,744	46,872
7	34,649	35,836	37,067	38,343	39,667	41,040	42,464
10	27,383	28,734	30,154	31,648	33,221	34,875	36,616
			Interest paid annually				
	55,556	55,814	56,075	56,338	56,604	56,872	57,143
			Interest paid semi-annually				
	57,692	57,831	57,971	58,111	58,252	58,394	58,537
			Interest paid monthly				
	59,603	59,627	59,652	59,677	59,701	59,726	59,751

The formula for this is:

$$\frac{\text{Deposit insurance limit}}{(1 + \text{interest rate})^{\text{years}}}$$

For deposits that compound more often than annually, get the annualized rate from appendix A-3. Suppose you can get a five-year 10% GIC with semi-annual compounding. The annualized rate is 10.25%, according to A-3. Restate that as 1.1025 and raise it to the power of 5. The result is 1.62889. Divide 60,000 by that to get 36,834.79. You can deposit $36,834.79, and all accrued interest will be within the $60,000 insurance limit.

10

Are You
Loansome Tonight?

DEBT CAN BE HELPFUL OR HARMFUL. IT ALL depends on how the money is used and how loan payments affect your mid- and long-term financial priorities.

Helpful debt would certainly include a home mortgage and tax-deductible investment loans. You're borrowing money to build financial security. It might also include a necessary big-ticket purchase such as a reasonably priced car.

Do I have to describe harmful debt? Just think about all the purchases you've financed and ask yourself — seriously — if they were worth the expense. Have they given you more freedom and flexibility, or less? Remember that interest costs can add 20-30% to the price you think you've paid. And every dollar spent on interest is a dollar you can't spend elsewhere.

Who's in Charge?

IN A FINANCIALLY perfect world, we would pay cash for all lifestyle expenses. That's the way it used to be. But most of us didn't grow up that way, and now we're willing to pay some interest to make life more comfortable. That's fine, as long as we keep the debts in check. Ideally, personal loan and credit card payments should eat up no more than 20% of your take-home pay. This strategy may help:

Before borrowing money:
1. Question the purchase. Do you really need the item now? If it's not

essential, list all the ways it will enhance your life. That exercise alone may change your mind.

Use budgeting techniques to reduce your need for borrowing. For example, set aside a sum each month to fund vacations and Christmas expenses. Buying Canada Savings Bonds through payroll deductions is a good idea for those who lack discipline.

2. Whenever possible, use cash for lifestyle spending and borrow only for investment or business expenses. The interest on investment and business loans is tax-deductible. For example, instead of investing a spare $5,000 in a mutual fund, put it against your car loan and borrow $5,000 for the investment. Either way, you'll owe $5,000. But the investment loan is tax-deductible, and the rate might even be lower.

3. Before making the purchase, set a deadline for paying off the loan. Write down and file this reminder where it will pop up occasionally.

4. Look for the cheapest, most flexible financing. Credit cards are the most convenient, but also the most costly. If you qualify, set up a personal line of credit, especially if you can use your home to secure it.

If you're in debt now:

1. List each loan that is not tax-deductible, the amount due and the interest rate. See if there is a prepayment penalty.

2. List all financial assets that can be cashed or sold — bank balances, Canada Savings Bonds, stocks, life insurance cash value, etc. Set aside enough money for an emergency cushion and leave your RRSPs intact. Take the rest and compare the after-tax returns on your investments to the after-tax interest due on your loans. Based on that comparison, liquidate holdings to pay down debt.

Few investments can compete with debt reduction. That's mainly because of taxation. When you earn one dollar, whether through employment or investments, you lose part of it to tax. Meanwhile, payments on your credit card, car loan or mortgage are made in after-tax dollars. If your marginal tax rate is 50%, you must take in two dollars to pay out one dollar in loan interest.

Suppose your marginal tax rate is 50% and you have an outstanding credit card balance that costs 16%. Look at table 10.1 at the end of this chapter. In the first column, find the credit card rate, 16%. Read across to the 50% marginal tax rate column, and you'll see that clearing the plastic is the same as earning 32% on a fully taxed investment like a Canada Savings Bond or treasury bill.

Seem unbelievable? Test it. At 16%, one year of interest on a $1,000 loan would be $160. So you need $160 after tax to service that debt. At 32%, one year of interest earned on a $1,000 deposit would be $320. Knock off 50% for tax and you're left with $160.

With debt reduction, you lose short-term use of the $1,000 in capital, but your net worth goes up and your monthly cash flow will improve as loan payments fall or end. As cash flow improves, you can rebuild your capital and get off the debt treadmill by paying with cash instead of credit.

That's why once an emergency cushion has been set and RRSP contributions have been made, accountants and financial planners nag clients to reduce or pay off debts that are not tax-deductible before turning to more traditional investments.

Start your debt liquidation drive by going for the highest-priced loan, probably your charge or credit card. Charge cards generally charge 28.8%, but that compounds monthly, so the true rate is 32.9%. Ouch! Credit cards from financial institutions normally don't compound, but they still charge very high rates. Several institutions offer low-rate cards but don't actively promote them. You can check credit card rates and costs at a federal government web site: http://strategis.ic.gc.ca/oca.

Once the plastic is cleared, work down through your other loans. Look at the interest rates, not the amounts due. People tend to get mesmerized by the size of their home mortgages and ignore other loans. A mortgage is probably the cheapest loan you have.

3. If you can't liquidate enough assets to clear your loans, plan a get-out-of-debt campaign. Allocate a portion of each paycheque to debt reduction. For reinforcement, total up your outstanding loans and mark the figure on a graph. Update the chart monthly so you can see your progress.

Consider consolidating loans if the new rate will be lower than the current blended one. Understand that consolidation plans typically cut the monthly carrying cost by extending the payback period. While consolidation costs less each month, you can wind up paying more over the long term. So pay off the loan as quickly as possible.

Many people consolidate by rolling other debts into their home mortgages. That plan can work well since mortgage rates are usually the cheapest form of personal debt. But mortgages tend to run many years. If you don't give priority to clearing the debt consolidation portion, you'll likely forget about it and ultimately wind up no better off.

Be careful. Many people who turn to debt consolidation end up still deeper in the hole. Bankers tell me most bad-debt write-offs in personal lending come from consolidation loans. Apparently, having just one loan

> doesn't seem as troubling as having three or four, so the borrowers
> consolidate and then go out and pile on still more debt.

If you chronically spend more than you earn, you must rethink your life as a consumer. You are probably a spendaholic, and that means trouble — if not today, then tomorrow.

If your spending bothers you, don't carry credit cards. To avoid temptation, put them in a plastic tub of water and stick the tub in your freezer. Getting at the cards means waiting for the ice to thaw. Or, lock up your cards in your safe deposit box.

If you can barely pay your bills and fear you're about to go under, see if your community has a credit counselling service. Look in the phone book, or call your local United Way office or provincial consumer affairs department. These non-profit services help people work out personal budgets and serve as a go-between in negotiating repayment plans with creditors. If you have just one or two creditors, approach them directly and honestly explain your situation. Almost all creditors would rather wait a bit for their money than lose it altogether.

If you can't pay your bills, consult the credit counselling service before seeking bankruptcy protection. Your provincial government might offer an option called "orderly payment of debts" (OPD). That's a provincially administered section of the federal Bankruptcy Act. To be eligible, you must have a job or employment prospects, must have no business debts, and must be able to pay off your bills in three years unless creditors agree to a longer term. OPD consolidates certain loans under a court order, with interest capped at 5%. Your creditors cannot garnishee your wages. OPD is not available for tax bills, alimony, mortgage payments or overdue utility bills. Nor is it offered in every province.

If there really is no way out, your last resort is a trustee in bankruptcy. The Bankruptcy Act was streamlined in 1993 to provide a less onerous process for those who owe less than $75,000, not including home mortgages. The trustee in bankruptcy or other administrator will total all your assets, review your income stream, arrange counselling, work out a budget for you and present your creditors with a "consumer proposal" outlining how you plan to pay them. Your creditors get 30 days to object. The trustee can sell off almost anything you own. Provincial laws let you keep certain personal and work-related property. The type and amount of protected property vary across the country. Proceeds from the sale of unprotected property will be used to pay the trustee's fees — which will probably run $1,000 or more — and then your creditors. While your consumer proposal can offer reduced payments to settle most loans, alimony, child support and legal fines are still due in full. Understand that bankruptcy is not an easy out. Among other consequences, you could lose your retirement savings. The bankruptcy will also be noted on your credit-rating file for seven years.

Plastic Fantastic

CREDIT CARDS: Boon or burden?

Canadians hold more than 60 million credit cards, according to federal consumer officials. That's nearly three for each adult. Visa and MasterCard account for about half the cards in circulation.

It's easy to dump on credit cards. The interest rates are extremely high. Since you have to pay only 3–5% of the outstanding balance, you can quickly rack up massive debt without realizing it. And studies have found that people buy up to 40% more when they pay with plastic.

But when used properly, cards offer the utmost in convenience, provide free bookkeeping and can even make money for you. These ground rules can help you get the most from your plastic:

1. Have just one or two cards. Gone are the days when people were impressed by a wallet full of plastic. The more cards you have, the harder it is to control them. The Credit Counselling Service of Metropolitan Toronto has found that its cash-strapped clients average six cards each. One of the big danger signals is when you carry several cards so you can "max out" one and still keep spending.

   As their ads keep pointing out, VISA and MasterCard are now accepted virtually everywhere. Do you really need more specialized charge cards?

   Do you pay annual card fees? On how many cards? What are you getting for that money? Need I say more?

2. Pay your full bill on time to avoid high interest charges. There are two ways in which that interest is calculated — the "posting date" method and the "statement date" method.

   Banks, trust companies and credit unions normally base their interest calculation on the date each transaction hits the institution's system — the "posting date." Suppose you charge $500 worth of items on June 19 and they're posted on June 20. On June 30, your monthly statement date, you're sent a bill due July 21. If you pay in full by July 21, no interest is charged; you got a free loan from June 19 to July 21. Note that credit card issuers use the date payment is received — not when it was mailed.

   Suppose you make only a partial payment. If you have an outstanding balance — even just one dollar — you'll face interest on the entire $500 from June 20. Maybe you returned a $50 item on June 29 and the credit did not appear on the June 30 statement. Pay the full amount on the statement. If you apply the credit yourself, you will have an outstanding balance and face interest on the full $500. The same goes if you dispute a charge. First pay and then argue.

There is no grace period for "cash advances" when you borrow money on your card. The interest meter starts ticking as soon as you get the money and runs until payment is received. The same goes for convenience cheques, which are special cheques for use at merchants who don't accept your card. You write the card number on the cheque and the charge is posted to your account, activating the interest meter at your steep cash advance rate.

The "statement date" method is used by most charge cards — those issued by retail stores, oil companies and travel firms. They base interest charges on the day your monthly bill is generated. It might be a set date or something like the second Monday. Check your cardholder materials or call the client service line.

Rates on these cards are exorbitant — generally 28.8%. That's compounded monthly, so the annual return is 32.9%. As before, if you pay in full and on time, no interest is due. If you don't, you are charged interest only back to the statement date, not the posting date.

Many people believe American Express charges no interest. Not so. If you don't pay within 30 days of being billed, the meter starts ticking at 30% — and you'll get snarky letters.

If you've always had an interest-bearing balance on your card and are now paying it off, ask if the issuer charges "residual" (or "trailing") interest. That's interest covering the period between the statement date and the payment date. If so, pay a little extra to make sure the interest meter is turned off. Otherwise, your next statement will still contain an interest charge.

If you're overwhelmed by the thought of having a clear credit card balance, consider that about half of all cardholders pay their bills in full and on time.

3. Take advantage of the "float." That's the interest-free loan if you pay on time. Several years ago I wanted just over $5,000 in broadloom. The store offered no discount for cash but did accept credit cards.

After ensuring I had enough credit available, I timed the purchase so the charge would be posted to my account one day after the statement date. That meant I would not be billed until the following month and then would get three weeks to pay. In effect, I got an interest-free loan for seven weeks — as long as I paid in full on time. Meanwhile, I parked my $5,000 cash in a term deposit that came due in time to pay the credit card bill. I not only made money off the float, but also earned 5,000 airline points.

Bankers understand the float better than anyone. That's one reason why they've spent a fortune developing "debit card" systems. A debit card looks like a credit card, but the money is transferred from your chequing-savings account to the merchant the moment you make your purchase. Not only do you lose the float, but your friendly financial institution may hit you with a service charge on each transaction.

A skeptic at the start, I now like the debit card's convenience and have heard very few tales of woe. There were over 3 billion debit card transactions in 1997, up 48% from 1996. Just make sure your account holds the minimum balance required to avoid transaction fees. And be aware that you may face steep penalties if your account allows overdrafts and you spend more than you have. Just because the computer says a purchase is OK doesn't always mean the cash is there.

4. Each spouse should have a credit card in his or her own name. Joint cards can present problems when a marriage breaks up or a spouse dies.

5. Don't use your card's cash advance feature as a regular source of financing. There are cheaper alternatives such as personal lines of credit.

6. Keep track of your charges. It's easy to lose control — especially if you have more than one card. Some people tell me they're willing to pay extra for an American Express card because it requires full payment each month. They see it as external discipline. That's hardly a reason to spend money on card fees. Tracking needn't be a big deal.

    Put a letter-sized envelope and a sheet of paper inside a folder. Each night stick your charge slips in the folder, but not in the envelope. Once a week, add up the outstanding slips. Write the figure on a piece of paper and keep a running tally. If you don't think you can pay your balance in full, temporarily stop using the card. Your running tally can easily be built into the budget discussed in chapter 4. After adding the slips to your total, put them in the envelope.

    When your monthly statement arrives, verify it against the slips in the envelope. Then staple the slips to the statement and file for future reference. Credit card accounting systems are amazingly accurate, but mistakes do occur. Report any error to the service number printed on the statement. Record the date and time of your call plus the name of the person who handled it. If it's a major error, send a letter noting the problem and the details of your call.

7. Protect yourself from fraud. Your liability is set by the agreement you signed, not by law. Under that agreement, it's probably $50, but only if you notify the issuer as soon as you suspect your card has been lost or stolen. If your card is stolen, your homeowner's or tenant's insurance may cover up to $1,000 of unauthorized charges. Here are some ways to play it safe:

- Sign your card as soon as you receive it. Destroy old and unwanted cards.

- Never lend your card. When using the telephone, give your number only if you know the merchant is reliable. Speak softly so the number cannot be heard by others. Never — ever — give your number to an unsolicited telemarketing caller.

- Never leave a card in your car or hotel room.

- Verify the charge slip before signing it. Always make sure you get back your own card, especially in busy stores and restaurants — and especially during the hectic Christmas shopping season.

Gold Cards: A Bright Idea?

A gold card might be worthwhile, but take a few minutes to read the cardholder's material — not just the glossy advertising.

Typically, you pay an annual fee of $100–$150 in return for a basket of features. Make sure your card provides the features you need. For example, most gold cards provide collision damage waiver (CDW) for rental cars, but some limit that to Canada and the United States.

A bank executive told me that her test of a focus group found that holders of a heavily advertised gold card thought they had "free" features when, in fact, these were options — available at an extra cost. No matter what card you have, even if a feature is included, check the cardholder booklet for conditions and exclusions. Don't just assume you're covered. Note that most cards have dropped the out-of-Canada medical insurance that used to be a standard freebie.

A frightening point: I find many people assume their credit card CDW includes liability if they're driving a rental car and hurt someone. Nope. That CDW only covers physical damage to the rented vehicle; it is not third-party liability insurance. Your own car insurance might transfer your liability coverage to a rental car, at least in Canada and the United States. Ask your agent. Otherwise, ask the rental company how much liability coverage comes with the car. You may find there is little or none unless you take optional — and costly — daily liability coverage.

Cards that grant airline points are very popular, but see if you have to pay your bill in full each month to receive the points. You don't want to shell out $100 a year or more for the card fee and not get the goodies. See how many points you'll need to go where you want. Say you pay $100 a year for a card that grants one flier point for each one dollar charged. If a "free" ticket requires 20,000 points, how long — at $100 a year for the card — will it take you to charge $20,000?

The same goes for cards that offer discounts on cars or mortgages. Also consider if such deals would deter you from shopping around when it's time for the major purchase. You may find that even with credit card points, one car model may not be as good a deal as another. Your points would then be useless.

Some gold cards pay a cash rebate on everything you charge. That's a lot cleaner than running the risk of the airline or carmaker point schedule rising before you can claim your reward. Also, if the card is used enough, the rebate can more than cover the annual fee. All this assumes your merchant doesn't offer discounts for cash. More and more stores do. If federal and provincial sales tax total 15%, a 2% discount is worth $2.30 for every $100 purchased. That's 2.3%. Why settle for a 1% credit card rebate?

Some issuers charge hefty fees for spousal cards. That's gouging. Others provide the second card either for free or for a nominal cost. Shop around. No law says you must take a credit card from the same place you bank.

Credit Limits

Your credit limit is not cast in stone. If you're making a big-ticket purchase or heading off on a trip, you may be able to get a temporary bump-up just by phoning the issuer's client service line.

To a certain extent, issuers routinely accept foreign charges that are over the limit. The cutoff varies among institutions. Note that you may face a surcharge when using your credit card outside Canada. Or, the issuer may first convert the amount to U.S. dollars and then to Canadian dollars.

Your charges may be rejected if you alter your pattern too much without contacting your institution. Many issuers have anti-fraud computer systems that track your spending and get cranky if you start charging too much too quickly.

Other Personal Loans

THIS SECTION is about personal loans in general. See chapter 11 for car loans and chapter 17 for mortgages.

There are two main types of loans — instalment and demand.

With an instalment loan, the lender extends money for a certain amount of time with a fixed schedule of monthly payments. The interest rate may be fixed for the life of the loan or only for a part. Or the rate may vary, based on market conditions. With a variable rate, your monthly payment stays constant but the split between interest and principal will shift. If rates plunge, repayment of principal will speed up and the loan will be paid off sooner than expected. If rates soar, repayment of principal slows down. The loan then takes longer to pay off and costs more. Often, you have an option to switch to a fixed rate at any time.

With a demand loan, the institution can demand full repayment any time, but usually that doesn't happen. The loan rate will depend on the amount borrowed and what security, if any, you put up.

The "personal line of credit" (PLC) is a very popular form of demand loan. It's a pre-authorized lending limit. You know you'll be able to borrow money when you need it, but you're not stuck with interest bills on idle cash. You pay no interest until you tap the line of credit.

The best time to apply for credit is before you need it, especially now that job security seems to be an outdated concept. If you set up a PLC while you're working, you'll have that much more cushion if you become unemployed.

Once your application is approved, the institution sets your limit and gives you a book of special cheques or a credit card. To borrow money, just write a cheque or use the card. The interest meter starts ticking as soon as the debit hits the system. Once activated, a PLC usually requires monthly payments. The contract may allow interest-only or require interest plus some principal. Repayments can be made any time in any amount — without penalty.

PLC rates are normally pegged to the institution's "prime rate" and float up and down. The rate depends on whether the PLC is secured or unsecured. The home equity line of credit is a popular and useful form of PLC. Your loan limit is secured by a mortgage on your home. That should get you a low rate. Setting up the mortgage will, however, require hundreds of dollars in legal fees. To minimize or avoid that cost, set up the PLC at the same time you take out your basic mortgage.

Other Sources of Credit

INVESTMENT DEALERS provide an often overlooked line of credit. If you have a "margin" account, you can borrow against the value of your holdings. You can use that loan for anything, not just investing.

The margin limit is based on the type of security and its market price. For example, you can borrow up to 50% of the value of a stock trading at $2 or more, and up to 70% if the stock is worth at least $5 and eligible for options trading.

The money is available with one phone call to your broker. You'll pay a floating interest rate that is usually just above or below the prime rate. Repayments can be made any time in any amount.

The disadvantage of this line of credit is that you'll be in trouble if your loan is near your limit and your account value falls sharply. You will then face a "margin call" because the account's value will be less than the loan limit. That means you get a fairly short amount of time to put up enough cash to bring the balance in line. Otherwise, the broker will do that by selling securities. Say your account's market value is $10,000. With a 50% margin limit, you could borrow $5,000. But if your account's market value then falls to $9,000, the 50% margin limit means you would have to deposit $500 cash or have the broker sell $500 worth of securities.

Bookkeeping will be awkward if you use this facility for both tax-deductible investment borrowing and non-deductible personal loans.

Certain types of life insurance policies let you borrow against their cash value. If your policy was issued before 1968, the interest rate may be quite low. Even on newer policies, it might be less than rates on conventional consumer loans. But the policy could be cancelled if the cash value falls below a certain point and you miss a premium payment.

You may face an income tax bill if you borrow more than your policy's "adjusted cost base." That's generally the sum of the premiums you paid. Consult your insurer.

Cash-value loans also reduce your insurance coverage. If you die before the loan is repaid, the outstanding balance and accrued interest will be subtracted from the death benefit. Although that possibility sounds awful, consider the alternative situation where you take a bank loan and then die. Your family will get the full insurance payout, but must use part to pay off your debts. Is there really a difference?

Credit Bureaus

WHEN YOU apply for a loan, the lender will most likely check your credit bureau record. Credit bureaus are privately run companies that collect vast amounts of data about how we handle the credit accounts we already have.

They're governed by provincial legislation except in Alberta and New Brunswick. The legal standards vary, but the basic principles are that the data must be accurate and you must be given a chance to review and correct your file.

Two companies dominate the Canadian credit rating market for individuals — Equifax Canada Inc. and Trans-Union of Canada Inc.

Using information from the credit granters, credit bureaus rate each one of your accounts on a standardized nine-point scale. The best rating — "one" — indicates you pay on time or within 30 days.

The rating will rise one point for each 30 days that the payment is late. You're often considered a bad risk if your accounts are rated "three" or higher. You get a "three" if you are two payments past due or have a balance overdue by 60-90 days. Even if your accounts are paid up, your rating may still suffer if your payments were consistently late.

If a credit granter has repossessed an item, you get an "eight." If the account has been declared a bad debt or turned over to a collection agency, you get a "nine."

Your credit file contains basic personal information plus a list of your current and previous credit accounts going back six years. There is no overall credit rating. Rather, each account has a code indicating your current payment status and your worst position in the past. The file does not contain personal gossip but does list legal and collection action taken by creditors.

The file may not contain all your accounts since it's up to credit grantors to provide the information. Home mortgages, for example, are often excluded because lenders don't want to tip off their rivals.

It's a good idea to check your file once a year. Also check it after a major change such as the death of a spouse or divorce, and before you apply for a large loan. If you're turned down for credit, ask the lender for the name and phone number of the credit bureau used.

Equifax and Trans-Union will send a copy of your file for free. For details on how to request that, call Equifax at 1-800-465-7166 and Trans-Union at (416) 291-7032.

Check the report carefully. In 1991, serious errors were found in 13% of the credit files checked by the CBC television program Market Place. Minor flaws were found in almost half. Negative entries can creep in when someone has the same name; "seniors" and "juniors" in the same family are a common problem. So is the situation where a marriage has broken up and one spouse finds the other's bad marks on his or her file.

The credit bureau will have a procedure for correcting the file. Even when the information is accurate but less than complimentary, you may be able to attach an explanation.

Beware of ads for companies that claim they can fix up your credit rating. They may charge $1,000 or more to do a records check and correction that you can do yourself — free, or for minimal cost — just by contacting the credit bureau.

When you apply for credit, don't lie. The financial institution will not only reject you, but will also note that fact in its records. When the next institution does a credit bureau check, it can find out who else requested a report on you. Bankers call each other to share information. If you think that's an unfair invasion of privacy, consider that the system runs on trust. Deadbeats abuse that trust and cost everyone money. Would you lend money to an absolute stranger?

TABLE 10.1: **Debt Reduction as an Investment**

This table shows what you would have to earn on a fully taxed investment like a Canada Savings Bond or treasury bill to match the return from reducing a loan.

| Loan Rate | Marginal tax rate | | | | | |
| | 25% | 30% | 35% | 40% | 45% | 50% |
			Equivalent pre-tax investment return (%)			
5%	6.7	7.1	7.7	8.3	9.1	10.0
6%	8.0	8.6	9.2	10.0	10.9	12.0
7%	9.3	10.0	10.8	11.7	12.7	14.0
8%	10.7	11.4	12.3	13.3	14.5	16.0
9%	12.0	12.9	13.8	15.0	16.4	18.0
10%	13.3	14.3	15.4	16.7	18.2	20.0
11%	14.7	15.7	16.9	18.3	20.0	22.0
12%	16.0	17.1	18.5	20.0	21.8	24.0
13%	17.3	18.6	20.0	21.7	23.6	26.0
14%	18.7	20.0	21.5	23.3	25.5	28.0
15%	20.0	21.4	23.1	25.0	27.3	30.0
16%	21.3	22.9	24.6	26.7	29.1	32.0
17%	22.7	24.3	26.2	28.3	30.9	34.0
18%	24.0	25.7	27.7	30.0	32.7	36.0
19%	25.3	27.1	29.2	31.7	34.5	38.0
20%	26.7	28.6	30.8	33.3	36.4	40.0
21%	28.0	30.0	32.3	35.0	38.2	42.0
22%	29.3	31.4	33.8	36.7	40.0	44.0
23%	30.7	32.9	35.4	38.3	41.8	46.0
24%	32.0	34.3	36.9	40.0	43.6	48.0
25%	33.3	35.7	38.5	41.7	45.5	50.0
26%	34.7	37.1	40.0	43.3	47.3	52.0
27%	36.0	38.6	41.5	45.0	49.1	54.0
28%	37.3	40.0	43.1	46.7	50.9	56.0
29%	38.7	41.4	44.6	48.3	52.7	58.0
30%	40.0	42.9	46.2	50.0	54.5	60.0

The formula for this calculation is:

$$\frac{\text{loan rate}}{(1 - \text{marginal tax rate})}$$

What if the alternative investment earns capital gains or dividends that are taxed more lightly than interest? Just look up the appropriate marginal rate in appendix B-1. Say your marginal rate for capital gains is 37% and the loan rate is 16%. Take 0.37 from 1 to get 0.63. Divide the loan rate — 0.16 — by 0.63 to get 0.254, or 25.4%.

11

Deals on Wheels

THERE IT IS: V-6, SPORT STYLING, LEATHER interior. You'd give anything to own that car. But should you?

This chapter is about options — not the ones on the car, but the financing options that face the buyer. Next to a house, a car is the largest single purchase most people make. Depending on your financing, the total cost can easily run at least 20% more than you think. At 8%, a $20,000 loan repaid over five years costs about $24,336 in principal and interest.

There are four ways to buy a car: pay cash, get a bank loan, use dealer financing or lease.

The best method is to pay cash. One gambit is to bargain your price without revealing you have the money. Dealers turn a profit on financing, so they may agree to a lower price in the expectation you'll use their package.

Even if you lack the full amount, put down as much cash as possible. Are there Canada Savings Bonds or term deposits you can redeem? Car loan rates are normally far higher than rates paid on savings. Even if they're equal, remember you will lose some of the savings interest to tax. Meanwhile, your loan interest is paid in after-tax dollars.

The dealer may present a computer projection showing you would save money by hoarding your cash. Take the $20,000 mentioned above. The computer may show that at 6% a year, it would grow to $26,765 over five years. That's $1,265 more than the total cost through financing. But that's a pre-tax calculation. Taxed at 40%, your five-year accumulation would be $23,869 — that's less than the car loan. And if you tapped the deposit for loan payments, the five-year accumulation would be far less.

Consider using part of your emergency fund to self-finance the car. Then pay back the fund monthly instead of making interest-bearing loan payments to a stranger.

If cash is the most straightforward approach, next comes the bank loan. Be ready for a thorough credit check. The lender has to be careful because the car that's pledged as security is a depreciating asset; every year it loses value. Car loans are structured like home mortgages; interest consumes much of the early payments. For a $20,000 five-year loan at 8%, interest gobbles about one-third of the first year's payments. The interest cost plus depreciation means that for the first two years or so the loan is "upside down." The car will be worth less than the outstanding loan. The lender obviously wants to make sure you're a good risk because it won't benefit much by seizing the car.

Table 11.1 at the end of this chapter shows monthly payments for standard payback periods, or amortizations. Suppose you have to borrow $14,322 at 8%. The table shows the cost per $1,000, so divide $14,322 by 1,000 to get 14.322. Go to the table's 8% row and read across to the applicable amortization. If the loan will run three years, multiply 14.322 by 31.34 to get your monthly payment of $448.85. Multiply 14.322 by 128.09 to get the loan's total interest cost — $1,834.50. Most home mortgage computer programs will also calculate car loans. The big difference is that car loans compound monthly while conventional home loans compound semi-annually.

Take the shortest amortization you can afford. As shown in table 11.1, a longer payback period lowers your monthly payment but costs more overall.

Dealer financing is really just another form of loan. The money ultimately comes from a finance company.

Shop for a bank loan before you shop for your car. Many lenders grant pre-approved loans for 30-60 days. You then know your exact loan cost and can see if the dealer will beat it. If so, you're not obligated to use the pre-approved loan.

In slow markets, auto companies offer buyers cut-rate financing, rebates and cash-back deals. The cost of these offers is normally shared by the dealer and the automaker. Clearly, it's in the dealer's interest to try marking up the initial price to cover at least part of the incentive.

Cut-rate financing can certainly look appealing, but watch for limits on the amount of the loan and its term. Often there's a choice between the cut-rate loan and a rebate that cuts the price. Depending on how it's structured, that rebate, by cutting the price, might save you sales tax.

Suppose you want to finance $10,000, and standard financing for 36 months costs 8%. You're offered either a 4% loan or a $1,000 rebate. Calculations from table 11.1 put the total cost of the 4% $10,000 loan at $10,628. If you take the rebate, you cut the price by $1,000. So your loan falls to $9,000. At 8% for 36 months, the total cost is $10,153. The 8% loan with rebate actually costs less — and you might even save some sales tax.

But this $1,000 rebate was quite generous. The cash-back offer may just reflect the amount the dealer/automaker would have had to pay to get a finance company to provide the cut-rate loan. It would cost about $614 to buy down $10,000 from 8% to 4%. (You can calculate that precisely if you have mortgage software that does "discounting." The concept is the same as a vendor take-back mortgage, but with monthly compounding. Or use table 11.1 for a rough estimate. Subtract the total interest cost for the cut-rate loan from the cost for a normal one. That gives us $652.)

Be careful if the cash-back offer pays off only after you buy the car. Since that rebate doesn't lower the price, it doesn't cut the sales tax.

Compare offers from several dealers, but set uniform standards. Get the price for the car you want — nothing more, nothing less. Subtract your down payment and trade-in allowance, if any. Add taxes and dealer preparation charges. If you want extras like rust-proofing, make sure each quote includes them — and nothing more.

Some tips:

- Be wary of low advertised prices. They're aimed at getting you into the showroom. The price may be for a stripped-down model not even in stock.

- Salespeople have quotas and may be more willing to bargain at the end of the month.

- Once you have a few cars in mind, call your insurance agent. Rates vary from model to model, depending on how well they survive collisions. The Vehicle Information Centre of Canada compiles statistics on insurance claims for specific car models. It was established by car insurance companies, but publishes free consumer guides — including a list of safety features on new cars. Write to 240 Duncan Mill Rd.; Suite 700; Don Mills, Ont. M3B 1Z4. Or phone (416) 445-1883. Ask your agent for the cost of insuring the car for its full replacement cost, not just the depreciated value. That extra coverage is available from lenders as well as auto insurance companies.

- The Automobile Protection Association, an aggressive consumer group, says it can provide members with the true dealer cost of most cars, based on information it gathers from friendly outlets and leasing companies. The APA has offices at:

292 Saint Joseph Blvd. West 2 Carlton St. #1319
Montreal, Que. H2V 2N7 Toronto, Ont. M5B 1J3
Phone: (514) 272-5555 Phone (416) 204-1444

- In some cities, independent brokers will, for a flat fee, shop for both your car and your loan. The service includes negotiating the price.

- Some leasing companies will sell new cars outright, passing on their bulk discounts. Contact the APA for referrals.

- Want to know what your present car is worth? See if your banker or public library subscribes to Canadian Red Book. Published monthly by Maclean Hunter, it's a survey of wholesale used-car prices.

Whether bank- or dealer-financed, the loan is subject to consumer-oriented disclosure laws. You'll know your exact cost and the fees, if any, involved in paying off the loan early.

Leasing

LEASING IS a far different prospect. It's the most complicated way to get a car. And since leasing is largely unregulated, it calls for the greatest degree of sophistication and research.

The big appeal is a low monthly payment and often little or no down payment. In very slow markets, manufacturers may offer incentives that push the underlying cost of a leased car lower than a purchased one. Also, credit approval is easier to get if you lease.

Leasing can work well if you keep cars just a short time. That way, you pay sales tax only on the monthly payment. You can also turn in the car without hassle. But short-term ownership is very expensive. A normal car can lose half its value over the first three years and 25% over the next two. With short-term trading, you continually bear that steep loss.

Many self-employed people believe leasing offers tax advantages, but tax rules were changed in 1991. Leasing and financing still have different write-off formulas, but the net effect is about the same. Ask your accountant. In most of the cases they examined, chartered accountants Price Waterhouse found little difference between leasing and conventional financing.

Don't get carried away by the cash flow benefit of a low monthly lease payment. As with any other easy payment scheme, you can easily wind up paying more in the long run.

Remember that you don't own a leased car. You really rent it long-term. Your payments cover the leasing company's vehicle cost and financing charge. With bank or dealer loans, you know the car's actual cost. That may or may not be the case with leasing. That's a key difference since lessors often claim they pass along the fleet discounts they get when they buy vehicles.

For years, leasing was unregulated. The industry made lots of claims about how leasing could save consumers money, but refused to provide the information required for a fair evaluation. In 1995 British Columbia implemented ground-breaking consumer protection legislation that, among other things, required leasing companies to disclose the vehicle price and the interest rate on which the deal was based. It also prohibited dealers from claiming that leasing is a money-saving form of financing.

With help from two consumer groups, the leasing industry then developed voluntary national disclosure standards and began phasing them in on Jan. 1, 1997. Federal and provincial officials say they hope to put those standards into law by the end of 1999, but for now car leasing is officially regulated only in B.C. and Quebec.

You can't directly compare the low monthly lease payment with a standard monthly loan payment. When you buy a car, your loan finances the full difference between the price and whatever you put down. At the end of the loan you own the car. With a lease, you own nothing.

You could theoretically create your own lease by amortizing your loan longer than you plan to keep the car. When the car is sold, proceeds of the sale are used to pay off the outstanding loan. You minimize monthly payments, but run the risk that the unknowable resale price will be less than the loan balance. Lease companies achieve the same end in one of two ways:

- An "open-end" lease sets the residual value upfront. At the end of the lease you can buy the car for that amount or turn it in. If you turn it in, the car will be auctioned. If it sells for less than the pre-set value, you'll have to compensate the lessor. Be careful. The lessor can low-ball the monthly payment by inflating the residual value. You'll then face a whopping lump-sum payment at the end of the lease. However, if the car can be sold at the end of the lease for more than the residual value, see if the contract requires the lessor to compensate you.

- A "closed-end" lease shifts the residual value risk to the leasing company. But you're not off the hook. The contract will set a mileage limit and bill you for each extra kilometre. You may also have to pay for any repairs required to sell the car.

So, with a car loan, you finance a car. With a lease, you finance the use of a car. For an apples to apples comparison, assume you will buy the car at the end of the lease, suggests consumer advocate Robert Lo Presti, developer of the CarCalculator, a nifty $49 Windows computer disk that compares car financing deals. It's available through Rob's web site at http://www.carcalculator.com or by phoning 1-800-647-8693.

A few years ago Lo Presti walked me through the basic calculation method by using an advertised deal on a Pontiac Grand Prix. The lease would run $299 a month for 36 months with a security deposit and other upfront totalling $2,861.

Lo Presti pointed out that this lease deal required more money going in than the 10% down payment required for a normal car loan. Lessors often promote their deals on grounds that they require little or no money down. Be careful; they make up the difference by charging higher monthly payments or boosting the buy-back value. It's a numbers game and the elements can be juggled many ways.

Another gambit is to fill the standard lease package with lots of high-margin options. If the customer balks at the monthly cost, the dealer can trim it by removing one option at a time. Before you talk money, get an itemized list of the car's add-on features and warranties.

Step 1: Calculate total cost of normal car loan

Get your best purchase price. That's the comparison's base so leasing starts with an edge if the lessor really does pass along a fleet discount. Lo Presti priced our sample Pontiac at $19,314 including freight and dealer preparation but not sales tax. At 15%, federal and Ontario sales tax brought the total cost at $22,211.

The advertised lease required $2,861 upfront. The 15% sales tax pushed that to $3,290. Lo Presti applied the same amount as a loan down payment, leaving $18,921 to be financed over 36 months. At 9%, table 11.1 indicates the loan will cost $601.69 a month or $21,661 overall. Including the down payment puts the total cost at $24,951.

Step 2: Calculate total cost of lease

Some lessors insist their financing is superior because you don't pay for the car's depreciation. In fact, as you'll see, you do. That's because part of the lease calculation works like a normal car loan, which blends principal and interest.

That's a key point since depreciation is the biggest cost of car ownership. With a normal car loan, you can minimize that yearly hit by getting the car paid off and then driving it as long as you can. The depreciation is then amortized over more years. If you buy a $20,000 car and sell it for $5,000 after five years, the amortized depreciation is $3,000 a year. If you drive it for 10 years and then scrap it, the depreciation is $2,000 a year. That's why consumer groups and many financial advisers urge people to take care of their cars and drive them into the ground.

But let's get back to the math.

Get the car's buy-back value from the lessor. It was $8,972 for our Pontiac.

Subtract the $2,861 in upfront fees and $8,972 buy-back from the pre-tax $19,314 price. The remaining $7,481 is then amortized just like a 36-month car loan. At 9%, the monthly payment is $237.90.

Next, calculate straight interest on the $8,972 buy-back. Divide 9% by 12 to get 0.75% a month. Multiply the buy-back value by that to get $67.29.

Add the two components to get $305.19. That would be the normal monthly lease rate with no breaks. Our Pontiac's $299 rate was subsidized by General Motors to boost business, Lo Presti explained. That often occurs in leasing. Sometimes it creates true bargains. Many times it does not.

With an auto loan, sales tax is due upfront on the purchase price. With a lease, it hits the monthly fee. At 15%, our $299 lease rate jumps to $343.85 or $12,379 overall.

Assuming the car is bought at the end of the lease, add tax to the $8,972 buy-back value. At 15%, that's $10,318. Add the $3,290 in upfront fees, $12,379 in lease payments and $10,318 buy-back for a grand total of $25,987.

Subtract the result from step-1 — $24,951 — from step-2's $25,987. Even though the lease was a special deal, it still costs $1,036 more than a normal car loan.

There is, however, a timing difference. The loan requires more money each month while the big hit on the lease — the buy-back — doesn't come until the end of the term. This is where Lo Presti's computer disk is handy. Using "present value" math, it adjusts the loan and lease cash flows for inflation. At 2% inflation, our Pontiac's lease plus buy-back costs $722 more than the car loan.

Note that this model used a 36-month lease. On longer terms the balance tilts even more in favor of conventional financing.

A lessor will point out that this assumes you have the cash to exercise the buy-back option. Many people don't and just continue to lease. That's foolhardy, says Lo Presti, because they continue to pay high finance charges on a rapidly depreciating asset. His conclusion: If you can't afford to buy the car, you can't afford to lease it either.

Control is another key concern. A lessor may set tighter insurance and service requirements than you would. And what if the car's a lemon? With conventional financing, you could sell the car and just pay off the loan. But a lease is usually very expensive to break.

Lease contracts are complex, and there is generally little consumer protection. So make sure these points are covered:

1. The contract should clearly outline all costs, including:

- down payment

- deposit

- monthly payment

- residual value

- administration or acquisition fees:
  – at start of lease
  – at end of lease

- the lease term in months

- the total of all monthly payments

- the total lease value for which you are responsible, including the residual value

- the sale price of the car

- the mileage limitation, if any:
  – how many kilometres per year?
  – what is the charge for each kilometre over the limit?
  – is that charge payable yearly or at the end of the lease?

2. Is the lease open-end or closed-end? How will the car be sold when you return it? Can you find an alternate buyer if the lessor's price is too low?

3. What happens if:

- you want to cancel the lease early? (Hefty penalties often apply.)

- you miss one or more payments?

- the car is stolen or destroyed?

4. Restrictions:

- Can neighbors and friends use the car? (Some contracts allow just immediate family or employees.)

- Are there special maintenance requirements? (For example, must all servicing be based on the manufacturer's specifications?)

- Is permission required to take the car outside Canada?

5. What insurance must you carry? The lessor may require more coverage than you would buy on your own.

Those who don't have computers that will run Lo Presti's disk can turn to the APA for a lease versus loan analysis. The service costs $5 per run for non-members. Send the association the following data and a stamped, self-addressed envelope:

- car's normal price

- monthly lease payment

- number of monthly payments

- sum of the trade-in allowance and all down payments and/or deposits

- sum of the residual value and all costs at the end of the lease.

Always remember that a leased car does not belong to you. If you take out a car loan and times get tough, you can sell the car and repay the loan. With a lease, you have nothing to sell and are caught in a monthly-pay contract that may cost a lot to cancel.

TABLE 11.1: The Cost of a Car Loan

This table shows the monthly payment for a $1,000 car loan. It also shows the total interest cost over the loan's life.

	Amortization									
	24 months		30 months		36 months		48 months		60 months	
Interest rate —%	Monthly payment	Total interest	Monthly payment	Total interest	Monthly payment	Total interest	Monthly payment	Total interest	Monthly payment	Total interest
1	42.10	10.45	33.77	12.97	28.21	15.49	21.26	20.55	17.09	25.63
2	42.54	20.97	34.20	26.04	28.64	31.14	21.70	41.36	17.53	51.66
3	42.98	31.55	34.64	39.22	29.08	46.93	22.13	62.46	17.97	78.12
4	43.42	42.20	35.08	52.50	29.52	62.87	22.58	83.79	18.42	104.97
5	43.87	52.92	35.53	65.88	29.97	78.95	23.03	105.40	18.87	132.28
6	44.32	63.70	35.98	79.36	30.42	95.20	23.49	127.25	19.33	160.00
7	44.77	74.55	36.43	92.96	30.88	111.56	23.95	149.39	19.80	188.09
8	45.23	85.45	36.89	106.64	31.34	128.09	24.41	171.85	20.28	216.53
9	45.68	96.44	37.35	120.44	31.80	144.79	24.89	194.43	20.76	245.48
10	46.14	107.49	37.81	134.35	32.27	161.60	25.36	217.43	21.25	274.77
11	46.61	118.58	38.28	148.33	32.74	178.59	25.85	240.53	21.74	304.59
12	47.07	129.77	38.75	162.43	33.21	195.75	26.33	264.08	22.24	334.77
13	47.54	141.01	39.22	176.65	33.69	213.01	26.83	287.68	22.75	365.26
14	48.01	152.32	39.70	190.94	34.18	230.37	27.33	311.61	23.27	396.05
15	48.49	163.67	40.18	205.35	34.67	247.91	27.83	335.89	23.79	427.39
16	48.96	175.04	40.66	219.80	35.16	265.76	28.34	360.32	24.32	459.20
17	49.44	186.56	41.15	234.50	35.65	283.40	28.86	385.28	24.85	491.00
18	49.92	198.08	41.64	249.20	36.15	301.40	29.37	409.76	25.39	523.40
19	50.41	209.84	42.13	263.90	36.66	319.76	29.90	435.20	25.94	556.40
20	50.90	221.60	42.63	278.90	37.16	337.76	30.43	460.64	26.49	589.40

The formula for this is the same as that used for the home mortgage amortization discussed in chapter 17. However the interest here is compounded monthly.

12

Keep the Cash Flowing

WHAT WOULD HAPPEN TO YOU AND YOUR family if you were injured in a car crash or suffered some medical problem that kept you off work for months?

Disability coverage is often the most neglected — yet most critical — personal insurance need. It provides money to cover your bills when you can't work because of illness or injury. Without it, your savings could easily be exhausted within a year, maybe just a few weeks.

Most people feel life insurance is important. Yet before age 65 you are more than twice as likely to become disabled for at least 90 days as you are to die. Consider the possibilities: car wrecks, job-related or sports injury, heart attack or stroke, cancer, burns. The list goes on and on.

Most disabilities are not permanent. On average, if a case runs more than 90 days, the person is likely to be disabled for two and a half to five years. On the one hand, that's good news; people do return to work. On the other: Without adequate insurance, the victim has no doubt lost his or her retirement savings, home and all other financial assets.

Don't confuse disability coverage with critical illness insurance, a fairly new product. A critical illness policy only covers certain diseases such as cancer or heart attack. Though common, those events are not your only risks. Also, critical illness policies pay a lump sum benefit, not continuing income.

Disability insurance programs are designed to replace 60-85% of your income. Even if you have several plans, insurers won't replace your entire income because certain benefits are tax-free and because the partial salary provides incentive to get back to work.

The disability safety net has several elements. The most basic element consists of government programs:

- **Workers' Compensation.** Administered by provincial agencies, WC pays tax-free benefits for work-related illness and injury if your employer belongs to the program.

- **Employment Insurance.** EI applies only if you qualify for it. The benefits are taxable and fairly low. Self-employed people are not eligible for EI.

- **Canada/Quebec Pension Plan.** Taxable benefits are low and paid only if the disability is severe and prolonged.

The second element consists of employer-sponsored group plans. They provide the main coverage for most employees. Most plans have two parts. Short-term disability may run as long as 52 weeks. Long-term disability then kicks in until you return to work or reach retirement age.

Check your benefits booklet; don't just assume your coverage is adequate. Full benefits may run just two years and be capped well below your income level.

More importantly, this coverage normally ends when you leave your job. Some employers have begun providing coverage through the severance period for those who are dismissed. Unlike group life insurance, disability insurance is normally not convertible to an individual policy. If you have a health problem, a new individual plan may be hard to get and will likely be quite expensive.

Many people who quit their jobs take a week or so off before joining their new employer. Remember that you're not covered during that time. To bridge the gap, include unused vacation or overtime in your notice period instead of taking a cash payout. Or see if your new employer's plan will cover you as soon as you leave your current job.

Be careful when changing jobs. Some employer plans — mainly at small firms — exclude conditions for which you sought medical attention in the two or three months before you entered the group policy.

Consider topping up employer-sponsored coverage with your own plan. That way, you're always protected. Your alumni or professional association may offer group coverage at relatively low cost. For the utmost in protection, consider an individual policy.

Individual policies — the safety net's third element — are tailored to your needs. They can be expensive, but there are several ways to trim costs. If you have group coverage, see about supplementing it with a "bare bones" individual plan. Pay a little extra for a "future insurability" rider. That guarantees that if you leave your group plan, you can increase the individual policy without a new medical review.

There are three types of individual policies:

- **Non-cancellable.** The policy and its price are fixed. You're covered even if your health changes. This is also called "non-cancellable guaranteed renewable."

- **Guaranteed renewable.** The insurer must renew the policy, but can boost premiums for everyone in the same class, not just you.

- **Commercial.** The deal is reviewed at each anniversary. The insurer can boost rates or even refuse to renew.

Disability insurance is marketed by life insurance companies. Unfortunately, the policies are complex and they're hard to sell — so many agents are not well versed in them. Shop around.

It's very easy to buy group creditor disability insurance through the lender when you take out a mortgage, car loan, credit card or other consumer debt. Perhaps too easy. First consider if you really need that extra insurance. You might have enough other coverage or sufficient assets to cover the debt. If not, compare the cost of the new piecemeal plan to that of boosting current coverage. Make sure you read the fine print of the creditor plan. You might be excluded because of a pre-existing condition, if you're 65 or older, or if you're self-employed. How stringent is the definition of disability? Does the insurance apply only in the unlikely event you're totally and permanently disabled? Is the premium payable directly, or must it be part of the loan and subject to loan interest? Be aware that if you renegotiate the loan, you will likely have to reapply for the insurance and complete a new medical questionnaire.

To evaluate current and planned disability coverage, ask these questions:

All plans

- Are there any limitations or exclusions?

- Are benefits paid on a partial disability without first having a full disability?

- What is the maximum benefit as a percentage of salary? Is there a dollar limit? Is there an "all sources" rule that caps payments from all plans?

- Can coverage be increased without a new medical review?

- When would benefits begin? Are there different waiting periods for accidents and illness? What happens if you return to work and then suffer a relapse or a new disability? Extending the waiting period, perhaps from 90 to 180 days, can be a good way to cut the cost of an individual policy.

- How long do benefits run? Are they taxable? The benefits are tax-free if you paid the full premiums. Many employers fund the short-term disability plan and have employees pay for the long-term coverage. That way, tax applies only to benefits paid for the first few months. Some employers pay the full cost of the short- and long-term group coverage, but add that amount to your taxable income each year. In that case, your only cost is the income tax due yearly, and any disability benefits would be received tax-free.

  A wrinkle: if you're an executive or in a small company, the employer might agree to pay for your own individual policy. That becomes a taxable benefit for you, but any benefits would be received tax-free.

- Are benefits indexed for inflation?

- Is there a "waiver of premium"? That means you don't have to pay for the insurance while you collect benefits. Must you be totally and permanently disabled for it to kick in?

- How is disability defined? This key point is tricky and highly contentious. Are benefits tied to your inability to do your own job, any job related to your training or experience, or any work at all?

  Some individual plans are based on loss of income, not ability to work. Consider the case of a commissioned salesman who is ordered to slow down after having a heart attack. A loss-of-income plan would top up his earnings, at least for a while.

- Do loss of speech, hearing, sight or at least one limb qualify as total disability?

- What benefits are paid during rehabilitation? How much is paid if you return to work on a trial basis?

Employer and association group coverage

- Does coverage continue during a strike or leave of absence?

- Under what circumstances can the plan be cancelled?

- Will your employer top up your disability annuity if its insurer fails and the annuity payment is beyond the $2,000 monthly coverage limit for the ComCorp life insurance consumer protection plan? That became an issue when Confederation Life Insurance Co. failed in 1994. Confed was a big group insurance supplier.

- Is the association coverage offered for just a set term? Is renewal guaranteed without evidence of good health? How much will the premium increase at renewal? Is that schedule guaranteed? For how long?

- Are benefits reduced for older members?

Individual coverage

- Is the policy guaranteed non-cancellable and guaranteed renewable to 65 without medical evidence of insurability?

- Are benefits payable if you can work, but not at full speed?

- If you are self-employed, how can the plan meet your tax and business needs? Individual policies can be tailored to pay deferred income tax, bank loans and office overhead.

- Are premiums refunded if you're claim-free for a certain amount of time? How much extra does that feature cost?

Be totally honest when you apply for disability insurance or file a claim. A major disability means big bucks for the insurer, so your file will be carefully checked.

Consult your broker about any condition that might affect your ability to work. A medical problem doesn't automatically lead to rejection. The insurer may still issue a policy but exclude or limit coverage for that condition. In 1995, a Saskatchewan court upheld an insurer's refusal to pay disability to a man who did not disclose what turned out to be symptoms of multiple sclerosis. Significantly, the man did not intend to deceive the insurer; he thought he had a temporary condition that was successfully treated.

Reviewing a claim can be time-consuming. Before filing, make sure you understand the process and have your doctor complete all required forms. The insurer may require you to see a designated doctor. For a long-term disability, expect periodic reviews. If your claim is rejected or benefits are cut off, you should have the insurer send its reasons to your doctor. You are entitled to an appeal.

13

Medical Insurance: Don't Get Tripped Up

TRAVEL CAN BE HAZARDOUS TO YOUR financial health if you run into problems with your personal health while in another country or even another province.

No — repeat, no — Canadian resident should set foot in the United States without out-of-Canada medical insurance. Your provincial medicare plan will pay only one-fourth to one-third of the cost of emergency care at an American hospital or doctor's office. Alberta and Saskatchewan pay foreign hospitals only $100 a day. British Columbia pays just $75.

Many people consider that when booking vacations, but forget they run the risk of accidental injury during an afternoon outing for shopping.

Check the benefits booklet from your employer, union or retiree benefits plan. You may already have coverage. See if your employer's plan covers personal as well as business travel. If you rely on coverage that comes with a credit card, check if it applies to all trips or only when you charge a ticket or car rental on the card.

Provincial medicare cutbacks have led to a proliferation of private travel medical insurance plans. They vary widely in price and, more importantly, coverage. Read the fine print. Remember that the premiums you pay qualify for the medical expenses tax credit — a bit of relief for retirees who can easily spend $1,000 or more to cover winter sojourns down south.

Here are some points to check:

- Are you excluded because of a pre-existing condition? Many plans won't cover any condition for which you've had treatment within 90 days before leaving Canada. Some plans extend that exclusion period to as much as one year — or even longer.

  No plan will cover a condition that is not stable at the time you leave. Many seniors and others with chronic ailments get a predeparture checkup. In some cases, the insurance might even require that.

  Some plans add an age test. Past a certain age, they won't cover any pre-existing condition, even if it was stable before you left Canada.

  If you're on maintenance medication, does that affect your coverage? For example, you might take medication to control your blood pressure. Would you be covered for a heart attack that may or may not be related? If the medication is changed just before you leave, will you fall under the exclusion for pre-existing conditions?

- Are planned activities covered? Many plans exclude high-risk pursuits such as mountain climbing, parasailing and scuba diving.

- What is the cap on benefits? Many plans limit payments to $1 million, but a few offer only a few thousand dollars of coverage.

- What is the duration of coverage? Make sure you check this if you rely on credit card insurance. Forty-eight days used to be standard, but that has been cut back considerably, to as little as 17 days — or dropped altogether.

  If you extend your trip, can you extend your coverage? How?

  Those who visit the United States often can buy blanket policies that automatically cover each trip. Snowbirds who go home temporarily for Christmas may find it cheaper to buy a blanket plan than one for each leg of their sunbelt sojourn.

  Your provincial medicare plan might also want advance notification of any long trip. Failure to notify does not mean the province won't cover you. Rather, processing a claim may take longer if the province decides to verify you were not away for more than the standard minimum residency requirement.

- Who pays when you're released from hospital or the doctor's clinic? Many insurance plans have direct-billing arrangements with certain hospitals and doctors in popular destinations like the U.S. sunbelt. If you are treated elsewhere — or your plan has no direct-billing setup — you will have to cover the bill yourself, file a claim with your provincial medicare plan and only then file a claim with the private insurer. It often takes months to clear up the paperwork. Meanwhile, you're out of pocket for the cash paid upfront. If you were discharged without making full payment, expect snarky collection letters from the U.S. hospital and doctors. Medicine is a business in the United States. Never forget that.

- Does the insurer have a 24-hour toll-free phone line for emergencies? You may need it for referral to a hospital or doctor if your plan has "preferred provider" contracts. Any hospital will need it to verify your coverage and billing arrangement.

  A very important point: Your plan may set a deadline for notification through that line — often within 24 or 48 hours of the emergency. If the call is not made, the insurer may sharply limit your coverage

- Does your employer-sponsored plan have a lifetime limit? Some cap coverage as low as $25,000. When shopping for a private plan, ask if there's a "subrogation" clause. This means the private plan will cover only what the group plan doesn't. One claim could wipe out a group plan with a low lifetime limit. That's less of a worry if the travel plan follows Canadian Life and Health Insurance Association coordination guidelines.

One way to save money on health insurance is through a plan with a fairly high deductible. Discounts may run about 15%. Odds are you can muster $500 or $1,000 in an emergency.

Another potentially big money-saver is a new concept called "managed care." These American-style plans may cost 40% less than traditional Canadian ones. Along with facing a deductible, you are required to use certain hospitals if you need treatment. Those hospitals have agreed to let the insurer audit their treatment procedures and billing on both a general and a case-by-case basis. As soon as it's safe, managed care plans whisk patients with major problems back to Canada where medicare takes over.

A key feature of managed care is often misunderstood. Many snowbirds assume it means a heart attack victim might have to be shuttled across town to an authorized hospital. Not so. For true life and death emergencies, the insurer provides full coverage at the closest hospital and then moves the patient once he or she is stabilized.

There are super-low-priced catastrophic plans that cover just enough hospital care to stabilize you for return to Canada, maybe 72 hours' worth or a maximum of $10,000. Is the dollar cap in Canadian or American currency? Intensive care can run more than US$4,000 a day.

Don't try to stack free credit card coverage, using one card for 21 days and a second card for another 21. All card coverage starts when you leave home. Don't try to top up individual coverage from one company with insurance from another. First, you face a jurisdictional battle between the two insurers. Second, if you have a problem during the first coverage period, the top-up plan may exclude that as a pre-existing condition. Top-ups sold by your credit card issuer are designed to extend the card's free coverage but may be more expensive than a separate whole-trip travel policy.

Travel insurance changes a lot from year to year. Don't assume one plan is automatically a good deal; shop around. The Canadian Life and Health Insurance Association sends out a list of insurers and associations selling out-of-Canada coverage and their toll-free numbers. Call 1-800-268-8099 (Toronto: 777-2344).

Out-of-Province Medical Insurance

IF YOU have a medical emergency outside your province but in Canada, your provincial medicare plan will normally cover most or all of the bill under interprovincial direct payment agreements. Unless you're from Quebec.

Quebec's medicare plan will pay only as much as a Quebec hospital or doctor would receive. As a result, some hospitals require Quebec residents to pay their full bills in cash or use private insurance, and then claim reimbursement from Quebec's plan when they return home. For example, while getting a ski injury treated in Banff, one of my colleagues noticed a sign stating the hospital would not accept Quebec medicare cards.

Normally, blanket out-of-Canada plans like those on credit cards automatically provide out-of-province coverage.

14

Life Insurance: How Much and What Kind?

THE LIFE INSURANCE INDUSTRY HAS DONE a fantastic job of shaping and reshaping insurance to meet a wide range of needs. But that means a fairly simple concept has become quite complex.

Since this is a personal finance book, I've ignored business-related reasons for buying insurance. Here are common family-oriented reasons:

- To provide cash for direct death expenses. That includes the funeral and repayment of any debts.

- To help your dependants maintain their standard of living if you die prematurely.

- To maximize the after-tax value of your estate. For example, some people buy extra coverage to ensure the family cottage doesn't have to be sold to pay capital gains tax due at death.

- To equalize bequests among survivors. If one heir gets an entire house or business interest, others may get the equivalent in cash through insurance payouts.

- To provide a bequest to a charity.

- To provide an alternative form of tax-sheltered savings.

Unfortunately, many insurance agents get carried away with the scope of their products, and clients end up with confused objectives. The most critical objectives are the first two — to cover death expenses and to provide for your dependants. For most young families, those are the only insurance concerns. These people should focus on getting the right amount of coverage for the money they have available and put off estate planning concerns until they are in their 40s and more financially comfortable. If you have young children, you probably need far more insurance than you think — and far more than you have now.

Try this three-step assessment. It and the analysis that follows have quite a bit of number-crunching. They make heavy use of the tables at the back of this book. For easy reference, you might want to first photocopy appendices A-1, A-2, and A-6 through A-10.

Step 1: Cash available and required at death

A. Determine the value of your estate. Add up all investments and estimate the market value of cars or other assets that could be sold without hurting your family's lifestyle. You did much of this in compiling your net worth statement in chapter 3. Include your home only if it would be sold. Include your RRSP only if it would be cashed in. Remember, the RRSP can be rolled tax-free to your spouse's RRSP. If there is no spouse, there may be an eligible dependant. See chapter 23. If a rollover is not possible, the RRSP money will be withdrawn, added to your final year's income and fully taxed.

Add any lump-sum death benefit from your employer's pension plan. Some employers also pay a tax-free $10,000 death benefit.

Add the lump-sum death benefit from Canada/Quebec Pension Plan. The maximum payment is $2,500.

Add any existing life insurance such as group coverage at work.

Ignore the accidental death insurance you get on credit cards, other financial products and certain association memberships. Your family doesn't need any more money if you die in a plane crash than if you die of a heart attack.

Total cash available = $ _____ .

B. List your debts. Your survivors should be able to pay off all liabilities, including the mortgage on your home. Is that loan or any other major consumer debt insured under group insurance sold through the lender? If so, don't count it as a debt. (When talking out a loan, don't assume the lender's insurance plan is cheaper. As group coverage, it's priced to cover the added risk of smokers and those in poor health. If you're in good shape and have other insurance needs, you may do better under your own policy.)

Subtotal/Debts = $ _____ .

C. Estimate funeral costs. Funerals need not be a major worry or a huge expense. Throughout Canada there are non-profit memorial societies. With cooperating funeral directors, they help people plan dignified yet inexpensive services. If there is no listing in your phone book, write to Toronto Memorial Society; 55 St. Phillips Rd.; Etobicoke, Ont. M9P 2N8. It will put you in touch with your local society.

   The average funeral bill from an Ontario mortician is about $5,000. Add to that the cost of flowers, newspaper notices, thank-you notes, long-distance phone calls, family travel and miscellaneous expenses.

   That amount also does not include the purchase, opening and closing of a grave. Many people are turning to cremation, which costs just a few hundred dollars.

   Some people — often older folk — prepay for their funerals. The money is put in trust and earns interest. Be careful if you might move far away. Some funeral directors make full refunds, but others don't.

   There is another — most generous — alternative. Consider donating your body for transplantation and/or medical research. The medical centre then handles the cremation. The donor authorization is attached to your driver's licence. Non-drivers can get forms from their doctors or local hospitals. Make sure you discuss this option with your family and executors. Often, hospital personnel don't check drivers' permits, even though time is critical for some organs. Also, even if you've signed a donor card, your family can override that after you're dead. Make sure they understand your wishes.

Subtotal/Funeral = $ _____ .

D. Estimate taxes due at death. The self-employed may have to worry about deferred income tax.

   There could be a big hit from capital gains tax. But that's deferred if your spouse inherits your property. No payment is due until he or she sells the property or dies. If your property does not go to a spouse, all stocks, bonds, mutual funds and other investments — except your tax-free principal residence — are deemed to have been sold on your day of death. Capital gains tax is levied on any "profits."

   Family cottages are a growing problem. They've been soaring in value. That could produce a capital gains tax bill so high that the property must be sold to pay off Revenue Canada. But see chapter 19 before piling on insurance to cover that. The same goes for U.S. estate tax facing those with sunbelt homes or other substantial American holdings.

Probate fees will be due if your will is confirmed by the court. They vary widely, depending on your province and the size of your estate. Consult your accountant, insurance agent or lawyer.

Subtotal/Taxes = $ _____ .

Total liabilities (B + C + D) = $ _____ .

E. Subtract total liabilities from total assets in A. The result — hopefully positive — represents a cash pool available to support your dependants.

Cash pool = $ _____ .

Step 2: Income replacement

Until your kids are grown, your family will have to replace 50-80% of your after-tax income. What are your spouse's near , mid and long-term job prospects? The more financially independent your spouse, the less insurance you'll need. Don't forget that Canada/Quebec Pension Plan pays survivor benefits. The maximum 1998 payments were $410.70 a month for a spouse under 65 and $446.87 for one older. The monthly payment for each dependent child was $169.80. Those payments are taxable. There might also be an income stream from your employer's pension plan.

Say your family would need $30,000 annually for the next 15 years. How much capital is required to fund that? If there's already enough savings to fund the first year, use appendix A-7. Otherwise, use appendix A-8. Let's say the $30,000 can be invested at 5% a year after tax. On A-7, the factor for 15 years at 5% is 10.3797. Multiply that by 30,000. You need $311,391. To index that payment stream for inflation, use appendix A-9. For 3% indexing, the factor is 12.9054. So the required capital is $387,162.

Your capital requirement = $ _____ .

Step 3: The income gap

Subtract step 1's cash pool from step 2's capital requirement. The difference represents the amount of income replacement insurance you need.

Income replacement insurance required = $ _____ .

Don't buy insurance you don't need. Use your money for RRSPs, emergency savings, a home, or prudent investments. Many agents push insurance as a university-funding vehicle. There are better alternatives. See chapter 31.

Should a non-working spouse be insured? That depends on the family responsibilities. Will outsiders have to be hired to care for the children and home? For how many years? Insurance may be advisable if the kids are small, but probably not if they're teenagers.

Should a child be insured? Not unless the family depends on his or her income. As noted above, funeral costs need not be onerous. As tragic as it may be, the death of a child actually reduces the parents' financial responsibilities. Insurance on a child's life will look very inexpensive. That's because there is little statistical chance the child will die.

Should a young single person worry about insurance? Probably not — especially if your employer already provides enough group coverage to pay death expenses. Insurance agents often pitch coverage to singles three ways:

- *It's a good tax-sheltered savings vehicle.* RRSPs are better. They offer the same tax-sheltered growth, but the contributions are tax-deductible. Also better are debt reduction, home ownership and well-chosen investment funds, some of which are sold by insurance agents.

- *Lock in a low price now; the cost goes up as you age.* That sounds attractive, but is meaningless if you calculate the "present value" of the two payment streams over the coverage period. That's discussed later in this chapter. Even without fancy math, on $100,000 coverage, there is as little as $13 a month difference between buying at 25 and 35. Buy insurance when you need it, not before.

- *Buy while you're healthy in case your condition changes.* First, that assumes you'll need insurance in the future. If you don't have dependants, you need very little insurance. Second, if you come from a generally healthy family and lead a healthy life, odds are your condition won't change. That's why the insurance cost is low. This could, however, be good advice if you are in a high-risk group for diabetes, heart attack, cancer and similar conditions.

Step 4: Special needs

The first three steps meet the most critical objectives — to provide cash for direct death expenses and help dependants maintain their standard of living. Here are some special needs, but consider them only after covering those first two objectives and your other financial priorities.

1. **University funding.** As a legacy, you could boost insurance coverage to pre-fund your kids' university or college education. See chapter 31.

2. **Spousal retirement.** Were you and your spouse going to depend on your pension in retirement? If so, your spouse will likely need investment money to cover that loss. The amount will depend on his or her age and employment prospects.

   Estimate the annual income needed to supplement government and employer benefits. Use appendix A-1 to determine the inflation-adjusted value of that income at your spouse's retirement. Then, depending on the payment's timing and indexing, use appendices A-7 through A-10 to determine the capital needed at retirement. Let's say that's $200,000. Go back to A-1 and find the factor for the years left till retirement and a reasonable after-tax growth rate. Say 25 years and 5%. The factor is 3.3864. Divide $200,000 by that to get $59,060. That's how much must be invested today to generate $200,000 in 25 years at 5% growth.

3. **Pension maximization.** Agents make these proposals to members of Registered Pension Plans who, on retirement, must choose between a full pension that ends when they die and a reduced one that runs until they and their spouses both die. This has been a big issue for couples where one partner has the pension membership and the other doesn't. Let's use an example where the husband has the pension.

   With "pension max," the husband takes the full single-life pension and uses part of the higher payout to buy life insurance. If he dies first, the insurance payout will support his wife. If the wife dies first, the husband can cancel the insurance and still collect his full pension. Had a "joint and survivor" pension been taken, he would be stuck with the lower payout.

   One agent told me this can work if the pension reduction is high — say 40% — and if term-to-100 or universal life insurance is purchased before age 55. After that, the insurance is too expensive.

   But another veteran agent was highly critical of pension max. His biggest concern is the wife's lack of income security if the husband dies first. Women normally outlive men. With a joint-pension, the wife knows how much she will get. That amount may even be indexed for inflation. The pension plan may also provide generous medical coverage and other fringe benefits. The pension max retirement income can't be known in advance because it will come from an annuity purchased with the husband's life insurance payout. Annuity rates vary with interest rates, and can't be predicted accurately. That income probably won't be indexed either. Indexed annuities are expensive. Also, when the retiree dies, the spouse may lose any right to the other's non-pension RPP benefits.

Carefully analyze any comparison your agent provides. Pension benefits are paid in pre-tax dollars, while insurance premiums are paid in after-tax dollars. Make sure the pension max projection deducts income tax from the higher single-life pension before the insurance premium is paid.

After writing a condemnation of pension max, American personal finance writer Jane Bryant Quinn received letters from angry insurance agents. She invited them to submit plans. Ten did. Two financial planners — working independently — did a math and tax analysis. They found only one plan worked "passably well," and it used an unusual policy that paid the agent a minimal sales commission.

Bryant Quinn echoed the income security concerns of the agent I spoke with. She also warned that if the husband owns the policy and the marriage goes sour, he can cut off the wife by dropping the coverage or changing the beneficiary.

The decision on which form of pension to take is irrevocable. Since your spouse may have to live with it for decades, consider getting an analysis from an independent financial planner or accountant before signing up for pension max. Your adviser will need a detailed proposal from your insurance agent and the terms of your pension plan.

4. **Charitable bequests.** Want to leave money to a charity? Consider giving the group an insurance policy on your life now instead of leaving a bequest in your will.

When you die, the charity will collect the death benefit. That payment will likely be much greater than you could give on your own. Plus, you get a tax break now; the premiums paid qualify for the charitable donation tax credit.

Keep your objectives clear and your insurance plan straightforward. It's very easy to cloud the issue with special group coverage for loans, projections of million-dollar cash-value savings pools by age 50, and dire warnings about the tax collector forcing a sale of the family cottage.

Remember that your first priorities are to have adequate disability and life insurance, a maximized RRSP, and home ownership or an alternative investment fund. Until you meet those priorities, focus only on basic insurance needs. The cottage may hold great emotional value, but saving it from the tax collector won't mean beans if your family doesn't have enough money to live on.

Is Group Insurance from Work Enough?

BREADWINNERS SHOULD not rely solely on employer-sponsored group coverage. That coverage is tied to your job, and job security has become an outdated concept. Consider getting your own supplemental policy or group coverage through a professional, alumni or social association.

If you lose your job, you normally get a set amount of time to switch your group coverage to an individual policy, but the new rate will probably be quite high. If you don't already have your own coverage, go shopping. If you lack time, take the conversion to make sure you're covered and then shop. After getting your own policy, cancel the converted one.

Employers often provide $25,000 of group life insurance as a taxable benefit. Many people buy more — often three times their yearly salary. That may or may not be a good deal. If you're a non-smoker in your 40s or 50s you might do better on your own.

Group insurance from your professional or alumni association may or may not be a good deal. Shop around. Note that future rates on individual policies can be fixed, but group insurance rates tend to be based on one-year renewable terms. Whether that's a concern will depend on the demographic composition of the group. Check rates for the past few years. Also compare current rates for older members to those guaranteed in an individual policy.

Many agents make much of the risk that an association's insurer could refuse to renew the group policy, but nobody has presented me with a case in which that actually happened and the association was unable to get coverage elsewhere. In one case, rates rose 30% — but that was on top of a very low base.

Shopping for Insurance

BUYING LIFE insurance is difficult. Policies come with confusing names and all kinds of features. There is also a wide range in the level of knowledge and professional commitment among life insurance agents. I've met quite a few who are true professional advisers. Several hold prominent positions in Canada's financial planning community. I've also had dealings with agents who lived down to the stereotype.

Some agents are tied to just one company. Others can sell insurance for several, and many of them subscribe to computer services that churn out quotes for a whole range of insurers. Canada's major quote services are Compulife Software Inc. of Kitchener, Ontario and Toronto-based Compu-Office Software Inc. Toronto-based Best Financial Network includes the CompuOffice service.

Prices on some policies vary by as much as 200%. But there are often wrinkles, so look at more than basic price. Some agents quote a basic price to get the sale and only then add high-margin options. In particular, consider the stability of the company. The life insurance industry has a consumer protection plan in case a company fails, but the coverage limit on a life insurance policy is only $200,000. See chapter 9.

Several independent agencies do financial ratings of life insurance companies. They include Toronto-based TRAC Insurance Services, Montreal-based Canadian Bond Rating Service and Toronto-based Dominion Bond Rating Service. Your agent should have access to their reports and be able to explain them.

Some Canadian insurers are also rated by American services: A.M. Best Co., Duff & Phelps Credit Rating Co., Moody's Investors Service, Standard & Poor's Corp., and Weiss Research Inc.

Price Determinants

Your initial premium — or cost — is based on your age, health and the amount of coverage.

Non-smokers get huge discounts — often at least 40-50% on term policies, a bit less on others. Normally, a "non-smoker" hasn't lit up for one year before buying the policy. If you smoke, many companies will sell you a smoker's policy now and reprice it if you quit and stay weed-free for at least 12 months. Some companies charge pipe and cigar smokers less than those who smoke cigarettes and cigarillos. It's all based on mortality statistics. When you apply, don't lie about smoking. Investigators check out death claims, and courts have upheld insurers' refusals to make payouts when it was discovered that the deceased did smoke at the time the policy was issued.

The amount of coverage affects your unit cost because of "banding." That's a volume discount. A $500,000 policy may cost just a little bit more than one for $400,000.

It's best to pay one annual premium. Insurers charge more for monthly instalments. Checking one random quote, I found the monthly payment plan 8% more expensive.

Types of Life Insurance

THERE ARE two basic types of life insurance — renewable term and permanent. Renewable term was designed to meet specific temporary needs — for example, covering the family while the kids grow up. Permanent is lifetime insurance and can be useful for estate planning.

Renewable Term

Most people can meet their basic insurance needs with term insurance. A term policy is no-frills; it simply insures your life for a set amount of time.

Term insurance is sold in chunks. It is available in one-year increments, but policies usually run five or 10 years at a time. Note that although a policy may have a 10-year term, you can cancel it early.

This is the least expensive form of life insurance, and "10-year term" is usually the best buy. It's especially good when young parents must stretch limited paycheques to support small children and a big mortgage.

Some agents say buying term insurance is like throwing money away because there's no value unless you die. There is value — the protection against unexpected death. One agent told me renewable term is a terrible buy because only about 2% of policies ever pay death benefits. I suggested such a finding is good news, because it means few people die prematurely. I asked if he had fire insurance on his house. He did. I asked if that was a terrible buy. He considered it a prudent purchase. So how is that different from renewable term, I asked. He moved on to another point — quickly.

Make sure your policy is guaranteed renewable without evidence of good health. Normally, policies can be renewed to age 70 or 75. When that term ends, you're uninsured.

Also make sure the future rates are guaranteed; they should be shown in a table term-by-term.

A good term policy should also be guaranteed convertible to a term-to-100 or cash value policy. (See the following section of this chapter.) Conversion means if you later find you need lifetime insurance, you can switch without providing evidence of good health. Many agents advise young clients — especially those with families or new businesses — to start with guaranteed renewable and convertible term to maximize initial coverage at an affordable price. If they still need insurance years later, they can switch to term-to-100 or universal life.

But don't pay too much extra just for convertibility, some agents advise. That feature's value will depend on the rates and conditions of the new policy at the time you convert; they're not guaranteed in advance. If the new policy is outrageously expensive or not very good, the conversion feature isn't worth much.

Permanent Life Insurance

These policies run as long as you do, or to age 100. In each case, you really buy guaranteed renewable term insurance. However, permanent policies have level premiums while renewable term goes up in price at each renewal.

Whole-life

Whole-life is the most traditional form of life insurance. The big sales appeal is the level premium. Some insurance agents portray that as a bargain. In fact, you overpay in the early years to create a tax-sheltered fund that subsidizes the escalating cost later on.

That fund is the "cash value" or "cash surrender value." The big problem is that for the first 10 or 20 years it can make the whole-life coverage far more expensive per $1,000 of coverage than with a renewable term policy. In the worst case, the consumer is sold a whole-life policy that doesn't provide enough coverage. Agents can earn four times more on a whole- life policy than on renewable term providing the same death benefit.

Understand that the cash value is part of the policy's pricing. It is not savings. An agent may play up the fact that you can borrow the cash value. But you'll be charged interest, and your insurance coverage will be reduced by the value of the outstanding loan and its interest. Years ago, interest rates on these loans were very low. Not now, except for those old policies. You might also have to pay income tax if you borrow more than a set amount. Consult your insurer. The tax paid will be deductible after you repay the loan.

Some people stop paying premiums and let the cash value cover the policy cost. But that can reduce coverage, unless the pricing was designed upfront for premiums to stop at a certain point. A "paid-up" policy is one designed in such a way that you prepay the full cost over a certain number of years. Again, this is a function of having overpaid early on to create a cash value fund.

Paid-up plans are inherently flawed since they rest only on future assumptions. Plans sold in the 1980s have not earned the returns projected, so premiums have been extended or coverage reduced. Lawsuits have led insurers to adopt better voluntary standards for illustrations. Those standards apply to all sales materials that refer to future values, premiums or features. The agent must provide at least two projections, one with a basic scenario and one using less favorable assumptions. The illustrations are also supposed to clearly indicate what is and isn't guaranteed.

If you cancel a term insurance policy, you get back nothing since you bought the insurance only on a pay-as-you-go basis. If you cancel a whole-life policy, you get the cash value that's no longer needed to subsidize future premiums. Part of that payment will be taxable because it includes the tax-sheltered earnings on your premium overpayments.

If you keep the policy and die, the cash value disappears when the death benefit is paid. That's because it was designed to be part of any death benefit and was factored into the premium you paid for that coverage.

Universal Life

Universal life is a newer, far more flexible, form of whole-life insurance. It has become quite popular, especially among business owners (who need permanent insurance anyway) and the wealthy (who look for tax-sheltered savings). Others should be careful. Consider UL only after you've made full RRSP contributions and have reduced your non-deductible debt. Both can offer more tax-effective returns than UL.

Like whole-life, UL has two components — insurance and a tax-sheltered cash-value "side fund."

The insurance death benefit may remain level or automatically increase every year to offset inflation or cover growing wealth.

The side fund is one pot of money, but think of it as having two parts. The first part is the cash value discussed above — a subsidy that keeps the policy cost level. The second is a more flexible savings account that permits withdrawals — not just loans. Those withdrawals can encroach on the first part of the fund, but you run the risk of having your coverage reduced or even cancelled if there's then not enough interest earned to cover your premium.

The long-term performance of a UL policy depends on the insurance cost, administration fees and the side fund's earnings. When considering UL, make sure all fees, commissions and expense charges are detailed in the contract and guaranteed for the life of the policy. Future rates for the insurance component should also be guaranteed and should be competitive with rates on renewable and convertible term insurance.

Some UL policies are based on rates for one-year term, some on 10-year term and some on term-to-100. Some policies may cite two sets of rates, the one in use and a guaranteed maximum.

Check withdrawal fees and surrender charges. They can be onerous in the first few years.

Money in the UL side fund is normally put in interest-bearing GIC-type deposits. The interest compounds tax-free until withdrawn, when the tax becomes due. That's a very powerful feature over long periods of time. Under federal rules, the maximum size of this tax-sheltered fund is limited by the amount of insurance.

UL money can also be put in investment pools that are similar to mutual funds, but you don't get a special tax break. Every investment fund — whether run by an insurer or a regular mutual fund — provides tax-sheltered growth since capital gains are not taxed until you sell your units.

You may find that returns on a UL bond fund reflect a non-standard index. A UL equity fund may reflect just part of the growth in a standard stock market index by excluding its dividend component.

Make sure the contract has interest rates guaranteed into the future. Ask for actual rates paid in the past five years and compare them to similar investments. Some UL policies let you vary the premium paid. They rely on the investment earnings to make up any shortfall. If you don't watch carefully and investment earnings fall, you could end up losing coverage. As with whole-life insurance, make sure you understand whether any projection is based on interest rates that are truly guaranteed or only assumed.

Term-to-100

Term-to-100 insurance is a hybrid between term and cash-value policies. It's very popular among those who need permanent insurance.

Like renewable term insurance, you just buy coverage against death, in this case until age 100. On some policies, the face amount is paid out at that time. On others, the coverage just ends.

Normally, you get back nothing if you cancel, though some policies build a small cash value and even reach a paid-up stage at some point.

Like cash-value insurance, the premium stays level because you pay more in the early years to subsidize the cost later on. In the policy's early years, term-to-100 can cost twice as much as renewable term, but it's still less than whole-life or universal.

Many insurers have lost money on term-to-100. Some no longer sell it. Others have raised prices.

"Features"

Cash-Value "Dividends"

There are "participating" and "non-participating" policies. Participation means the client participates when the insurer pays a dividend. But that dividend is not the same as a dividend paid by any other successful business. It's really just a rebate. When the policy quote is issued, the insurer builds in a surcharge. If the company's overall actuarial assumptions pan out, this charge is paid back. But if they don't, it gives the insurer a cushion. So you really participate in the risk.

There can be a problem if the pricing of your policy assumes a certain level of dividends. Dividends cannot be guaranteed. If they don't materialize, you'll have to pay more or do with less coverage.

Accidental Death

Some policies pay twice as much for accidental death. So what. If you die in a plane crash, your family doesn't need any more money than if you have a fatal heart attack. In the meantime, that feature may be costing you 70 cents to $1 for each $1,000 of insurance.

Credit cards often provide free death and dismemberment insurance if you charge your bus, train, plane or ship ticket. Before travelling, make sure the card booklet and/or insurance policy are easy to find. Any free insurance is good, but don't count it as part of your insurance needs assessment.

Waiver of Premium

This feature covers the policy premiums if you become disabled, and some waivers also cover job loss. On one quote I have, it adds about 5% to the cost of a $250,000 policy for a 35-year-old male. On another, it adds 22%! Agents normally tack on this rider after clinching the deal, so the added cost is not part of the quote you get upfront. Since the price varies so much, you may find this waiver makes one policy more expensive than a competing one with higher basic insurance rates.

Read the rider carefully before signing up. You may find the definition of disability very tight. The rider may pay off only in the rare situation that you are totally and permanently disabled. There may also be a six-month waiting period. Do you have your disability policy, as discussed in the previous chapter? That might be a more effective way of covering your life insurance premium.

"Freedom 55"

Sponsored by London Life Insurance Co. — now part of Great-West Life — this has been the most successful marketing campaign ever launched by a Canadian financial company. It may be Canada's most successful marketing campaign — period.

But there is no such product. "Freedom 55" is just a concept aimed at getting you to sit down with an agent and hear about the company's range of insurance policies, RRSPs, RRIFs, GIC-type deposits and investment funds. London Life's products are remarkably similar to those of its competitors. If you respond to the Freedom 55 bait, get alternative quotes too.

Buy Term and Invest the Difference?

TERM INSURANCE supporters concede there is a problem with sharply increasing premiums at later ages, but argue that insurance needs normally decline as you grow older. That's because your kids grow up and your savings increase. The fewer dependants you have and the greater your wealth, the less need there is for insurance.

That's true, say cash-value proponents, but they add that even after you retire you may need insurance for estate planning and to supplement retirement income.

"Termites" respond that for most families, estate planning is a secondary priority. They also argue that the estate-planning aspect is undermined when cash-value insurance is also sold as a retirement fund, since retirement income withdrawals can reduce the death benefit available to pay death taxes and bequests. Term advocates also stress that for retirement security, an RRSP provides better tax breaks than cash-value insurance at less cost overall.

Some term promoters suggest taking the money you save on insurance premiums and putting it into a well-run mutual fund. If you still need insurance in later years, you can tap the mutual fund to cover the higher price of term renewals or conversion to a level-premium policy. If you don't need insurance, you can put the fund to other use.

Cash-value supporters say this strategy may work in theory, but people lack the discipline to invest the difference each month or year. Termites counter by suggesting that you have RRSP or mutual fund deposits automatically deducted from your bank account, or that you might voluntarily increase your monthly mortgage payment. Cash-value supporters then argue that people tend to tap such funds for luxuries instead of letting them grow. Insurance surrender and withdrawal fees discourage early withdrawals, they insist. Term supporters reply that forced savings is not a good reason to buy costly insurance.

Cash-value supporters also argue that, unlike universal life deposits, mutual fund returns are not guaranteed. But those pressing "buy term and invest the difference" reply that universal life guarantees can be misleading and then cite at least a half-dozen funds with excellent long-term records.

Cash-value supporters point out that the alternative mutual fund will be taxed when you die, reducing the money left for your survivors. Insurance proceeds are not taxed. Some termites concede the point and agree that term-to-100 or universal life is better for the long haul, but they cycle back to the argument that most working stiffs don't need insurance for the long haul.

Comparing Term and Cash-Value Insurance

THIS SECTION may seem a bit complex. But if you master the concept you'll be able to cut through the fog that envelops so many insurance sales presentations.

To evaluate the long-term cost of term and whole-life insurance, think of your premiums as an "annuity due" for the insurance company. That's a stream of periodic payments made at the start of each period. Calculating the present value of the two streams provides a standardized value for each insurance type.

Our Model Case

I obtained whole-life and 10-year term quotes for John, a 35-year-old non-smoker, who wants $250,000 of insurance. The quotes came from one of Canada's largest and most stable insurers. (Any agent can probably produce a better variation — it's amazing how policies can be mixed and matched and altered. My quotes are just used for illustration.)

John's life expectancy, based on appendix C-1, is just over 40 more years — to about age 75. That doesn't mean John will die at 75. It means he has a 50% chance of being dead by then. That's often misunderstood.

The normal whole-life policy would cost $1,390 a year for 20 years. Then it would be paid up; the insurance would continue, but no more premiums would be due — if the insurer's investment return assumption pans out. The alternative is 10-year term insurance guaranteed renewable and convertible. The yearly rates, guaranteed, are $385 for the first 10-year term, $810 for the second, $1,750 for the third, and $4,213 for the fourth. Notice that the term policy's annual cost is lower during the first half of the 40-year period. Then it soars.

For the calculations, John must assume a "discount rate." That's the after-tax rate at which his money could reasonably grow if invested. Maybe 5%. That assumption is not critical in valuing the payment streams, since it's applied to both policies. But it is critical for a "buy term and invest the difference" analysis.

Step 1: Whole-life policy: $250,000 at death

Use appendix A-8. Find the factor that corresponds to John's 20-year payment stream and 5% discount rate. It's 13.0853. Multiply that by the $1,390 yearly premium to get a present value of $18,189.

That's how much — growing at 5% after-tax — it would take to fund a 20-year series of $1,390 payments. It's equivalent to putting money in the bank, writing a cheque and letting the rest grow until the next cheque is due one year later.

Note that with this paid-up policy, the insurance will run for John's life — likely 40 more years — but payments will be required for just 20 years. That assumes policy dividends will be received as projected. They are not guaranteed.

Step 2: Term insurance policy: $250,000 at death

This analysis is more difficult because it involves a series of annuities, each with a different payment. Over his 40-year remaining life expectancy, John could buy four 10-year terms. Use the factors in table 14.1 at the end of this chapter:

A Term	B Factor from 14.1	C Annual premium	B x C Present value
1 (10 years)	8.1078	$ 385	$ 3,122
2	4.9775	810	4,032
3	3.0558	1,750	5,348
4 (10 years)	1.8760	4,213	7,904
Total Present Value			$20,406

So the whole-life policy would cost $18,189 in today's money, while the term cost would be $20,406. For this 40-year insurance need, the whole-life policy's tax-sheltered cash value subsidy makes it cheaper. According to one agent who is an outspoken advocate of renewable term, permanent life is frequently cheaper if, in fact, you do need long-term coverage.

But perhaps John is buying insurance because he and his wife have just had a baby and they want to cover the child-rearing period. Let's price the same alternatives for 20 years.

Just eyeballing the rates tells us the term policy is cheaper, but there's a wrinkle. If John cancels the whole-life policy, he'll receive the cash value. So let's do the numbers.

We already know the present value of the whole-life policy for 20 years is $18,189. If John cancels at that point, the guaranteed cash surrender value is $30,000. Part of that is taxable, but only the insurance company can determine how much. Your agent can get a printout showing the "adjusted cost base." The taxable portion is the difference between the cash value and the ACB. In this case, the taxable portion is $10,987. Let's knock off 50% — $5,494 — for tax. Deducting that from the $30,000 leaves John $24,506. That's in future dollars. Use appendix A-2 to get the present value. The factor for 20 years at 5% is 0.3769, so multiply the two figures to get $9,236. Subtract that payment-received from the $18,189 paid out. The whole-life policy's net cost in today's money is $8,953.

For the term policy's present value, just add the $3,122 and $4,032 above to get $7,154. So without even investing the difference, the renewable term policy is a better buy for just 20 years of coverage.

Want to measure the value of "buy term and invest the difference"? In this case, the "difference" is $1,005 in each year of the first term and $580 in each year of the second.

In appendix A-6, find the 10-year factor for the after-tax 5% discount rate we've been using. It's 13.2068. Multiply that by $1,005 and you'll see the alternative investment will be worth $13,273 at the end of the first term. That money will grow for 10 more years, so go to the 10-year row in appendix A-1. Multiply the money by the 5% factor — 1.6289. The 20-year accumulation for those 10 yearly investments will be $21,620.

During the second term, the annual premium gap was $580. Using the 13.2068 factor from appendix A-6, you'll see that this series of deposits will grow to $7,660. Add that to the $21,620 from the first set, and the total fund equals $29,280.

That, of course, is in future dollars. As with the whole-life cash value above, use appendix A-2 to find the present value. The factor for 20 years at 5% is 0.3769. Multiply that by $29,280 to get the present value of $11,036. Subtract that from the premium's present value $7,154 — and you'll see that John can pay for 20 years of term coverage and still have $3,882 in the kitty — assuming he invests the full difference and makes no withdrawals.

I didn't levy tax on growth of the yearly "difference" because our discount rate was already an after-tax assumption.

Replacement

REPLACEMENT IS when you cancel a policy from one insurer and go with another. It happens a lot, usually with people switching from whole-life insurance to term policies for much higher coverage at the same annual cost.

Agents are required to fill out special forms, informing the first insurer that the client intends to scrap the policy. Industry spokespeople say this practice ensures the client gets a comparison of both policies.

It also helps discourage agents from churning commissions by constantly replacing policies, misleading people into unnecessarily dropping good coverage.

Interestingly, it gives the current insurer an in-depth view of the other's policy — and a chance to offer a better deal. "Replacement often ends up in knock-down drag-out brawls between companies," one agent told me.

Expect your whole-life agent to defend his or her policy by citing the array of features you would give up. For each one, ask these two questions:

1. Why do I need that?

2. Is it available on a renewable term or term-to-100 policy?

Write down the replies and verify them with your new agent. Yes, this will take some time and bother. But life insurance is a major expense every year — and a critical part of your family's safety net.

De-mutualization

Several life insurance companies have announced plans to "de-mutualize." That means they want to change their form of ownership.

Currently, as "mutual" companies, these insurers are owned by policyholders, specifically those who own "participating" whole-life coverage. Under de-mutualization, the insurers would become public companies owned by shareholders, who can buy and sell their shares on a stock exchange.

When the transformation occurs, participating policyholders will be entitled to shares of stock plus a windfall payment that reflects value that has built up inside the company. If you hold such insurance, wait for that windfall before canceling or replacing your policy.

TABLE 14.1: Present-value Factors for Term Insurance

Calculating the present value of a term insurance policy is tedious, so I've simplified things. Each term has a set premium. For example, the annual cost for a 10-year term policy might be $385 for the first 10 years, then $810, $1,750, and $4,213.

1. Assume a discount rate, the after-tax rate at which your money could grow if it was invested instead of being spent on insurance. Let's say 5%.

2. Find the first-term factor for your discount rate. It's 8.1078. Multiply the first term's annual premium by that factor. [$385 x 8.1078 = $3,122] Then multiply the second-term premium by the second term's factor, etc.

Present value of 10-year term insurance

Term	1%	2%	3%	4%	5%	6%	7%	8%	9%	10%	11%	12%	13%	14%	15%
1	9.5660	9.1622	8.7861	8.4353	8.1078	7.8017	7.5152	7.2469	6.9952	6.7590	6.5370	6.3282	6.1317	5.9464	5.7716
2	8.6600	7.5162	6.5377	5.6986	4.9775	4.3564	3.8204	3.3567	2.9549	2.6059	2.3022	2.0375	1.8063	1.6040	1.4266
3	7.8398	6.1659	4.8647	3.8498	3.0558	2.4326	1.9421	1.5548	1.2482	1.0047	0.8108	0.6560	0.5321	0.4327	0.3526
4	7.0972	5.0582	3.6198	2.6008	1.8760	1.3594	0.9873	0.7202	0.5272	0.3873	0.2856	0.2112	0.1568	0.1167	0.0872
5	6.4250	4.1495	2.6934	1.7570	1.1517	0.7585	0.5019	0.3336	0.2227	0.1493	0.1006	0.0680	0.0462	0.0315	0.0215

Present value of five-year term insurance

Term	1%	2%	3%	4%	5%	6%	7%	8%	9%	10%	11%	12%	13%	14%	15%
1	4.9020	4.8077	4.7171	4.6299	4.5460	4.4651	4.3872	4.3121	4.2397	4.1699	4.1024	4.0373	3.9745	3.9137	3.8550
2	4.6641	4.3545	4.0690	3.8054	3.5619	3.3366	3.1280	2.9348	2.7555	2.5892	2.4346	2.2909	2.1572	2.0327	1.9166
3	4.4377	3.9440	3.5100	3.1278	2.7908	2.4933	2.2302	1.9973	1.7909	1.6077	1.4448	1.2999	1.1708	1.0557	0.9529
4	4.2223	3.5722	3.0277	2.5708	2.1867	1.8631	1.5901	1.3594	1.1640	0.9982	0.8574	0.7376	0.6355	0.5483	0.4738
5	4.0174	3.2355	2.6117	2.1130	1.7133	1.3922	1.1337	0.9252	0.7565	0.6198	0.5088	0.4185	0.3449	0.2848	0.2355
6	3.8224	2.9305	2.2529	1.7368	1.3424	1.0404	0.8083	0.6296	0.4917	0.3849	0.3020	0.2375	0.1872	0.1479	0.1171
7	3.6369	2.6542	1.9434	1.4275	1.0518	0.7774	0.5763	0.4285	0.3196	0.2390	0.1792	0.1348	0.1016	0.0768	0.0582
8	3.4604	2.4040	1.6764	1.1733	0.8241	0.5809	0.4109	0.2916	0.2077	0.1484	0.1064	0.0765	0.0551	0.0399	0.0289
9	3.2924	2.1774	1.4461	0.9644	0.6457	0.4341	0.2930	0.1985	0.1350	0.0921	0.0631	0.0434	0.0299	0.0207	0.0144
10	3.1326	1.9721	1.2474	0.7926	0.5059	0.3244	0.2089	0.1351	0.0877	0.0572	0.0375	0.0246	0.0162	0.0108	0.0072

15

Insurance: From Fender-Benders to Fires

THIS CHAPTER IS ABOUT AUTO AND HOME insurance. Not whether you need it — you do — but how to get good value.

Auto Insurance

AUTO INSURANCE is a major expense. It accounts for 12-20% of the average yearly cost of car ownership, according to management consultants Runzheimer Canada Inc. And the figures are bound to rise. More crowded roads mean more accidents. Smaller, more complex cars carry higher repair bills. Medical costs are soaring. So are theft and vandalism rates in some areas. Indeed, insurance industry researchers have developed a system to rate particular models based on accident, repair cost and theft statistics.

Make sure you have adequate coverage at a fair price — when you first buy your policy and at each renewal. Several years ago I cut my renewal cost by about 20%, simply by reading my policy and phoning my broker to discuss the coverage. Before that, I routinely wrote a cheque each year, continuing coverage established when the car was brand new.

If you do nothing else, read your policy. Surprisingly, many policies are now in plain English. Make sure you understand:

- Just who is covered while driving your car?

- What happens when you drive somebody else's car? His or her coverage will probably apply. But if it doesn't — or it's inadequate — to what extent will your policy cover you?

- What happens if somebody riding in your car is injured?

- What post-accident expenses are covered? Legal fees? Replacement rental car?

Your ability to shop around depends on where you live. Drivers in British Columbia, Manitoba and Saskatchewan have to buy insurance from public plans. Quebec has a hybrid system. A public plan insures basic liability, while private firms insure the vehicles and offer top-up liability coverage. Auto insurance is privately run elsewhere.

All policies provide basic standardized coverage, so you can easily compare prices. Talk to a broker who deals with a range of insurers. Don't just take the cheapest rate. Some companies are much better than others at paying claims.

Ask the broker about the insurers' financial stability. Toronto-based TRAC Insurance Services, mentioned in the previous chapter, rates property and casualty insurers and sells brokers its report. The property and casualty insurance industry has a fund to compensate consumers if a member insurer fails. There is more on that at the end of this chapter.

Here are some points to discuss with your agent or broker:

- **Use and mileage.** Those who drive to work pay more than those who use the car only for pleasure. Tell your broker if you retire, join a car pool or switch to public transit. The same goes for any change in the family, perhaps divorce or a child leaving home. Total yearly mileage may also affect the rate.

- **Select rates.** Does the company have preferred rates for those with long term claims-free records? What's the savings? If you're one or two years away from that threshold, switching insurers now may not pay in the long run. Some companies allow one minor accident without raising your premium.

There are three basic sections to an auto insurance policy.

Arguably, the most important is liability coverage. This pays others' claims if you cause an accident. Provincial minimum requirements range from $50,000 to $200,000, but $1 million is generally recommended. Some people carry more, especially if they drive in the United States, where court awards tend to be high. Some people believe a judgment can't be higher than their insurance. Wrong. You're liable for anything over the insured amount.

Make sure you're protected against uninsured and underinsured motorists. That protection is automatically included in policies sold in Ontario, New Brunswick and Alberta, according to the Insurance Bureau of Canada, an industry association. Elsewhere it's an optional rider. While every province requires that vehicles be insured, the IBC estimates as many as 5% are not.

The second section of the policy provides "accident and medical payments." Accident benefits coverage pays a cash settlement if you die or lose income because of a car crash. It's compulsory in most of the country. Medical payments coverage handles accident-related medical expenses not covered by provincial medicare. That can include U.S. hospital bills if you're injured while driving south of the border.

The third section is collision and comprehensive coverage.

Collision covers damage to your car if you have an accident. It is essential for new cars but less important for autos getting on in age or in poor shape. Many drivers don't realize that if their car is a total write-off they only get its book value, based on standard surveys. As the car ages, with each renewal reconsider whether it's worth insuring for collision. One broker told me she would keep coverage on a five-year-old car but not an eight-year-old one. If you have an old car in mint condition, ask about getting it appraised and insuring that value. Collision insurance is required by government plans in Saskatchewan and Manitoba.

A new car starts depreciating as soon as you leave the dealer. If it's financed and you total it, you still have to repay the loan but the insurer won't pay you the full amount. Ask your agent about a depreciation protection rider. It covers the car's full purchase price during the first few years. Your lender probably also offers this coverage.

The cost of your collision coverage is heavily affected by the "deductible." That's how much of a claim you would have to pay yourself. Review your deductible at each renewal. Set it as high as you can; if you have an accident, you can cover the deductible by tapping the emergency cushion discussed in chapter 5. Going from $250 to $1,000 may cut your annual cost by about one-third.

Comprehensive coverage protects your car against theft, fire and mishaps like vandalism and broken windshields — basically, events beyond your control. Many drivers don't file claims, fearing their rates will rise. Comprehensive claims don't drive up your premiums, though frequent filings may lead the insurer to insist on a higher deductible. As with collision, set your deductible as high as possible. For two decades many policies have had $50 deductibles. Think about past inflation; $50 today is a lot less than $50 10 years ago. If you could afford to cover $50 on your own then, you can afford to cover far more today.

Are you shopping for a new car? Consult your agent or the Vehicle Information Centre of Canada, mentioned in chapter 11. Insurance rates vary among models, based on their crash "survivability" and average repair cost.

Do you ever drive outside Canada? Your coverage should apply in the United States. If going elsewhere, consult your agent before leaving home.

Do you ever rent cars? In most cases, your auto policy's liability and accident benefits coverage would back up whatever insurance comes with the rental car, but possibly only in Canada and the United States, and probably only if the rental car is used for pleasure trips, not business ones. Consult your agent.

Your collision coverage probably applies to rentals only if your own car is inoperable because it's being serviced or repaired. There is a rider, called SEF 27, that transfers collision and comprehensive coverage from your car to a rental or borrowed one. But it's limited to Canada and the United States, your car must be idle, and it applies only to personal use, not business trips. Some policies automatically include this rider. It's an option on others.

Be careful if you rely on your credit card's collision damage waiver. Your card's CDW may not cover fire or theft. Some cards limit CDW to Canada and the United States. Luxury cars are not covered; there should be a list of these in your cardholder booklet. Nor are vans like the one you rent when moving. The CDW may run only 31 days per rental.

Most importantly, your credit card does not provide liability insurance. The rental car likely comes with some liability coverage, but it may be a very small amount. If you hit someone, you'll be on the hook unless your own liability insurance applies or you buy the daily top-up coverage offered by the rental agency. That daily coverage is expensive, but outside North America it may be your only option.

Home Insurance

I KNOW a fellow whose apartment was robbed. Cleaned out. He had no insurance. He thought his stuff was covered by his landlord's policy. It wasn't.

Another friend had a laundry room fire in his condominium apartment. Fortunately, he and his wife were not hurt. There was substantial smoke damage, but they had a good insurance policy. Their insurer moved them to an excellent nearby hotel for two weeks or so, paid for all their clothes and linen to be cleaned, and restored their apartment to its original condition — even matching the wallpaper. Aside from the horror of the fire, their only problem was straightening out which bills were payable by their insurer and which by the condo corporation's.

Whether owner or renter, you need home insurance. It protects you from loss caused by burglars, fire, tree limbs falling on the neighbor's car, a visitor slipping on your patio and all kinds of other threats.

These policies are inexpensive compared to life and car insurance. An apartment renter might pay as little as $150 a year. A house or condo owner might pay $300-$500. These policies are easy to set up, and automatic renewals make them easy to ignore. A little bit of effort can generate full value at a fair price.

Insure for full replacement cost with automatic inflation adjustment. Otherwise, you'll just get the depreciated value. Insurance brokers can easily calculate a home's replacement cost based on its size, construction and any special fittings. If you own a high-priced house, you'll find the estimated replacement cost low. That's because much of your home's market value is the land, which can't be stolen and won't burn down. Don't overinsure the building.

If you do major renovations, build an addition or buy expensive art or some other fitting, tell your insurance agent. If you don't, those investments probably won't be adequately covered.

If you own a condominium, you are responsible for the interior of your unit. The condo corporation is supposed to have insurance for common elements. Its insurance also covers your walls, floor and ceiling, but only for the original state as built by the developer. Alterations and even seemingly minor decoration like wallpaper would not be covered. Make sure your insurance provides for them. Your condominium owner's policy may also cover up to $5,000 or $10,000 of certain special assessments levied by the condominium corporation for property damage or a liability settlement.

Shop around. One survey of eight companies found a price spread of 21-31%, depending on the home's value. Home policies are often sold through brokers who represent a range of insurers. But look beyond price. Unlike car insurance, home policies are not standardized. There are three types of coverage:

- "Standard homeowners" covers the building/apartment and contents only for perils that are specifically named — fire, lightning, water damage, theft, burglary, etc.

- "Broad form" covers the building/apartment against all risks, but the contents are insured only against named perils.

- "Comprehensive form" covers both building/apartment and contents against all risks.

That seems straightforward, but just what's covered varies among companies. For example, one policy might automatically cover damage from sewer backup while another makes that optional. One might cover freezer spoilage due to a power failure while another doesn't. Clearly, that feature isn't worth much if you don't keep a lot in your freezer. Consider your needs. Even comprehensive all-risk policies contain exclusions. Fortunately, most insurers have small pamphlets that outline their basic policies. Your agent or broker can fill in the fine points.

Make sure to ask about special limits, a common problem when claims are filed. Your off-the-shelf policy may cap any payment for items like jewellery, silverware and computers. You can increase the amount by adding specific endorsements.

Make sure your liability section covers any maids, nannies or other domestic help.

Policies normally protect your belongings against theft or loss even when they're outside your home — for example, in your car or a hotel room. But coverage outside your home may be limited to 10% of your personal property coverage limit. Review that part of your policy and make sure you don't buy other insurance that duplicates it. For example, if you have a child at university, his or her belongings may already be covered by your policy. Also see if your possessions are covered during a move.

To document what you own, make a video of each room, noting the cost, purchase date and serial number of each valuable item. Keep the video in your safe deposit box along with sales receipts for the big-ticket purchases. If it won't fit in the deposit box, keep the video in your desk at work or have a friend hold it.

Check your obligations for when temporarily away. Must the water be turned off? How often must someone check the place? What happens if you vacate the house, perhaps because you've moved and can't sell it?

Every policy has a deductible — the amount of a claim you must pay yourself. That's often $100 to $1,000, with most people taking $200. Set it as high as you can. Going from $200 to $500 could knock 20% off your cost. If there's a loss, take the extra $300 from your emergency fund. Review your deductible every few years.

Don't be afraid to file a claim for fear your rates will rise. Your premium is based on the type of dwelling and coverage, not the frequency of claims. What if you have five break-ins in two years? The insurer might increase your deductible or limit you to standard form coverage. If you keep losing bikes, they might be excluded. Only rarely does an insurer refuse to renew a policy.

Some companies give discounts to claims-free customers. Some routinely cut renewal rates by 5% or so. A few grant discounts for homes that are less than 10 years old. Your age can matter too. With some insurers, those as young as 50 qualify for seniors' discounts. You might get a discount if the same company insures your car and home. Most companies give credits if you have a burglar alarm with a central call-in feature, not just one that goes off and annoys your neighbors. Some insurers give discounts if you belong to Neighborhood Watch or have paid off your mortgage. That marks you as a more responsible person. Some also cut rates for non-smokers.

Do you run a home-based business? More and more people do. Discuss that with your insurance agent. Certain professionals like lawyers and accountants may be able to get limited business contents and liability coverage under their homeowner policies. Others, however, may need separate coverage. Without it, valuable equipment would not be covered if adjusters find the invoice was made out to a business.

And, once again, talk to your broker about the financial stability of any insurance companies you're considering.

Consumer Protection

THE INDUSTRY-RUN Property and Casualty Insurance Compensation Corporation pays policy claims and premium refunds if a member company goes bankrupt. A policy claim must be filed before the bankruptcy or within 45 days. Payment, handled by the company's liquidator, is capped at $200,000 with a deductible of at least $500, depending on your policy.

Suppose you were at fault in a car accident that injured several people and your insurer has gone under. Knowing the industry fund caps payments at $200,000 per occurrence, the victims are likely to sue you personally. You can ask the liquidator of your insurer to defend you.

This industry-run fund does not cover public auto insurance plans in British Columbia, Manitoba, Saskatchewan and Quebec.

For more information, contact the Property and Casualty Insurance Compensation Corp.; 20 Richmond St. East; Suite 210; Toronto, Ont. M5C 2R9. Phone (416) 364-8677.

16

Home Is Where the Heart Is

BE IT EVER SO HUMBLE, ALMOST EVERYBODY wants one: a home, the great North American dream.

The best — most indisputable — reasons for buying a home are lifestyle and security. You can do almost anything you want with a home you own. As long as you pay your bills, nobody can kick you out. You're not prey to a landlord's whims. Eventually your mortgage will be paid off. While rents normally rise each year, the only shelter costs for someone with a paid-off home are maintenance and taxes. That's indeed a great comfort in retirement.

Sure, big maintenance bills — a new roof or furnace — hit every so often, but one rule-of-thumb is that, over time, maintenance averages out to about 1% of the home's value each year. Many people who sell their houses and move to condos complain about high maintenance fees. But they're probably funding a much higher level of service — for example, 24-hour security, snow removal and full athletic facilities. A fair-sized chunk of those fees — in Ontario, at least 10% — is invested as a reserve for common area redecoration and replacement of roofs and mechanical equipment. Few homeowners have such a contingency fund.

Property taxes have been soaring in many areas, but they hit both owners and renters. Tenants pay indirectly through their rents. Taxes on rental buildings may be even higher than on owner-occupied dwellings, though provincial rent control laws may limit any increase that landlords can pass on.

Home ownership definitely works. But is it a good financial investment? That used to draw an unqualified "yes." Now, it's a "maybe."

First, there's a tax break. Any gain on the sale of your principal residence is tax-free. That's a substantial benefit, but to liberate that tax-free money you have to borrow against your equity, or sell and then rent or buy a cheaper place.

The principal residence tax break also works only if your home sells at a profit. Many don't. Markets in smaller communities depend heavily on the fate of a few dominant employers, sometimes just one. It's no secret that corporate Canada is restructuring. Big city markets like Toronto, Calgary and Vancouver have been quite volatile, with up or down bursts. Swings of 20% or more a year have not been uncommon. Those who bought and sold at the right times made tons of money. Those who didn't got clobbered.

Real estate gains are magnified by leverage — the use of borrowed money. Let's say you buy a $200,000 home (ignoring fees and taxes) with $50,000 down. That's 75% leverage. You sell the house for $225,000, pay off your $150,000 loan and pocket $75,000 — your $50,000 initial investment plus $25,000 pure profit (again ignoring fees).

That's greater leverage than you're allowed in the stock market. Unlike the stock market, if your house value plummets you don't have to inject more cash, so long as you stay with the same lender.

But leverage can hurt. Say you have to sell your $200,000 house because of divorce or a new job in another city. You get only $175,000. You pay off the $150,000 loan, are left with $25,000 and have lost half your down payment. Unlike other investments, you must absorb the full loss; you can't apply it to past or future capital gains. Volatile markets make it tough for those who have to sell.

Fervent real estate believers argue that prices must rise over the long term because "God doesn't make land anymore." But government bodies do, all the time, by rezoning. So do developers. Some keep building up by erecting high-rise condos. Others build out by expanding suburbia's borders during boom times. Suburban growth will likely increase as communications technology makes it less necessary for offices to be in the city.

Increasingly, analysts are bearish about real estate because of the life cycle of the baby boomers. Prices soared in the '80s, when boomers flooded into the market as first-time buyers and then quickly traded up. Now, the analysts say, boomers are set for a while, and the next big shift in places like Toronto may be a marked downturn around the year 2000, when boomers start selling out and moving to retirement havens.

Key to this vision is that the baby boomers greatly outnumber the generation that followed. This vision is one of a double whammy. Big-city prices fall as boomer vendors glut the market, while prices in those already booming havens like Victoria explode with boomers bidding against each other — much like they did in the '80s.

Real estate believers say job creation is more important than the movement of baby boomers, and they point to Canada's outlook for continued economic growth. Some believers also cite immigration as salvation, but real estate values are highly localized and immigrants tend to cluster in just a few areas.

Other bearish analysts say all you have to do is consider the outlook for inflation. Real estate is an inflation hedge. In the late '70s, the smart money said to buy the most expensive house you could handle because inflation would drive up the price and reduce the real cost of your mortgage. The smart money was right.

As the go-go '80s ended and we headed into a low-inflation environment, many in the smart money set sold their urban mansions, rented luxury homes or condos and put their cash into the capital markets or retirement getaways. As I write this, it seems they were right again. I have a few boomer friends who know where they want to retire. They now rent their big-city dwellings and have put their money into getaway farms and cottages — all within easy commuting. Though used only on weekends and holidays, those properties still qualify as tax-free principal residences.

If you don't live in a potential retirement haven, enjoy your home as a lifestyle investment. But don't expect it to make you rich.

Is Rent Really Money Down the Drain?

HOMEBUYERS AND tenants both pay rent. The buyer rents money through a mortgage. The tenant rents space. One rule-of-thumb says a property's annual rent should be at least 10% of its cost. Few, if any, big-city properties rent for that much. Thus, tenants generally pay less each month during the first 10-15 years than someone who buys a home and sticks with it. But what do renters do with that extra money? Spend it.

Homeowners, meanwhile, have a big advantage. Part of each mortgage payment constitutes forced savings. Eventually the house will be free and clear, while the tenant still pays escalating rent.

Maybe you rent now but plan to buy a home in a few years. Or perhaps you just don't want a home. Either way, consider this: Price a home you would like to own, get the monthly cost for the mortgage and taxes, and add a bit for maintenance. Suppose this "notional home cost" totals $1,600 a month and your rent is $1,000. Open an automatic monthly $600 mutual fund investment plan. If possible, open the account with a lump sum equal to the fees and taxes involved in purchasing the home. Ideally, also stick in an amount equal to the home's down payment.

The automatic bank debits get the short-term renter used to the higher cost of home ownership. Meanwhile, the long-term renter builds an investment fund for retirement or an unplanned future decision to buy a home, perhaps when prices are depressed. Remember, residential real estate is highly cyclical.

If you're a prospective homeowner, it may be best to put your deposits into a money market or mortgage fund. Why risk a major capital loss if you might need the money for a home in a year or so?

If you're a long-term renter, you'll probably want to put the cash in an equity fund with a solid long-term record. You may not get the principal residence tax break, but your fund will qualify for the capital gains tax break. Don't sweat market ups and downs. Monthly investments average your cost. Holding at least five years tends to reduce risk. Consider that house values also change daily, but the figures aren't published.

Every year or so, review your notional home cost for changing mortgage and property tax rates. Bump up maintenance by the overall inflation rate. Then adjust your investment plan.

Every so often, the media report on studies that show home ownership beats renting. Those studies are funded by the real estate industry. You'll find they have renters investing in guaranteed income certificates (GICs) or the Toronto Stock Exchange. Neither has been a stellar investment over the past decade or so.

To recap: Home ownership is great in terms of lifestyle and security. A paid-off home works wonders for any retirement plan. Whether ownership beats renting in the mid-term depends on where you buy, what you buy, whether you'll have to sell at the wrong time and what you would do with your spare money as a tenant. No investment is a sure thing.

Home Runs Take Team Spirit

SO YOU want to buy a home. First, line up your team.

The Agent

Most homes are sold through real estate agents, who collect a commission on the sale price. Usually, that fee is paid by the vendor — the seller. There is a legal principle that agents work for the people who pay them, so your agent may technically be working for the seller. Some areas now allow buyer-paid agents.

As in any commissioned sales force, there are excellent agents and horrible agents. If you have a good one, tell your friends and co-workers. More importantly, don't go to an "open house" without him or her. Otherwise, if you decide to buy that place, your purchase can be claimed by the agent running the open house, not your own.

Set your criteria and target price before linking up with an agent. That will save you and the agent time and trouble. On meeting your agent, cite a shopping price 5-10% lower than your target. Agents routinely show clients higher-priced homes in hopes they'll fall in love with one.

Ask the agent if there are any wrinkles in pricing your desired home. For example, condominiums tend to be priced per square foot. Agents have access to computer services that list prices for all homes sold in your area. Don't make an offer without checking.

If the agent doesn't follow your criteria, try another. While vendors sign contracts, buyers are not committed to agents. Be patient. Your home is invariably the largest single purchase you'll make. And it's truly one you have to live with.

When you select a home, check the listing form for the name of the vendor's agent. If two agents do a deal, the commission is split. If one agent serves both sides, it's not, and the agent may then be willing to shave the commission to clinch the sale. That gives the vendor leeway to cut the price and still come out even. An agent who has both sides of the deal might also be willing to tell you the seller's bottom line to save time and trouble.

The Lawyer

Find a lawyer versed in residential real estate deals; he or she can probably give objective advice about prices in your community.

Get a copy of the standard "agreement of purchase and sale" or "offer to purchase" form used by real estate agents in your area. Have your lawyer add his or her pet clauses. The only blanks will then be the names of the vendors, the property's address, the price and the closing date.

The wording of your offer is critical. In real estate law, only written agreements count. Real estate agents are well versed in writing out offers, but they might not put in clauses as tightly worded as your lawyer's.

For example, the agent's clause might state only that your deposit will earn interest. Only at closing, three months later, do you learn that the money — up to 10% of the home's price — was kept in his or her company's trust account at a miserly yield. Instead, your lawyer might produce a clause requiring the money to be put into a term deposit and even holding the vendor responsible if it's not.

Your lawyer can also give you an idea of all the fees and taxes involved in closing the deal. These can run as high as 3% of the purchase price.

Your lawyer can also provide referrals to other members of your team.

The Lender

Most financial institutions offer pre-approved mortgages. Some charge for this service. The maximum loan and the interest rate are set in advance. You're protected if interest rates start rising but, depending on the lender, you may not benefit if they fall — at least not automatically. Ask before you sign. Pre-approval does not obligate you to take that lender's mortgage.

Check out features as well as rates. See the next chapter.

The Home Inspector

I hired a home inspector when I bought my first house in 1978. Though well-established in Britain, home inspection was then a fledgling field in Canada. The industry has grown substantially since then, both in size and in quality, but is still unregulated.

There is a voluntary association with a code of ethics. The Canadian Association of Home Inspectors requires members to pass three exams and perform at least 250 inspections. Call (613) 475-5699.

If you buy a resale home, make the offer conditional on getting a home inspection. Since time will be tight, perhaps just three days, line up your inspector beforehand. Contact at least three firms. Fees vary widely, but may run about $250–$500 — that's small change compared with the price of fixing a major flaw.

Find out precisely what the inspector will check. The list should include every major structural and mechanical area, except appliances.

Ideally, the inspector will estimate the cost of any major repairs. Make sure the inspector has errors and omissions insurance, in case a serious flaw is missed. Also be sure the inspector isn't really a renovator out to drum up business.

Accompany the inspector to see what's wrong; you can get valuable advice. But don't expect the inspector to give an opinion about the property's price.

If the inspection turns up major flaws, renegotiate the deal or walk away. If your offer was made conditional on a satisfactory inspection, you won't lose your deposit.

Setting a Closing Date

MOST BUYERS and sellers set their closing date for the end of a month. If you can, avoid the rush by going for a mid-month closing. Most real estate deals involve a chain of transactions with several houses changing hands that same day. Your local registry office will be very busy. Just one snag at a lawyer's office or the registry can leave one or more buyers with a loaded moving truck and no place to go until the next day. Also, movers typically charge more at month-end.

17

The Getting, Feeding and Killing of Mortgages

PEOPLE NEED MORTGAGES TO BUY HOMES, and lenders are eager to provide them. Financial institutions find residential mortgages very profitable and low risk. But not everyone qualifies.

Debt Service Tests

INSTITUTIONS NORMALLY don't approve loans if the mortgage payments, property taxes and heating total more than 30-32% of the applicants' annual income, not counting irregular income like overtime. That's called the "gross debt-service" ratio.

A second test, "total debt-service" ratio, calculates the cost of carrying the home plus all other loans as a percentage of income. Limits are 37-42%.

Down Payment

FOR A conventional mortgage, you must put down at least 25% of the home's appraised value. If you don't have that much, you have two options:

- You can take a first mortgage for 75% of the appraised value and a higher priced second mortgage for the rest. The second mortgage would be arranged by a mortgage broker for a fee.

- Or you can put down as little as 5% and get just one "high-ratio" mortgage from your conventional lender. The rate and most features will be the same as for a normal loan, but you have to buy special insurance arranged through your lender.

   That insurance — from the federal government's Canada Mortgage & Housing Corporation (CMHC) or privately-run General Electric Capital Canada Inc. — protects the lender against default. It does not protect you. You must insure the full loan, not just the high-ratio part — the difference between your down payment and the 25% limit. The insurance rate depends on the size of your down payment and could run as high as 3.75% — that's $3,750 on a $100,000 mortgage. Payment is due upfront. If you don't have it, your lender will add it to your mortgage. That makes it even more expensive, since you'll pay interest on the outstanding balance.

Price both options. Even with a higher rate and broker's fee, a second mortgage might be the cheaper route, especially if you can repay it quickly.

The 5% Down Plan

UNDER A special CMHC program, you can put down as little as 5%. But the loan size is limited based on regional thresholds. The loan has to be insured; that's expensive. And while borrowers can select any term, the debt service test requires them to have enough cash flow to meet the payments due on a three-year term.

   Even if you qualify, think twice before signing on. Just because a program is government backed does not mean it's financially prudent. Why do you have just 5% to put down? Is your income really good enough and stable enough for you to buy and maintain a house? Remember, when you consider taxes and maintenance, home ownership costs more than renting, at least for 10 years.

The RRSP Home Buyers' Plan

A FIRST-TIME home buyer can borrow up to $20,000 from his or her registered retirement savings plan (RRSP), interest-free. You qualify if you've signed a home purchase agreement and neither you nor your spouse owned a home in the previous five years.

   The loan must be repaid within 15 years. Revenue Canada will bill you for equal payments but you can pay more any time. The sooner the loan is repaid, the better. That's because your RRSP will lose interest in the meantime.

   Repayments can be made at any institution and you do not have to make the same type of RRSP investment. Say you cashed a GIC when the plan began in 1992. You could now buy mutual fund units. All that matters is that the money goes into an RRSP.

Repayments are not considered RRSP contributions, and therefore provide no tax deduction. If a repayment is skipped, the money is considered an RRSP withdrawal. It's taxed as income for that year and can't go back into the plan.

The Home Buyers' Plan (HBP) has been very popular, but I suspect many — maybe most — of the applicants don't appreciate the damage it can do to their retirement savings. It's significant that provincial pension regulators — who are most concerned with future financial security — don't allow Home Buyers' Plan withdrawals from locked-in RRSPs.

Understand that an HBP withdrawal is not free money. Your cost is the interest your RRSP gives up and all the future growth on that money. The younger you are, the greater that cost. If you take the full 15 years to pay back the loan, decades of lost future growth on that money could make your withdrawal far more expensive than any conventional mortgage.

The cost of the withdrawal will rise still higher if the required repayments prevent you from making new RRSP contributions. You will then lose the tax deductions on those contributions as well as decades of compound growth.

There is also a problem with lack of diversification. A home already dominates most people's wealth. An HBP withdrawal increases that concentration just when several major real estate markets face uncertain prospects. Contrary to widespread belief, a home is not a surefire investment.

The analysis is complex. If you have a computer, consider getting PowerMath for RRSPs, a reasonably priced software package from Speakman + Todd Publishing Inc. (1-800-268-5212).

A study by Bank of Montreal Private Client Services concluded:

- RRSP withdrawal is worthwhile if the mortgage would not otherwise be repaid before retirement.

- RRSP withdrawal is worthwhile if the mortgage rate is higher than the RRSP's growth rate, *provided the person pays off the mortgage early by making the same monthly payment as if no RRSP money were available. That also assumes money saved from the early payoff is invested, not spent.*

- RRSP withdrawal is not worthwhile if the rates are similar and the mortgage will be repaid before retirement.

Even studies done for the real estate industry found the plan works only if all savings generated by the higher down payment are invested, not spent.

The plan may work well if you have limited income and face a quandary between saving for a home and putting money into an RRSP. Let's face it; you would probably forego the RRSP. This way, your money goes into the RRSP system but you still get to use it for a home.

For the plan's first two years, borrowers were barred from making tax-deductible RRSP contributions in the same year as their withdrawals. But that rule was relaxed in 1994. Now you lose your deduction only if an RRSP contribution is made less than 91 days before your withdrawal.

The plan can also work well if you fall just shy of the 25% down payment required for a conventional mortgage. The question in that case is whether the RRSP's lost growth is less than the extra money you would have to pay for a second mortgage or special default insurance. If you take this route, pay back the RRSP as quickly as possible.

The plan can work very well for a retiree who qualifies as a first-time buyer and who would have tapped the RRSP anyway. Note that the home need not be a house. A mobile home may qualify — as long as it's bought in Canada.

Mortgage Shopping

THERE'S A lot of interest in mortgages, but check more than the rate. These considerations affect your mortgage cost:

- **Amortization.** That's the payback period for the entire loan. Most new mortgages have 25-year "ams." Say you start with a 25-year amortization and an 8% rate set for one year. The lender's computer assumes you'll pay 8% for 25 years and calculates a constant monthly payment. That payment is a blend of principal and interest. The interest compounds semiannually. At first you'll owe a lot of money, so nearly all the payment will be interest.

    One year later you renew for another year at 7.5%. Your amortization is now 24 years. Your new payment is based on the assumption you'll pay 7.5% for 24 years. The next year's renewal is based on a 23-year am, etc.

    Must you start with, and stick to, a 25-year am? No. A shorter payback period will cost more each month because the loan's repayment is compressed. But the loan will be repaid sooner, so you'll pay less interest overall. At 8%, a 25-year am for $100,000 costs $763.21 a month, with interest totalling $128,966 over the 25 years. A 20-year am costs $828.36 a month, but total interest falls to $98,805.

    If you run into a cash crunch, your lender might extend the am. That would cut your monthly payment but cost you more overall because the loan's repayment will take longer.

- **Term.** That's the period for which your rate is set. Lenders used to set the mortgage rate for the full amortization. Now, most mortgages carry rates set for six months to five years. Some lenders also offer seven- and 10-year terms.

  Normally, rates are higher on long terms. First-time buyers and those near the financial edge are often advised to go long. It may cost more, but they can breathe easier. Many veteran homeowners always go short. Volatile financial markets can make that choice emotionally tough, but these people usually save money over time. Others hedge by taking two- or three-year terms.

  Predicting interest rates is a perilous pastime. Even professionals can't do it accurately on a consistent basis. Sometimes economic trends are clear. When they're not, use the amortization table in table 17.1 (at the end of this chapter) to price your alternatives. When you pay more for a longer term, you buy security. That cost difference is like an insurance premium. Consider also that if you lock in an affordable payment, you have leeway to budget for prepayments. Later in this chapter you will see that, over the long term, prepayments are worth more than a slightly lower rate.

- **Split mortgage.** Some people hedge their bets by taking split mortgages that divide the loan over several terms — perhaps one-third in a one-year term, one-third in a three-year and one-third in a five. The mortgage rate is then averaged. But this scheme ties you to your lender. When one term comes due you won't be able to move your mortgage to get a better deal elsewhere.

- **Open mortgage.** You can get out of an open mortgage any time without penalty. Just pay off the loan. That's handy if mortgage rates fall. Rates on open mortgages are higher than on closed ones.

- **Closed mortgage.** You can't get out of a closed mortgage until the term is up, unless the lender agrees. In that event, expect to pay a stiff penalty.

- **Fixed rate.** Just what it says. A fixed rate is set for the full term. Some lenders let you switch to a new rate during the term's last year, but you have to pay an adjustment fee.

- **Variable rate.** Just what it says. A variable-rate mortgage (VRM) is tied to the lender's prime rate or some other floating measure. Your payment stays level. When rates fall, you automatically pay back more principal. When they rise, you pay back less. Clearly, this option requires monitoring. Normally, you can switch to a fixed rate any time without penalty. Not all lenders offer variable rates.

Be aware that fixed-rate mortgages compound semi-annually, but VRMs compound monthly. That means the variable rate is a bit higher than you think. Appendix A-3 converts both types to an annualized rate. For example, 7% compounded semi-annually is 7.123%, while 7% compounded monthly is 7.229%.

VRMs also have lower loan limits — 70% of appraised value instead of 75%. That provides a cushion. Otherwise, if rates soar and you don't change your payment, you could end up owing more than you borrowed. The unpaid interest keeps getting added to your loan balance.

Some lenders offer capped VRMs that protect you from rising rates beyond a certain level. But these loans often carry too high a base rate. Also, the rate on some gets locked in once it hits the cap while on others it's free to float back if interest rates fall.

Borrowers become mesmerized by rates, but rates are only part of the story. You won't find much difference in rates among lenders because the institutions tap pretty much the same capital pool — mainly GICs and bonds called mortgage-backed securities. But still shop around. A half-point difference can save you nearly $400 a year on a $100,000 loan. Just appreciate that lenders can shave rates only so much.

The big area where lenders vary is in features. Over time, the right features can save you far more than trimming the rate a half-point here and a quarter-point there.

Check for "portability" and "assumability." Most people move before the mortgage is paid off. Portability lets you transfer the loan to your new home. Assumability lets your buyer assume the mortgage if he or she qualifies. Some lenders guarantee these features in the contract. Others allow them as policy, but policy can change any time. Without these two features, the lender could keep you on the hook for interest payments until the term is up. Even if there is an assumability clause, see if you could still be held accountable if the new buyer defaults.

Ask about refinancing if interest rates plummet. Refinancing is covered later in this chapter.

If your deal doesn't close on the first of a month, you'll owe interest from the closing date to the first of the month. Ask about the "interest adjustment date." Some lenders deduct that amount from the loan advanced at closing, which means you have to come up with a few hundred bucks extra before you can take possession. Other lenders add the interest to the amount due on the first of the month, so your first mortgage payment will be higher than you expected. Still others avoid the interest adjustment by scheduling your first payment exactly one month after closing.

The Prepayment Spiral

Definitely check prepayment privileges. Prepayment is the best way to save money on your mortgage — and one of the best investments you can make. Regular payments chip away at your mortgage. Prepayments chop.

When you make a prepayment, you set off a compounding spiral that can knock years off your amortization and save tons of money. Suppose one year ago you began an 8% $100,000 mortgage with a 25-year amortization. You've just won $11,000 in a lottery. After blowing $1,000 for a glorious night on the town, you go to your lender and make a $10,000 prepayment. This single payment will cut 5.7 years off your am, saving you $41,990 of interest.

Here's how the prepayment spiral spins around. The lender's computer hacks your prepayment off the outstanding balance, but does not reduce the scheduled payment amount. When the next payment arrives, the computer checks the new outstanding balance and says: "Gosh, that payment is too high, but I don't think I'll send back a refund. No, I'll use it to reduce the outstanding loan." The process repeats again and again and again — each time a scheduled payment is received. By saving you interest, your prepayment earns a tax-free return equal to the mortgage rate. Go back to table 10.1 in chapter 10 and compare that return to the equivalent return you would need on a taxable investment.

There are three types of prepayment:

- **Annual.** You can pay off a certain amount without penalty, usually up to 10 or 15% and sometimes 20%. Some lenders base the limit on the original loan amount, while others use the current balance. Some allow prepayments only at the yearly anniversary date; others accept them on any regular payment date.

- **Ad hoc bump-ups.** Some lenders let you boost any scheduled payment by as much as 100%. Really good plans then let you skip or reduce future payments, as long as you don't fall behind the original payback schedule.

- **Accelerated payment mortgages.** The standard mortgage has monthly payments, but virtually all lenders will let you pay weekly, biweekly or twice a month. Matching your mortgage payment to the timing of your paycheque is convenient. However, whether you save money depends on how the mortgage is structured.

    For you to save a pile of money, the lender should calculate the monthly payment and then divide it by four for weekly payments, or by two for biweekly ones. On our 8% 25-year $100,000 mortgage, these biweekly payments will chop the payback by as much as five years, saving up to $30,479. That's not magic. Your biweekly payment is $381.61, or $9,921.86 for the year. That's $763.34 higher than the normal plan's annual total. Without realizing it, you make the equivalent of 13 monthly payments each year.

Note, however, that for a biweekly mortgage some lenders multiply the normal monthly payment by 12 and then divide by 26. Here, your biweekly payment is $352.25, a bit less than before. Your 25-year payback period falls only to 24.86 years, saving you $1,248.

There is yet a third method. The loan is amortized over 25 years, with a total of 650 biweekly payments. Each payment works out to $351.63. The payback period is still 25 years. You save just $403 off the normal monthly plan.

Any lender should be able to construct the mortgage the way you want, but you have to ask.

Bruce's 4-Step Mortgage Paydown Tango

If buying a home is a dream come true, paying it off may seem like a fantasy when you look at your first mortgage statement. But clearing the loan early may be a lot easier than you think if you follow this four-step plan. If you do all four steps, you'll pay off your loan in less than half the original time without having to save up whopping amounts for lump sum prepayments. But any step will work without the others.

Let's say your dance partner is a run-of-the-mill $100,000 mortgage amortized over 25 years. We'll assume an 8% rate for the first five years and then 7% at each renewal. Total interest over the 25-year payback is $115,907.

Step 1. When the interest rate falls from 8 to 7% at the end of the first five-year term, book the lower rate but don't change your payment. The minimum monthly payment may have dropped from $763.21 to $708.81, but if you continue to make the payment you're used to, the extra $54.40 a month will reduce your total amortization to 22.2 years and cut your total interest cost to $103,489 — a savings of $12,418. Even if you split that $54.40 between the mortgage and some other need, you can still do well.

Step 2. Instead of a monthly-pay mortgage, take an accelerated payment schedule set up to maximize savings. The biweekly payment for the first five years will be $381.61. Continue to pay that when you renew at 7%. Your total amortization has now been cut to 18.6 years and your total interest cost has fallen to $84,254 — a savings of $31,653.

Step 3. Index your payment to growth in your income. This step was very powerful when 5% pay raises were the norm. Right now, we'll assume 1.5% a year. This is a wonderful technique because you bump up your payment, but it stays constant as a percentage of income. So you haven't reduced your purchasing power. Our three steps have now cut the amortization to 15.7 years. The total interest cost is $73,241 — a savings of $42,666.

Step 4. Make an RRSP contribution and use the tax refund it generates to pay down the mortgage. Since a new homebuyer is often strapped for cash, we'll start step 4 midway through the second year. Say the refund is worth $3,500.

Just one such payment in year-2 will shave the amortization to 14.9 years and trim another $5,836 off the total interest cost. Make a payment every subsequent year, and the amortization falls to 10.7 years. The total interest cost — which began at $115,907 — will be $49,312.

These calculations were done on MORGIJ2, an amortization software package produced by Different Products Ltd. of Burlington, Ontario (905-639-0387). Due to rounding and formula variations, results may differ slightly from those produced by lenders or by other software. If you have a computer, you'll find such software to be a great investment. Packages range from $25 to $100. Or build your own with a spreadsheet. The math is discussed in appendix D at the end of this book.

Don't use the amortization functions in spreadsheet software like Lotus 1-2-3 or the pre-programmed keys on standard business calculators. They're set up for U.S. mortgages, which compound monthly.

Bruce's Muffin-a-Day Mortgage Paydown

This is for those who can't tango. How about setting aside just $1 a day — the cost of a fattening muffin — to pay down your mortgage?

I took the above base case — a $100,000 mortgage with normal monthly payments at 8% for five years and then 7%. I increased each monthly payment by $30. Just that amount cut the amortization from 25 years to 22.6 and saved $12,940 of interest.

Warning!

Since large amounts are involved, many people focus only on their mortgages. But a mortgage is usually the cheapest loan around. First pay off credit cards, then tackle car and other consumer loans if their rates top the mortgage rate. Even if they match, go for the other loans. Remember that standard mortgages compound just semi-annually while consumer loans compound monthly.

Mortgage Life Insurance

Expect a sales pitch for special life insurance to cover the loan if you get a mortgage from a financial institution. If you don't smoke or have a major health problem, it may be cheaper to buy a regular, more flexible, term policy from an insurance agent. For one thing, you keep that policy even if you change lenders. Mortgage prepayments reduce your coverage under a lender's plan but your premium may not go down unless you ask. Also, the lender's plan may not apply if you rent out the home. You are *not* required to buy the bank's insurance.

Cut-Rate Mortgages

When the market is slow, real estate agents find that cut-rate mortgages can drum up business. But such deals may just be smoke and mirrors if you don't understand the concept.

Say the current mortgage rate is 8% and the vendor feels a buyer would jump at 5%. The vendor tells a lender: "Set the rate at 5% and I'll make up the difference with an upfront lump-sum payment."

The lender then calculates the "interest rate differential." The IRD is the present value of the income stream the lender gives up by setting the rate at 5% instead of 8%. Using a complex calculation, the difference between the two rates is projected over the mortgage term and then adjusted for the time value of money. The lender doesn't care if the buyer pays just 5% because the upfront payment can be invested so the overall return is the same.

If mortgage rates are 8%, a lender needs about $11,435 upfront to break even on granting a $100,000 five-year 5% mortgage amortized over 25 years. The vendor then has a choice: absorb that cost, or try adding it to the price of the house. What do you think will happen?

A savvy buyer should determine the buy-down amount. Ask any lender or mortgage broker. Or calculate it yourself with mortgage amortization software that can handle buy-downs. If you don't have a computer, see if your public library or office supply store has a book of "mortgage value tables." That book explains how to do this exercise manually. Don't confuse it with the book of standard mortgage amortization tables.

Once you know the cost of the buy-down, suggest the vendor reduce the price by that amount while you arrange your own financing. You might even boost the amount by a few hundred dollars since the vendor would likely have to pay the lender or a mortgage broker a fee in addition to the actual buy-down payment. Whether you take the cut-rate mortgage or bargain down the price, your mortgage cost is about the same. But shaving the price will save the vendor money on the agent's commission while the purchaser saves money on sales and/or land transfer tax.

Refinancing when Mortgage Rates Fall

To understand this section, you must understand the difference between a mortgage's term and its amortization. That was covered earlier in this chapter.

In 1996, as mortgage rates sank to their lowest level in 40 years, homeowners rushed to pay off their current loans and replace them with new ones. That's called refinancing. Most found themselves at their lenders' mercy because their contracts did not mention refinancing. Some lenders refused. Others charged whichever was greater: three months' interest or the interest rate differential discussed above.

The IRD is the fairest arrangement, since it's based on the lender's lost income. When a mortgage is near the end of its term, a flat three-month penalty produces an unfair windfall to the lender. Early in the term, it produces an unfair windfall for the borrower.

Unfortunately, the IRD concept is not regulated. In 1984, then-Finance Minister Marc Lalonde tabled legislation mandating a standardized IRD formula for all mortgages. But it died when his government was defeated and has not been reintroduced despite pleadings by the Canadian Bankers' Association. The major banks use the proper calculation, but they differ on whether a surcharge is added. Some other lenders use different formulas.

Instead of the greater of the two, some lenders require just an IRD while others want just three months' interest. Which method is better depends on the rate spread and where you stand in the amortization.

Since it reflects the interest the lender will be giving up for the rest of the term, the IRD is lowest when there's a narrow rate spread and you're well into the term. For example, take a $100,000 mortgage amortized over 23 years at 8%. With one year left, the IRD would be $1,869 if the new rate is 6% and $3,793 if it's 4%. If the term has two years left, the IRD would be about twice as high.

In the same case, the standard three-month interest penalty would be about $1,965 no matter what the new rate or how long is left in the term.

Since it's a flat charge, this penalty is affected only by where you stand in the amortization. The farther along you are, the lower the penalty. That's because the interest component of your monthly payment falls with each passing year.

Three years into the term, CMHC-insured mortgages become open, with a penalty of three months' interest. You might think your mortgage is closed when it's not; consult your agreement or lender. The three-month rule may not apply to GE mortgage insurance, which follows the lender's prepayment policy.

By law, mortgages issued for more than five years also become open, but at the five-year mark. You'll then face a flat penalty of three months' interest if you pay off the loan early.

Blend-and-extend refinancing has become popular. The lender re-books your loan at a current rate but for a longer term. The old and new rates are blended. Your payments fall and the lender gets to keep your business past the normal term. Whether you really win depends on how the rates are blended. That's not standardized. Without realizing it, you'll likely pay the full interest due for the current term. Generally, these deals really work only if mortgage rates have bottomed or if you use your new cash flow productively, perhaps to pay down the mortgage or other more costly loans.

Before refinancing, check the impact of keeping your current rate but making a lump-sum prepayment with cash that would have been spent on the penalty. Compare the end-of-term balance on that to the balance you'd have from a new, lower-rate mortgage. If your lender charges an IRD, you will likely find that prepayment beats refinancing.

If refinancing, try to make a lump-sum prepayment before the lender calculates your penalty. That will reduce the balance on which the refinancing fee is based. Don't pay a refinancing penalty if your term is almost up. At renewal, every mortgage can be paid off without penalty.

Mortgage Math

Mortgage math is tedious, so most people use amortization tables like the one in table 17.1. It shows the monthly cost for each $1,000 borrowed. Suppose you want a $100,000 mortgage at 8% amortized over 25 years. Multiply 100 by the factor 7.63. The monthly blended payment — principal and interest — is about $763.

If you're mathematically inclined — or compulsive — and want to build a mortgage table, see appendix D at the end of this book.

TABLE 17.1: Monthly Cost of a $1,000 Loan

This table shows the monthly payment for each $1,000 of a standard mortgage loan with semi-annual compounding. Say you start a mortgage amortized over 25 years with a five-year term at 8%. During that term you will pay $7.63 a month for each $1,000. When you renew after five years, your payment will be based on a 20-year amortization. If you then take a three-year term, your next renewal will be based on a 17-year amortization.

Amortize (yrs)	Mortgage Rate														
	3.0%	3.5%	4.0%	4.5%	5.0%	5.5%	6.0%	6.5%	7.0%	7.5%	8.0%	8.5%	9.0%	9.5%	10.0%
25	4.73	4.99	5.26	5.53	5.82	6.10	6.40	6.70	7.00	7.32	7.63	7.95	8.28	8.61	8.9
24	4.87	5.12	5.39	5.66	5.94	6.22	6.52	6.81	7.11	7.42	7.74	8.05	8.38	8.70	9.03
23	5.01	5.27	5.53	5.80	6.07	6.36	6.64	6.94	7.24	7.54	7.85	8.16	8.48	8.81	9.13
22	5.17	5.42	5.68	5.95	6.22	6.50	6.79	7.08	7.37	7.67	7.98	8.29	8.60	8.92	9.25
21	5.34	5.60	5.85	6.12	6.39	6.66	6.95	7.23	7.52	7.82	8.12	8.43	8.74	9.05	9.37
20	5.54	5.79	6.04	6.30	6.57	6.84	7.12	7.41	7.69	7.99	8.28	8.59	8.89	9.20	9.52
19	5.75	6.00	6.25	6.51	6.77	7.04	7.32	7.60	7.88	8.17	8.47	8.76	9.07	9.37	9.68
18	5.99	6.23	6.48	6.74	7.00	7.27	7.54	7.82	8.10	8.38	8.67	8.96	9.26	9.56	9.87
17	6.25	6.50	6.75	7.00	7.26	7.52	7.79	8.06	8.34	8.62	8.91	9.19	9.49	9.78	10.08
16	6.56	6.80	7.04	7.29	7.55	7.81	8.07	8.34	8.62	8.89	9.17	9.46	9.75	10.04	10.33
15	6.90	7.14	7.38	7.63	7.88	8.14	8.40	8.66	8.93	9.21	9.48	9.76	10.05	10.33	10.62
14	7.29	7.53	7.77	8.01	8.26	8.52	8.77	9.03	9.30	9.57	9.84	10.11	10.39	10.68	10.96
13	7.74	7.98	8.22	8.46	8.70	8.95	9.21	9.47	9.73	9.99	10.26	10.53	10.80	11.08	11.36
12	8.27	8.50	8.74	8.98	9.22	9.47	9.72	9.97	10.23	10.49	10.75	11.02	11.29	11.56	11.83
11	8.90	9.13	9.36	9.60	9.84	10.08	10.33	10.58	10.83	11.09	11.35	11.61	11.87	12.14	12.41
10	9.65	9.88	10.11	10.34	10.58	10.82	11.07	11.31	11.56	11.81	12.06	12.32	12.58	12.84	13.10
9	10.57	10.80	11.03	11.26	11.49	11.73	11.97	12.21	12.46	12.70	12.95	13.20	13.46	13.71	13.97
8	11.72	11.95	12.17	12.40	12.64	12.87	13.11	13.34	13.58	13.83	14.07	14.32	14.57	14.82	15.07
7	13.20	13.43	13.65	13.88	14.11	14.34	14.57	14.81	15.04	15.28	15.52	15.76	16.01	16.25	16.50
6	15.19	15.41	15.63	15.85	16.08	16.31	16.54	16.77	17.00	17.23	17.47	17.71	17.94	18.18	18.42
5	17.96	18.18	18.40	18.62	18.85	19.07	19.30	19.53	19.75	19.98	20.21	20.45	20.68	20.91	21.15
4	22.13	22.34	22.56	22.78	23.01	23.23	23.45	23.68	23.90	24.13	24.35	24.58	24.81	25.04	25.27
3	29.07	29.29	29.51	29.73	29.95	30.17	30.39	30.61	30.83	31.05	31.28	31.50	31.72	31.95	32.17
2	42.97	43.19	43.41	43.63	43.85	44.07	44.29	44.51	44.73	44.95	45.17	45.39	45.61	45.83	46.05
1	84.69	84.91	85.13	85.36	85.58	85.81	86.03	86.26	86.48	86.70	86.93	87.15	87.38	87.60	87.82

18

Money from Your House: Moving Forward in Reverse

IF A MORTGAGE ENABLES YOU TO GET A house, a "reverse mortgage" enables you to get money out of one without having to sell or move.

Operating in Europe for about 40 years, the concept is fairly new in Canada. Vancouver chartered accountant William Turner launched it in 1986 as a way to help cash-short retirees remain in their homes. Plans have since been refined for use by younger homeowners with temporary cash needs.

The idea is that you borrow a pile of money, with your home as security. The loan's interest meter starts ticking immediately, but no payments — interest or principal — are due until the home is sold, you move out or you reach the end of a pre-set term. You remain the property's owner, and the agreement normally prohibits the lender from forcing you out as long as the property is maintained, taxes are paid and fire insurance is kept in place.

Perhaps the most straightforward reverse mortgage is a plan developed in 1990 by Cataract Savings & Credit Union of Niagara Falls, Ontario. It was subsequently offered by other Ontario credit unions. The home secures a line of credit, which the client can tap as needed. The loan can be fully or partly repaid any time. Otherwise, the interest builds. The plan is meant to run no more than 10-15 years and involves a considerable amount of financial counselling by credit union staff.

More complex — and better known — are the plans offered by

Turner's Vancouver-based Canadian Home Income Plan Corp. (1-800-563-2447), directly and also through a few banks. As well, some financial planners do deals on a local scale. They market "reverse annuity mortgages." A RAM is a two-part deal. The mortgage generates a pool of cash, much of which is used to buy an annuity. The annuity pays monthly income for life or a set term.

That income is effectively tax-free. It does contain taxable interest, but that is offset by the interest accruing on the mortgage, which Revenue Canada treats as a tax-deductible investment loan.

In some cases, reverse mortgages have been granted without annuities attached. That was done when an aged homeowner wanted to pay off a regular mortgage, freeing up money otherwise spent on principal and interest payments. There have also been cases where seniors who didn't need extra money to live on effectively pre-sold their high-value homes by putting reverse mortgages on them. The money was then used to help their children buy homes of their own or meet other major expenses. In effect, the kids got their inheritance ahead of time.

The desire to leave an estate is a key consideration in deciding whether to take a reverse mortgage. You're really spending your home equity — no matter what the salesperson projects for growth in the home's value.

As survivors of the Great Depression and World War II, today's seniors place priority on leaving an estate and are inherently reluctant to take on debt. Because of those factors as well as the reluctance of well-known banks and insurance companies to get involved, the reverse mortgage has been slow to catch on. But many analysts believe it is the product of the future. Baby boomers are quite comfortable with debt and, having been consumers instead of savers, many will have to tap their home equity to generate retirement income.

Some boomers have already used reverse mortgages to cover a short-term cash flow crunch, perhaps due to recession-related unemployment. Their payment-free loans were advanced for just a few years, but the concept is associated most closely with retirees who own homes that are fully or mostly paid off.

The reverse mortgage lender bets that when the home is eventually sold there will be enough equity to repay the loan and all interest. If not, most plans make the lender — not the borrower — absorb the loss. Some borrowers take less income in return for a guarantee that their estates get at least 20% of the home's value when the property is sold.

If they don't want to sell the house, heirs can pay off the mortgage with their own money.

Long-term deals — especially the life annuity version — can be risky for the lender. There may be no return for 10, 15 or 20 years or more. Meanwhile, the compounding interest may outrun the home's value if real estate prices fall, stay flat or rise less than anticipated.

To cover those risks, lenders charge premium rates for the mortgage and offer the arrangement only in markets with a history of rising prices. They also use conservative assumptions in setting loan limits. For example, a 60-year-old couple may be able to borrow only about 30% of the home's appraised value. The limit climbs about 10 percentage points for each additional 10 years of age, so an 80-year-old couple might borrow about 50% of their home's equity.

With a reverse annuity mortgage, the older you are, the better the deal becomes. Loan limits for older borrowers are higher because the mortgage is expected to be repaid sooner. With interest compounding over less time, there's less risk of it outrunning the home's value. Older clients also receive higher annuity payments. That's because they can buy larger annuities with their larger loans. As well, life annuities make higher monthly payments to older people, since the payout is expected to cover a shorter period of time. In one comparison, a 75-year-old got 80-100% more per month than a 65-year-old.

The financial stability of the annuity issuer is a key concern. Life annuities are issued only by life insurance companies. In the event a member issuer goes bankrupt, the life insurance industry's consumer protection plan covers annuity payments only to $2,000 a month. Term annuities are issued by a variety of institutions and may not be protected at all. Don't worry about the mortgage side of the deal. If the original lender goes under, another will take over that contract.

A reverse annuity mortgage is a complex arrangement. Setup fees are high, running $1,000 or more. Even if not required by the plan, you should get independent legal advice. There should also be a "cooling off" period in which you can change your mind. That often runs 60-90 days. After that, expect steep fees if you want to get out of the deal early. You will also probably owe an astounding amount of interest.

Don't underestimate the impact of compounding. In chapter 6 we saw how "the rule of 72" can work for you when you're a saver. Here, you're a borrower and it works against you. Each month your unpaid interest is added to the outstanding loan and the new interest is calculated. Divide the mortgage rate into 72 to see how long it takes the total loan to double.

19

Getting Away: Homes Away from Home

THE CANADIAN FLAG SHOULD BE REDESIGNED. Replace the maple leaf with the silhouette of a cottage. That's Canadian living!

Statistics Canada estimates that at least 638,000 Canadian households own vacation homes. From 1985 to 1991, the number of vacation homeowners grew by about 4,500 a year. That rate was expected to triple during the 1990s.

This chapter offers some shopping tips for those who want cottages and some tax tips for those who have them. We also look at the U.S. estate tax, an issue for snowbirds with sunbelt properties — and even for some Canadians who never cross the border.

Shopping

COTTAGE COUNTRY is filled with legal restrictions. Definitely consult an experienced local real estate agent and lawyer. Some points to check:

- Who maintains the access road? How old is it? Some new roads wash out in the first spring runoff. Where's the closest ploughed road in winter?

- How is the area zoned and what are the local building restrictions? While the cottage may seem fine now, building limits might prevent you from enlarging it.

- If the land is on a lake, what agency governs it? If the lake is part of a conservation area, powerboats and docks may not be allowed. That's good or bad news, depending on what you consider leisure. Get the water tested for pollution. Check potential problems such as an abandoned factory upstream.

- Are any Aboriginal groups pressing land claims in the area?

- Have city slickers been driving up taxes by demanding good roads and urban-type amenities?

If buying vacant land, check the availability of water that's safe to drink and find out how much neighbors paid to dig their wells. How much would it cost to run power and phone lines to your building site? Check the rules for septic tanks and other sewage facilities.

It's often harder to arrange a mortgage on a cottage than on a city home. The loan rate will also be more expensive. Look into mortgaging the equity in your city home and using that cash to buy the cottage. Mortgaging raw land can be difficult. Again, get local advice.

Tax Collector and Golden Pond

When a Canadian dies, his or her executors file a tax return for that final year. They must list all capital property as though it were sold on the day of death. Revenue Canada then levies capital gains tax. That rule hits cottages, ski chalets, investment real estate and vacant land — any personal real estate aside from a principal residence. Sunbelt condos and other foreign retreats get hit too, but they have special wrinkles, discussed later in this chapter.

This is probably of greatest concern to people determined to pass on their cottages to their children and grandchildren. If there's a spouse, he or she can inherit the property tax-free. But the full holding is then taxable when that spouse dies and it all goes to the kids or somebody else.

This can be serious stuff. A ramshackle cottage bought for a song in 1972 — when capital gains tax began — may well be worth several hundred thousand dollars today. There are, however, some ways to ease the sting.

Did you and your spouse own two properties before 1982? Until then, many couples had the city home in one name and the getaway in the other. Both properties then counted as tax-free principal residences. That break still applies for gains to 1982 when Ottawa changed the double-residence rule. Even if the properties were held jointly before 1982, Revenue Canada will let you change that retroactively. That way, capital gains tax would apply only to growth in the property's value since 1982.

Some people who bought a cottage or rental property before March 1, 1992 were able to make part of the increase in its value tax-free under the $100,000 lifetime capital gains exemption. That break was killed in 1994 but those who got in on time now have a tax-saving legacy. If you "crystallized" your property, leave a record for your heirs. If you inherit a property, check the deceased's past tax returns.

Without proper planning, children of today's cottage owners may have to sell the properties to pay the tax bill due on their inheritance.

One straightforward option is to buy life insurance to cover the anticipated tax bill. Get "permanent" insurance, perhaps term-to-100. If you have a spouse, get a "joint and last survivor" policy that pays out only after both of you die. That's when the tax bill will hit, assuming the first spouse to die leaves his or her share in the cottage to the other. Insurance death benefits are paid tax-free without going through probate.

Other options are complex and carry lots of tax and legal implications. Common ones include:

- Transfer the cottage now to the kids or a trust. You'll face tax now on any capital gains not covered by the 1982 tax break or the 1994 capital gains crystallization, but any future growth will be taxed in the others' hands.

  These transfers are very tricky. You must ensure you retain the right to use the property. Tax rules affect such issues as who will pay for the upkeep and whether it's a gift or sale. Are the kids in stable marriages? If you're not careful, half your beloved cottage could wind up in the hands of an estranged son- or daughter-in-law.

- For the year of disposition, claim the cottage as your principal residence for certain years and the city home as principal residence for others. The mix-and-match rules are incredibly complex.

For these and still other options, you definitely need good professional advice. For a good rundown of the possibilities, read *Second Property Strategies* by John Budd, a Toronto-based chartered accountant and estate planner.

Sunbelt Dreams and the Tax Collector

U.S. CONDOS and other vacation homes have an irresistible appeal for Canadians. It's always great to get away from the cold north and it's almost your patriotic duty to fantasize about wintering down south in retirement. Except for health insurance, the sunbelt cost of living is low, and though real estate prices are rising in some areas, they are still cheap by Canadian standards.

Nonetheless, accountants and financial planners often advise clients to rent, not buy, unless they really can spend a lot of time there. Why tie up money in a property that's often empty? Vacant homes invite burglars and vandals. Land-use controls are generally looser in the United States. That means your neighborhood's character could change radically in a few years. It also leads to overbuilding, so sunbelt prices have not risen much by Canadian standards, even in popular areas.

If you rent, you'll probably find a good range of accommodation at reasonable rates — at least by Canadian standards.

If you buy a unit and rent it out, tenants are supposed to send 30% of their rent to the Internal Revenue Service as withholding tax. That's unless you make a one-time election and then file a yearly U.S. tax return reporting the rent as income. In that case, you'll pay U.S. tax on any rent that exceeds mortgage interest, maintenance fees and other deductible expenses. The tax return route is best. After expenses, you rarely owe any tax. Even then, Revenue Canada will give you credit for the U.S. tax paid.

A Toronto accountant who specializes in cross-border tax planning told me sunbelt rentals cause more grief for his clients than any other U.S. tax issue. Many Canadians ignore American tax rules in the belief Uncle Sam's Internal Revenue Service doesn't know about them. But IRS agents check sunbelt property tax records and keep tabs on local real estate managers and syndicators. Filing a U.S. return is no big deal if you don't owe any tax or get Canadian credit.

If you sell the unit, the IRS will withhold 10% of the proceeds. You must then file a U.S. tax return reporting the capital gain or loss. If the property is held jointly with your spouse, each of you must file a return. If there is a profit, you face U.S. capital gains tax that may not be creditable here if you have used the Canadian capital gains exemption.

The U.S. Estate Tax

Feel overtaxed now? You ain't felt nothin' yet. If you're a Canadian with substantial U.S. property, Uncle Sam may join Ottawa in taxing what's left when you die.

Even worse, that tax is in addition to any Canadian tax due. Normally, Canadians get full credit for tax paid in the United States. But not in this case, because there's no Canadian estate tax to offset the American one. Revenue Canada's "death tax" is a capital gains levy only on asset appreciation. The U.S. death tax is a full-blown estate tax on the full market value of the taxable property. The two taxes are different.

The U.S. estate tax is levied only on American property, but Uncle Sam's reach can extend across the border. Taxable holdings include:

- U.S. real estate.

- Shares of U.S. companies — even if held in a Canadian brokerage account. A U.S. tax official told me these shares create a major problem for Canadians. The Internal Revenue Service gloms on to them when your heirs or executors ask the transfer agent to change the ownership.

  Some brokers say you can avoid the U.S. estate tax by having securities registered under your brokerage firm's name, a widely used practice called "street name." That way, the transfer agent doesn't know who owns the stock. A U.S. tax official confirmed that "street name" stocks are hard to catch. He warned, however, that not reporting such transactions is illegal and questioned whether a trust company or other professional executor would break the law.

  Do you work for an American company and hold shares in its deferred profit-sharing plan? An IRS official told me a tragic tale. When a man in Alberta died, nearly all his retirement savings consisted of company shares in his U.S. employer's profit-sharing plan. The widow lost a substantial portion to Uncle Sam's estate tax. The man had lots of time to cash his shares before he died, thereby avoiding the levy. But he didn't know they would be taxed.

- U.S. government and corporate bonds.

- Possibly interests in any limited partnership that does business in the United States.

- Goodies such as boats, furnishings in a U.S. residence and club memberships.

U.S. estate tax does not hit financial institution deposits or life insurance payouts. It does apply to mutual funds like Janus or Vanguard that are based in the United States, but it does not apply to U.S. funds that are sold by Canadian marketers. It also does not apply to shares of foreign companies that trade on U.S. exchanges as American Depository Receipts.

U.S. estate tax became a major concern for Canadians in 1988 when Washington jacked up the rates to the point where total Canadian and American tax could easily gobble up more than half a property's value at death. Americans were given a credit that exempted US$600,000 worth of assets but the credit for Canadians covered only US$60,000.

In late 1995, the U.S. and Canada adopted an agreement that generally puts Canadians on the same footing as Americans.

Under the agreement, a Canadian's U.S. estate tax credit will be based on how much of his or her wealth was held in U.S. assets. Say your sunbelt condo, U.S. stocks and sunbelt bank deposits account for half your worldwide wealth. Your estate would get half the U.S. credit — enough to shield US$300,000 in property. Note that the bank deposits count in the proration even though they're not subject to estate tax.

Your credit may be doubled if your spouse inherits your property. Previously, that applied only if the spouse was a U.S. citizen.

Many Canadians will generally face U.S. estate tax only on their real estate holdings. That's because the proposed agreement excludes investments such as stocks from the estate tax net if the person's total worldwide wealth is less than US$1.2 million.

Even if your estate has to pay U.S. tax, there may be credit available from Revenue Canada. But that credit will apply only to the extent there's Canadian tax due on U.S.-source income during the year of death.

The bottom line is that the proposed agreement will eliminate the threat of double taxation for most middle-class Canadians. But it's not 100% effective in all cases.

If the 1995 agreement doesn't provide enough relief for you, planning can ease or eliminate your estate tax exposure. But most options require professional advice. They include:

- Sell the vacation property. Rent instead. How often do you spend time there anyway?

- Buy life insurance to cover the anticipated tax bill. Let's hope your age and health still allow you to get affordable coverage. If your estate is growing, get coverage that can be increased without evidence of good health.

- Acquire property jointly with your spouse or others. But each owner must pay for his or her share.

- Sell or give away U.S. property before you die. Aside from the timing problem, there could be gift or capital gains tax complications. See an adviser now.

- Slap a "non-recourse" mortgage on the property. Such a mortgage is secured only by the property itself. It's deducted from Uncle Sam's taxable value. If, however, you don't need financing, then what do you do with the borrowed cash? There are potential income tax concerns. Get advice.

- If your total wealth is more than US$1.2 million, keep U.S. stocks and bonds in a Canadian holding company. This, too, requires professional advice.

Canadian "Offshore" Reporting Rules

In 1996, Ottawa drafted tough reporting rules in response to talk that Canadians were shipping huge sums of money outside the country to avoid or evade tax. You may have heard that you must report your foreign vacation getaway if it cost more than $100,000. Not so. There is an exclusion for "personal use" property such as a sunbelt condo — unless it's rented out — and for "active business" property. But over the $100,000 threshold, you will have to file a special return with Revenue Canada to report foreign bank and brokerage accounts as well as foreign trusts and any foreign corporation in which you and related people hold at least 10% of any class of shares. This reporting requirement is scheduled to take effect in 1999.

20

Retirement: Winding up the Gold Watch

TWO YEARS AFTER RETIRING, A FELLOW IN my hiking club was telling us how he was still excited by his freedom and his ability to enjoy it.

"A lot of men can't handle retirement," remarked an older woman. "They devote their lives to their jobs and can't handle life as retirees or living on a pension."

"I know," the fellow remarked. "But I planned for it."

"When did you start?" the woman asked.

"The day after I began work — forty years ago," he said, laughing.

In retirement, will you enjoy Golden Pond? Or be up the creek without a paddle? Planning should start as early as possible — at the latest in your early 40s — and build as you near the big day. Too many people leave it until their late 50s. That's too late, considering the sums and lifestyle decisions required.

There are four sources of retirement income:

1. **Government benefits.** Canada/Quebec Pension Plan, Old Age Security and Guaranteed Income Supplement. See chapter 21.

2. **Employer-sponsored retirement plans.** See chapter 22.

3. **Individual RRSPs and RRIFs.** See chapters 23-26.

4. **Unregistered investments and savings.** See chapters 27-30.

The retirement planning process has two phases — capital accumulation and capital withdrawal.

The capital accumulation phase runs from now to just before you stop full-time work. Key objectives are:

- Get cash flow under control and pay off all debts by retirement.

- Set up and follow a systematic long-term savings plan.

- Make sure your current and future safety net is in place with a cash cushion to handle emergencies, adequate disability insurance to replace income until retirement age, and enough life insurance to cover current needs as well as future estate planning.

The capital withdrawal phase starts at retirement. Its objectives are:

- Tap savings in an orderly manner.

- Maintain a satisfactory lifestyle and preserve good health.

How much you need for retirement will depend on the age at which you hope to retire, your life expectancy and your desired lifestyle.

Appendix C-1 contains Statistics Canada's basic life expectancy figures. An average 40-year-old man can expect to live past 75. An average 40-year-old woman will likely live past 80.

More than 100 years ago, Prussia's Count Otto von Bismarck set the normal retirement age at 65 when he created the world's first publicly funded pensions. It was a cynical ploy; average life expectancy was then about 48.

We still tend to view 65 as the normal retirement age, but it's not. A 1997 Statistics Canada survey found that 71% of retirees had stopped work before 65, and 34% retired before 60. Analysts cited widespread employer cutbacks during the early 1990s and historically high levels of personal savings.

Many of us dream of early retirement — often as early as age 55. If that includes you, first do a reality check:

- The 50s are often a person's peak earnings years. If the mortgage is paid off and the kids have left, you can save up a lot of money.

- The sooner you retire, the longer your money must last — and the more exposed you are to inflation. Use appendix A-9 to see how much capital is required to fund retirements of varying lengths. Suppose you want $20,000 a year pre-tax for 20 years to top up government and employer pensions. You want inflation-indexing at 2%. During retirement, your money can earn 7% in a tax-sheltered RRSP or RRIF. The factor for those parameters is 12.5665. Multiply that by $20,000. If you retired today, you would need $251,330 to cover 20 years. For 30 years, you would need $310,916.

Check the impact of inflation in appendix A-2. Think $100,000 is a lot of money? At 2% inflation, it will be worth about $67,300 in 20 years; at 4% inflation, just $45,640.

- Early retirement means reduced pension income unless your employer offers a special deal.

- Replacing employment benefits such as medical and dental insurance or a company car could be expensive.

Of course, early retirees often keep working by starting new careers. But beware of the "antique shop syndrome." That's when you think it would be nice to run a specialized business, but jump into it without the required knowledge. Those with careers in large organizations often think they can run a small business — then have trouble coping without the backup they're used to. Instead, can you continue your current career on a part-time or seasonal basis? The workplace is becoming incredibly flexible.

That's good, because most baby boomers — consumers supreme — will find they can't afford the retirement lifestyle they expect. Forget "Freedom 55." It's marketing hype.

Lifestyle is the wild card. A rule-of-thumb says retirees need 70% of their pre-retirement income. That figure's based largely on the assumption you'll save money on office clothing, commuting and lunches. If you now wear jeans, walk to work and brown-bag it, take that into consideration.

The 70% guideline is also based on lower taxes, since pensions are lower than salaries. As well, it assumes you don't need as much income because there won't be deductions for group insurance, Canada/Quebec Pension Plan and unemployment insurance. But ever-rising tax rates and new levies mean that within a few years a well-off pensioner could be shouldering the same tax load he or she had as a worker.

The 70% standard evolved when retirees led fairly placid lives. But improved health means today's retirees can pursue more vigorous — and expensive — hobbies and travel. When you stop work you gain about 2,000 hours of free time every year. Filling them can cost a bundle. You could easily need 80-100% of pre-retirement income. Or more.

Many people assume they'll finance retirement by selling their homes and trading down. Maybe their folks did that. But baby boomers face a double whammy. First, while lots of family-type homes will be put up for sale, demographics indicate there will be fewer family-type buyers. We could have the 1980s real estate spiral — in reverse. Second, lots of boomer retirees will be bidding up the price of housing in popular retirement havens. We could have the 1980s real estate spiral — repeated. Good luck.

That assumes you want to sell at all. Many retirees prefer to stay put. Aside from renting out space, the only way to get money out of your home then is a "reverse mortgage." See chapter 18.

Several studies have found that healthy retirees generally maintain the values and lifestyles they developed during their working years. Continuing contact with friends and family is important; many retirees who move to distant low-cost areas return home. Loneliness is one factor. Another is that low-cost areas often lack the services and amenities city folk expect. Always try before you buy; rent a retirement haven home for a while before pulling up stakes for good.

All is not gloom and doom — if you put time on your side. The sooner you start planning, the better off you will be. First, you will find saving easier because you have a goal. Second, you will accumulate more because of long-term compounding. Say you make a $5,000 RRSP contribution at the start of each year and it earns 8%. That will grow to $247,115 over 20 years — and to $394,772 if you continue for 25. The extra five years generates almost 60% more growth. Check it out in the tables in appendices A-5 and A-6. Third, the longer your investment timeframe, the more risk you can assume to get a higher return. A one percentage point difference may not seem like much, but redo the previous calculations at 9%. You'll see a gain of about 13% in the 20-year fund and 17% in the other. Remember, as discussed in chapter 6, compounding is exponential.

Want to retire? Get to work.

TABLE 20.1: Retirement Planning

If you have a computer, you will find an increasing array of inexpensive retirement planning software. Prices range from $25 to $100. Check your local computer store or *Canadian Moneysaver* magazine, which often reviews financial planning software and sells several programs. Its phone number in Bath, Ontario, is (613) 352-7448. If you have a spreadsheet package, you can use the math in this book to build a pretty sophisticated planning worksheet.

For those without computers, here's a worksheet adapted from the Ernst & Young/Financial Post Guide to Retirement Security, a video and guidebook produced in 1990. It can help you determine how much you should save — in addition to your expected RRSP contributions. You'll need the following information:

- Total value of your current unregistered savings and investments.
- Total value of your current RRSP.
- How much you would get from the Canada/Quebec Pension Plan if you retired today. In 1997 the maximum was $8,842 for a 65-year-old. Early retirees must deduct 0.5% for each month before 65 that they stop work. For example, a 60-year-old would deduct 30%.
- How much you would get from Old Age Security. Benefits are revised each quarter. The 1997 payments were about $4,750. That's payable from age 65, but higher-income recipients must repay whichever is less: the OAS benefits received or 15% of net income over the "clawback" threshold. In 1997 that was $53,214. Many baby boomers don't include OAS in their calculations.
- How much you will get from other government retirement benefits, such as the Guaranteed Income Supplement for low-income retirees.
- How much you will receive from employers' pension plans. If you are in a defined-benefit plan, there might be a projection on your yearly statement. If not, consult your employer's human resources officer. If you have a defined-contribution plan, you must project the future value yourself as with an RRSP. Follow the instructions in step 3.

To use this worksheet, you must know how to use the compound growth table that's in appendix A-1. That's explained in chapter 6.

Step 1: Figuring How Much Retirement Income You'll Need	You	Spouse
See appendix A-1 for step 4's multiplier. It's the factor at the intersection of your years to retirement and the average annual pay raise you expect. Line 6 uses the traditional assumption that in your first year as a retiree you will need 70% of your pre-retirement income. Feel free to use any percentage you find appropriate.		
1. Current annual income	$	$
2. Years to retirement		
3. Expected annual pay raises	%	%
4. Multiplier		
5. Pre-retirement income (multiply line 1 by line 4)	$	$
6. Retirement income needed (multiply line 5 by 70%)	$	$
Step 2: How Your Current Savings and Investments Will Grow		
In looking ahead, make a reasonable assumption about how much your current savings and investments will grow each year on an after-tax basis. For example, a 50% bracket taxpayer earns 3% after tax on a 6% Canada Savings Bond. The multiplier for line 9 comes from appendix A-1.		
7. Total value of current savings and investments	$	$
8. Average annual after-tax growth rate	%	%
9. Multiplier		
10. Value of savings at retirement (multiply line 7 by line 9)	$	$

Step 3: How Your Current and Future RRSP Savings Will Grow

For line 12 use the pre-tax growth rate, since RRSPs grow on a tax-sheltered basis. Make a reasonable assumption. The multiplier for line 13 comes from appendix A-1. In line 15, estimate a constant amount you will contribute to your RRSP each year — for example, $5,000. Depending on whether you contribute early or late each year, line 17's multiplier will be found in appendix A-5 or A-6.

11. Total value of current RRSP	$
12. Average annual growth rate	%
13. Multiplier	
14. Value of current RRSP funds at retirement (multiply line 11 by line 13)	$
15. Annual RRSP contributions in future years	$
16. Average annual growth rate	%
17. Multiplier	
18. Value at retirement of future RRSP contributions (multiply line 15 by line 17)	$
19. Value of all RRSP funds at retirement (add lines 14 and 18)	$

Step 4: What Will Your Pension Be Worth?

Get this information from your yearly pension statement or your employer's human resources officer.

20. Annual pension amount (defined-benefit plans)	$
21. Annual pension amount (defined-contribution plans)	$

Step 5: What Will Your Government Pension Plan Be Worth?

Enter the government retirement benefits you expect. Canada/Quebec Pension Plan, OAS and the low-income supplements are fully indexed for inflation. Line 27's multiplier is in appendix A-1 at the intersection of the years until retirement and the inflation assumption in line 26.

22. Annual C/QPP	$
23. Annual OAS	$
24. Other benefits	$
25. Projected annual benefits in current dollars (add lines 22, 23 and 24)	$
26. Average annual inflation	%
27. Multiplier	
28. Benefits at retirement (multiply line 25 by line 27)	$

Step 6: Adding up Your Retirement Income

Here we add up all of your retirement income sources to see if you'll have enough or whether there will be an income gap.

For simplicity, we'll assume you'll draw an equal amount from your RRSP/RRIF each year — in effect, an annuity. Estimate how many years of income you'll need. Appendix C-1 contains life expectancy data. In appendix A-7, find the factor at the intersection of those years and the rate at which you believe your money will grow. That's the divisor for line 33. For example, the factor for 25 years at 6% is 12.7834.

If line 35 exceeds line 36, you will have enough income for your first year of retirement. So enter zero on line 37. If line 35 is smaller than line 36, you will have an income gap. Enter the difference on line 37. Note that this calculation assumes none of your capital will be spent prior to retirement.

29. Future value of savings (enter line 10)		$
30. Retirement income from savings (multiply line 29 by line 3)		$
31. Future value of RRSP funds (enter line 19)		$
32. Average annual growth rate	%	%
33. Divisor		
34. Annuity income from RRSP (divide line 31 by line 33)		$
35. Total projected retirement income (add lines 20, 21, 28, 30 and 34)		$
36. Retirement income target (enter line 6)		$
37. Income gap (subtract line 35 from line 36); if line 35 exceeds line 36, enter 0 on line 37. Otherwise, make line 37 a positive number.		$

Step 7: How Much More Savings Are Needed to Close the Gap?

Divide line 37 by line 8.

38. Savings needed (divide line 37 by line 8)	$

Step 8: How Much Will You Have to Save Each Month?

The divisor for line 39 comes from appendix A-5. It's the factor at the intersection of the years until retirement and your expected after-tax growth rate from line 8.

39. Divisor	
40. Future annual savings to reach goal (divide line 38 by line 39)	$
41. Future monthly savings to reach goal (divide line 40 by 12)	$

Step 9: How Much Income Will You Need Five Years into Retirement?

Here you take your original retirement income target and figure how much more income you'll need to maintain your standard of living as prices go up after you retire. Assume an inflation rate and find line 43's multiplier in appendix A-1 at the intersection of that rate and five years.

42. Retirement income target (enter line 6)	$
43. Multiplier	
44. Income target five years after retirement (multiply line 42 by line 43)	$

Step 10: Where Will the Money Come From?

First adjust your government pension plan benefits for inflation. Multiply the benefits on line 28 by the multiplier used on line 43. Then add up your other retirement income.

- If line 48 is greater than line 44, you face no income gap. Congratulations! You've completed the worksheet.
- If line 48 is less than line 44, you will face an income gap five years after retirement.

45. Government pension benefits five years after retirement.

(multiply line 28 by line 43) $

46. Annual pension amount — defined benefit only

- If your pension does not increase with inflation, enter line 20 $

- If your pension is indexed for inflation, multiply line 20 by line 43 $

47. Income from savings (add lines 30 and 37) $

48. Total income five years after retirement (add lines 21, 34, 45, 46 and 47) $

49. Annual income gap five years after retirement (subtract line 48 from line 44) $

Step 11: How Much More Savings Do You Need to Make up for the Shortfall?

This step determines the total savings needed to cover the income gap shown on line 49.

50. Additional savings needed after five years of retirement (divide line 49 by line 8) $

Step 12: How Much Must You Save Each Month to Make up the Shortfall?

Line 52 shows how much you'll have to save each month to avoid an income gap five years after retirement and maintain your standard of living. If it's a huge amount, see if you can reasonably save more and/or earn more on your money. Consider part-time work in retirement. Perhaps scale back your desired lifestyle or even delay retirement a bit. With long-term compounding, an additional year's growth can be substantial.

51. Divide the additional savings needed by the divisor from step 8 (divide line 50 by line 39) $

52. Determine the amount to be saved each month (divide line 51 by 12) $

21

Retirement Plans: Will You Still Feed Me?

IN THE '50s, '60s AND EARLY '70s, INFLATION was of piddling concern, government debt loads were generally kept in check, there were even budget surpluses, and Canadian factories and resource projects hummed along.

Step by step, we built a high-cost social welfare state promising cradle-to-grave security. But politicians did not fully consider future funding and the impact of at least two major demographic changes: (1) Canadians are living longer than anyone expected; and (2) baby boomers have had a remarkably low birth rate — their boom was followed by a "baby bust." Together, those factors mean seniors — those over 65 — are the fastest growing segment of our population. By 2025, actuaries expect Canada to be transformed from a relatively young nation to one of the oldest among industrialized countries. Our demographics may resemble those of Florida today.

During the 1980s, Ottawa's chief statistician wrote a paper showing that pension, health and education programs were all affordable in spite of the demographic trends — if there was rapid economic growth. But that didn't occur. Instead, our federal and provincial governments financed the system by piling on debt. Our governments became credit card junkies, borrowing ever-greater amounts just to cover interest on earlier loans.

Now, our governments are putting their financial houses in order and the social welfare state is being cut back. Today's retirees get fewer tax breaks and other benefits than those of a few years ago. Tomorrow's retirees will get even fewer.

Government has stated openly that individuals must start assuming more responsibility. In 1989, when it released legislation overhauling the retirement savings rules, the Finance Department stated: "In less than 20 years, the children of the baby boom will begin to reach retirement age. In 40 years, nearly 30% of Canada's adult population will be over 65, compared with less than 15% today. A sound tax framework is needed to encourage the increased private saving that is required now to meet pension needs later."

Government benefits are aimed at providing a basic pension fully indexed for inflation that replaces no more than 40% of pre-retirement earnings for those at the average industrial wage. In 1998, maximum benefits from the Canada or Quebec Pension Plan and Old Age Security totalled about $13,800. While that was about 40% for someone who earned the average wage of about $34,500, it was a far lower percentage for anyone earning more. The more money you need in retirement, the more you must look to other sources of funding.

Canada/Quebec Pension Plan

BETWEEN THEM, the Canada and Quebec Pension plans cover every Canadian who does paid work, whether as an employee or self-employed. Employees and their employers split the cost of contributions. The self-employed pay both sides themselves. Contributions are not based on full income, but rather on "year's maximum pensionable earnings," a measure of the average wage.

CPP covers people everywhere but Quebec. The two plans are very similar, and are integrated so those who move between provinces do not lose benefits.

C/QPP retirement benefits depend on your record of contributions and when you start taking benefits. In 1997, the maximum CPP benefit payable at 65 for a new recipient was $8,937 a year. C/QPP is still payable, even if you retire outside Canada.

If the amount doesn't seem like much, consider this. C/QPP benefits are fully indexed for inflation, with adjustment once a year. If your RRSP earns 8% and inflation averages 3%, you would need about $113,000 to fund the same income stream for 20 years. See appendix A-9.

You must apply for government benefits; they do not begin automatically. Contact Human Resources Development Canada and/or the Quebec Pension Plan a few months before you become eligible.

You can start benefits as early as 60 or wait as late as 70. For an early start, the payment is reduced by 0.5% for each month before age 65. That's 6% a year. Take it late and your payment goes up by the same factor. Here's a rule-of-thumb method used by some CPP staff in advising people:

1. Determine how much you would get if you were now 65. That figure is available from your local income security office. Let's say it's $744.79 a month.

2. Reduce that by 0.5% for each month you start early. Starting at 60 cuts it by 30% — or $223.44 — to $521.35.

3. Multiply that by the number of months until age 65: $521.35 x 60 = $31,281.

4. Divide that by $223.44, the reduction from step 2. That's 140.

5. Divide that by 12. The answer — 11.7 years — is your approximate break-even point. So waiting until 65 can make sense if you expect to live past 76.7.

Many financial advisers recommend starting C/QPP early. That means RRSP funds can stay tax-sheltered longer. It also ensures you get some payback for all the years you contributed. When you die, the only payout is the survivor's death benefit. That will be no more than $2,500 plus a monthly income based on the survivor's age. A disabled spouse would get more.

Consider waiting if you don't need the money to live on, are in good health and find yourself in a high tax bracket. The C/QPP benefit and any earnings on it will be taxed. The benefit could also increase your exposure to the OAS/Senior's Benefit clawback discussed later in this chapter. Waiting means your benefit will be higher when you do start collecting C/QPP. You might even find that the extra 0.5% per month plus indexing beats the after-tax income you would make if you took the money early and banked it.

Other planning opportunities include:

- **Income-splitting.** You can have up to half your benefit paid to your spouse and taxed at his or her rate. The actual split depends on your credits and marriage duration.

- **Working in retirement.** CPP requires you to be "substantially retired" when benefits begin. The general interpretation is that a 65-year-old's employment income should be less than the CPP benefit. But after benefits start, you can work all you want. Just make sure your employer does not deduct CPP contributions from your pay. Nobody past 65 has to make CPP contributions.

- **Pension inversion.** That's when inflation rises by more than the average wage. It means people who start C/QPP late one year could end up with slightly higher benefits than those who wait until the new year. Each fall, CPP's client service officers get an indication if this will occur. Call your local income security office.

- **The dropout.** C/QPP computers automatically exclude low- or no-income months for up to 15% of your credited years dating back to January 1, 1966, when the plans began. That helps people who took off time to raise children or go to school. It can help or hurt early retirees. On the one hand, if you are 60 or over and always made maximum contributions, you can start benefits early and still get the full payment. On the other, say you leave or are thrown out of work early — perhaps at 55 — and don't get another job. When you apply for C/QPP, your benefit will be reduced if those zero-credit years are more than 15% of your record.

Changes Coming

Increasingly, baby boomers fear C/QPP won't be there when they retire. Many believe the plans are bankrupt. That's not true, but C/QPP have not been working as intended.

CPP and QPP were designed as "pay as you go" plans, not pre-funded pensions. Contributions from active workers pay benefits for current retirees. It's much like any government program where one group of people pays taxes to fund services or benefits for others.

But C/QPP have become more generous than originally planned, and demographic projections point to an imbalance in cash flows. There were 16 contributors supporting each recipient when C/QPP began in 1966. Now the ratio is 5-to-1 and it may be just 3-to-1 when C/QPP turns 50 in 2016.

To shore up the plans, in early 1997 Ottawa and the provinces agreed to nearly double contribution rates by 2003. While that made big headlines, it was simply a speedup of increases set back in 1991. For 2003, the new schedule calls for workers and their employers jointly to pay 9.9% of covered earnings. The prior schedule called for 10.1% in 2016. The new rules also freeze at $3,500 the income level that's exempt from contributions.

On the benefit side, pensions will be based on average earnings for the last five years of work, not the final three. That's in line with common practice for private pension plans. Disability and survivor benefits will be tightened, and the lump-sum death benefit will be capped at $2,500. Those who turned 65 or started CPP pensions before 1998 are not affected by the benefit rule changes.

Critics have made much of the state of the CPP reserve fund. That's a red herring. The reserve is just a contingency fund; it was never meant to finance the plan though new rules will give it a greater role in the future. There have also been calls for CPP to be scrapped in favor of mandatory RRSPs. But those proposals do not adequately explain how workers will be paid for the benefits they've been promised so far.

C/QPP cannot go bankrupt, because their main asset is the ability to tax — just like a school system. Rather, the issue is how much tomorrow's workers should be taxed to support people who have thus far not paid as much as they should have.

Old Age Security

OLD AGE Security and its low-income supplements are funded out of general tax revenues. OAS starts at 65. It is not related to employment. Everyone with at least 10 years of Canadian residence since age 18 qualifies for at least a partial pension. For a full one, you need 10 years of residence immediately before applying. Those born after July 1, 1952, will need 40 years of Canadian residence after age 18.

OAS benefits are fully indexed for inflation. For 1998, OAS paid about $4,800, but those with net income over $53,215 faced a "clawback." Their payments are reduced by 15% of net income over $53,215, so those at the $84,500 level lose all their OAS. The clawback threshold is indexed only to the extent the prior year's inflation rate rose by more than 3%. So, each year more middle-class retirees face the reduction originally set for just "high-income" people. You can reduce, or even beat, the impact of the OAS clawback, but it takes planning.

Meanwhile, low-income retirees may qualify for extra payments: the Guaranteed Income Supplement and Spouse's Allowance. GIS and SPA benefits are tax-free and fully indexed for inflation. But the benefit is cut by $1 for every $2 of other income. GIS pays about $5,600 for a single pensioner. SPA adds up to $8,400 for widows and widowers of OAS recipients. Several provinces also pay low-income supplements.

In 1996, the federal government proposed revamping the program in 2001 by replacing OAS, GIS, SPA and the pension and age tax credits with a new Senior's Benefit for those who were under 60 at the end of 1995.

The Finance Department estimated that 75% of seniors would do as well or better under the new plan, but the proposal was quite complex and ran into heavy criticism. In mid-1998, Finance Minister Paul Martin yanked it. "The existing OAS/GIS system will be fully maintained," he declared. But he added that this decision was based on the long-range benefits expected if governments continue to balance their budgets and reduce their debt loads. If they don't, he warned, seniors' pensions will have to be reviewed, especially as the baby boomers retire.

Many of today's seniors oppose any reduction at all — even the current OAS clawback — on grounds that they've paid for their benefits through a special tax. Indeed, there was a line on the income tax return for Old Age Pension tax until 1972, but that money was never intended to be set aside for the future.

When OAS was designed in the late '40s, federal finance officials were concerned that costs could quickly rise out of control if the public demanded higher pensions and politicians failed to say no. They favored the self-funding model set for unemployment insurance in 1940, but the government had no way to collect contributions from large blocks of workers who were not required to file tax returns.

So the designers decided to create a special OAS fund with earmarked income tax revenue. OAS was launched in 1952 with funding from a "2-2-2" formula. The government allocated for funding two percentage points of the 10% manufacturer's sales tax, which was eventually replaced by the goods and services tax. The new program was also allocated revenue from a 2% increase in the corporate tax rate. And there was the new individual OAP tax, a 2% levy on taxable personal income with a cap of $60.

OAS was intended to be self-supporting with current tax collections funding current benefits. But it wasn't. The fund ran a $100 million deficit for 1953 and averaged shortfalls of about $50 million over the next six years. Tax hikes in 1959 and 1965 put the program into the black, but its surplus peaked at $242 million in 1996 and then dwindled because of benefit improvements. The fund was down to about $7 million in 1971.

In 1972, as part of a bid to simplify the tax system, the OAS fund was wound up and the special tax allocations were paid into general revenue. Finance continued to estimate cash flow for five more years, but found a solid run of deficits ranging from $87 million in 1972 to $538 million for 1974.

In all, the program ran a deficit of $740.5 million for 1952–76, the period when separate records were kept. While today's seniors did pay a special Old Age Pension tax, it was never enough to finance the benefits they now get.

By the way, many retirees hail 1995 when seniors forced Brian Mulroney's conservative government to scrap a bid to reduce inflation-indexing for OAS pensions. But that was less of a victory than people remember — Ottawa simply raised the tax on gasoline to finance the cost of full OAS indexing.

Foreign Government Plans

CANADA HAS social security treaties with the United States and more than two dozen other countries. C/QPP credits and OAS residence years can be integrated with credits in the foreign plan to meet eligibility levels. You might end up with a Canadian pension, a foreign pension or even both. This is called "totalization." Consult a federal income security office.

22

Pensions: The Older You Get, the Better It Looks

I REMEMBER, AS A LONG-HAIRED YOUNG man, declaring, "I don't care about a pension." Friends expressed similar sentiments. Now we're in our 40s and 50s. Some of us are bald. And our sentiments sure have changed.

There are several types of employer-sponsored retirement plans. Many employers have more than one type.

Registered Pension Plans

WE TEND to think of RPPs when we think of pensions, but some fear they are an endangered species. RPPs are heavily regulated, can be very expensive for employers to administer, and cover less than 50% of the Canadian workforce.

Most RPPs fall under provincial pension legislation and the federal Income Tax Act. Those for employees of federally regulated industries such as banking and transportation fall under federal pension legislation. So do pensions in Yukon and the Northwest Territories.

During the 1980s, "pension reform" swept across the country and the legislation was updated. Efforts were made to standardize the various acts, yet many differences continue.

One of the key improvements under pension reform dealt with "vesting," a critical but often misunderstood concept. Vesting is when you get the right to the benefits that have been bought by your employer's contributions. Before pension reform, that generally occurred only after you were 45 and had 10 years of service. Therefore, many job-hoppers accrued no pensions. Now, all jurisdictions have earlier vesting — generally after just two or five years of service or plan membership. Your employer might vest all credits at the earliest date. Or pre-reform credits may still be under the old "45-and-10" rules. Although you take title to the employer's money, you usually can't cash any credits until 10 years before normal retirement age, as defined by the pension plan. In most cases, that early retirement age is 55. Even then, controls ensure the money is used for lifetime retirement income — the idea in the first place. On leaving your job, options for the vested credits are:

- Leave them in the plan and, upon retirement, collect a pension based on them.

- Transfer them to your new employer's plan if it will accept them. That's rare, except among public-sector plans.

- Buy a life annuity starting no earlier than 10 years before the pension plan's normal retirement age.

- Transfer them to a "locked-in" RRSP, also called a locked-in retirement account (LIRA). This is the most popular choice.

From an investment point of view, a LIRA is virtually the same as a normal RRSP. But special controls protect your future retirement income. For example, most plans do not allow any withdrawals until age 55.

Technically, no withdrawals can be made from a LIRA. To draw income, you must transfer the money to a life annuity, or to a Life Income Fund (LIF). By the end of the year in which you turn 69, you must switch to an annuity or a LIF, whether you want income or not.

Originally, a life annuity was the only "maturity option" for a locked-in RRSP. But then Quebec pioneered the LIF concept. The LIF delays mandatory annuitization until age 80. In the meantime, you control the money but face minimum and maximum yearly withdrawal limits. The maximum limits ensure the plan provides lifetime income.

In 1993, Alberta introduced an alternative LIF that does not require an 80-year-old to buy an annuity. Instead, the retiree keeps control of the money and continues with yearly minimum and maximum withdrawals until death. The money then goes to a named beneficiary or the person's estate. This arrangement, also approved by Saskatchewan, is called a Locked-in Retirement Income Fund (LRIF).

Many people resent the lock-in and try to get around it. But it's there to protect you. The RRSP program has shown that too many people are quick to rob the future in order to buy toys today. Locked-in plans ensure that pension plan money originally meant for retirement really is used for that purpose.

Younger people who leave defined-benefit pension plans are often surprised by the low value of the money transferred to a LIRA. That amount is based on an actuarial calculation. Given certain assumptions about interest rates, it's the amount that must be invested today to fund the pension you were promised. The younger you are, the more time that money has to compound. So today's amount may be quite small. Based on the math, the amount is fair, but you must manage it prudently to do as well as the pension plan you left.

Don't put regular RRSP contributions into a locked-in plan. They could become locked in.

Other key pension rules are:

- Generally, the employer must have paid at least half the cost of the pension benefits due when you quit, retire or die. If you quit a plan and have paid more than half your share, your excess contributions will be refunded.

    Some employers pay the plan's full cost. For employees, these plans are "non-contributory." In a "contributory" plan, the employee shares the cost. For an excellent plan, the employee's tax-deductible contribution may run as high as 9% of pay.

- Generally, after two years of service employees must be eligible to join the pension plan. In some cases, part-timers qualify too.

- On marital breakup, your spouse is generally entitled to half the pension credits earned during your marriage, but determining their value may require complex legal wrangling. In some provinces, the spouse can't access those credits until you reach retirement age.

- Generally, at your retirement you and your spouse get a choice between a full pension that covers only your life or one that pays benefits until both you and your spouse die. To fund the "joint and last survivor" option, you get a lower monthly payment. The choice is really your spouse's; he or she has to sign a waiver for you to take a single-life pension.

There are two types of RPP — defined-benefit plans and defined-contribution plans. Defined-contribution plans are also called money purchase plans.

Defined-Benefit Plans

The defined-benefit plan is the traditional pension plan. Members are promised a specific dollar amount of pension based on years of service and salary. The employer is responsible for ensuring there is enough money to meet that commitment. An actuary values the plan and its potential liabilities at least every three years. If a deficit exists, the employer gets a certain amount of time to top up the fund. If there is a surplus, laws and rules vary on what, if any, access the employer has to it.

If the employer decides to wind up the plan — or goes bankrupt — the available money is used to secure promised benefits through the purchase of annuities. Members can also transfer vested credits to LIRAs. First dibs go to current retirees and anyone eligible to retire. If there's not enough money for the others, benefits for younger members may be reduced. Ontario has an employer-funded pension guarantee plan. Note that pension laws require employers to make regular contributions and file periodic reports with regulators. Also, the money is not held by the employer. It is held in trust by a custodian bank, trust company or insurance company.

Most defined-benefit plans use one of three methods to calculate the retirement pension:

1. **Final-average.** Good plans average the salary for your last three or five years. That's multiplied by the "accrual rate" — capped by law at 2%. That amount is then multiplied by your years of service.

2. **Career-average.** The same calculation, but using average earnings during your entire time with the employer. These plans periodically adjust past earnings for inflation.

3. **Flat-benefit.** Often set up for unionized blue-collar workers, this plan is based on service, not wages. The monthly benefit equals a flat amount times years of service.

If your pension is "integrated" with the Canada/Quebec Pension Plan, your monthly payment will be reduced by whatever you get from C/QPP. That may be done directly, or indirectly through the pension calculation formula.

Public sector pension plans are normally indexed for inflation. Such indexing is far less common in the private sector.

Highly paid employees have a special concern. Those earning more than about $86,000 a year will probably not receive the full benefits they're due under their pension plan's formula. The law limits defined-benefit RPP payouts to $1,722.22 times the member's years of service. The cap was imposed to ease the government's revenue loss. RPP contributions and earnings are tax-sheltered until paid out. By capping payouts, the rules limit plan funding, thereby controlling the amount of tax-sheltering.

That means the well-paid face a pension gap. Employers must use other ways to top up the limited RPP benefit. Several options are available, all requiring specialized professional advice:

- **Pay as you go.** The pension top-up is not pre-funded. After the employee retires, the employer treats the top-up as an operating expense. This route means the employee's entitlement is unsecured in the event of bankruptcy or a major change in management.

- **Retirement Compensation Arrangement (RCA).** RCAs let the employer pre-fund the promised pension. But to ensure there is no tax sheltering, Revenue Canada collects 50% tax on contributions and annual earnings. The tax is later refunded without interest as benefits are paid out. An RCA sponsor can't avoid the tax on contributions, but can escape the tax on earnings by investing in certain life insurance products. The employer can also minimize the cost and tax bite by using a "letter of credit" instead of cash. That's an agreement in which a chartered bank guarantees to pay the pension top-up if the employer defaults. The price of this guarantee depends on the employer's credit rating, but is far less than pre-funding.

- **Secular trust.** Each year before retirement, the employee is paid a special bonus on condition that the after-tax amount be put in a trust until retirement. This option provides the same security as an RCA, but is easier to administer.

  Significantly, secular trusts qualify for the normal tax breaks on capital gains and dividends. RCAs don't. Then again, the 50% RCA tax is refunded as benefits are paid out. The secular trust bonus is taxed at the employee's marginal rate, which may be above 50%, and is not refunded.

  If the employer uses tax-effective life insurance investments, death proceeds can effectively flow tax-free through a secular trust to the employee's beneficiaries. They would be taxable if paid out of an RCA.

- **Employee profit-sharing plan (EPSP).** EPSPs are more often used for stock-purchase plans, but can fund supplementary pensions. They offer the same security and tax breaks as a secular trust but have been around much longer, so their legal status is clearer. EPSP contributions must come from current or retained profits, so this option won't help employees of public sector or non-profit bodies.

Defined-Contribution Plans

While a defined-benefit RPP has one big pot of money for all members, a defined-contribution plan has individual accounts. Every year your employer will contribute an amount that probably equals 3-6% of your pay — subject to certain limits set by federal tax rules. You may contribute too. You can normally choose how the money is invested. Common options include GIC-type deposits, stock funds, bond funds and balanced funds.

These plans are similar to RRSPs in that the level of your retirement income is not known in advance. It's determined only at retirement, when the money in your account is used to buy an annuity. Thus, your pension will depend on how well your account was managed and on annuity rates at the time you stop work. In a defined-benefit plan, the employer carries the risk that the investments won't do well and that annuity rates at retirement will be low. In a defined-contribution plan, you carry those risks. Poor performance and low annuity rates mean less retirement income.

Also, your retirement income won't be indexed unless you buy that option as part of your retirement annuity.

During your career this pension money is held in trust, just as it is in a defined-benefit plan. But since the employer makes no future promise, there's no concern about underfunding or bankruptcy.

Unlike defined-benefit plans, which generally require at least two years of membership or service, many defined-contribution plans have immediate vesting.

Deferred Profit-Sharing Plans

DPSPs are similar to defined-contribution RPPs in that your retirement income can't be known until you're about ready to stop work. But you cannot make contributions, and the employer's limit is half that for a defined-contribution RPP. Also, your employer is not required to contribute if there was no profit for the year. Unlike an RPP a DPSP lets you withdraw the money before retirement age.

Individual Pension Plans

An individual pension plan is a defined-benefit RPP set up for one person. Initially developed for incorporated business owners, it is also marketed to senior executives as a more flexible alternative to their company pension plans.

Originally, IPPs let people as young as 40 tax-shelter far more than with an RRSP. But the 1995 and 1996 federal budgets ended that and pretty much limited their appeal to those over 55 and those who want the ironclad creditor-proofing available under pension laws.

Be aware that IPPs are less flexible than RRSPs when it comes to withdrawals and income-splitting strategies like spousal contributions. IPPs' fees are also much higher and they must comply with complex pension and tax laws. Specialized professional advice is a must before — and after — you buy.

Group RRSPs

Though very popular among employers, group RRSPs don't exist. Technically, that is.

A group RRSP is really a collection of individual plans administered on a group basis by a financial institution or mutual fund company. The employer normally pays the administration fees and deducts contributions from employee pay. In lieu of offering a formal pension plan, an employer might increase salaries on condition that the extra money goes into the RRSP.

Within the group arrangement, individuals get a choice of how the money is invested within a family of investment funds and/or fixed-rate deposits.

Group RRSP money is not locked in by law, but most employers impose penalties or controls to discourage withdrawals before retirement. Any money the employer puts up would vest immediately.

Many employers offer voluntary group RRSPs as a supplement to their pension plans. The voluntary plans offer convenient savings through payroll deductions. Sometimes they're a good deal because you save on fees, but that's not always the case. Make sure the plan has the product range you want, and compare the cost and complexity to what you would set up on your own. Your employer may have a conflict of interest in promoting the plan if it has promised the plan administrator a certain membership level.

The Best Plan

SO WHAT'S the best plan? That depends on the employer's generosity, your age and your investment temperament.

The defined-benefit plan's strength is security. Retirement income is set in advance and is guaranteed. Very good plans are indexed for inflation. The big weakness for the employee is that the "pension adjustment"

— discussed later in this book — means RRSP limits are unfairly reduced for younger members and those in a plan that is not top-of-the-line. Also, vesting may not occur for as long as five years. And, the employer could go bankrupt, leaving some benefits unfunded.

A defined-contribution plan offers a great deal of control over the investment, but no promise at all about future income. Ironically, while pension fund managers are seen as stodgy, history has shown they invest more aggressively than most individuals. Their portfolios are typically 35-55% in stocks, while individuals tend to favor fixed-rate deposits. Many defined-contribution plans have immediate vesting.

Defined-benefit and defined-contribution RPPs are both creditor-proof. In each case you can take vested money with you when you leave the plan, but it must generally stay invested until you are at least 55.

Deferred profit-sharing plans often depend entirely on the employer's health; annual contributions are not required if there is no profit.

Group RRSPs vest immediately. You get considerable control over the investment. That could be a plus or a minus. RRSP withdrawals are not locked in by law. But there is no guarantee of your future income level, the employer can cancel or alter the arrangement at any time, and group RRSPs do not have the same ironclad creditor-proofing as pension plans.

If given a choice, some advisers say, a young employee in the 20s or 30s should invest aggressively in a money-purchase plan. That's a defined-contribution RPP and/or RRSP. For young people, those plans are allowed the highest levels of tax-sheltered contributions. Once past 40, switch to a defined-benefit RPP. Tax-sheltered funding for a defined-benefit plan increases as you near retirement — to make sure there's enough money to fund the promised benefit. Also, as you approach retirement you will probably appreciate the certainty of knowing exactly how much your pension will be.

23

RRSPs: Rules and Wrinkles

THE FINANCIAL WORLD IS FULL OF IRONY. RRSP rules are aimed at giving those who don't have employer pension plans the same scope for retirement savings as those who do. Otherwise, they must rely heavily on Canada/Quebec Pension Plan (C/QPP) and other government benefits designed to replace no more than 40% of the average industrial wage. These people should be pouring money into RRSPs. Yet several studies found pension plan members were more than twice as likely as non-members to have RRSPs.

Pension plan members are generally full-time employees in high wage industries, so they have more disposable income, suggested Statistics Canada analyst Hubert Frenken, one study's author. He added that their pension plan membership may make them more aware of the need to save for retirement.

RRSPs offer great tax breaks. They can also be incredibly sophisticated investment vehicles. This chapter reviews the basic rules, the tax breaks and some wrinkles. The next one deals with RRIFs (Registered Retirement Income Funds), essentially RRSPs in reverse. Then we look at investment concepts.

Who . . .

. . . may contribute to an RRSP? Almost anyone with "earned income." There is no minimum age. If your baby earns money as a model, part can go into an RRSP. Say your teenager works part-time at McDonald's and doesn't earn enough to file a tax return. Have him or her file one anyway to create RRSP contribution room for use now or in a few years. Under new rules, a full-time student can even take an interest-free loan from his or her RRSP.

There is an upper age limit for RRSPs. You cannot contribute to your own plan after the end of the year in which you turn 69. But even after that, you can make contributions to your spouse's plan if you still have eligible income and your spouse is under 70.

What . . .

. . . is eligible earned income? First, note that the system works on a one-year lag. For example, contribution limits for 1999 are based on 1998's earned income and pension plan membership.

The earned income list includes wages and salaries, net rental income, royalties and taxable alimony and separation payments received. The person who paid the alimony or separation and claimed a tax deduction must subtract that amount from his or her earned income. Tax-deductible rental and active business losses must also be subtracted.

Canada/Quebec Pension Plan retirement benefits don't count as earned income. But C/QPP disability benefits do. Taxable disability benefits from private plans also count, because they are considered a form of taxable employment income. Tax-free disability benefits don't count.

Net research grants count, but scholarships and bursaries don't. Other significant items that do not count are:

- Investment income. That includes dividends business owners pay themselves. If incorporated, consult your accountant about the best mix between salary and dividends.

- Pension income.

- Employment Insurance benefits, though supplemental unemployment plan payments do count.

- Business income from a limited partnership.

- Severance payments. But there is an important exception. See this chapter's section on "wrinkles."

If you lived outside Canada for part of the year, get Revenue Canada's T1023 earned income worksheet.

Where . . .

. . . can a contribution be made? At any financial institution or investment dealer.

Banks, trust companies, credit unions and life insurance companies offer a choice mainly between fixed-rate deposits and investment funds. Normally there is no annual administration or trustee fee.

Mutual fund companies let you open one "umbrella" account in which you can divide your money among several types of funds. You may be charged a yearly trustee fee, perhaps $25 or $50.

Investment dealers offer the widest range of choice. In addition to fixed-rate deposits and mutual funds you can buy foreign and domestic bonds, shares in companies and "derivatives" that represent a stock index or a basket of stocks. These self-directed plans normally carry an annual administration fee of $100-$200. Banks and trust companies also offer self-directed RRSPs. If you have a self-directed plan, the RRSP can fund your mortgage, as discussed in chapter 25.

When . . .

. . . can contributions be made? Any time during the year or 60 days after December 31. Most people procrastinate, so January and February have become "RRSP season."

Under old rules, if contributions weren't made by the deadline, the opportunity was lost. Now, "carry-forward" rules allow unused RRSP limits to be kept for later years. See the "wrinkles" section of this chapter.

Do you wait until the last minute? Shift forward to maximize your growth. Say it's February 28, and you've just made your contribution for the prior year. Can you do the one for the current year now? If your plan averages 8% growth, shifting forward — and keeping that schedule every year — will boost its ultimate value by 8%. If you put in $5,000 a year, your normal end-of-year pattern will produce a pot worth $365,530 after 25 years. Contributing the same total amount, but on a start-of-year pattern, will produce a pot worth $394,772. See appendices A-5 and A-6.

If you lack the cash to double up now, borrow it or set up a monthly contribution plan. Gradually boost each deposit so within a few years your budget can handle one lump sum early on. Many people use the tax refund they get in spring or summer as an RRSP contribution.

The same "early bird" concept applies to your career. Thanks to long-term compounding, the sooner you start saving for retirement, the easier it is overall. Suppose you will need $500,000 by age 65 and that your money will average 8% growth. If you're now 25, you have 40 years to build your fund. You must save $1,787 each year. If you start saving at 35, you must sock away $4,087 each year to meet that target. Start at 45 and you must save $10,117 every year. For your own case, divide your target by the applicable factor from appendix A-6. For end-of-year deposits, use table A-5.

Here's another example. Twins Mary and Larry turn 21 on January 1. Mary starts contributing $1,000 a year to her RRSP. At 30, after the deposits total $10,000, she stops. Larry then starts and continues every single year until they turn 60. Mary's total cost is $10,000. John's is $30,000. Mary's fund will be larger.

Don't you wish you could turn back the clock?

Why . . .

. . . contribute to an RRSP? To save tax for the current year. To save future tax on investment income. To build financial security.

How . . .

. . . much can you put in? There is a three-step calculation.

First, take whichever is *less*: $13,500 or 18% of "earned income" for the prior year. The $13,500 limit runs until 2004. It's scheduled to rise to $14,500 in 2004 and $15,500 in 2005. Then it will be indexed to growth of the average wage. So, to contribute $13,500 you must have had earned income of at least $75,000 in the prior year.

Second, subtract your "pension adjustment" for the prior year and any "past service pension adjustments." The PA is the deemed value of credits earned in any employer-sponsored plan. A PSPA is an adjustment for certain retroactive upgrades in a defined-benefit pension plan.

The PA concept integrates employer pension and personal RRSP limits under one tax-shelter umbrella, equal to 18% of earned income. If you have no employer plan, there is no PA and you get your full RRSP limit. If there is a modest employer plan, you get a modest PA and a high RRSP limit. If there is a good employer plan, you get a high PA and a low RRSP limit — or none at all.

Your employer is responsible for calculating your PA and reporting it on the T4 tax slip you get in February. You are supposed to be advised of PSPAs as they are determined. In some cases, a PSPA determination could force you to withdraw money from your RRSP to make room in the tax shelter for the improved pension credit.

PAs for defined-contribution registered pension plans and deferred profit-sharing plans are simply the total of all contributions in the prior year. For defined-benefit plans, a special calculation values the promised benefits. PAs are discussed further in the "wrinkles" section.

The third step in calculating your RRSP limit is simply to add on any unused limit from prior years since 1991.

Sally is calculating her RRSP limit for 1998. Earned income for last year was $74,500 and deposits to her defined-contribution RPP totalled $3,000. She takes 18% of $74,500. That's $13,410, well within the year's dollar limit. She subtracts $3,000 for her PA. That leaves $10,410. She has $5,000 of "room" carried forward from last year, so she can make a total tax-deductible contribution of $15,410.

Good news! Revenue Canada does this entire calculation for you and prints your RRSP limit on the "notice of assessment" sent after it processes your tax return due April 30. Your current year's RRSP limit is based on the data in that return. This means you should know your current year's limit by June or July. If you lose that notice, just use a touch-tone phone to call Revenue Canada's computerized TIPS telephone information service. The number is in your phone book.

If you don't want to wait, do your own calculation. If required, make an adjustment after hearing from Revenue Canada. There is a $2,000 penalty-free over-contribution cushion for those who make mistakes. That's also discussed in the "wrinkles" section.

. . . With what?

If you lack cash for a contribution, consider borrowing. Many banks and trust companies offer cut-rate loans for that purpose. Although the RRSP is an investment, the loan's interest is not tax-deductible. But if you pay off the loan within a year, your plan's growth should offset the interest cost.

The RRSP contribution will generate a tax refund that can be used to pay off the loan. Say you already have some cash for your contribution, but not enough. Here's how to determine the break-even point where your tax refund should cover the loan:

$$\frac{\text{Available cash}}{1 - \text{marginal tax rate}} - \text{Available cash}$$

Say you have $3,000, and your marginal tax rate is 51%. Subtract the marginal rate from 1 to get 0.49. Divide $3,000 by that to get $6,122. Subtract the $3,000 cash on hand. The result — $3,122 — represents your top-up loan. If you borrow that much and add it to your available cash and then contribute the full $6,122, your tax refund should be about $3,122 — enough to pay off the loan.

In late 1996 several institutions began offering multi-year "catch-up" RRSP loans. They can work well if your income is high enough for your catch-up contribution to generate a high- or middle-bracket tax deduction, if you use the tax refund to reduce the loan and if you can afford to pay off the balance while still making future RRSP contributions.

With a self-directed RRSP, the cash-strapped can make a "contribution in kind." You simply put an RRSP-eligible investment like stocks, bonds or mutual fund units into the plan. Be careful. The transfer will trigger a capital gain if the holding is worth more than what you paid. But Revenue Canada won't recognize a capital loss if it's worth less. For a GIC to be a contribution in kind, it must be "transferrable and assignable." The transfer value equals the amount of principal plus accrued interest.

RRSP Tax Breaks

Tax break #1: Tax deferral

RRSPs get the same tax treatment as employer-sponsored Registered Pension Plans. Government delays taxing contributions — and their investment earnings — until the money is withdrawn from the plan. That could be 50 years or more down the road. Ideally, you'll be at a lower tax rate in retirement than when the money was first earned.

In reality, however, middle-class retirees often stay in the same tax bracket. Frequently, that's because of insufficient planning. But an RRSP is still a good deal, since you can make money on dollars that are really the government's. In effect, you get two interest-free loans through the upfront tax deduction and the tax-sheltered growth.

Suppose your RRSP contribution limit this year is $10,000 and your marginal tax rate now and for the next 25 years is 50%. You buy an interest-bearing investment compounding at 8% per annum. Your annual growth outside the RRSP is 4% because your 8% interest is fully taxed. Inside the RRSP, growth is 8%. Here's what would happen with that $10,000 of income:

	No RRSP	RRSP
Income	$10,000	$10,000
Income tax @50%	(5,000)	0
Available for investing	5,000	10,000
Value after 25 years @4%	13,329	
25 years @8%		68,485
Income tax @withdrawal	0	34,242
Net amount	$13,329	$34,242
Annualized after-tax growth on original $10,000	1.2%	5.0%

Even that example understates the power of the RRSP by assuming it's fully cashed in 25 years. The tax shelter could run decades longer — even after you die, if your spouse is named as RRSP beneficiary. Compound growth is an inverted pyramid; the longer the timeframe, the larger the pot at the end.

Tax break #2: Income-averaging

Suppose you're well paid but plan to give it all up and just travel next year. You are now in the top tax bracket. A $10,000 RRSP contribution would save you about $5,000 in tax for this year. Next year, with little or no other income, you could withdraw the $10,000 tax-free and never pay the $5,000 Ottawa gave up.

There is, however, a steep opportunity cost and you may regret this withdrawal later in life. (I do!) The money might be liberated tax-free, but you give up decades of future tax-sheltered growth. At 8%, saving $5,000 in tax today means giving up $58,485 in tax-sheltered growth over the next 25 years.

Tax break #3: Income-splitting

This break is for those who are married — formally or common-law. "Spousal RRSP contributions" are a long-term income-splitting strategy that shifts income to the spouse with the lower tax rate.

Say a retired couple has $60,000 of income in retirement but only one person earns it. It's taxed at the top rate. If they each earn $30,000, total income is the same but it's taxed at the low rate.

Every year you can put all or part of your RRSP limit into a plan for your spouse. Your limit stays the same; you just use it differently. You still get the tax deduction, but the money and its earnings are taxed in your spouse's hands when taken out. A spousal contribution does not affect your partner's own RRSP contribution limit. Income-splitting can work well in these situations:

- One spouse is a homemaker with few ways to build savings.

- Both spouses work, neither has a pension plan and one earns far more than the other.

- One spouse has a good pension plan while the other has none or a less generous one. The pension plan member should consider spousal contributions even if he or she earns less than the other. The idea is to balance total retirement income. While the lower-paid spouse earns less now, his or her pension plan might be good enough to reverse the situation in retirement.

- One spouse's RRSP is far larger thanks to earlier investing, higher contributions or better growth. Say both are 35 and one RRSP has $30,000 while the other has $10,000. Growing at 8% a year, today's $20,000 gap will widen to $201,253 at age 65. Remember: Two retirees with balanced income will likely pay less tax than if one has substantially more than the other.

- One spouse is in line for a large inheritance that can be put away for retirement. He or she should top up the other's RRSP to balance future income.

- Both spouses now work but one plans to take off time for child-rearing, education, travel or some other purpose. If that spouse earns little or no income while off, RRSP money deposited now can then be withdrawn at little or no tax.

  But tricky rules apply. Withdrawals made during a "holding" period are taxable for the contributor, not the recipient. That period runs two years after the year the contribution is made. The key is the year of contribution, not the tax year for which it applied, as illustrated here:

Contribution date	For tax year	Holding period ends
Dec. 30, 1998	1998	Dec. 31, 2000
Jan. 2, 1999	1998	Dec. 31, 2001
Jan. 2, 1999	1999	Dec. 31, 2001

The spouse can avoid this by having one RRSP for spousal money and one for personal contributions that can be withdrawn any time. Other exceptions are:

– If the marriage fails and the spouses live apart.

– If either spouse becomes a non-resident for tax purposes.

– If either spouse dies.

– If the recipient spouse transfers the money to a Registered Retirement Income Fund and makes only minimum withdrawals, or to an annuity that cannot be commuted for at least three years.

– If the recipient spouse makes a withdrawal under the RRSP Home Buyers' Plan and does not make the required repayment.

A spousal contribution immediately becomes property of the recipient spouse. On marital breakdown, however, it is subject to asset-splitting rules under provincial family law. Common-law couples should be careful; if they break up they may not be subject to provincial asset-splitting rules.

Wrinkles in RRSP Rules

HERE'S A grab-bag of handy points. Some can be worth big bucks.

Carry Forwards

There are two RRSP carry-forwards:

- The best-known one applies when you decide not to contribute your full limit one year. The unused entitlement can be used later — there is no longer any time limit. There is no form to fill out. The people at Revenue Canada automatically track it. The running balance is updated each year when they print your RRSP limit on the notice of assessment of your tax return. At first glance, this seems wonderful. But consider:

  – Will you really have the cash for a catch-up? Amassing thousands of dollars will require discipline.

  – A carry-forward can cost you substantial long-term growth. At 8%, putting off a $5,000 contribution for five years will cost your plan $10,937 over 25 years. See for yourself. Use appendix A-1. If we do the deposit now, $5,000 will compound for five extra years. The multiplication factor at row 5 and the 8% column is 1.4693. So the value after five years will be $7,347 — $5,000 of capital plus $2,347 of growth. Over the following 20 years, the row-20 factor tells us the $2,347 would grow to $10,937.

- The second carry-forward is a tax-planning device. You can make a contribution one year, but not claim the tax deduction for it until a later year — ideally when you're in a higher tax bracket. The deduction's value goes up with your marginal tax rate.

Over-Contribution Cushion

The RRSP contribution rules are so complex that officials set up a penalty-free zone for those who make mistakes. Normally, if you put too much into your RRSP, the excess is taxed at 1% per month. But under this cushion, you can put in up to $2,000 too much without being penalized. That's a cumulative lifetime limit. That's very handy for members of defined-benefit pension plans who want to make RRSP contributions right at the start of the year, before their employers report their pension adjustments.

Others — who are less concerned about pension adjustments — may wish to use this cushion to bump up their plans. Although the over-contribution is not tax-deductible, its earnings are not taxed until withdrawn. Here are some strategies:

- Advance contribution. Make the over-contribution now. At a future point, tell Revenue Canada to count it in that year's normal limit. The money then becomes tax-deductible and your over-contribution limit is reset.

    Here's an example. You're now 40. You put $2,000 extra into your RRSP. There is no tax deduction at this point since the $2,000 is an over-contribution. You've also used up your $2,000 cushion.

    Roll forward 20 years to your first year of retirement. Though not working, you can make an RRSP contribution based on income in your final year of employment. You'd like the tax deduction, but you're tight on cash because your new pension is less than the salary you were used to. Aha! Instead of putting in $2,000 cash, tell Revenue Canada to apply that 20-year-old $2,000 over-contribution to your current limit. You then get the standard RRSP tax deduction and your over-contribution cushion is reset to $2,000. Meanwhile, at 8% the 20-year-old over-contribution has increased the value of your plan by $9,322.

- Age 69. Say you're 69. You can't have an RRSP after this year. But if you still earn eligible income, you can make tax-deductible spousal contributions. What if there's no spouse? You could over-contribute now and write it off against RRSP-eligible income after this year.

- Do you have a child or grandchild who's at least 18? Though there may not be any RRSP-eligible income, he or she still has an over-contribution entitlement. Give him or her $2,000 for an RRSP contribution. At 8%, the RRSP will be worth $74,464 when the 18-year-old is 65.

Excess contributions beyond the $2,000 limit are taxed at 1% per month. You can ask Revenue Canada for permission to withdraw the overage. Depending on the case, that withdrawal might be taxed as income.

The over-contribution cushion used to be $8,000 but the 1995 federal budget reduced it, effective for 1996. Those who had made past over-contributions were supposed to report them by filing schedule-7 with the 1994 tax returns due in 1995. Revenue Canada then counted the amount over $2,000 as part of their normal contribution for 1996 and later years.

If you didn't report your over-contributions, you can ask Revenue Canada to recalculate your RRSP limits. Or do nothing and forget about ever deducting that money. You will face a double tax bite since after-tax money went in and will be taxed again on withdrawal, but the tax-sheltered growth can offset that second bite after a certain number of years. See table 23.1 at the end of this chapter.

Severance Payments

IF YOU leave your job, part or all of your severance may qualify as a "retiring allowance." It can then be rolled into your RRSP without affecting your normal limit for the year. That can be done directly on a tax-free basis, or you can receive the after-tax amount, write a cheque to your RRSP and claim a deduction on the year's tax return. There is no carry-forward on this contribution. The deadline is 60 days after year-end.

You can transfer to your RRSP $2,000 of retiring allowance for each year of service before 1996 with your employer and any related one. A partial year — even one day — qualifies for the full $2,000. There is an additional $1,500 for each year before 1989 not covered by vested pension credits.

Say you joined your employer in 1985 and waited one year to join the pension plan. Suppose you leave next year and are paid a severance. You will be able to roll up to $23,500 of it to your RRSP as a retiring allowance. That's $2,000 for each of the 11 years you put in to the end of 1995 plus $1,500 for the year for which you have no vested pension credits.

In the past, a big retiring allowance rollover could have exposed you to the alternative minimum tax. But no more: RRSP contributions were exempted from the AMT rules by the 1998 federal budget. You might even be due a refund if you paid AMT as far back as 1994.

You could lose the retiring allowance rollover entitlement if you quickly return to your employer as an "independent contractor."

Survival tip: If facing unemployment, do a direct retiring allowance roll to your RRSP but keep a fair chunk readily accessible in case you have to withdraw it for living expenses.

A tip for those facing early retirement: If your employer has a defined-benefit pension plan, you might be allowed to boost your pension by buying credits for past service. Ask your employer if that purchase will generate a "past service pension adjustment." A PSPA can reduce your normal RRSP contribution limit or even force you to withdraw RRSP assets. To avoid that PSPA, put money into your RRSP as a retiring allowance rollover and then transfer it to the pension plan for use in purchasing the past service credits.

Withdrawals

There are no penalties on RRSP withdrawals. The amount is just added to your income and taxed accordingly. But think twice about tapping this nest egg. Except for the Home Buyers' Plan and educational use, RRSP withdrawals can't be put back into the tax shelter. So you could lose substantial future growth. See chapter 17.

Withholding tax is levied on withdrawals:

Withdrawal	Outside Quebec	Quebec
$0-$5,000	10%	21%
$5,001-$15,000	20%	30%
$15,000+	30%	35%

This is not a special tax, but a prepayment of income tax. You will likely owe still more, based on your marginal tax rate, when you file your return. To minimize withholding tax, make several $5,000 withdrawals instead of one big one.

Loan Collateral

Can an RRSP or RRIF be used as collateral for a loan? Not if your plan was issued by a bank, trust company or credit union. That's a "depositary" plan. If your plan was registered as a "trust," you can use it to secure a loan if your administrator agrees. But your income for that year will be increased by the value of the collateral, so you'll pay more tax. When you repay the loan, you'll get an offsetting deduction minus any amount the lender seized for non-payment. So, overall it's not a good idea, unless you repay the loan within that year.

Pension Adjustments

What would you say if your employer told you your future pension will be cut from $1,000 a month to $700, but there will be new bells and whistles like inflation-indexing? You might say "thank you." That is, if you have the discipline to make RRSP contributions.

RRSP contribution limits for members of defined-benefit pension plans are reduced by a pension adjustment, based on a special formula:

For 1998: 9 x (accrual rate x pensionable earnings) – $600
Pre-1998: 9 x (accrual rate x pensionable earnings) – $1,000

That formula attaches a value of $9 to every $1 of credit you earn. It assumes you have a quality pension like the indexed one for federal civil servants, and that you will put in a full career. Those assumptions mean your PA is really too high — and your own RRSP limit too low if your pension is only so-so. The PA is also too high if you're young and your employer's current defined-benefit plan contributions are fairly low since long-term growth can fund much of the promised benefit. Most people don't realize that until they leave their job and see the pension amount they can take with them.

To address that problem, some employers are redesigning their pension plans. They are reducing the cash pay out since its "accrual rate" boosts the PA. And they're adding or improving benefits like indexing or survivor pensions that don't affect the PA. The pension's overall value stays the same, but the lower PA lets you put more into your own RRSP.

The 1997 federal budget included a major change that much of the media overlooked. Before, people who left their jobs and/or pension plans before retirement got no compensation for the RRSP contribution room they lost because of their PAs — even though early departees don't get the full value of the pension credits those PAs measure. Now, a new "pension adjustment reversal" (PAR) will restore that lost room, starting with people who moved in 1997. Their former employers must calculate the amount due going back to 1990. The PAR they report will increase the individual's RRSP limit, often by thousands of dollars. Unfortunately, there's no compensation for the RRSP growth they gave up.

Past Service Pension Adjustments

Past service pension adjustments apply only to certain defined-benefit pension plan upgrades for credits earned after 1989. The rules are confoundingly complex; be glad your employer has to master them, not you. Some key points to watch:

- Ask about the PSPA before you make extra pension contributions to "buy back" pension credits for 1990 on. The same goes if you leave your employer, then return and go to reinstate your pension credits.

- Carefully read any memo from your employer that mentions PSPAs. A PSPA determination may reduce your RRSP room. If so, you might have to withdraw RRSP money to get the pension improvement.

PSPAs may sound silly, but they are aimed at curbing the taxpayers' loss from double-dipping. Without them, employers could offer low quality pensions — or none at all — to let staff maximize their own RRSPs. Then, the boss could later bring in super tax-sheltered pensions covering those very same years.

Death

If your spouse is named as your RRSP/RRIF beneficiary, your plan can be rolled into his or hers when you die. Otherwise, it will be cashed and taxed. Your estate may also save money if your institution will do a transfer to a named beneficiary without probate.

The same rollover can be done if you have no spouse but a dependent child or grandchild who is physically or mentally infirm. Any other dependent child or grandchild under 18 can receive a tax-free rollover to buy an annuity that makes taxable payments until age 18. If your estate is named RRSP/RRIF beneficiary, the plan will be cashed and taxed.

Problems arise when the contract for an RRSP or RRIF names one beneficiary and a will names another. Make sure yours jibe — or leave the designation out of the will.

If you die before using up your RRSP limit, your executors can do that for you — up to 60 days after year-end. That contribution generates a tax deduction for your final return and boosts the rollover to your beneficiary's tax-sheltered plan. Make sure your will grants authority to do that. Otherwise, another heir could challenge it.

Keep a record if you make an over-contribution that you plan to deduct in the future. Your executor can claim the deduction on your final tax return as part of your normal RRSP limit. If you haven't used up your $2,000 over-contribution cushion, your executor can — assuming there is a rollover beneficiary who will live long enough for earnings to offset the tax due when he or she withdraws this already-taxed money. That break-even point is shown in table 23.1.

Your RRSP or Home Mortgage . . .

Where should your money go? Here's a rough guide. Consider the mortgage only if it costs at least two percentage points more than what your RRSP can earn. That's unlikely in the current climate. Your RRSP also provides a last-resort emergency fund and diversifies your wealth.

TABLE 23.1: Breaking Even

This table shows the point at which earnings on an RRSP over-contribution offset the extra tax bite on withdrawal.

Tax rate in:	27%			41%			45%			47%			50%		
Interest rate:	6%	7%	8%	6%	7%	8%	6%	7%	8%	6%	7%	8%	6%	7%	8%
Tax rate out:							RRSP over-contribution break-even point (years)								
27%	20.4	17.7	15.6	13.7	11.9	10.5	12.6	10.9	9.7	12.1	10.5	9.3	11.4	9.9	8.8
41%	33.7	29.1	25.6	22.5	19.4	17.1	20.5	17.7	15.7	19.7	17.0	15.0	18.6	16.0	14.2
45%	38.1	32.9	28.9	25.4	21.9	19.3	23.2	20.0	17.6	22.2	19.2	16.9	20.9	18.1	15.9
47%	40.5	34.9	30.7	26.9	23.2	20.4	24.6	21.2	18.7	23.5	20.3	17.9	22.2	19.2	16.9
50%	44.1	38.0	33.4	29.3	25.3	22.3	26.8	23.1	20.3	25.6	22.1	19.5	24.1	20.8	18.4

24

Catching the dRRIFt

ALL GOOD THINGS MUST COME TO AN END. You can close your RRSP at any time, but you must do it by the end of the year in which you turn 69. You can cash the plan and pay tax on the full amount. Not a good idea. Or, preserve your tax shelter by using the money for a RRIF or an annuity. Any of these options can be combined.

Your RRSP institution can easily convert your plan, and might even pay a premium to keep the business. But it pays to shop around. Since this money can be placed for very long time frames, you can find a fair-sized variance in rates and terms.

There are RRIF/annuity brokers who specialize in this field and represent a wide range of issuers. Many subscribe to computer database services that can churn out quotes in seconds. Normally, RRIF/annuity brokers receive fees from the financial institution, not the client. They often advertise as "retirement planners."

Keep security in mind. Make sure you understand the deposit insurance rules. Few 75-year-olds can afford to lose money if an institution fails.

Registered Retirement Income Fund

THE REGISTERED Retirement Income Fund (RRIF) is the most popular option. It's really an RRSP in reverse. An RRSP is a tax shelter where you can put in a certain amount each year. A RRIF is a tax shelter where you must take out a certain amount each year. While the law sets a minimum withdrawal limit, there is no maximum. But the more you take out early on, the sooner your fund will run out.

The RRIF withdrawal rules changed in 1993 after Ottawa decided to let the plans run past age 90. Plans opened before 1993 fall under the old rules until the age on which withdrawals are based hits 78. That could be your age or the age of your spouse, if younger.

Each year's minimum withdrawal rate is based on the age at January 1. If there's a younger spouse, you can use that age to prolong the tax shelter. The withdrawal rate — shown in table 24.1 — is applied to the account balance at January 1, though the withdrawal does not have to occur until the end of the year. The longer you delay, the more tax-sheltered growth you get. Note that a 72-year-old must earn at least 7.38%. If not, you eat into your capital.

TABLE 24.1: Minimum RRIF Withdrawal Rates

| Age at Jan. 1 | ~~~ RRIF opened ~~~ | | Age at Jan. 1 | ~~~ RRIF opened ~~~ | |
	pre-1993	post-1992		pre-1993	post-1992
65	4.00%	4.00%	80	8.75%	8.75%
66	4.17	4.17	81	8.99	8.99
67	4.35	4.35	82	9.27	9.27
68	4.55	4.55	83	9.58	9.58
69	4.76	4.76	84	9.93	9.93
70	5.00	5.00	85	10.33	10.33
71	5.26	7.38	86	10.79	10.79
72	5.56	7.48	87	11.33	11.33
73	5.88	7.59	88	11.96	11.96
74	6.25	7.71	89	12.71	12.71
75	6.67	7.85	90	13.62	13.62
76	7.14	7.99	91	14.73	14.73
77	7.69	8.15	92	16.12	16.12
78	8.33	8.33	93	17.92	17.92
79	8.53	8.53	94+	20.00	20.00

The Rogers Group

RRIFs offer the same investment choice as RRSPs. Those who want the most control can have self-directed plans.

RRIF deposits must be structured so you have enough payout to meet the yearly withdrawal requirement. As a result, issuers are flexible. There are many formats and combinations.

If you go for fixed-rate GICs, see if the institution is able to pay out only the required withdrawal while keeping the rest invested at full interest. When shopping for a RRIF deposit, look beyond the quoted rate. Depending on how withdrawals are handled, you may earn less than you think. Also, the quoted rate may not include administration fees or other charges.

Narrow the field to three or four institutions. Get a projection from each, using an identical sample case. For example, assume $50,000 is deposited for exactly 10 years with a $300 withdrawal on the first of each month starting December 1. Be precise. Warned one broker: "There's lots of playing around; make sure it's an apples-to-apples comparison." After 10 years, there will be money left in the account. The institution with the highest balance is the one with the most favorable setup.

Mutual funds are ideal for RRIFs because you can redeem as many or as few units as you need. Just make sure you won't face any stiff redemption fees.

Your minimum withdrawal does not have to be taken as cash. You can take it "in kind." Suppose you don't need cash for expenses. You could, for example, transfer mutual fund units from your RRIF to a regular investment account. The same goes if you don't wish to sell shares of a certain company.

In chapter 23's "wrinkles" section, see the discussion of death. The beneficiary rollover rules also apply to RRIFs.

Many seniors resent the rule that whatever is left in their RRIF when they die is taxed. Many financial advisers make a lot of money by selling life insurance to cover that bill. Due to the way insurance is priced, such a plan can work well for couples who buy coverage that pays out on the second death. But it may be a wash or even a money-loser for a single person who lives just a bit longer than the average life expectancy for his or her age group and gender. Have your adviser compute the "present value" of both the anticipated tax bill at death and the pre-tax cost of all the insurance premiums due in the meantime. And consider that the insurance will benefit your heirs, not you, so ideally they should pay the premiums.

Annuities

IN RETURN for a lump sum, an annuity issuer agrees to pay you a certain amount every month. There are "term-certain" annuities that run for a set time, often to age 90. And there are "life" annuities that run as long as you do. Life annuities are sold only by life insurance companies, though chartered banks keep trying to get permission to offer them.

The key point with an annuity is that you give up control of your money. Many people don't like that, but others do want a hands-off arrangement. Those with small retirement funds may prefer the security of knowing a life annuity can't run out — especially if they're in good health and come from a long-lived family.

A single-life annuity pays income for as long as you live. A joint-life annuity runs until both you and your spouse die. It's often said about annuities that when you die, your estate gets nothing. Not quite. Most people take reduced monthly payments in order to guarantee payouts for a set time, usually 10 or 15 years. If death occurs during that time, the present value of the remaining payments is paid as a lump sum. If no guarantee is purchased, no payout is made.

Definitely get several annuity quotes before buying. Payouts vary widely. (If an issuer doesn't want much annuity business at the time, it doesn't drop out of the market; it just slashes its payouts.) Don't base your decision only on a quoted interest rate. There are different ways of structuring the payout. Compare the actual amount paid each month.

Annuity payouts depend on your age and on interest rates at time of issue. The higher each factor, the better you'll do. "Deferred annuities" let you lock in a high interest rate, but you don't take payments for several years. One insurance executive told me that back in 1981, a 45-year-old client set up a life annuity deferred for 20 years. When that man is 65 he will start receiving life-long payouts based on something like 15% a year.

Some planning points:

- You can divide your money between an annuity and one or more RRIFs, each meeting a specific objective. For example, you could set up an annuity for secure income and use a RRIF to top it up for inflation.

- It's easy to switch from a RRIF to an annuity, but often impossible to go the other way. Because of required withdrawals, a RRIF will reach peak value at a point that can be determined in advance. At that point — around 86 for an 8% RRIF — some people annuitize if interest rates are high.

- If you're willing to take less initially, you can have annuity payments that rise up to 4% a year to offset inflation. If today's low interest rates persist, that means an indexed annuity might provide better inflation protection than a RRIF.

- RRIFs can leave money for your estate. Life annuities have no estate value unless guarantees are purchased. A term-certain annuity would make the remaining payments or lump-sum equivalent.

- Security is the big reason for buying an annuity. Deal only with solid companies and make sure your contract is within limits for the insurance industry's ComCorp consumer protection plan. See chapter 9.

Prescribed Annuities

PRESCRIBED ANNUITIES are purchased with unregistered funds — those not from an RRSP or RRIF. They can look very attractive for people over 70 because they generate more after-tax income than a GIC. But make sure you understand why that happens; there's no magic.

A normal annuity payment is a blend of taxable interest and tax-free return of capital. Usually, payments in the early years have far more interest than capital. But in a prescribed annuity, the issuer is allowed to level that blend. Thus, payments in the initial years contain more tax-free capital than otherwise. That's why the after-tax cash flow looks good.

Eventually, the balance will tilt the other way and each payment will contain more taxable interest than otherwise. But many people die before then.

As with any other life annuity, a prescribed annuity involves giving up your capital. That means — unlike a GIC — the annuity leaves nothing for your estate unless you buy a period of guaranteed payments and die during that time. To overcome that situation, many RRIF/annuity brokers package a prescribed annuity with a life insurance policy. For example, $50,000 going into an annuity would be matched with a $50,000 insurance policy. Since the annuity pays out more cash than a GIC, some of that money can be used to pay the insurance premiums. When you die, the insurance pays $50,000 tax-free to your survivors. That way, they end up in the same position as if your $50,000 had been put into a GIC. Or, your adviser can team the annuity with a quality mutual fund

Charitable Gift Annuities

CHARITABLE GIFT annuities are prescribed annuities sold by about 50 non-profit organizations, including the United Church, the Salvation Army and McGill University. More than $100 million worth have been issued.

Say a 70-year-old man buys a $10,000 annuity from his church or university. He hands over the money in return for periodic income. The charity invests the money and makes a monthly payment that contains interest as well as a return of capital. When the purchaser dies, any capital left is released for charitable use. These annuities tend to pay less than annuities from commercial issuers.

At this point, the annuity is a straight investment transaction; there are no tax breaks. But many buyers generate tax breaks by taking still lower annuity payments. They let the charity keep more of their capital instead of paying it out. Say our friend's initial $10,000 is scheduled to be repaid at the rate of $725 a year over 13.8 years. That's his life expectancy, according to a special Revenue Canada table used for pre-scribed annuities. But instead of $725, he takes just $349 a year, so the projected capital return falls to $4,816. The $5,184 difference becomes a donation that qualifies for the charitable tax credit. A tax receipt for the full amount is issued upfront.

Charitable gift annuities are not backed by any consumer protection plan or deposit insurance, but they have been issued for about 100 years and there has never been a default.

For more information, write to: Canadian Association of Charitable Gift Annuities; 10 Carnforth Rd.; Toronto, Ont. M4A 2S4. Phone (416) 598-2181.

If your favorite charity does not issue its own annuities, consult your insurance agent. He or she can arrange for the charity to sell you one from a regular insurance company.

25

Tending Your Nest Egg

THERE IS ONE CARDINAL RULE FOR RRSP/ RRIF investing: Don't buy anything you don't understand. No investment is risk-free. Each type gains or loses in a given market condition.

Even with a "risk-free" GIC, you take the chance that your money won't keep up with the cost of living and that you won't get the rate you need when it's time to renew. That first concern is called "inflation risk." The second is "reinvestment risk." This doesn't mean GICs are bad — only that you must factor those risks into your game plan.

Historically, stocks have delivered above-average long-term performance. Over 40 years — 1956–97 — the Toronto Stock Exchange 300 Index averaged 11.2% a year though the actual fluctuation ranged from 44.8% to –25.9%. Based on past data, Dr. Moshe Milevsky of York University estimates that a diversified portfolio of Canadian stocks has a 60% chance of beating the real return of "safe" GICs or Canada Savings Bonds for any one-year period. The stocks have an 82% chance of winning over a 10-year period and a 95% chance over 35 years. A portfolio split evenly between Canadian and U.S. stocks would do even better.

Note the importance of time and patience. People who buy shares or funds they don't understand often lose money, especially those who speculate. A hot tip may work once or twice, but the inevitable stumble typically proves devastating. If you now think of your RRSP as speculative fun money, you won't on retirement eve. Bet on it. That plan is your own pension. You should be at least as prudent as the professional who runs an employer's defined-benefit plan. Actually, your risk is higher. With its many members, the employer's plan has future liabilities spread over a wide timeframe. Your RRSP has just one member and one retirement period.

Table 25.1 at the end of this chapter shows why it's not wise to gamble with RRSP/RRIF money. Say you need 8% average annual growth, but in the first year your investment just breaks even. To get back on track over the next two years, it must average 12.2%. That's 52.5% better than you expected when you bought in. If you make a dud investment outside your plan, you can save up more cash and try again. But contribution limits make your RRSP a finite pool and a RRIF can't be topped up at all. So if one investment fails, everything else must work harder.

Table 25.1 also shows that time makes it easier to overcome a loss. That's why young people can invest more aggressively. Unfortunately, they don't — because schools teach little about money management. Worse, 50-year-olds who think they know about investing often take extraordinary risks when they realize they don't have enough savings for the retirement they want. Usually, they end up further behind.

Overall Strategy

VIEW ALL your investments — RRSP/RRIF and unsheltered — as one portfolio. Then balance that portfolio between fixed-income and equities (stocks) based on your risk tolerance, objectives, knowledge, timeframe and opinion about where the economy is going and how that will affect the markets.

A common mix has fixed-income and equity components varying between 40% and 60% each, with cash running 5-20%. Cash includes equivalents such as money market funds, Canada Savings Bonds and treasury bills. Fixed-income and cash normally rise as you approach retirement, but there are no concrete rules for the actual percentages. Investment dealers and mutual funds often publish updated guidelines.

One very rough rule-of-thumb is to determine your equities level by subtracting your age from 100. A 30-year-old's portfolio would be 70% in stocks or equity mutual funds.

It's best to keep interest-bearing investments inside your RRSP/RRIF so the annual income is not taxed. Equities should ideally be outside since RRSP/RRIFs don't get the dividend tax credit and capital gains tax breaks.

If your RRSP/RRIF is your only investment pool, divide that between fixed-income and equities. Over the long term — decades — stocks have produced higher returns than interest-bearing investments.

Mutual funds have become extremely popular investment vehicles. A mutual fund is not an investment class, but a way to invest in one — stocks, bonds, mortgages, etc. If your portfolio balance calls for 70% equities, a fund that invests in stocks would fall within that 70%.

Fixed-Income

FIXED-INCOME investments like GICs and bonds offer steady returns through interest. Some trade on secondary markets, where you can get back more or less than you paid. That depends on how interest rates have moved since you invested. If rates are up, you will lose money because your resale investment must compete with more generous new ones. If rates are down, you will make money because your resale investment pays more than the going rate. That's easy to say, but hard to understand. Make sure you do.

Short-Term Money

Financial institutions offer daily interest RRSP savings accounts that don't tie up the money. But those accounts may pay just 1% or less. Money market funds may yield three or four times that return, but often require higher initial amounts.

Some institutions offer monthly deposit RRSP investment plans. Money is automatically taken from your bank account and parked in a savings account until there's enough to buy a GIC. Check the savings account rate. You could have a money market fund make the same withdrawals and then move the money to a GIC yourself.

Canada Savings Bonds (CSBs), sold by the federal government every October, can be held in RRSP/RRIFs. The rate is set once each year, often at around the chartered banks' one-year GIC rate. CSBs can be cashed any time, but newly issued ones pay no interest if redeemed in the first three months. After that, redeemed CSBs pay interest only to the end of the prior month, so the best time to cash one is on the first day of the month. Some investors buy them to lock in a base rate for the year and then redeem them if a better opportunity comes along. If a CSB bought outside an RRSP/RRIF is then moved inside, the transfer value equals the CSB's original cost plus accrued interest. In 1997 Ottawa introduced RRSP bonds that are just like CSBs, but they pay a bit more because they're cashable just once a year.

Guaranteed Investment Certificates

GICs have long been a popular RRSP/RRIF investment. Easy to buy. Easy to understand. But not wrinkle-free:

- Index-linked GICs base their interest on growth in a stock market index. Your capital is guaranteed but you don't get the market's full growth because the index used does not include dividends on the underlying shares. Potential gains may also be arbitrarily capped at 20–40% of the market's gain over the GIC's term. Your exposure to market peaks and valleys depends on whether the GIC measures index growth just between two dates or with a rolling average. Instead, consider dividing money between a regular GIC and an equity mutual fund.

- If you deal with one institution, your total portfolio may be fairly large. Is the total value still within the $60,000 deposit insurance limits?

- At what rate does the money compound — the original one or the one at each anniversary? In 1993, major institutions began offering escalator GICs. These earn a higher rate each year. The advertising, of course, plays up the final-year rate. But check the true blended rate over the full term. Don't be misled.

- Some GICs and escalating CSBs let you out before maturity, but early redemption means you'll get a much lower blended rate overall since their rates start low and then rise gradually.

- At maturity, will there be a fee if you transfer the money elsewhere or cash out? How are transfers handled? Does the institution issue a post-dated cheque or wait until the maturity date to send the money? You'll lose interest if the money is not immediately rolled into your new deposit elsewhere.

- Before transferring money to get a higher rate, see if your current institution will match the competition. Branch managers often add 0.25% or 0.5% to keep the account.

- Does the institution pay a bonus to attract deposits? What about to keep maturing deposits?

- Is the GIC cashable before maturity? Most life insurance company deposits are. Depending on whether interest rates are higher or lower, you'll lose a bit or gain a bit through a "market value adjustment." These deposits also come in terms longer than five years, the limit for bank and trust deposits insured by the Canada Deposit Insurance Corporation (CDIC).

- Do you have a self-directed RRSP/RRIF? GICs in it are not individually registered as RRSPs the way they are if you deal directly with the issuer. The issuer books them as regular GICs. When institutions fail, others snap up their RRSP/RRIF portfolios. But if the regular deposits aren't wanted, holders are paid off by the CDIC and may have to reinvest elsewhere at a lower rate. That happened to Standard Trust GICs in self-directed plans, but not those bought directly from Standard. On the other hand, self-directed plans aren't charged transfer fees when a deposit matures and money is moved to another institution.

A GIC bought by your self-directed plan might not be covered by deposit insurance. Some brokers buy "jumbo GICs" and slice them up for retail sale. They pay a bit more because they are not insured. Ask your broker before placing the order.

Committed GIC investors should know about deposit brokers, the travel agents of the financial industry. Brokers track rates and features daily. With one stop — even a phone call — you can check GICs from dozens of institutions. The broker does all the paperwork and collects a fee from the issuer; you pay nothing. The broker's computer tracks your maturities and sends reminders.

These brokers are generally unregulated, so write your cheque directly to the institution. There is a voluntary national association with a code of ethics. Call the Federation of Canadian Independent Deposit Brokers at (519) 825-7575 or visit their web site at: http://www.incan.com/fcidb/index.html.

Real Return

GIC investors freaked out in 1991-92 as deposit rates plunged below the magic 10% mark. To no avail, bankers and others tried to explain that the "nominal," or stated, rate matters less than the "real return" — the rate after subtracting inflation. When GICs paid 10-11%, inflation was running 5-6%. So a $100 deposit returned about $105 in purchasing power after one year. As inflation fell to 1.5%, GIC rates fell to 6%. The real return stayed pretty constant; the investor got back about the same purchasing power.

If your retirement projections use 8% growth and 3% inflation, you automatically assume a 5% real return.

After I wrote about real return in The Financial Post, one reader sent a letter stating any fool could see that $10,000 growing for 25 years would total $108,347 at 10% and just $54,274 at 7%. He ignored the future purchasing power. GIC rates track inflation. So getting 10% at each renewal means inflation would be running about 5%. Using appendix A-2, we can see that with 25 years of 5% inflation, this $108,347 will be worth $31,995 in today's purchasing power. The 7% GIC rate assumption implies average inflation of 2% for 25 years. At that rate, $54,274 will be worth $33,080 in today's purchasing power.

Most economists believe we're in a low-inflation era. But inflation, of course, can surge as it did before. To guard against that, vary your deposit terms so money keeps coming up for renewal. This is called . . .

... The "Staggered Maturities" Concept

It is also called "ladder GICs." It counters the inflation and reinvestment risks cited above. Even professionals concede that, on a regular basis, nobody can accurately predict mid- and long-term interest rates. This technique lets you average the ups and downs, riding the inflation/reinvestment rate wave.

Initially, spread money evenly over each term — say one through five years. Each subsequent year, put renewal and new money into a new five-year term. Long-term deposits normally pay more. You will then have a mix of deposits with varying rates and maturities. Here's how to measure the portfolio's overall yield:

A Deposit	B Accrued value	C Portion of porfolio	D Yield	E Weighted return
Due Jan-30-94	$ 7,637	0.1745	0.1125	0.0196
Jan-30-95	6,947	0.1587	0.1100	0.0175
Jan-30-96	11,411	0.2607	0.1050	0.0274
Jan-30-97	7,771	0.1776	0.0875	0.0155
Jan-30-98	10,000	0.2285	0.0775	0.0177
	$43,766			0.0977

Column B is the value from your periodic statement. Or use this formula to estimate the amount:

$$\text{Cost or value at last statement} \times \left[(1 + \text{interest rate})^{\left(\frac{\text{days elapsed since statement}}{365} \right)} \right]$$

For column C, divide B's value by the portfolio's total. Column D is just the deposit's interest rate. To arrive at column E, multiply columns C and D. Adding up E, we see that even with a new $10,000 deposit earning 7.75%, the plan is still growing at 9.77%.

Strip Bonds

Strip bonds are also called "zero-coupons." If you like GICs, you will love strip bonds.

To hold strips in an RRSP or RRIF, you will need a self-directed plan at an investment dealer, trust company or bank. Administration fees run $100-$200 a year. Your plan should hold at least $35,000-$40,000 to absorb the fee. That fee is no longer tax-deductible.

Strips are created when an investment dealer buys a large bond from a government or corporation. Bonds normally "stripped" for the RRSP/RRIF market are issued by the federal and provincial governments, as well as by crown agencies such as Ontario Hydro and Quebec Hydro. Some are denominated in foreign currencies.

The coupons for each semi-annual interest payment are stripped away from the bond and individually sold to individual investors. The bond itself — called a "residual" — is often sold to institutional investors.

Each coupon is redeemable for a set amount at a future date, for example $10,000 in 20 years. Your price, which includes broker commissions, is "discounted" from that maturity value based on current bond rates for that term. If a $10,000 20-year coupon is priced to yield 8% semi-annually, it should cost about $2,083. Always ask if the yield quoted is semi-annual or annual. Record that yield for tracking; the one on your confirmation slip and statements is the bond's rate at issue, not your yield.

Strips come in virtually any maturity to about 30 years. That makes them ideal for long-term retirement savings. If you buy government or crown agency issues, your money is fully government-backed — unlike GICs, which have a $60,000 deposit insurance limit.

Your strip coupon pays no interest between now and maturity. You get that upfront through the discounting calculation. If you buy a mid- or long-term strip, this means you face no reinvestment problem for 10–20 years. You will face substantial inflation risk, but can hedge that by creating a ladder of strips with staggered maturities. Also, diversify among different issuers to hedge the risk of default.

Unlike GICs, whose terms normally run in multiples of one year, strips come with all kinds of terms. If not careful, you can end up with maturities all over the calendar. Table 25.2 presents a way to control that from happening and to keep your money evenly distributed.

At purchase, strips normally pay a bit more than GICs. You can then lock in that yield long-term. But your money is not locked in. As discussed in chapter 6, you can sell a strip early, scoring an extra gain if interest rates have fallen or a loss if they've gone up. This market value — reported on your brokerage statement — can be quite volatile. Don't worry if you plan to hold on until maturity, as you would with a GIC that must be held until maturity.

If you don't want a self-directed RRSP/RRIF, long-term staggered maturities are also available through life insurance deposits. But your deposit is less secure than with a government-guaranteed strip.

Ordinary Bonds

RRSP investors have a reinvestment problem with the income stream from ordinary bonds, as opposed to strips. You collect interest twice a year, probably a few hundred bucks each time. How do you reinvest a small sum at a decent rate?

That reinvestment problem means most bondholders don't get the yield they were quoted. In quoting an 8% yield, the broker assumes every interest payment will be reinvested at 8%. But you may do better, or worse. Strip bonds avoid that uncertainty since there is no interest stream to reinvest.

RRIFers can create monthly interest income by purchasing six bonds. Each bond pays interest twice a year. Snowbirds can buy bonds denominated in U.S. dollars and other currencies.

RRSPers might use a quality bond to secure the plan's capital, and then put interest payments into a more risky mutual fund. The same gambit works with GICs that pay monthly or semi-annual interest.

Investment dealers sell a "retirement savings bond," which is geared to the RRSP/RRIF reinvestment scenario. It's a strip bond for a set period and then starts paying interest. Remember that bonds with distant maturities carry substantial inflation risk.

Several years ago the federal government issued "real return" bonds that adjust the principal — not the interest payments — for inflation. These bonds can be purchased through any investment dealer. In early 1993, one investment dealer took some of those bonds and turned them into real-return strips for RRSP investors. At maturity in 2021, each coupon will pay out $10,000 in 1993 purchasing power.

Mortgage-Backed Securities

Reinvestment is even more of a problem for RRSP investors with mortgage-backed securities (MBSs), since these bonds make monthly payments. But that negative becomes a big positive for RRIFers who want periodic income. The monthly income — guaranteed by the federal government — makes the MBS ideal for RRIFs.

A mortgage-backed security takes virtually all the risk out of investing in mortgages. The issuer assembles a large portfolio of residential mortgages, ideally spread over the country. Each investor owns a slice of that portfolio.

Every month the investor gets a payment containing interest and some principal. Many MBS pools are "open." That means borrowers can make prepayments, which are passed on to the investors. That tends to happen when interest rates fall. Unfortunately, the investor must then put the money elsewhere. About a third of MBS pools are "closed." They yield a bit less, since the monthly income stream is totally predictable.

MBSs normally yield a bit more than Government of Canada bonds with the same maturities. They may yield a bit more or less than monthly-pay GICs. MBS yields change constantly as they trade in the bond market. GIC rates move more slowly.

Since bonds and MBSs trade actively, you can sell before maturity. It's hard or impossible to cash GICs early (unless they're from a life insurance company). You need a self-directed plan to hold bonds and MBSs. You don't for GICs. MBSs and government/crown corporation bonds are 100% government-guaranteed, while GICs are insured for only $60,000 per CDIC member institution.

Bond and Mortgage Mutual Funds

Bond and mortgage mutual funds are discussed in the chapter on mutual funds.

Your Own Mortgage

You can borrow home mortgage money from your self-directed RRSP/RRIF. That means you would pay yourself interest, and your plan would earn more than with a GIC.

However, these arrangements are usually worthwhile only if you can fund a substantial portion of your mortgage. That's because there are costly fees. The higher the loan, the easier it is to absorb the fees. Your plan administrator will charge several hundred dollars to set up the arrangement, and that's on top of the normal legal fees involved in creating a mortgage. You will also be charged annual administration fees. And you must buy special default insurance, which costs as much as 2.5% of the loan amount.

According to one rule-of-thumb, you should consider funding your own mortgage only if you have at least $50,000 of RRSP money. If you have less, consider a mortgage shared between your RRSP and your spouse's. Some institutions charge double administration fees for both plans, but others charge only one set of fees.

A mortgage from an RRSP must be comparable to those from regular lenders. You cannot give yourself a cut-rate loan or unduly favorable prepayment privileges. Some people actually find the most expensive mortgage rate on the market and use that for their plan to boost their tax-sheltered savings.

An RRSP/RRIF mortgage also carries the problem of having to reinvest monthly payments.

Equities

TO HOLD stocks, your RRSP or RRIF must be self-directed. You should also have quite a bit of money to diversify your selection.

Growth stocks move down as well as up, sometimes very quickly. But your registered plan does not get the benefit of the tax breaks for capital gains and losses. Quarterly dividends on blue chip common and preferred shares can also be a problem.

How, then, do you get a decent rate when reinvesting amounts that dribble in periodically? Some share issuers offer dividend reinvestment plans (DRIPs) that use dividends to buy fractional shares and even let you make lump-sum purchases — all commission-free. DRIPs can be a great idea outside an RRSP or RRIF. If they're inside, however, you'll likely find your plan's administrator charges a hefty fee for the bookkeeping involved in each reinvestment. Note that your registered plan does not benefit from the dividend tax credit.

Fortunately, investment dealers have created "split shares" that solve this dividend problem. The underlying security is a share of a blue chip company or bank. One part of the split share is purchased by an investor who wants capital growth. The other is bought by an investor who only wants the dividend.

Mutual Funds

Mutual funds and segregated ("seg") funds — the life insurance industry's equivalent — offer an easy, effective way for RRSP/RRIF investors to invest in capital markets.

Mutual and seg funds offer monthly investment plans, often called PACs for pre-authorized cheques. Such plans offer the RRSP investor several benefits:

- **Paying yourself first**. Automatic deductions from bank accounts or paycheques free you from having to muster cash for your annual contribution. It may be the only way many people will ever make their full contributions.

- **Timing**. The sooner money goes into an RRSP, the more tax-sheltered growth you get from a fixed-income holding like a bond or mortgage fund. (Returns on equity funds depend more on market performance.)

- **Dollar cost averaging.** Investing the same amount each month, you automatically buy more units when the market is down and fewer when it's high. By averaging cost, you reduce risk of capital loss. This method also frees the long-term investor from the anxiety of market ups and downs.

RRIF investors often set up "systematic withdrawal plans." They're the opposite of PACs. You automatically take out a certain amount each month. The normal assumption is that unit values will continue to rise, preserving the fund's base. But if they should plunge — that's possible with an equity or a bond fund — level-dollar withdrawals can eat into your capital.

Since they provide diversification and professional management, mutual funds should reduce your investment risk. But check out what you are buying. Read the prospectus and portfolio summary as well as newspaper coverage. A high-flying equity fund may be mostly in resource stocks, even though it's not listed as a resource fund. Resource stocks are volatile. Some exposure may pay off for your RRSP/RRIF, but do you really want most of your own pension fund in them?

Or, perhaps you already have a U.S. equity fund, so you buy an international fund to diversify. But that fund might be 60% in U.S. equities. Do your homework.

Periodic distributions from mutual funds can be automatically reinvested without charge, so you need not worry about idle cash. But sales and redemption commissions can be a concern, since they're normally deducted from your finite tax-sheltered pool. If you have a self-directed plan, consider the following:

- **Upfront sales commission.** First, buy fund units outside the plan so you're not using RRSP money to pay the sales fee. You hope they will rise in value. Then, once you have a paper gain, move them into your RRSP as a "contribution in kind" or into the RRSP/RRIF as a swap for cash. Your broker may charge a "swap fee." Remember that on such transfers, Revenue Canada will recognize only a capital gain — you get no benefit for shifting in units that have lost value.

- **Redemption fee.** "Back-end" funds carry redemption fees instead of upfront sales commissions. Don't sell these funds inside your RRSP/RRIF. Swap them out of the plan in exchange for cash. Then sell them. That way, the redemption fee reduces your taxable gain or boosts your capital loss.

Management fees — deducted directly from the fund — are unavoidable. Instead of purchasing equity mutual funds, some people buy TIPs and SPDRs (pronounced spiders) or similar derivatives. TIPs (Toronto Index Participation Units) trade on the Toronto Stock Exchange and represent holdings in the 35 largest Canadian companies. SPDRs (Standard & Poor's Depository Receipts) trade on the American Stock Exchange and reflect the companies in the Standard & Poor's 500 index. The only fees are the brokerage commissions to buy and sell them. Since TIPs and SPDRs are based on large portfolios, you get the diversification of a mutual fund. You will do as well as the market, but no better. (Mutual funds, in contrast, tend to do better or worse.) A major disadvantage: Mutual funds reinvest distributions, but these "index participation units" don't.

Foreign Content

RRSP/RRIF MONEY is increasingly going global. Many Canadians lack faith in our dollar or want to benefit from booming economic growth in other parts of the world.

Appreciate, though, that going global means making two simultaneous investments — a bet in favor of the underlying security and one against the Canadian dollar. If the security does well and our dollar falls, you can do extremely well. You can still do well if only one of the two pans out. But if the investment's a dud and our dollar rises, your loss is compounded. Some mutual funds hedge against a rising Canadian dollar, but the cost of that protection cuts their returns a bit if the dollar goes up or stays flat.

Foreign mutual funds generally have better long-term records than Canadian ones. But that's due in good part to the 20-year decline of the Canadian dollar. Many analysts believe that decline may be about over.

One tax wrinkle favors keeping foreign investments outside your RRSP/RRIF. The capital loss tax break — available only for non-RRSP/RRIF holdings — can ease the pain of the above double-whammy loss.

Still, given the strong past performance of foreign investments — and strong long-term economic outlooks for areas like the U.S. — many, if not most, advisers recommend foreign holdings as part of your retirement plan. As of January 1, 1994, 20% of the "book value" of your RRSP/RRIF can be invested in foreign securities.

The book value is the cost of your plan's holdings — not your total contributions or the portfolio's current value. With every transaction — be it purchase, sale, dividend, transfer or contribution — the book value changes. You don't have to track it yourself. Just call your broker, mutual fund company or financial institution. The plan's administrator is required to track the book value and check if you're within the limit. If you're not, the excess faces a hefty penalty tax of 1% per month.

Check your status before a major purchase and after a major sale. Although the book value is a running tally, your administrator may compare it to the 20% limit just once a year. You could pile up a penalty without realizing it.

If you invest in mutual funds and automatically reinvest distributions, don't go right to the limit. If you do, the next reinvested distribution will push you into the penalty zone. Here's how. Say your book value is $50,000. Your foreign content limit is then $10,000. You put $10,000 into a global fund. The fund pays and reinvests a $1,000 distribution. That pushes the book value of your plan to $51,000, your 20% foreign limit to $10,200 and the book value of your foreign holding to $11,000 — $800 over the limit.

The foreign content limit applies to each plan on its own, not to all plans in your name. Suppose you have two plans, each with a book value of $20,000. At 20%, each plan has a foreign content limit of $4,000; you are not allowed to have $8,000 of foreign content in one and none in the other. That's one reason for consolidating your plans into one account.

In the past, investors in foreign content had to use self-directed plans with administration fees of $100 or more. But a number of mutual fund companies now offer umbrella accounts that let you mix any of their funds. Administration fees for such plans may run $25–$50 or be waived altogether.

Some mutual fund companies now routinely check the RRSP/RRIF accounts they administer and automatically shift money to one or more Canadian funds to keep you within the 20% foreign content limit. You designate those funds when setting up the account.

Mutual funds are an excellent way to invest outside Canada, especially if you want to put money into areas that require special expertise, like the Far East or international bond trading.

Alternatively, check out WEBs (see p. 239), which trade on the American Stock Exchange. Each WEB reflects a stock market index in one of 17 countries. As with TIPs in Canada and SPDRs in the U.S., you get the convenience and diversification of mutual fund investing but with much lower yearly management fees. Management fees on foreign mutual funds can be quite high. Be aware, though, that you need a full-blown self-directed plan to hold WEBs. That means you'll face an annual administration fee of about $125. If your foreign investment is modest, you may find that even with higher management fees, it makes more sense to hold mutual funds in a fund company plan that carries no administration charge.

You can also hold foreign stocks and bonds on your own in a

self-directed plan. In fact, some people do without realizing it. Even if purchased on a Canadian exchange, the shares of a company incorporated outside Canada are foreign property. For example, General Motors Corp. is listed on the Toronto Stock Exchange, but it's foreign property for an RRSP/RRIF because it's incorporated in the United States.

Your Canadian shares may turn foreign. In 1991, many registered plans held shares of Toronto-based Varity Corp., which used to be Massey-Ferguson. Those shares were Canadian property, but they changed status when Varity reincorporated as a U.S. company. Ottawa now grants time for investors to adjust their holdings — two years from the date of the corporate reorganization.

What about buying shares on foreign exchanges? You can do that, but only on certain ones approved by the government. That list includes the world's major exchanges and several smaller ones.

If the foreign content rules are too much to absorb, relax. There's an alternative. The same goes if you really want to max out on foreign investments. There are several ways to boost foreign content without exceeding your plan's limit:

- Buy RRSP-eligible "Canadian" mutual funds that are using their own 20% foreign content limits. The monthly mutual fund performance tables in newspapers such as The Financial Post and The Globe and Mail show each fund's level of foreign investment.

- Some funds are mostly or entirely foreign content, yet still qualify as "Canadian" property. Many buy Canadian-issued securities that are denominated in foreign currencies. Some buy stock index futures that represent foreign stock markets. Some invest in companies that benefit when the Canadian dollar falls. You could buy the same stocks yourself if you don't want a mutual fund.

- Buy Canadian-issued foreign-pay bonds on your own. Most investment dealers offer strip and ordinary bonds payable in U.S. dollars or other currencies. They come from the federal and provincial governments, utilities such as Ontario Hydro, and chartered banks. Bonds issued by international agencies such as the World Bank get the same treatment.

  As a retiree, do you plan to winter in the United States? You could buy strips or bonds that pay enough U.S. dollars to fund your three or four months down south.

- Finally, you're allowed $3 of additional foreign content for each $1 you invest in shares of a qualified small business corporation. However, many RRSP administrators don't allow those shares because of problems in valuing them.

Remember that your retirement spending will likely be in Canadian dollars, and with foreign content you assume currency risk as well as security risk. So, how much foreign content is enough? One technique is to think about your retirement. If you plan to spend 25% of your time down south, go for 25% foreign content. Several pension fund studies have found that 30% is a good overall level. Interestingly, that's the average foreign content level among British pension plans, which face no foreign-content limits.

TABLE 25.1: Recovering from a Loss

Annual growth target	First year's return	If you have this many years to get back on track									
		1	2	3	4	5	6	7	8	9	10
		Here's the average annual return (%) you'll need to meet your target									
8%	5%	11.1	9.5	9.0	8.8	8.6	8.5	8.4	8.4	8.3	8.3
	3	13.2	10.6	9.7	9.3	9.0	8.9	8.7	8.6	8.6	8.5
	0	16.6	12.2	10.8	10.1	9.7	9.4	9.2	9.0	8.9	8.8
	-5	22.8	15.2	12.7	11.5	10.8	10.3	10.0	9.7	9.6	9.4
	-10	29.6	18.3	14.8	13.0	12.0	11.3	10.8	10.5	10.2	10.0
	-15	37.2	21.7	17.0	14.7	13.3	12.4	11.8	11.3	10.9	10.6
10%	7%	13.1	11.5	11.0	10.8	10.6	10.5	10.4	10.4	10.3	10.3
	5	15.2	12.6	11.7	11.3	11.0	10.9	10.7	10.6	10.6	10.5
	0	21.0	15.4	13.6	12.7	12.1	11.8	11.5	11.3	11.2	11.1
	-5	27.4	18.4	15.5	14.1	13.3	12.7	12.3	12.0	11.8	11.6
	-10	34.4	21.6	17.6	15.7	14.5	13.7	13.2	12.8	12.5	12.2
	-15	42.4	25.1	19.9	17.3	15.8	14.8	14.1	13.6	13.2	12.9

TABLE 25.2: Strip Bond Organizer

RRSP Strip Bond Worksheet

Issuer	Due	Yield	Value today	% of group	Weighted yield	Year	Jan	Feb	Mar	Apr	May	Jun	Jul	Aug	Sep	Oct	Nov	Dec
Quebec	28-Dec-01	11.4%	7,851	12.5%	1.4%	2001												
						2002	20,000											
						2003												
BC	05-Sep-04	9.2%	9,729	15.5%	1.4%	2004									26,500			
BC	23-Feb-05	8.9%	10,779	17.2%	1.5%	2005		29,750										
Canada	01-Mar-06	10.4%	5,251	8.4%	0.9%	2006			18,750									
						2007												
Que Hydro	15-Feb-08	11.0%	11,721	18.7%	2.1%	2008		55,000										
Ont Hydro	27-May-09	10.6%	7,975	12.7%	1.3%	2009					40,250							
						2010												
Ont Hydro	15-Apr-11	9.8%	9,449	15.1%	1.5%	2011				50,625								
						2012												
						2013												
						2014												
Totals:			62,756	100.0%	10.1%													

Distribution by issuer:

— Quebec	$ 7,851	13%
— BC	20,509	33%
— Canada	5,251	8%
— Que Hydro	11,721	19%
— Ont Hydro	17,424	28%
	62,756	100%

The left side is the same blended yield calculation described on page 206 for GICs. The right side shows how much matures when. Over coming years, this person will fill in gaps and spread or condense the monthly maturity timing to match his or her eventual cash needs in retirement. Don't forget that strips can work well in RRIFs as long as there's enough available cash for the required yearly withdrawal. If using a computer, you can calculate the "value today" by setting up work columns for the purchase date and amount. This is the accrued value, not the market value. The formula is COST*[(1+YIELD)^([TODAY'S DATE – PURCHASE DATE]/365)]

26

Protecting the Pot

READY FOR A NIGHTMARE? AFTER SAVING for decades, you're almost ready to retire. But:

- Rushing through traffic, you hit a brain surgeon who's left paralyzed. She wins a judgment that exceeds your insurance.

- Your business fails. The bank goes after your assets for the loan you took out. Yes, you're incorporated, but the loan was personally guaranteed.

- A Revenue Canada audit discovers you've been cheating for 20 years. There's no time limit on tax evasion. You get a gargantuan bill for back tax, penalties and interest. You spend a fortune in legal fees to appeal, but lose.

Any of these scenarios could place your retirement fund in jeopardy. Many people believe their retirement funds are safe from creditors. Many of those people are wrong. Your nest egg may be a sitting duck. Compare yourself to the following people.

Bob has spent his career working for an employer with a Registered Pension Plan. His RPP credits — worth several hundred thousand dollars — fall under pension legislation that grants ironclad creditor-proofing except for spousal claims on marital breakdown. The same goes if Bob has an "individual pension plan." IPPs are simply one-person RPPs for incorporated entrepreneurs and highly paid executives.

Barbara works for a small firm. Instead of offering an RPP, her employer has a group RRSP. This plan does not fall under pension laws, so it's up for grabs unless the money is placed with a life insurer and Barbara meets certain conditions. (They're outlined below. See Betty's case.)

Bernard, who is self-employed now, spent years building pension credits in his prior employer's RPP. Last year he moved that money to a locked-in RRSP. That money and its earnings are protected by the legislation which governed the original pension plan. That protects it from most creditors, but Revenue Canada could argue that the federal Income Tax Act supersedes provincial pension law.

Betty has a plain-vanilla RRSP. It holds GIC deposits and an investment fund. In most provinces, Betty's RRSP — or RRIF — is up for grabs if she has it anywhere but a life insurance company. Deposits with insurers are creditor-proof under provincial insurance laws all across Canada — if the following conditions are met.

First, there must be a named beneficiary. Normally, that's a spouse, child, grandchild or parent. If it's anyone else, the designation has to be irrevocable — it cannot be changed.

Second, the creditor-proofing can be voided if Betty runs afoul of the federal Bankruptcy Act. An insurance RRSP deposit loses its protected status if the contributor goes bankrupt within one year of placing the money — or within five years if creditors show the money was needed to pay debts at the time of the contribution.

Even then, a creditor has to go to court. That's expensive, and unlikely if your creditor is Joe's Garage. It's very likely if you're on the hook to a big bank or Revenue Canada, the country's most powerful creditor. Their lawyers have been going after plans that life insurance companies sold as being "bullet-proof." Depending on the facts, rulings have gone either way, although a 1996 Supreme Court of Canada ruling substantially strengthened the insurance company shield.

Insurers and mutual fund companies have begun teaming up to repackage regular mutual funds as life insurance investment funds that work the same way but offer creditor-proofing. Marketing efforts for these funds focus on their capital protection guarantee, which kicks in after 10 years, but the creditor-proofing is really far more meaningful for someone like a doctor, lawyer or business owner who stands an above-average risk of being sued. But be careful — yearly management fees on these funds are quite high.

Prince Edward Island has extended the same degree of creditor protection to RRSPs and RRIFs sold by all vendors. Quebec provides creditor protection for fixed-term annuities from provincially chartered trust companies. British Columbia grants creditor-proofing at death to all RRSPs/RRIFs that have irrevocable beneficiary designations.

Creditors argue that unlike registered pensions, RRSPs and RRIFs are savings accounts that can be tapped any time for any amount. They say if that's the only cash available, they should be entitled to it. Otherwise, all of society pays. Deadbeats cost everyone a little more in taxes and prices.

That's true. But the current system is inherently unfair. Why should an insurer's GIC or investment fund be treated differently from a competitor's? We're not talking about life insurance that protects "widows and orphans" — the real reason the creditor-proofing was granted long ago.

Increasingly, RRSPs are used as surrogate pension plans. Real pension plans are creditor-proof. If they deserve that special status, shouldn't their proxies? Let's be totally cynical: Why should the generous defined-benefit RPP of a civil servant or politician be fully creditor-proof when the RRSP of a small entrepreneur is not?

Finally, bankruptcy law is aimed in part at giving the bankrupt a second chance. If your regular investment portfolio is seized, you can work hard, save up and replace it — at least in theory. But contribution limits make it impossible to replace a lost RRSP or RRIF.

One lawyer gave me a good idea. If a person goes bankrupt, give him or her a one-time election under which the RRSP or RRIF would be protected from creditors but also made subject to the same lock-in provisions as a registered pension plan.

If this concerns you — and I think it should — write your provincial and federal legislators. When 1930s gangster Willy Sutton was asked why he robbed banks, he replied, "that's where the money is." As baby boomers age, retirement funds are swelling . . . and creditors are giving them more and more attention.

27

Investing 101

THIS CHAPTER DEALS WITH SOME BASIC investment concepts. We'll look at risk, diversification, asset allocation and leverage.

Risk

AFTER READING this section, you may just throw up your hands in despair. I hope not. The idea is to be prudent, not paralyzed.

Forget about "risk-free" investments; they don't exist. Even rock-solid vehicles like guaranteed investment certificates (GICs) and Canada Savings Bonds carry risk. You'll see why a bit later.

Don't expect low-risk investments to make you rich. High-risk investments probably won't make you rich either. It's often said that the higher the risk, the higher the return. But that's the expectation — not necessarily the reality. Just ask the legions of people who have dropped bundles on penny stocks, commodities futures, speculative real estate and other sophisticated wheeling and dealing. Yes, there are people who do quite well in those areas over the long term, but they are generally professionals or financially sophisticated amateurs who thoroughly understand their investments and prudently calculate the risks. They don't gamble.

Before committing money, ask yourself two questions: (1) Do I understand what I'm buying? (2) What's the worst that can happen if this doesn't work?

The first question rests on a self-evident premise: If you don't understand why you're buying in, how will you know when to sell? The second question rests on the notion that each person has a unique risk level, determined by a variety of factors:

- **Investment attitude.** Are you passive, aggressive or in between? While you should never make an investment that keeps you awake at night, you can't afford to do nothing. Is the stock market risky? Yes and no. Stocks may soar and plunge, but the only value that matters is the value on the day you sell — everything else is a paper gain or loss. More learning and analysis will let you feel more comfortable. Consider more conservative strategies, such as "staggered maturities," "dollar cost averaging" and "value averaging." They're explained elsewhere in this book.

- **Age.** The further you are from retirement, the more risk you can assume. That's because you have more time to recover from any loss. Ideally, we should recognize that fact in our early 20s. Unfortunately, we usually don't learn it until our 40s or 50s. A common — and tragic — scenario occurs when a 50-year-old who has not been saving for retirement realizes that time is running out. He or she starts chasing high returns, but often compounds the problem by losing money on hot tips and poor gambles.

- **Family responsibilities.** A single 25-year-old can shoulder more risk than a 35-year-old who is feeding three or four mouths, a car loan and a mortgage.

- **Income and cash flow.** The more secure your job, the more risk you can take on — assuming your debts and lifestyle spending are under control. Obviously, the more you depend on investment income to meet daily expenses, the more careful you must be.

- **Commitments.** If you plan to buy a house next year, don't put down-payment money into the stock market now. Even if the market is soaring, there is no guarantee that all your money will be there when you need it. Remember, you save and invest to meet both short- and long-term goals. Always consider how those goals would be affected if your prospective investment goes bad.

- **Net Worth.** The greater your wealth, the more risk you can handle. Net worth is what you really own after subtracting debts; someone who seems to have a lot might be awash in a sea of credit.

  How diversified is your wealth? Maybe you're worth $1 million, but if almost all of it is in a home, in one mutual fund or in your employer's stock plan, you are very vulnerable to a setback.

- **Prudence pays.** The idea is not to avoid risk, but to manage it. You can amass more money with moderate but steady growth than you can with sharp ups and downs. A five-year investment growing steadily at 10% will match one that soars 25% in the first year and 20% in each of the next two years, then loses 15% and then gains 5%. Plug $100 into your calculator and see for yourself.

Greed and Fear

The cycle of greed and fear is the investor's worst enemy. It's based on the reality that no market goes up forever — stocks, bonds, real estate, you name it.

Markets are cyclical. They run on demand and supply. Prices rise as demand exceeds supply. But then, one of two things happens. Supply expands and then it exceeds demand; or prices rise so much that calmer heads prevail and people decide the item just isn't worth that much. Either way, prices fall.

Fortunately or unfortunately, depending on your viewpoint, markets overreact. They rise too high and fall too low. That's where astute investors and speculators make most of their money. They buy low, sell high, wait for the plunge and then buy low again. But this technique requires two skills most people lack: the ability to recognize true value, and the guts to go against the herd.

More often, people wait until an investment has racked up big gains. Then they rush in as the smart money is getting out. As the bandwagon starts rolling, media coverage attracts still more buyers — many of whom have little or no understanding of what they're getting. Public interest fuels prices. More people are convinced they must act or else lose out on the bonanza. The higher prices go, the more people get interested — and the more salespeople offer words of assurance. Toronto real estate agents were up in arms in 1989 when Wood Gundy economist Jeff Rubin warned that the area's booming housing market was poised for a 25% fall. "World class city," they shouted. "Can't happen!" But it did. The salespeople and their buyers focused only on market momentum, not on what was driving it.

Astute investors are usually gone by the time the inevitable correction begins. Others, with some knowledge, follow suit and still come out ahead. The latecomers hang on; they still believe in what they bought and expect a turnaround any day. Finally, hope gives way to despair. The investors who previously thought the market could only go up now feel it can only go down. So they bail out at the bottom — just as the smart money is moving in again.

Depressing, isn't it? Not if you resist the drive of greed and the despair of fear. Understand what you buy and look for steady, not stellar, gains.

Types of Risk

You can't avoid risk, but you can manage it. Appreciate that there are many types of risk and they affect different investments in different ways. Here are the major types:

- **Market risk.** That's the risk associated with just being in the market. A market plunge will hit the shares of even the world's best companies. You might own the nicest home on the best block in town, but an overall housing slump will reduce its value. What you paid for something is irrelevant; it's worth only what someone will pay when you go to sell.

- **Inflation risk.** That's the risk that your investment won't keep up with inflation. It's a major concern for those who buy GICs and other seemingly risk-free investments.

  Say you buy a five-year GIC that pays 6%. Remember that this income stream is fixed for five years. If inflation averages 3% a year between now and maturity, your "real return" is only 3%. Real return is the difference between the stated return and the inflation rate.

  Moreover, if that GIC is not held in an RRSP or some other tax shelter, you must pay tax on the interest each year. Say your marginal tax rate is 40%. That cuts your 6% GIC rate to 3.6% after tax (8 x (1.00 – 0.40)). Now subtract the 3% inflation rate and you'll see you're hardly making money — or at least purchasing power — on a risk-free GIC. The same goes for Canada Savings Bonds, though their rates are adjusted each year.

- **Reinvestment risk.** That's the risk that when your holding matures, you will have to reinvest at a rate that's too low to meet your needs. It was a big concern in 1996 when GIC renewal rates hit their lowest levels in 40 years.

- **Interest rate risk.** This is related to inflation risk. As inflation goes up, so do interest rates on newly issued bonds and other fixed-income vehicles. As interest rates rise, the market value of previously issued instruments fall. Conversely, as interest rates fall, those values rise. That is a big concern for an investor who has to sell a bond before it matures.

- **Currency risk.** This applies when your investment is made in foreign money. Perhaps you buy shares on the New York Stock Exchange, or purchase a mutual fund that invests outside Canada. When converted to Canadian dollars, your return gets an extra push up or down, depending on whether the Canadian dollar has gained or lost value. Canadians seem to believe our dollar can only go down. In fact, it moves both ways — in bursts.

- **Economic risk.** Some investments are more sensitive than others to changes in the economy. The auto industry is "cyclical." It tends to do well in good times and suffer during downturns. Utilities such as telephone companies are less sensitive.

- **Industry risk.** Some industries are inherently volatile because the dramatic pace of change means a whole generation of technology can quickly become outdated. Examples include the computer and health-care industries.

- **Company risk.** When you buy shares, you buy part of a business. Even in booming industries, poorly run businesses lose money over time.

- **Credit risk.** This is a prime concern for the income investor. What are the chances that the issuer of your bond will suspend interest payments or fail to pay back principal at maturity? What is the risk that dividends on your shares will be cut or skipped? Rating services assess those risks. See chapter 28.

- **Liquidity risk.** How easily can you get at your money without undue capital loss? A bank account is highly liquid and carries no risk of capital loss — if you're within deposit insurance limits. But it pays very low returns. Stocks and bonds are highly liquid and offer higher returns, but at greater capital risk. Residential real estate is liquid when the market booms, but you'll get hammered if you have to sell when the market is down.

- **Political risk.** Government action affects every investment, either directly, through changes in tax or zoning laws, or indirectly, through economic policy. The longer you hold your investment, the more you run the risk that politicians and bureaucrats will change the rules.

So, there are all kinds of risks — and no investment is immune. But there are ways to manage your investments so you reduce risk while still getting decent returns. Please read on.

Risk Management Strategies

1. **Know what you want.** Match your investing to your needs and goals. Divide your money into short-, mid- and long-term chunks. Assign each chunk to a set of goals and assume only as much risk as you need to generate the returns required. If your retirement plan requires 8%, why take on the added risk required to make 15%?

2. **Keep it simple.** Don't buy what you don't understand. Lay a strong foundation and then climb the pyramid shown in figure 27.1. It ranks investments according to risk, required knowledge and potential return. The higher you go, the higher the return should be. Don't feel compelled to reach for the exotic stuff at the top; many people have made lots of money with mid-range investments. The rankings are indicative, not absolute. For example, a preferred share issued by a major chartered bank

is arguably far more secure than a GIC from a small trust company that's over the deposit insurance limit.

3. **Diversify.** You can't count on the stock market alone to make you rich — especially if your money is in just one stock or even just in Canada. You can't count on your house to fund your retirement. Various economic conditions lend themselves to different weightings. These are routinely discussed in the financial media. Pay attention.

4. **Average.** Few people have the time, interest, knowledge, talent and discipline to "play" the markets and avoid the cycle of greed and fear. Even among professionals, very few produce above-average "long-term" returns. Active investing is hard work. Three proven strategies require little time and effort and should produce decent returns while reducing overall risk:

- **Staggered maturities.** This is a key strategy for people who buy GICs or strip bonds for RRSPs. Instead of trying to guess interest rates, evenly divide your money over a range of terms so part comes due each year. That way you're averaging ups and downs.

- **Dollar cost averaging.** Normally done with a mutual fund, this technique has you invest the same amount every month. You thus automatically buy more units when prices are low and fewer when they are high. This can work especially well with international mutual funds, since currency fluctuations make them volatile.

- **Value averaging.** You determine how much you want at a future date and the growth rate required to get you there. Periodically value your account and top up or draw down to get back on track.

5. **Think for yourself.** Be skeptical when your friend or colleague brags about some current success. A one-time hot tip may now be lukewarm or ice cold. A good broker or other salesperson offers good advice — and is able to explain why it's good advice. If you don't understand the explanation, seek clarification. If you don't understand the clarification, don't buy. If you don't understand the salesperson, deal with someone else. The same goes if the salesperson tries to rush you into buying. Investments are like buses — another will always come along.

Diversification

MOST PEOPLE are aware that investment money should be spread over a number of holdings. The worn but apt cliché is "don't put all your eggs in one basket."

FIGURE 27.1: Investment Risk Pyramid

Futures

Precious metals
Speculative stocks
Art & other collectibles

Resource limited partnerships
Investment real estate

Blue chip stocks/equity mutual funds

Quality mortgages
Quality preferred shares & convertible bonds
Bond & balanced mutual funds

Quality government & corporate bonds
Mortgage-backed securities
GICs

Canada Saving Bonds   T-bills   Money market funds

But diversification does not mean taking all your investment money and just dividing it over several equity mutual funds. It means you first divide your money into chunks matched against your short-, mid- and long-term goals. Then you divide each chunk among investment classes such as cash, fixed-income and growth. And then you divide each class into individual holdings.

Look at your total wealth and income, not just your stock portfolio or RRSP/RRIF. If you live in a one-industry town and work in that industry, both your salary and your home depend on that industry's health. If most of your investment money is in your company's employee stock purchase plan, you're really concentrated. Such plans can be great if the employer kicks in money, but periodically take your gains and move the money elsewhere.

If you own a home, you already have a substantial real estate investment in your local community. Why not diversify into other forms of investment, or at least into real estate not tied to your local economy?

The same goes for Canada. Your job, home and most — if not all — of your retirement savings depend on Canada's economic performance. Why not hedge your risk by investing money outside the country? International mutual funds make that very easy to do.

Don't, however, diversify too much. You must be able to keep track of your investments and their outlooks.

Asset Allocation

"ASSET ALLOCATION" refers to how you diversify your investment portfolio among the standard asset classes: cash and equivalents like money market funds and treasury bills, equities (stocks), and fixed-income (bonds and GICs). Some add real estate and tangible assets like gold or art.

For example, you might carve your investment pie into three slices: 10% in cash, 60% in equities and 30% in fixed-income.

A further refinement would divide one or more slice among geographic areas. For example, the equity component might be divided among Canada, the United States, a mutual fund that invests in "emerging" markets and a mutual fund that invests anywhere its managers find value.

The asset allocation concept is based on a 1986 study that financial analyst Gary Brinson summarized in the Financial Analysts Journal. Brinson found that about 90% of the performance difference between one portfolio and another was due to how the pie was carved, not the selection of individual investments.

Unfortunately, many financial salespeople use Brinson's finding out of context, and take an aggressive concept called "market timing" and repackage it as asset allocation. Market timing involves major moves to catch the right market at the right time. It is very difficult. Some academics argue it is impossible to do correctly over the long term. Asset allocation is not aimed at being in the right market at the right time. Rather, you're in most markets all the time, but with varying exposures.

There are two basic forms of asset allocation — passive and dynamic.

With passive — or strategic — allocation, you set a percentage for each category. Some categories do well. Others don't. Periodically, bring your holdings back into line with your fixed percentages by selling winners and topping up losers. How often? Several academic studies suggest rebalancing when there's a six or seven percentage point variance from your plan. The idea is that every category will have its day, and you're trying to buy low and sell high. Also, markets move in bursts and you ideally want to be in place before the takeoff occurs.

With dynamic — or tactical — allocation, you regularly alter your percentages, based on your assessment of the short- to mid-term outlook for each market. Investment dealers and mutual funds often publish updated recommendations.

The difference between market timing and dynamic asset allocation is easily clouded. Asset allocation is not a bid to get the biggest bang for the buck. Instead, its goal is to produce above-average long-term returns by going for steady gains while minimizing losses. One practitioner put it this way: "We're not out to get lots of home runs, but rather lots of doubles.

Batters who hit lots of home runs also strike out a lot. We aim to do well by consistently making money. No big swings up but no big swings down."

I watched an investment dealer's computer graphically display this concept. First, we fed in our requirements for growth, income and inflation protection along with a measure of how much volatility we could stand. Then we fed in the asset allocation of a model portfolio. Using historic returns along with mathematical principles developed by William Sharpe and Henry Markowitz, the system plotted our model portfolio in relation to the "efficient frontier" — the point at which we maximize returns while minimizing risk.

The computer told us that for our test case, a slight increase in international equities should produce a higher return with lower overall risk and volatility. When we increased the international equity component beyond the recommended level, the volatility levels rose and the projected return fell off. Very subtle stuff.

When discussing asset allocation with an adviser or salesperson, clarify whether the plan is based on major moves like market timing or on more subtle moves within an overall long-term strategy.

Also remember that financial researchers like Brinson, Sharpe and Markowitz base their studies on large diversified pension funds run by disciplined managers with long-term strategies.

For an excellent book on asset allocation, read *Risk is a Four Letter Word* by George Hartman.

Leverage

LEVERAGE IS when you buy an investment with borrowed money. Interest on that loan is tax-deductible. This is a very aggressive strategy. It magnifies both gains and losses.

Suppose you invest $1,000 of your own money. In the one-year scenarios given in the following chart, you can gain or lose no more than 20% — $200. The subsequent rows show what happens with ever-increasing loans at 8% compounded monthly. (Appendix A-3 tells us the annualized loan rate is 8.3%. I've assumed here you're in the 50% tax bracket, so the after-tax loan cost is 4.15%.)

| Borrow | Amount invested | After-tax loan cost | At these investment yields | | | |
| | | | 10% | -10% | 20% | -20% |
			one-year net gain/loss is			
$ 0	$1,000	$ 0	10%	-10%	20%	-20%
1,000	2,000	42	16	-24	36	-44
2,000	3,000	83	22	-38	52	-68
3,000	4,000	125	28	-52	28	-92
4,000	5,000	166	33	-67	83	-117

In the best case, leverage produces a 83% gain after you pay off the loan and its interest. In the worst case, your $5,000 investment is worth just $4,000 after one year. But the loan repayment and interest cost $4,166. So you've lost every single cent of your own $1,000 and you're still $166 in the hole. Note that with leverage, the downside risk is far greater than the upside potential — a maximum loss of 117% versus a maximum gain of 83%. Often, people come away from slick mutual fund presentations with the impression that their maximum loss would be the fund units. No. You're normally on the hook for the full amount you borrow. Read the agreement carefully; don't just take the salesperson's word.

Obviously, timing is everything. Leverage works wonders when markets are heading up, but proves devastating when the cycle turns. Real estate investments are typically very highly leveraged. That leverage produced millionaires in the 1980s and bankrupts in the early '90s — in many cases, the same people.

Stock market rules generally limit you to 50% leverage, depending on the price of the stock. For the most part, if you put up $1,000, you can buy shares worth $1,500. If your investment falls below the limit, you get a "margin call." You have to top up your account, or the broker will sell enough to put you back onside.

Mutual funds may qualify for 100% leverage, a seductive and dangerous gambit for novice investors. Some mutual fund salespeople have even encouraged older people to borrow against the equity in their paid-off homes and put the proceeds into aggressive stock funds. That's reprehensible.

Leverage can be a very powerful investment tool for those who have the stomach and the money to weather big downturns. Many don't, and feel compelled to unwind the plan at the worst time — after a big paper loss. Never underestimate the "cycle of greed and fear" discussed earlier in this chapter. And be conservative in your borrowing.

Weigh carefully any adviser's enthusiasm over leverage. The more you invest, the more the adviser makes in commissions. And the adviser will likely collect a referral fee from the bank for helping you set up the investment loan.

Although interest on an investment loan is tax-deductible, during the year you must pay interest at the full loan rate; your tax deduction doesn't save you money until you file your return.

Also be aware that you'll lose part of your deduction if you sell any of your holding and don't reinvest the full proceeds. Say you borrowed $100,000, which grew to $150,000. If you sell $50,000 worth of your holding and don't reinvest that full amount, only two-thirds of your future loan interest will be tax-deductible.

Leveraged investors got a major tax break in 1994. Tax rules were changed to let them continue to deduct loan interest after a leveraged investment is sold as long as proceeds from the sale are reinvested. Before, that deduction ended once the investment was no longer held. This tax break does not apply to real estate.

A Reality Check

IT IS extremely hard to make killings on the capital markets year in and year out. If it weren't, there'd be a serious shortage of investment professionals. They would all retire at 30. I know some very successful amateur investors. Each one has excellent analytical skills and discipline. But such people are uncommon.

Realistically determine how much growth you need. Assume only as much risk as that requires. In line with your knowledge, temperament and objectives, balance your portfolio to minimize risk. Forget about big scores; go for modest but consistent gains.

Understand what you're doing. That's hard amid all the hype. So try this approach. Before you buy, see if you can explain your decision in no less than 30 seconds and no more than one minute. The bottom limit rules out: "All I know is my broker said it's a great deal." The top limit will force you to crystallize your thinking. You'll sleep well at night, and most likely be wealthier in the long run.

Good luck! That enters into it too.

28

Strolling Through the Capital Markets

NON-INVESTORS I TALK TO INVARIABLY have a warped view of the stock market. Many believe it's full of speculators who make tons of easy money. Others believe it's a high-risk casino where almost everybody loses. The reality is in between. In large part, how you do depends on how well you do your homework, how much money you have to spend on diversification, and how long you can keep it invested.

Stocks of major and many minor companies trade on centralized exchanges. Canada's best-known exchanges are the Toronto Stock Exchange and the Vancouver Stock Exchange. Companies on the VSE are smaller and more speculative. The best-known U.S. exchanges are the New York Stock Exchange and Nasdaq, which is run by the National Association of Securities Dealers.

You must use a broker to buy shares on an exchange. The traditional stockbroker — who provides ideas, advice and research reports — is now called a "full-service" broker. There are many full-service firms.

"Discount" brokerage began in Canada in 1983. That field is now dominated by the Toronto Dominion Bank's Green Line Investor Services. Originally, discounters simply handled trades, but they've steadily expanded their services. For example, discounters now provide research reports at extra cost.

Several banks now run "deep discounters." They only execute trades. While the discount firms offer 24-hour service, deep discounters might not. Many other, smaller discount firms have been launched to capitalize on the growth of home computers and the Internet.

Stocks are also called equities. There are "common" stocks and "preferred" stocks.

Common Shares

When you buy a common share you buy a small piece of the business. In most cases, each share entitles you to one vote on major issues such as a takeover bid.

The value of your share will depend on how the market views your company's earnings. Even if the company is losing money, the share price can rise if the market foresees a turnaround. Even if the company is making money, the share price can fall. The market might expect a downturn for that industry. Or the company's earnings may be on a downward slope. Or the company can be doing well, but still not meeting expectations.

Besides getting capital appreciation, you may collect quarterly dividends, usually a few cents per share. These are discretionary payments. Often, companies boost dividends after profits increase. Banks and utilities have had excellent records for dividend growth.

Some companies pay high dividends even if profits stay flat or fall. Earnings may just be temporarily down, and the company wants to maintain its standing with institutional investors like pension funds. Or, the company might be controlled by a larger company that depends on those dividends.

There are four broad categories of common shares:

- **Blue chip.** These are shares of large, well-established companies. These companies normally pay quarterly dividends.

- **Growth.** These are shares of companies that have had above-average growth in recent years and are expected to continue that. Many of these companies do not pay dividends; instead, they use that money for expansion.

- **Small-cap.** These are smaller companies. Some grow at astounding rates — and so do the prices of their shares — because they have a "small capitalization." That means in relative terms, they have fewer shares on the market than other companies.

- **Penny.** These are highly speculative stocks that usually trade for less $1 a share. Many of them are listed on the Vancouver Stock Exchange.

There are two main ways to analyze a stock. "Fundamental" analysis examines the individual company's operation as a business, its standing in its industry and the prospects for that industry. "Technical" analysis rests on the assumption that patterns repeat themselves. So, using charts designed to measure market activity, you can predict stock price movements.

Historical data show that equities have delivered superior returns over long periods. But that's the overall market, not individual stocks. If you don't buy wisely, the market can rise while your stocks fall. If you do buy wisely, your returns can easily beat those from just about any other investment.

Peter Lynch insists amateur investors can handily beat the pros. He knows how the pros work. As manager of the gargantuan Boston-based Fidelity Magellan mutual fund, he piled up amazing returns year after year before retiring in his mid-40s to spend time with his family.

But Lynch's amateur investors are folks who pass up hot tips and get-rich-quick schemes in favor of research. They keep abreast of Main Street's buying habits by paying attention to what's going on at the mall. Then they delve into Wall Street's numbers to select the companies that make the most money selling those goods and services people want.

If that suits you, read his excellent books, *One Up on Wall Street*, and *Beating the Street*. Or contact the Canadian Shareowners Association by phone at (416) 595-9600 or on the Net at http://www.shareowner.ca. The association has a quick, user-friendly self-study course on how to analyze stocks. Consider joining an investment club. Small groups of people band together to do research and invest jointly. The CSA may know of one in your area, or help you start one.

Generally, to invest directly in stocks you need money and time. You will probably find it hard to build a well-diversified portfolio for less than $50,000. The Canadian Shareowners Association does, however, sponsor a low-cost investment program in which members can build diversified portfolios for fairly small amounts of money. This program is based on the use of "dividend reinvestment plans." Companies that offer DRIPs let investors who hold their stock buy more shares on a commission-free basis directly from the company. Sometimes, that purchase is limited to reinvested quarterly dividends. In other cases, you can make lump-sum purchases for thousands of dollars.

The Toronto Stock Exchange maintains a list of major Canadian corporations with DRIPs. Or contact *Canadian Moneysaver* magazine by phone at (613) 352-7448 or on the Net at http://www.canadianmoney saver.ca.

Direct stock investing requires considerable time. You have to select potential buys, research them and then monitor your holdings. You can't just rely on your broker; investment dealers are often quick to recommend "buys" but slow to act when they become "sells." Those dealers have an inherent conflict of interest because they underwrite corporate share offerings with one hand and advise the public with the other.

Once you buy a stock, you face a daily decision on whether to hold or sell it. I've done much better with mutual funds than with direct stock ownership. Most investors I know have had the same experience. Those who've done better with direct ownership generally pursue investing as a serious hobby, or focus on DRIPs of stocks with strong dividend records.

Preferred Shares

Preferred shares are a hybrid. While the appeal of a common share is capital appreciation, the appeal of a preferred share is steady income like you get from a bond.

Preferreds pay quarterly dividends. Their share prices rise and fall more as a result of interest rates than because of the earnings of the issuer's business — unless the issuer runs into trouble and can't pay the dividends.

If a company goes under, preferred shareholders rank ahead of common shareholders.

Some preferreds are redeemable, retractable and/or convertible. Redeemable shares can be called in by the company in exchange for a pre-set amount. Retractable shares give you the right to cash them at certain times for a pre-set amount. Convertible shares can be exchanged for common shares.

Independent agencies rate preferred shares according to the issuer's ability to pay the dividends due. Rating is discussed in the next section, on the bond market.

The Bond Market

IN DOLLAR terms, the bond market dwarfs the stock market. But you can't visit it — there is no exchange. The bond market consists of traders all over the world linked by telephone and computer. This "over-the-counter" market works around the clock, with single trades running millions of dollars.

This is where corporations, countries, provinces and cities borrow money. Institutional investors like pension funds and insurance companies buy those bonds. So do investment dealers who resell many of them to the public.

When you buy or sell a common or preferred share, your broker acts as your agent and tacks on a commission. When you buy or sell a bond, the broker acts as a "principal." That means the firm buys your bond at a "bid" price, adds a markup and then sells it to someone else at an "ask" price. Since they see no fee on their trade slips, some people believe there are no commissions on bonds. The commissions are built into the price.

Bond buyers have two concerns:

- Will the issuer be able to make interest payments on time and pay off the bond at maturity?

- Will the interest payments be enough to cover inflation?

Thus, the price of a bond is based on the credit status of the issuer, the bond's interest rate and the duration of the bond.

Independent agencies rate bonds according to how well their issuers can meet their obligations. Canada's top rating goes to the federal government. Although we keep talking about how Ottawa is broke, it still has the power to levy taxes and print money. The provinces range from Alberta at the top end to Newfoundland at the bottom. The lower the rating, the higher the interest rate that must be paid. The major Canadian rating agencies are Dominion Bond Rating Service and Canadian Bond Rating Service. The major American ones — Standard & Poor's Corp. and Moody's Investors Service — also rate Canadian bonds. These four agencies rate preferred shares too.

Their reports are sold to investment dealers and institutional investors. If you deal with a full-service broker, he or she can definitely tell you a bond's or preferred's rating. If you're a do-it-yourselfer, your public or university library might subscribe to a rating service. A bond or preferred issue's rating may change from time to time. Financial newspapers like *The Financial Post* and *The Globe and Mail* report changes.

There are two ways to make money on a bond. You can collect the interest, which is fully taxed. Or you can sell the bond before it matures for a capital gain or loss.

You can buy a brand new bond, called a "new issue." Or you can buy one issued some time ago. New issues are priced at "par," and you pay full price. The others are sold on the "secondary market" and are generally priced at a discount or premium.

When you buy a bond, the broker will quote a yield. The "current yield" is the bond's yearly interest — its "coupon rate" — divided by the price you pay. The "yield to maturity" is the result of a calculation that adjusts the current yield for any discount or premium on the bond's price. If the bond is bought at par, the two yields are the same.

Note that if your broker quotes a yield to maturity of, say, 8%, the broker is assuming all semi-annual interest payments will be reinvested at 8%. That's most unlikely.

The "secondary market" handles bonds after issue and before maturity. Prices fluctuate with interest rates. Your yield will most likely be different from the "coupon rate" when the bond was issued. When interest rates go down, prices of existing bonds go up. Say you paid $1,000 for a bond that pays $100 a year of interest until February 1, 2000. Your current yield was 10%. Suppose new bonds dated February 1, 2000 pay just $85 per $1,000 — 8.5%. Your bond is repriced to about $1,176 so the $100 in yearly interest reflects the current going rate of 8.5%.

When interest rates rise, bond prices fall as the old ones are equalized to pay the same yield as new ones.

Short-term bonds have up to three years left until maturity. Medium-term bonds run three to 10 years. Long-term bonds have more than 10 years left. The longer the maturity, the more volatile the price — both up and down. That's because the longer timespan carries more credit and inflation risk. Many traders say 10-year bonds are the most efficiently priced.

Financial newspapers print bond prices and yields, and broadcast reports might cite the price and yield of "benchmark" bonds — large issues that are actively traded. But those tables and quotes are for big-money institutional trades. Use them only as a guide.

There is a wide range of bonds. Some corporate issues are secured by physical assets. Others, called "debentures," are unsecured. If a bond is "redeemable," it can be "called." That means the issuer can pay you off early at a pre-set price. A "retractable" bond gives you the right to force the issuer to pay you off early. An "extendable" bond gives you the right to swap yours for a longer-term one at the same coupon rate or better. "Convertible" bonds can be exchanged for a company's common shares according to a pre-set formula. There are bonds that have floating rates and bonds denominated in foreign currencies.

The "money market" is a large part of the fixed-income market. That's where governments and corporations raise money for less than one year. The biggest item in this market is Government of Canada treasury bills. T-bills are issued for terms of 91 days, 182 days and 364 days, but the market is so big and liquid that you can buy a T-bill coming due on any date within the year.

T-bills do not pay interest as such. The price you pay is discounted by the quoted yield. If the going one-year yield is 8%, you would pay about $920 now and collect $1,000 at maturity. Brokers set minimums for T-bill sales. They range from $5,000 to $25,000.

Short-term notes from banks and corporations are sold on the same discounted basis, but their rates are higher than on T-bills since there is no government guarantee.

More and more, Canadians are buying strip bonds for their RRSPs and RRIFs. Like T-bills, strips are discounted upfront, so there is no cash flow until maturity. That's not a problem if they're held in a tax-sheltered RRSP or RRIF. If you hold them in a regular portfolio, you face a tax bill for each year's internal growth, but you're not getting any cash flow.

Still, some people buy strips as regular investments when they expect interest rates to fall in the next year or two. As noted, falling rates drive up bond prices. Strips can produce big trading gains when interest rates fall since they're more volatile than ordinary bonds. That's because they carry no income stream. When interest rates trend down, strip buyers are willing to pay extra to avoid the risk of having to reinvest periodic interest payments at ever-lower rates. When interest rates rise, strip buyers demand more of a discount since they won't be able to reinvest periodic interest payments at ever-higher rates.

Special Products

INVESTMENT DEALERS excel at packaging securities to meet special needs and investment strategies. Options and derivatives can provide protection for conservative investors and increased gains for aggressive ones. But they increase the cost and complexity of your decision-making. Perhaps the simplest special products are options known as "puts" and "calls."

When you buy a put, you buy the right to make someone else buy your shares at a pre-set price any time during a pre-set period. It's a form of insurance for investors who fear their stocks may fall in price but don't necessarily want to sell them at this time. Say ABC Co. shares are now worth $10 each. You might buy a put giving you the right to sell yours at $9.00 any time over the next three months. The person who sells the put is betting the stock price won't fall to that level.

(A person who believes a stock is poised for a fall might use an aggressive strategy called "short selling." That's a strategy, not a product. You sell a stock you don't own by having your broker arrange for you to borrow someone else's shares. After the price falls, you buy shares to replace the ones you borrowed — and pocket the difference between the price you received and the price you paid, less brokerage fees and any dividends due while the shares were borrowed. If, however, the share price goes up — not down — you can get clobbered because you'll have to pay more than you received.)

While a put is the right to sell a stock at a pre-set price, a call is the right to buy a stock at a pre-set price. If you own a stock, you can generate extra income by selling calls on it. For example, you might sell a call that lets someone buy your ABC shares — now valued at $10 each — for $11 any time over the next two months. If your plan works, the option will expire before ABC gets to $11. That way, you keep both the shares and the money paid for the option. The person who bought your call expected ABC's share price to rise. In that case, the shares could be purchased at the pre-set level and be immediately resold for more. That will normally produce a higher return than just purchasing the shares and waiting for the price to rise.

Your broker handles puts and calls through a clearing house called Trans Canada Options. Only certain shares are listed, mainly those of blue chip companies. TCO works like a stock exchange. Prices for a given option change constantly, based on bidding. Some people actively trade options, buying them with no intention of holding on until maturity.

Recent years have seen the creation of many "derivatives" with snappy acronym names like LEAPS and WEBS. The full names are irrelevant; nobody uses them because they're so awkward. LEAPs, for example, are Long-Term Equity Anticipation Securities.

At least that's descriptive. LEAPS are similar to puts and calls, but run much longer before expiring — up to two years. The purchaser anticipates the price of the underlying stock will appreciate over the long term. The seller wants protection in case the price of the underlying stock falls. WEBS are World Equity Benchmark Shares. Try guessing what that means! WEBS were introduced on the American Stock Exchange in 1996. There are 17 of them, each representing a country with a well-developed stock market. WEBS reflect the movements of those markets, so they offer foreign exposure without the complications of direct security ownership or the ongoing, generally high, management fees for international mutual funds. WEBS are like the Toronto Index Participation units (TIPs) and Standard & Poor's Depository Receipts (SPDRs) discussed in chapter 25. Please, no jokes about SPDRs and WEBS!

LEAPS and WEBS are just two examples. There is probably an option or derivative for every investment situation. They can be quite complicated, so make sure you get a full explanation from your broker. Read up on the subject yourself through investment newsletters or more specialized books. In addition to increased complexity, these products generally carry increased risk if there are deadlines. If you buy an option and it expires, you lose all the money you put out.

Mortgages

MORTGAGES ARE bonds. Some residential first mortgages are lumped into pools and sold as federally guaranteed mortgage-backed securities. MBSs trade on the bond market. They're discussed more fully in chapter 25, on retirement investments.

Other residential and commercial mortgages are traded locally through mortgage brokers. These are usually second or third mortgages. Mortgage brokers match up investors with cash and people who need money to buy buildings. Some real estate lawyers also do that. The ranking of the mortgage indicates that's where you stand in terms of repayment if the borrower defaults and the property is sold. Bear in mind that defaults rise as the economy — and real estate values — slump.

A common application: To help sell your house, you grant the buyer a cut-rate second mortgage. But the buyer's promise to make monthly payments doesn't help you get your new home; you need cash. A mortgage broker will buy that agreement from you at a discount and sell it to an investor who does want monthly income.

Investing in individual mortgages can be very risky. The security of your money depends entirely on one borrower and one property. If you buy a mortgage, do a credit check on the borrower. Also visit the property. That might sound obvious, but there have been numerous cases of investors losing their money because it was secured by poorly built or rundown properties nobody wanted.

Mortgage brokers often pool investors on one side and borrowers on the other. That reduces the impact of any one default, but the investment is still risky — especially if the pool is concentrated in one geographic area. In 1992, Ontario tightened regulations for mortgage brokers after a series of mortgage brokerage failures left investors high and dry. One of the reforms prohibited brokers from stating that an interest rate is guaranteed.

Before lending to a stranger, consider helping a family member. At least you know the borrower well and there's an emotional as well as financial reward. But that kind of mortgage carries a somewhat different risk. If the borrower runs into financial trouble, not only could you lose money, but the family could be ripped apart.

29

Mutual Funds: Everybody into the Pool!

MUTUAL FUNDS HAVE GOT TO BE ONE OF the most brilliant developments in the financial industry. By pooling their money, small — even very small — investors reduce their risk through diversification and by turning over the decision-making to professional managers. They also gain access to markets they couldn't touch or probably survive in on their own.

The mutual fund industry is exploding. Canada now has more than 1,500 funds. Assets under management grew from nearly $3 billion in 1968 to more than $300 billion in 1998

Fund Setups

THERE ARE two basic fund structures:

1. **"Open-end" funds,** which are the most common. They sell and redeem units constantly. The unit price is called the "net asset value." Each unit is a proportional share. To price it, the distributor divides the fund's total value by the number of outstanding units. This chapter focuses on open-end mutual funds.

2. **"Closed-end" funds,** which have a fixed number of shares and trade on the stock exchange like any other company. Unlike an open-end fund, the distributor is not required to buy back the shares. As a result, those shares often trade at a discount to the value of the underlying assets.

Occasionally a closed-end fund is wound up or converted to an open-end one. The share price then moves up to the full value of the underlying assets. Some advisers like these funds better than open-end funds, especially for investing in emerging markets and other illiquid areas. Since the managers don't have to worry about redemptions, they can take a longer-term view.

Within the two structures, there are several types of funds that reflect different investment categories. A mutual fund is not an investment on its own, but rather a way to invest. For example, instead of picking individual stocks on your own and then buying and selling them, you're hiring someone else — the fund manager — to do that for you. But you're still investing in stocks.

Appreciate that while a fund can reduce your risk, it does not eliminate it. Ultimately, each fund's performance reflects the characteristics of the underlying investments. The basic fund types are:

- **Money market funds.** These invest in high-quality short-term notes issued by governments, banks and corporations. Their unit price is normally fixed at $10. Monthly distributions automatically buy more units.

   A money fund's yield changes daily. Daily newspaper tables show two returns. The "current yield" converts the return for the previous day into an annual yield. The "effective yield" takes the return for the past seven days and compounds that over one year.

   Money funds pay far more than bank accounts. Some can transfer cash to and from chequing accounts, and some offer cheque-writing privileges. Make sure you face no redemption fees.

   Even if sold by a financial institution, a money fund is not covered by deposit insurance. There is no deposit insurance for any mutual funds. Later in this chapter we'll see how fund investors are protected.

   Some people use mortgage mutual funds as a higher-yielding alternative to money market funds. However, mortgage fund unit values do fluctuate a bit, and you can lose money if interest rates rise.

- **Equity funds.** These invest mainly in common stocks. Some invest mostly in Canadian issues, while some focus on the United States. Others invest in parts of the world such as Europe. Still others are global.

   Among U.S. and Canadian funds, "small cap" ones concentrate on smaller corporations. Others build more broad-based portfolios.

   You can attribute a large part of an equity fund's performance to its manager's style. "Top-down" managers predict which industries will do best in the coming part of the economic cycle and then seek the best bets in those industries. "Bottom-up" managers look first for well-run companies. Some funds are run by "growth" managers. These funds buy companies whose earnings are growing quite rapidly and whose stock may already be quite expensive. The fund manager believes further growth exists.

A few funds are run by "value" investors. These funds try to buy stocks that offer potential not yet recognized by the market — a task that requires considerable research and patience.

Growth-oriented funds usually do best in rising markets. Value-oriented funds are usually safer during market declines.

Over time, few actively managed funds consistently beat the index for the market in which they invest. So, more and more investors have been turning to "index funds" that simply reflect that market.

For example, an index fund based on the Toronto Stock Exchange 35 Index reflects movements in the shares of the 35 largest companies on the TSE. The fund manager makes no attempt to pick which of those companies are good buys and which are goodbyes. Similarly, a U.S. index fund based on the Standard & Poor's 500 Index will reflect movements in share prices for the 500 companies in the S&P 500.

So, index fund investors get the broad market's performance minus a bit for fees — and those fees are typically one-half to one-third the cost of fees for actively managed funds. Always remember that every dollar spent on fees is a dollar that can't grow in the future.

Some active managers are actually "closet indexers." That means their funds look much like the index for that market, yet they still charge active management fees. Each fund publishes its portfolio twice a year. To see if your manager is a closet indexer, compare that portfolio to the relevant index.

In 1997 the National Bank of Canada took indexing out of the closet when it launched the InvesNat Canadian Index Plus Fund and the InvesNat American Index Plus Fund. Though they've drawn little attention, I would not be surprised if these funds do well over time. Each one is 70–80% indexed while the rest of the money is actively managed. Management fees were set low to reflect the fact that indexing requires little effort.

- **Fixed-income funds.** These invest in interest-bearing securities. Most focus on Canadian securities, but some international ones are available. There are also funds that invest in foreign-pay bonds from Canadian entities. Bond funds trade government and corporate bonds. Mortgage funds trade residential and commercial mortgages. In each case, the interest payments provide an income stream for as long as the security is held.

While an individual is likely to hold a bond or mortgage until maturity, these funds trade them for capital gains. Key to their success is the manager's ability to predict interest rate movements and alter the portfolio's average duration.

Because they receive a steady flow of interest, fixed-income funds are normally less volatile than equity funds. But big moves in interest rates can cause big changes in fund values. The best time to buy is when the economy peaks and interest rates are high and will soon head down. The worst time is when interest rates have bottomed.

In 1994 many novice investors lost money because they bought mortgage funds as an alternative to safe but seemingly low-yield GICs. Mortgage funds are normally not very volatile but 1993-94 saw a big tumble in mortgage rates and then a spike up. Managers say you should buy a mortgage fund for a flow of interest income from the underlying loans, not for capital gains. The big gains of 1993 were quite unusual. While the sharp drop in 1994 hurt unit values, it did not affect the flow of interest. Normally, mortgage fund returns run about two percentage points above yields on treasury bills.

As you might expect, international bond funds get an extra kick — up or down — from fluctuations in currency rates. Some fund managers give up a little yield in order to hedge their currency risk.

- **Dividend funds.** These invest mainly in shares that pay dividends. If the fund is held outside an RRSP or RRIF, investors benefit from the dividend tax credit. Thus, on an after-tax basis, the fund's return is better than it looks at first. Some dividend funds hold lots of preferred shares with more stable dividends. Others favor riskier common shares. Increasingly, these funds also hold income trusts.

- **Balanced funds.** These invest in both stocks and bonds. The manager has wide latitude in determining the mix. Don't expect stellar gains; often the objective is just to outperform GICs.

- **Specialty funds.** These invest only in certain sectors. For instance, some funds invest only in oil and gas companies, and others hold gold and shares of mining companies. These funds are highly sensitive to the economic outlook for their sector.

  Real estate funds took a severe beating during the 1990 recession, and most funds suspended redemptions. It's easy for a stock or bond manager to sell securities to pay off exiting clients. It's much harder to sell an office building.

  To get around the redemption problem, most of those real estate funds were converted to "real estate investment trusts." REITs trade on the stock market. That makes commercial real estate easy to buy and sell.

New-style real estate funds avoid past valuation and redemption problems by investing only in totally liquid REITs and real estate company shares. They don't own buildings directly.

- **Fixed-payout funds.** These funds hold a mix of equity and fixed-income securities, and pay a set distribution each month. They were designed for people no longer satisfied with GIC returns. Check the fund's holdings; it may not be the truly conservative vehicle you think. If the fund does not earn enough, it maintains the distribution by simply returning some of your capital. Some funds have used capital return to cover up to 60% of their monthly payouts.

Who's Who

THERE'S A difference between fund distributors and fund managers. The distributor creates the fund, markets it to the public and handles administration. The manager makes the actual investment decisions. Often the distributor and manager are the same company, but sometimes they're not — especially for foreign funds. Having an outstanding Canadian equity fund does not automatically mean a company's foreign funds are great — and vice-versa.

Some people think they're buying mutual funds when they're not. They're buying "segregated funds" — or "seg funds," for short. These are investment funds from life insurance companies. The name refers to the fact that the money is segregated from the insurer's other assets.

Seg funds work just like open-end mutual funds. You can buy or sell units any time. Each unit represents an interest in a professionally managed pool. There are money market funds, Canadian and foreign equity funds, fixed-income funds, balanced funds — you name it.

Many seg funds are managed by the insurance company teams that also manage large pension funds. Some are managed by outside mutual fund managers on a contract basis. Some are actually repackaged mutual funds.

The fee structures are similar to those for open-end mutual funds, but often are a bit more costly.

Even though they are normally not tied to the sale of life insurance, seg funds are, technically, insurance contracts. That means they are governed by insurance regulators, not securities commissions. It also means seg funds offer two potentially valuable features:

1. Your investment can get the same creditor-proofing as other insurance

contracts. See chapter 26. When you die, the money can go directly to a named beneficiary without being taxed for probate. See chapter 32.

2. The insurer must guarantee a return of at least 75% of your capital after a "maturity date," typically 10 years from the time of deposit. Some funds guarantee 100%. Over 10 years, that guarantee doesn't mean much; you should have considerable capital growth at that point. But the guarantee also applies if you die before the maturity date. So if you die one year after investing, and the market is in a slump, your heirs will get back most, if not all, of your capital. The guarantee may look good, but actuaries reckon there's less than a 5% chance of any payout and it can sharply increase the fund's management fee, which eats into your returns. Advisers downplay the cost by expressing it as a tiny percentage of the account value. But that's a percentage of a growing pie, so the cost mounts over time. Also, the 10-year clock starts anew for each new purchase or a switch between funds.

Seg funds are sold only by advisers licensed to sell life insurance. Some life insurance companies offer regular mutual funds as well as seg funds.

For the rest of this chapter, I refer just to "mutual funds." But that includes seg funds too.

How Are Investors Protected?

IN A mutual fund, your security is as strong as the value of the underlying assets. No more, no less. Except for seg funds, there are no performance guarantees. If the fund's holdings fall in value, you lose money. That has been an unpleasant surprise for people who bought bond funds thinking they were just a higher-yielding way to hold GICs.

You are, however, protected if a fund company goes under. The stocks, bonds and any other fund assets are owned by the unitholders, not by the manager or distributor. Under securities regulations, those assets must be held in a custodian bank or trust company and be kept separate from the assets of the manager and distributor.

When a fund company goes out of business, another takes over its clients and their pooled assets.

There is also some protection against fraudulent or negligent salespeople. The Canadian Investor Protection Fund covers you if you buy fund units through a member investment dealer and the firm can't deliver your holding. Nova Scotia, Quebec, Ontario and British Columbia have provincial contingency funds that cover clients of independent mutual fund dealers.

Fees

MUTUAL FUND investors face three types of fees:

1. **Management fees** compensate the fund's manager and distributor. Every fund company deducts a percentage of the pool's assets. The deduction ranges from less than 1% for money market funds to 3% or more for international equity funds.

2. **Sales or redemption fees** provide compensation for the broker or other retailer who sells the fund.

3. **Special fees** may be charged in certain cases. Some funds levy a one-time fee to set up an account with them directly. Many charge annual administration fees for RRSP/RRIF accounts. Clients with systematic withdrawal plans might face a service fee for each payment.

Management Fees

Management fees are often expressed as a "management expense ratio" (MER). Say a fund's average assets for the year are $50 million. If the MER is 2%, $1 million is deducted from the pool to cover management expenses and fees. It's an automatic periodic deduction. For example, one-twelfth of the yearly fee might be deducted each month. Investors see no dollars-and-cents billing. The actual amounts are printed in the fund's semi-annual and annual reports. The only explanation of the fee is found in the fund's prospectus — which all investors get but hardly any read. Remember that the management fee is money out of your pocket.

When shopping for a fund, you can easily check the management expense ratios for the prior year. They are listed in the monthly performance tables printed by The Financial Post and The Globe and Mail. MERs on some funds may look higher than they really are if the fund did exceptionally well in the previous year and the managers qualified for a performance bonus.

Management fees are already factored into the returns that appear in those newspaper tables. But the higher the fee, the more a fund must make to yield a given net return in the future. Say two funds each gross 15% this year. The MER is 2% for one and 3% for the other. The return on the lower-cost one works out to about 12.85%. On the other, it's 11.78%.

That may not seem like much of a difference, but the first return is almost 10% higher. Say you invest $20,000 for 10 years. Such a gap would produce a difference of about $6,100. Management fees are the long-term investor's biggest cost of fund ownership. Those fees have risen sharply in recent years. To see the trend, consult your fund's annual or semi-annual report.

You may be able to negotiate a lower management fee if you invest at least $100,000 in one fund. That's one fund, not several funds within a family.

Some salespeople and publications say management fees are higher on "no-load" funds, which carry no sales fee. That is generally not true.

Sales Fees

Sales fees compensate the person and retail firm that sell you the fund. They do not directly benefit the fund manager.

There are three types of sales fee setups:

1. No-load funds charge no sales fee at all, though securities regulations allow them to levy a redemption charge if units are sold within 90 days of purchase. That's rarely done.

2. Front-end funds charge an upfront sales commission, or "load." The rate is negotiable and often ranges from 4% at full-service brokers to 2% at discounters.

3. Back-end funds charge no commission upfront, but collect a redemption fee if units are sold within a few years. These back-end loads are also called deferred acquisition, or deferred sales, charges.

No-load funds are usually sold directly by the fund distributor. A common example would be the funds sold by banks and trust companies. A few independent no-load companies deal directly with the public. Sometimes, brokers who normally sell loaded funds also sell no-loads. Their firms do that because of client demand or because they do investment business with the no-load fund company.

Salespeople often say loaded funds outperform no-loads. That may be true on a case-by-case basis, but the claim does not hold up as a generalization. Many journalists believe no-load investing always saves you money. That's true only if the no-load fund's management fee is lower than the fees on competing loaded funds. If you compare the management expense ratios, you may find little or no difference.

Front-end loads are fees subtracted from the amount you invest. Competition has driven down these fees sharply. They now run 2-4% at most brokerages. At 2%, if you place $5,000, you end up with $4,900 invested in the fund.

Back-end loads are redemption fees. The fund carries no sales fee upfront, so $5,000 gets invested. But you face a fee if you sell within a certain time — up to nine years. That fee may start at 5–6% and decline to zero as each year goes by. Some funds base the figure on the amount originally invested. Some use the market value of the units sold. Some use the lower of the two.

In the latest mutual fund sales wrinkle, a growing number of dealers and individual advisers offer funds in front-load format but with no commission. That's called "zero load." These dealers still make money because of "trailer" fees. A trailer is an annual fee that your adviser gets from the fund company. It's really a deferred commission. All loaded mutual funds pay trailers, but a front-load fund typically carries twice as much trailer as a back-end one carries — about 1% of your account value each year. So a zero-load dealer initially gives up money by waiving the upfront commission, but can do much better over time as your account grows.

For years, investors have preferred back-end funds over front-load ones. Now, zero-load offers the best of both worlds. Your full amount gets invested up front but there's no redemption fee to keep you in the fund.

If you don't buy on a zero-load basis, be aware that the mutual fund return tables you find in newspapers overstate the true returns of loaded funds. That's because they do not factor in the sales or redemption fees. To adjust those returns, assume a $100 investment and use this formula:

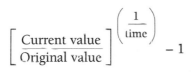

$$\left[\frac{\text{Current value}}{\text{Original value}} \right]^{\left(\frac{1}{\text{time}} \right)} - 1$$

Suppose the table shows a three-year return of 11.1% for AAA fund. The current value will depend on the load structure:

- **Front-end load.** Subtract the initial load from $100 and then compound that amount by the reported return for the period covered. If the load was 4%, we compound $96 at 11.1 % for three years to get $131.65.

- **Back-end load.** If it's levied on the full redemption amount, compound $100 by 11.1% for three years to get $137.13. If the redemption fee at that point is 4%, deduct that amount — $5.49 — to get $131.64.

  If that 4% back-end fee is based only on the initial $100 investment, calculate the amount due — $4 — and deduct that from the $137.13 compounded value to get $133.13.

Divide the current value by the original $100. Raise it to the power of 1 divided by the period covered, in this case three years. Then subtract 1.

Our adjusted returns are 9.6% for the front-end version and the first back-end one, and 10% for the other back-end version.

Choosing a Fund

EVERY PIECE of mutual fund advertising carries a warning that past performance is not indicative of future returns. Unfortunately, the ads are right. Yet virtually every investor and adviser picks funds based on past performance, and standard advice on fund selection is to look for one with a solid long-term record.

Performance figures are readily available. Each month *The Financial Post* and *The Globe and Mail* print tables showing how each fund did over selected periods. Be aware that for periods above one year, figures represent the *average* annual return compounded. One or two excellent or horrible periods can skew the average. Occasionally, these newspapers print returns for each year over the past 10 or 15 years. Or visit the *Globe*'s mutual fund web site at http://www.globefund.com.

There are also computer software packages that contain fund returns. They are sold by Portfolio Analytics Ltd., Southam Business Communications and BellCharts Inc. All are Toronto-based.

Compare a fund's returns to those of its group. Because of its narrow focus, a resource fund is far more risky than a broad-based equity fund. So its return should differ markedly. For each time period, all funds within a given group are customarily ranked by performance and the group is divided into fourths, called "quartiles." Those funds in the first and second quartiles posted above-average returns for that time period. But be aware that reporting services have not yet standardized fund classifications, so one service might assign a fund to a group where it's a second-quartile performer while a different service could compare it to a somewhat different group of funds and give it a third-quartile ranking.

Ideally, you should examine a fund's portfolio to see if it's in line with your objectives and view of the market. But funds release the information only quarterly or semi-annually — with a time lag of at least a month. Portfolio Analytics analyzes fund portfolios, and its findings are reported quarterly in *The Financial Post*. Its information is also used in the computer PalTrak disk.

Standard advice is to read the objectives printed in the fund's prospectus, but they tend to be motherhood statements that are remarkably similar from fund to fund. You're better off checking the financial press for interviews with the fund manager.

"Ethical" funds are becoming very popular. They rule out various investments such as tobacco companies but still have had excellent returns. I still wonder how much of this is just a marketing gimmick.

If you're considering an ethical fund, carefully review its screening standards and its portfolio. For example, the fund might hold stock exchange index units that contain companies that would normally be ruled out. Or there may be shares of banks that lend money to, and invest in, all kinds of companies — including cigarette and arms makers. You might even find companies that are big polluters yet qualify because they have clean-up programs. As well, there may be investments in countries you are not fond of.

Ethical standards vary from person to person, but you'll have to accept the fund's standards. For example, in mid-1998 one ethical fund had a large stake in a TV network that thrives on showing violent U.S. cop shows and sexist sitcoms. I don't find that very ethical. The best way to be an ethical investor is to pass up mutual funds and buy shares of companies that satisfy your criteria directly. To save on commissions and gain diversification, check out dividend reinvestment plans, discussed in chapter 28. Direct investing requires more time and effort, but it's the only way you can really be sure that your money is going where you want it to.

Going with past returns is usually a decent way to select a fund. If a fund has done consistently well, you can reasonably assume it has a system that works. Monthly tables in The Financial Post and The Globe and Mail make it easy to check that; above-average returns are printed in boldface. You need only scan for funds that have every period in bold ink.

The newspaper tables also indicate how volatile each fund is — how much its price moves up and down. Appreciate that funds that shoot up often correct and tumble. If a fund soars 40% one year and falls 20% the next, the total return is 12%. If a fund simply gains 10% each year, the two-year return is 21%. Be aware that the top-10 fund list for each year is often dominated by volatile specialty funds that seldom make it into top-10 lists for multi-year periods.

If you're eyeing a fund with good, steady performance, make sure it's still being run by the manager responsible for the gains. In several cases, winning managers have been lured away by other funds. When you buy into a fund, your most important purchase is its manager's expertise.

If you already own a fund and the manager leaves, you have a few months to decide whether to follow. That's because portfolio strategy doesn't change from day to day.

The ideal fund is one where the investment managers own part of the distributorship. Owners seldom walk.

Salespeople are an excellent source of information about the comings and goings of fund managers. They also have access to a lot of other information about the funds they sell.

But don't follow salespeople blindly. If their employer distributes funds, they may be under pressure to recommend them. Even if the employer claims to be "independent," be careful. In-house funds are a rapidly growing trend that's not always apparent since the funds may carry a different name than the dealer's. For example, advisers at Fortune Financial have shifted a considerable amount of money to Infinity Mutual Funds, a related organization.

Be aware that there is a trend toward consolidation of the financial planning industry. Some companies have been buying up smaller operations. Usually, the smaller firm continues to operate under its old name, but the deal is structured in such a way that the advisers have an incentive to sell the new owner's proprietary funds.

Few, if any, advisers really follow more than a handful of independent fund companies. Those groups compete vigorously for "shelf space." Some pay higher commissions. Most spend fortunes wining and dining advisers, and subsidizing their newsletters, seminars and other marketing efforts. There are even subsidized trips. In 1998 securities regulators imposed a new sales code that sharply limits these practices, but there are still loopholes — and the tough new rules do not apply to segregated funds, which fall under looser insurance regulation.

Also be aware that sales conduct problems are not confined to loaded funds and commissioned independent advisers — that banks also have a problem. It's called "tied selling." Tied selling occurs when a bank requires you to buy its mutual funds, deal with its brokerage arm or move over other business in order to get a loan. That's illegal, but I know it's done because a bank officer who didn't know my background tried pulling it on me. There is a subtle difference between tied selling and "relationship selling," which is legal. Relationship selling is when a bank offers a reduced-rate loan if you do other business with them. In other words, a bank should not look at your other business in deciding whether to grant a loan, but can look at your other business in setting the loan's rate.

Before you buy, ask your salesperson if the fund is experiencing "net redemptions." That means people are pulling money out faster than others are putting it in. Having to keep cash on hand for redemptions limits the fund manager's flexibility. To see for yourself, check several of the most recent monthly newspaper tables. Note the total assets shown on the oldest table. Then see if the assets — when adjusted by the month-over-month performance figure — are trending up or down.

If there's any departure from the trend in performance or assets under management, find out why. The reason may not be negative.

Here's an example of how a good fund can still suffer asset deterioration. For several years the Templeton Growth Fund, an above-average performer, experienced net redemptions. There were two reasons. One was that Templeton's commission structure had not kept up with the times, and salespeople were sending clients elsewhere. The other was concern that John Templeton was getting too old. As it turned out, Sir John had not been actively involved in stock selection for several years, so concerns about his age were groundless.

Don't be afraid to ask questions. In addition to getting a sales commission, your broker or agent will likely receive a "trailer fee" from the fund company every year you're in that fund. Trailers are supposed to compensate the adviser for providing ongoing service. Make sure you get that service.

Tracking Your Fund's Performance

THE MONTHLY performance tables that appear in newspapers are the bible, but also the bane, of mutual fund investors. They are the bible because, for most people, they offer the only cheap and easy way to see how a fund does on a regular basis. They are the bane because they rarely reflect reality — for two reasons.

First, the calculations assume just one investment was made precisely one month, six months, one year, three years, five years and 10 years before the valuation date at the prior month-end. If you invested at any other time, your cost base will be different and so will your return.

Second, as mentioned earlier, these tables do not factor in sales or redemption fees. The shorter the timeframe, the more those fees cut into your return. (The tables do factor in fund management fees.)

Commercially produced computer disks will store your own fund data and calculate returns. There are several on the market for $50–$100. The best deals might be Quicken or Microsoft Money. These kinds of software can handle your budgeting, organize your financial records and track your investments.

Calculating investment returns is much trickier than you might think. Just ask the Beardstown Ladies, an investment club in the U.S. The women sold 800,000 copies of a book that explained how they averaged 23.4% a year from 1984–93. But an audit by an accounting firm discovered a goof in their calculations. Their true return was just 9.1%.

Even if you don't goof, there are several recognized ways to calculate returns. It can easily get quite arcane but, significantly, Canadian mutual fund companies have agreed on a standard method for implementation in 1999. That will clear the way for most, if not all, of them to start reporting a personalized return for each client.

Reducing Your Risk

DCA AND VA are two methods mutual fund investors can use to hedge their risk.

DCA stands for "dollar cost averaging." You invest a fixed amount at regular intervals — for example, $100 on the first day of each month. The best way to do this is to authorize a mutual fund company to tap your bank account for a set amount each month. You then automatically get as many units as that money will buy.

This plan fits nicely with the "pay yourself first" savings concept discussed in chapter 4. It also protects you from the cycle of greed and fear because emotion doesn't enter the picture; you mechanically buy more when the market is low and less when it's high. Note that DCA investors actually benefit from volatile markets. The more the market dips, the more units they can buy at a lower price.

DCA is essentially defensive. Theoretically, you can do far better if you devote enough time and attention to jumping in and out at the right moments. But relatively few people have the time, attention span, discipline or good luck required to buy low and sell high.

DCA also works well for those who lack a wad of money to commit at once, but can spare a bit each month. Most funds require just $50 a pop. Some accept even less.

VA stands for "value averaging." It's ideal for mid- to long-term investing programs like your kids' college education or your RRSP. VA is the brainchild of Michael Edleson, an assistant professor at Harvard Business School. He analyzed DCA as a tool for his own long-term investing and refined it.

While DCA concentrates on the amount going in each month, VA focuses on your progress toward a set goal.

The investment vehicles are an equity fund and a money market fund. Since few fund managers beat the market over the long term, Edleson suggests using an index equity fund that reflects the entire market — not just a portfolio of selected stocks. If you want to try to beat the market, at least use a well-diversified equity fund. The equity and money funds should permit no-fee switching back and forth. To make this method more convenient — especially for an RRSP — set up a monthly DCA plan with cash going right to the money fund. Then transfer it as required.

To get the system going, determine the amount needed at a future date — perhaps $100,000 in today's money on retirement day in 20 years. Next, make assumptions for your investment return and inflation. Then, using a computer, plot a "value path."

The value path shows what your account should be worth each month to be on track. There are three components: (1) the plan's starting value, increased by your assumed return for the period; (2) your scheduled deposit, adjusted for inflation; and (3) growth on the new deposit.

At each investment date — monthly, quarterly or annually — compare the account's actual value to the value path. If the equity fund is higher than the projected value, redeem enough units to bring the two in line. Park the cash in your money fund. If the equity fund is below target, tap the money fund and/or inject new cash to buy enough units to put it back on track.

This system forces you to sell into rallies and reserve cash for the inevitable downturn. VA is "buy low, sell high" while DCA is "buy low, buy less high." Markets tend to overreact, heading both up and down. VA and DCA take advantage of this phenomenon by mechanically buying more when the market has fallen too far on the downside. But VA also takes advantage when the market rises too much because it forces you to take profits when you get ahead of your plan. DCA does not.

Edleson ran hundreds of tests using U.S. stock market data from 1926 to 1991 and found VA beat DCA more than 90% of the time.

Both systems are essentially defensive. You do not maximize your returns. But you do free yourself from worry about ups and downs.

Table 29.1 shows a sample spreadsheet and Edleson's formulas for plotting the value path. You fill in the "Inputs" section. The computer calculates the results in the "Work Area" and plugs them into the "Value Path," which shows your plan's monthly target value.

Those who build their own models will find these value points a bit high at first and then a bit low in the middle years. Edleson generalized his formulas so people could use them with calculators. Don't — it's incredibly tedious.

Edleson explains VA and stock market risk in *Value Averaging: The Safe and Easy Strategy for Higher Investment Returns.* The book, almost impossible to find in Canada, is published by Chicago's International Publishing Corp.

By the way, this concept is a simplified version of how defined-benefit pension plans work. Every so often an actuary calculates how much money the plan should have to meet projected liabilities, and the fund is adjusted accordingly.

How Mutual Funds Are Taxed

IT'S EASY to get confused about the tax rules for mutual funds.

First, the rules for funds held in RRSPs and RRIFs are simple. There are no tax considerations until the RRSP/RRIF money is withdrawn.

Then it's fully taxed as ordinary income.

Confusion hits when you use a mutual fund for non-registered investing. "Dividends" are not necessarily dividends and could end up being taxed at three different rates. Dividends that are dividends may not qualify for the dividend tax credit. You can have taxable capital gains even if you didn't sell during the year. And you can owe tax even though you never saw any cash.

What's going on?

During the year, mutual funds trade securities to score capital gains. They also receive dividends on shares they own, and collect interest on cash and bonds they hold. Those are the fund's internal earnings. The funds then pass them on to unitholders. That way, the unitholders — not the fund — are taxed on these earnings.

Many funds call this payout a "dividend." This is a misnomer. "Distribution" is a more appropriate term. While the distribution is paid as a single amount — say 76 cents per unit — it may have several components: capital gains, interest, Canadian corporate dividends that are eligible for the dividend tax credit and foreign corporate dividends that are not. The fund company itemizes these components on a T3 or T5 tax slip due in February.

Each component carries whatever tax breaks would apply had you earned it directly. The capital gains distribution is taxable for you at the capital gains rate and is eligible for the capital gains exemption credits discussed in chapter 7. If you received Canadian-source dividends, you can claim the dividend tax credit.

Interest and foreign dividends are fully taxed in your hands. The T3 or T5 may show that foreign governments withheld tax from your fund's foreign earnings. You can claim a credit for that on your tax return. Accountants say many people fail to claim that credit.

Most fund investors have distributions automatically reinvested. Reinvested distributions don't pass through your hands, but you're still taxed on them. In Revenue Canada's eyes, you got the money and immediately used it to buy new units. It is important to keep track of reinvestments because they increase the tax cost that determines the capital gain or loss when you ultimately redeem your units.

Periodic mutual fund purchases — whether direct or through reinvestment — fall under Revenue Canada's "identical property" rules for capital gains and losses. Your tax cost is averaged with each purchase.

Say you buy 100 units at $10, another 100 at $11 and still another at $12. The average unit cost is then $11. Say you sell 100 units at $13. You can't choose which 100 units were sold; your taxable capital gain is based on the spread between the $13 sale price and $11 average cost.

When a partial sale occurs, units retained keep their pre-sale cost base and the averaging resumes for new purchases. Some fund companies track that for you. If yours doesn't, keep your own running tally. It's explained very well in Revenue Canada's free capital gains tax guide. If you don't keep track, you'll face a tedious exercise — or pay more tax than required — after you redeem units.

Think twice about purchasing a mutual fund just before December 31 or some other distribution date. Say the $10 unit value includes $1 of capital gains scored by the fund. You'll pay $10 per unit and shortly thereafter receive the $1 distribution. When that money is paid out, the fund's unit value will fall to $9, so you'll have $9 in the fund and $1 in your hand. But you won't be even since you'll owe tax on that $1 distribution unless the fund is held in an RRSP or RRIF.

Management fees are not directly tax-deductible for you as an investment counsel fee. You get the benefit indirectly when the fund deducts those fees from its taxable income. That portion stays invested instead of being paid to you as a taxable distribution.

Labor-Sponsored Funds

VENTURE CAPITAL funds sponsored by labor unions may look appealing because a 15% tax credit saves you $750 in federal income tax on a $5,000 investment. The provinces, except Alberta and Newfoundland, pay matching credits.

These funds are supposed to invest in companies whose shares do not trade openly. So far, they've been slow to do that. A parliamentary committee has expressed concern and the Ontario government has retroactively imposed stiff investment quotas with heavy penalties. As the funds invest, the risk of losing money goes up. As well, high management fees eat into your account. The tax credits cushion you but new buyers must now stay in eight years to keep the tax break.

Take reported returns with a grain of salt. Labor funds are not as tightly regulated as mutual funds and their valuation methods are not standardized.

Promoters hype the tax savings by adding in the RRSP deduction, but that's due on any RRSP investment. Meanwhile, salespeople earn higher commissions from these funds than real mutual funds.

If you buy a labor fund, hedge your risk by putting the tax credits in a GIC or quality mutual fund.

In August 1998, Ottawa reversed part of a 1996 cutback on labor-fund tax breaks, and provincial governments were expected to follow suit.

Officials raised to $5,000 the maximum yearly investment that qualifies for the 15% federal tax credit. They also said they will scrap a rule that made labor-fund investors who sell their shares wait up to three years before they can reinvest and claim new tax credits.

Ottawa will also give labor-fund investors a $3 increase in their RRSP foreign content limit for every $1 held in a labor fund. That's the same break given to people who invest directly in shares of small privately held corporations.

Here's one idea for a parent: Put $5,000 of RRSP money into a labor fund and put the $15,000 of extra foreign content into a well-run U.S. or international mutual fund. Meanwhile, the labor fund purchase will generate a $2,000 tax credit outside the RRSP. Contribute that to a Registered Education Savings Plan for your child in order to qualify for the new $400 federal RESP grant.

TABLE 29.1: **Value Averaging Spreadsheet**

	A	B	C	
1	INPUTS:			KEY FORMULAS (Lotus 1-2-3)
2				
3	GOAL IN TODAY'S $:	100,000		Cell Formula
4	VALUE NOW $:	6,500		
5	YEARS TO GO:	20.00		B11 B3*((1+B7)^B5)
6	ANNUAL RETURN:	10.00%		
7	ANNUAL INFLATION:	5.00%		B12 B5*12
8				
9	WORK AREA:			B13 ((1+B6)^(1/12))-1
10				
11	Future value $:	265,330		B14 ((1+B7)^(1/12))-1
12	Months to go:	240.00		
13	Monthly return:	0.80%		B15 @AVG(B13..B14)
14	Monthly inflation:	0.41%		
15	R:	0.60%		B16 B12/(1-(1+B15)^B12*B4/B11)
16	T:	267.7		
17	t:	27.7		B17 B16-B12
18	C:	$198.51		
19				B18 B11/(B16*(1+B15)^B16)
20	VALUE PATH:			
21				B24 A24+$B$17
22	Months from now	Index #	Value points	
23				C24 $B$18*B24*(1+$B$15)^B24
24	0	27.7	6,500	+
25	1	28.7	6,775	In this case, we're starting with $6,500. After one
26	2	29.7	7,053	month the value path indicates the account should be
27	3	30.7	7,334	worth $6,775. After three months the equity fund should
28	4	31.7	7,619	be worth $7,334. If it's really worth $8,334, redeem
29	5	32.7	7,906	$1,000 worth of units and park the money in the money
:	:	:	:	market fund. If it's worth $6,334, add $1,000 to the
:	:	:	:	equity fund.
:	:	:	:	
v	v	v	v	
266	240	267.7	265,330	

30

Shelter from a Tax?

PREVIOUS CHAPTERS HAVE ALREADY DEALT with several tax shelters: RRSP/RRIFs, capital gains investing, the tax-free principal residence, universal life insurance and labor-sponsored investment funds. This chapter will focus on limited partnerships and income trusts.

Limited partnerships are often called "tax shelters," but they're really a way for a company to sell its tax losses. In the past, this arrangement was commonly associated with real estate. Now, hot LPs focus on energy development and films — high-risk projects where the startup cost is large and payback takes a long time.

Business expenses are tax-deductible, but that's meaningful in the current year only if the business makes more than it spends. A limited partnership lets a new business raise money from those otherwise unusable tax deductions. LPs raise money from individuals in exchange for two forms of return — potential future gains from the project itself, plus the tax deductions the project's promoter can't use now because costs are high and revenue is low or non-existent.

Limited partners are only financial backers; they are not actively involved in the project.

These deals boomed in the 1970s and 1980s. But they've been largely undermined. First, Ottawa really tightened up on the tax rules. In particular, "at-risk" rules limit the investor's tax deductions to the actual investment — the amount he or she stands to lose if the underlying project fails. Second, the go-go nature of the '80s masked a lot of poorly conceived and implemented projects overloaded with high fees. Investors lost a ton of money as recession-depressed resource prices plummeted and an overbuilt real estate market plunged. Many, perhaps most LPs, ended up costing investors far more than the tax benefits they gained.

Limited partnerships are still around, but there are not as many of them. Here are some points to ponder before investing in one:

- Does the investment make sense as a business project? If there were no tax benefits, would you still buy into it?

  Real estate limited partnerships have three sources of income: rent, proceeds from the final sale, and the tax breaks. Check the projections in the offering memorandum. Clearly, the rent stream is most important — and a key consideration in whether Revenue Canada challenges you. There must be a reasonable expectation of profit without counting on capital appreciation.

  Film limited partnerships often finance TV productions. Television is a very risky medium. Promoters frequently take the edge off by including a revenue guarantee backed by a chartered bank, perhaps secured by GICs.

- How solid and experienced is the general partner? The general partner is the organization that put the project together and bears responsibility for running it. Will the general partner be involved on an ongoing basis?

- What stage is the project at? If it hasn't been built or developed, you run the risk that it never will be — or will be done poorly. If it has been finished, is it currently functioning as a business? How well?

- Is the partnership buying a property or contract already owned by the promoter? Is the price unduly inflated? Ideally, it should be no more than 12-20% above the promoter's acquisition cost.

- Is there a cash flow guarantee? Who guarantees it? Is it secured? Odds are the general partner is a corporation without any assets.

- What happens if something goes wrong? Under what circumstances would you have to kick in more cash? If others default on their capital calls, are their interests forfeited to the general partner or divided among all syndicate members?

- How liquid is your investment? Odds are there is no secondary market for your share, so plan to hold for five to 10 years. If the project is a condominium, does the agreement give you the right to exchange your partnership unit for an actual suite that you could then sell? Ideally, these exchange rights are staggered over several years. If not, everyone could sell at once, glutting the market.

Clearly, limited partnerships are complex. They often involve major financial commitments — perhaps $50,000 in cash plus a note for another $100,000 or so. You're just inviting trouble if you buy one without independent review by an accountant or experienced financial planner. Remember that the investment firm recommending the deal is probably getting a good-sized commission or fee — at least 10% of the total amount raised, according to one rule-of-thumb.

Don't expect much sympathy from regulators if a deal goes sour. These deals are often sold as "private placements." That means the buyers are expected to have a considerable level of financial sophistication.

The most reliable LPs have been those created by mutual fund companies to raise money for sales commissions. Due to tax rule changes there are no new ones, but existing mutual fund LPs are available on the secondary market and some even trade on the Toronto Stock Exchange. These have run their course as tax shelters and now offer only attractive, but fully taxed, income.

Income Trusts

THESE SECURITIES, also called royalty trusts, took off in the mid-1990s because they met two needs. First, they offered a way for companies to sell mature assets or raise money from new sources. Second, they offered income-oriented investors high tax-advantaged yields.

Basically, a trust is created and raises money from the public. That money is used to buy one or more business assets. Each trust investor then owns a small bit of those assets. There are trusts for many industries, including oil and gas wells and pipelines, shipping terminals, office buildings and hotels, coal and iron ore mines, timber lands and electrical generation. The trust arranges for the continued operation of these assets and distributes most of the income to its investors.

These trusts provide tax-advantaged income, not direct deductions like LPs do. You face no tax today on part of each trust distribution because tax rules for that particular type of business allow a certain amount of income to be treated as a tax-free return of capital. This varies among industries. But as a return of capital, tax-free distributions reduce your adjusted cost base and thereby increase your capital gain or reduce your capital loss when you actually sell the holding — or when the trust is wound up if it has a pre-set life. So you may be getting only tax deferral, not absolute savings.

Although these deals are aimed at income-oriented investors, they are really more like equity investments such as common shares. That's because your income will depend on how well the underlying business is run and on the market price for the goods or services it produces. Unlike bonds, trust distributions are not fixed and there is no maturity date or principal amount to be repaid.

Here's a very important point to consider: Is the trust based on a depleting asset such as a mine or a continuing asset such as an office building? If the trust owns a depleting asset, your income will vanish as the resource runs out — unless the trust acquires more properties.

Also look into who runs the underlying business — the trust or a hired management company that may well be related to the trust's creator. This is a big issue for real estate investment trusts. Internal management — by the trust itself — presents less risk of conflict of interest.

As well, check out the trust's future business strategy. Will it just run the current asset, buy more assets that already exist or get into the more risky business of developing new assets?

Tax Wrinkles

CONSULT A tax adviser before making substantial limited partnership investments. The projected tax losses may be so high that you'll face problems with the alternative minimum tax.

Also, tax projections in LP or trust explanatory material assume the investor is a top-bracket taxpayer. The projected tax savings are less valuable for those in lower brackets.

31

Family Ties

ROMANCE: WHAT A WONDERFUL WORD! Just saying it brings a smile to your face. Try it. Say "romance." See what I mean? This chapter looks at love — or at least some of its financial aspects.

Marriage Contracts and Cohabitation Agreements

HOW WONDERFUL it would be if every couple lived happily ever after. But more than a third don't — and that's just the count among legally married couples. Throw in all the common-law couples who throw in the towel and you'll have quite a fair segment of the population.

Increasingly, financial advisers urge couples to sit down at the start of the relationship and work out a contingency plan for dividing the assets if the partnership ends. That means a marriage contract for those tying the knot and a cohabitation agreement for those who choose to live common-law.

This planning may not be a worry for the typical young couple just starting out with little in the way of property — unless one spouse has a professional licence or other asset that may become lucrative a few years down the road. It certainly should be a concern for those who do own tangible property, especially a house or shares in a family business. Each province has family laws that govern what happens to a couple's assets if they split up. The laws vary widely, but the underlying premise is that marriage is a financial as well as a social partnership. A common-law relationship may or may not be a financial partnership. The key point is that if you and your loved one don't consider that at the start of your relationship, you'll face a potentially unfair forced legal division at the end (if it should come to that). Even worse, there could be years of court action costing a fortune. Invariably, family lawyers are the only winners when parting couples dig in their heels.

By drafting an agreement upfront, the two of you can devise your own settlement — overriding those parts of the law that don't fit your situation. But for the agreement to be valid, each person must make full financial disclosure and get independent legal advice. Unfortunately, lawyers have found those two requirements can be enough to scuttle planned marriages. I find it amazing that a person is willing to share his or her life, but no financial details.

Appreciate that family law is a specialized area, so consult a lawyer who's well-versed in it, especially if there is anything out of the ordinary about your relationship.

Before getting to the legalisms, work out these points yourselves:

- What debts does each person have? When will they be paid off? Will that be with individual or joint money? If one spouse currently pays alimony and/or child support, how will that be covered during the new marriage?

- What kind of lifestyle do the two of you anticipate? Work out now what's considered a necessity and what's a luxury. Where do you plan to live? If there are children, will both spouses continue to work? Whose career takes precedence if one spouse faces a transfer?

- Who will pay family bills? Will you pool all earnings? Some couples contribute to a family fund for common expenses like shelter, but keep individual control of the rest of their money. If you do that, will family fund contributions be equal or a percentage of each person's earnings? Some couples just pay bills based on a preset division. For example, one covers the rent while the other buys the food.

If the two of you can't agree on those issues, there's no point in paying lawyers to draft a formal agreement. There may not even be any point in continuing your relationship.

Issues to discuss with your lawyers include:

- Precisely what do each of you own? Even if you feel a legal agreement now will spoil the romance, at least itemize your net worth, assemble documentation and tuck it away. Years later you could be very grateful you took the trouble. Provincial law may exclude that wealth from equalization — that's asset-splitting — if you can prove it was yours before the marriage. Otherwise, your spouse could end up with half.

    Houses are particularly tricky. In some provinces, unless there's an agreement to the contrary, the value of the matrimonial home gets split

50-50 on breakup — even if one spouse owned it outright before the wedding.

If one or both spouses hold business or partnership interests, definitely get legal advice. Take the case of an Ontario woman who, on her wedding day, held $100,000 worth of common shares in her parents' business. By the time of her divorce 10 years later, those shares had increased in value by $900,000. Under provincial law her estranged husband was entitled to half — even though he had had no involvement with the business. Had this woman seen a lawyer before her wedding, there would have been several ways to keep much or all of that growth out of the equalization pot.

Many professional firms now require prospective partners to have agreements in which their spouses sign away any right to the partnership interest. That keeps the firm from getting embroiled in a bitter separation dispute and having their financial data made public as evidence. Often, lawyers arrange "asset trading" in which property of equivalent value — such as full title to a house — goes to the spouse who gives up his or her stake in the business.

- Are you expecting a sizable gift, inheritance or insurance payout? Such payments received during a marriage are normally not subject to division on breakup. But the earnings on that money might be, unless the donor specifies that the earnings are not to be shared. You may also have to be able to trace the earnings on the money, so it's best to segregate it from other funds. Many people err in using this cash to pay off mortgages, buy cars or cover other big-ticket purchases. Later, if there's no agreement overriding family law, they're chagrined to learn the common property must be split 50-50 even though their money paid for most of it. Preventive legal advice is always cheaper than fighting after the fact.

- Who will hold title to assets acquired during the marriage? That's particularly important for common-law couples, who may not have the protection of family law equalization.

- What support obligations would there be on breakup? Family law clearly makes formally married people responsible for each other, unless they agree otherwise. Although common-law spouses are generally not covered, courts have required support payments in some cases.

  Issues such as pension credits and the rights of survivors to be involved in administering an estate may be the least of romantic thoughts, but can become a huge concern when a long-term relationship ends.

- Some people include sections governing the education and religious training of children not yet born. Issues of child custody and access after breakup are addressed in a separation agreement at the time of a marital split, not in the upfront marriage contract or cohabitation agreement.

The arrangement need not override all family law rules. Perhaps the two of you simply want to remove a house or business interest from required equalization. Some couples exclude personal investments and pension credits. Some go for a "staggered" setup, where equalization rights are phased in as the years go by.

Have the agreement reviewed after moving from one province to another. It may not comply with the new province's law. Some agreements also provide for automatic renegotiation on the birth of a child, upon a major career development or at a pre-set date.

Separation and Divorce

WHEN THEIR marriage breaks up, most people probably consult a family lawyer. Tax advisers can also be helpful. This section looks at breakups from a tax perspective.

Tax-planning advice can be critical if one of the spouses owns a business or significant capital investments such as real estate or stocks. In dividing assets, the transferred holdings can be valued at either their original cost or fair market value.

If the transfer is done at cost, no tax applies. But there's a big wrinkle. If the recipient spouse sells the asset before the divorce is finalized, Revenue Canada's attribution rules hold the other spouse responsible for the full tax bill, since the couple was still technically married. If the asset is sold after the divorce, the recipient spouse would be stuck with the full tax bill.

If the transfer is done at fair market value, the transferor spouse will be taxed that year on any accrued gain, but that cost could be factored into the settlement so both spouses end up sharing the tax bill as well as the asset. That's a lot fairer.

What about support payments?

For decades, alimony and child support was generally tax-deductible for the spouse who wrote the cheque and taxable for the one who received it. That's still true for alimony but not necessarily for child support.

First, alimony. To be deductible, payments must be made periodically under a court order or written agreement. They can begin before being put in writing, but the papers must be in place by the end of the next year. The spouses must live apart for the rest of the year the payments begin. If they move back together before year-end, the payments will not be deductible.

The payor can't attach any strings but the deductible allowance can include direct payments to others for certain expenses such as shelter.

A lump sum payment is neither tax-deductible for the payor nor taxable for the recipient. The same goes for periodic payments beyond those set in the settlement or court order.

If you receive taxable support, the money counts as "earned income" in calculating your RRSP contribution limit. So some of it can be tax-sheltered.

The child support rules were changed by the 1996 federal budget. Agreements signed before May 1, 1997 stay under the old rules; payments are tax-deductible for the payor and taxable for the recipient. That's if the agreement has not been changed since April 30, 1997. If it has, the new rules apply.

Under the new rules, child support is neither tax-deductible for the payor nor taxable for the recipient. There are also standard amounts based on the average cost of raising a child in each province and the payor's gross income. Extra payments are allowed for special child-care, medical, educational or recreation expenses. Courts can also raise or reduce payments for "undue hardship."

If you're due support, you have a vested interest in your former mate's health. Ask about including life and disability insurance in the settlement. Make sure the policies can't be cancelled or the beneficiary changed.

Parenthood

HOW MUCH does it cost to raise a child? A lot. Any parent can tell you that. But staff in the home economics section of Manitoba's agriculture ministry can tell you right down to the penny.

Each fall they compile a list of "basic goods and services necessary to maintain physical and social well-being." Then they go to popular stores to price that list. They seek well-made items that offer "good value." They keep fads and fashions in mind, but do not go for costly designer labels.

The survey results — shown in table 31.1 at the end of this chapter — generally reflect prices in Winnipeg. Costs for certain categories would no doubt be higher in larger cities like Toronto, Montreal and Vancouver. When I printed these results in *The Financial Post*, they set off big conversations and even disputes. Some people find the costs too low, some too high.

Onalee Nagler, who supervised the survey before retiring, used the data in raising her own daughter, Lara. For example, Lara was responsible for buying her own clothes with a budget based on the survey. Onalee found Lara dressed "competitively with her peers" but was much more careful about what she bought. By the time Lara entered university she was well-versed in budgeting and personal money management.

Note that:

- Having two children does not double the cost, since some of the expenses are based on family units and other purchases can be shared or reused.

- The survey does not include the cost of hockey or other expensive pursuits. Nor does it provide any savings for postsecondary education.

- The categories are explained in notes that accompany table 31.1.

Teach Your Children Well

IN 1987, an aggravated mother wrote to *The Washington Post*, urging its readers to "just say no" to their children's demands for luxury goods. Her breaking point came while lining up to buy her teenaged daughter a US$150 sweater.

I don't have kids, so I don't watch Saturday morning cartoons. But I'm told that time slot has the television schedule's highest concentration of commercials. When consumption dominates so much of society, how do you teach children the value of money? Start with an allowance as early as age 5, suggests Chris Snyder, a veteran Toronto financial planner and devoted family man. But don't just fork over cash:

- Before setting the amount, sit down with the child and work out guidelines for what the money should cover. Don't dictate what to buy, but agree on the areas so the child appreciates that he or she will have to budget.

- Base the allowance amount on the expenses covered, not what other children get.

- Don't tie the allowance to routine chores. First of all, washing dishes and making beds are a part of family life. Second, if the chores are not done, you face the prospect of having to hold back money meant for daily living expenses. That's tough.

  Do pay the kids for jobs you would pay to have done by others — for example, cutting the lawn, painting the house or cleaning out the garage.

- Kids value money more when it's their own. When they run short, give them a loan — not a grant. Insist that it be paid back.

Teach children about the fundamental economic concepts of "marginal utility" and "opportunity cost," suggests Gary Rabbior, head of the Toronto-based Canadian Foundation for Economic Education and author of a school workbook called *Money and Youth*.

Marginal utility simply asks: "How much value am I getting for this item?" Opportunity cost asks: "What do I sacrifice by using money one way instead of another?"

"If we teach kids to always consider those two questions, we'll at least teach them to pause and think instead of just responding to others," says Rabbior. "Most of the kids I teach have never really had any instruction on how to make an effective decision with all its trade-offs."

Here are some activity suggestions from Chris Snyder:

For ages 6-9:

- Go to an auction and explain the workings of supply and demand.

- Teach comparison shopping at the supermarket.

- Explain how banks work — not just how they take in money, but also what they do with it. Most banks have special accounts for children and booklets that explain the banking business.

For ages 10-12:

- Discuss the effectiveness of advertising.

- Use energy conservation to teach the value of saving money. Let the kids monitor your hydro bills and look for ways to reduce consumption. (Isn't every parent's refrain: "How many times have I told you to turn off the light when you leave a room?")

- If you have a GIC or term deposit maturing, let your child shop by phone for the best rates.

For teenagers:

- Have your child research the family's next major purchase. (Maybe ask for a verbal businesslike presentation.)

- Discuss all entries on a pay slip, especially the deductions.

- Go through a tax return, explaining how much tax is paid and how it is used. (Try not to be too cynical.)

If you would like to interest your young child in investing, buy him or her a few shares of a company that's popular with kids. Irwin Toy Ltd. is one of the most popular stocks among those who buy just one share. The company has a special program for its child shareholders and lets them play with toys at its annual meeting.

Other popular picks are McDonald's Corp., Walt Disney Co., Toys "R" Us Inc., Fisher-Price Corp. and Hasbro Inc.

Older kids might appreciate a share or two of movie theatre chain Cineplex Odeon Corp., or Nike Inc., Apple Computer Inc., Microsoft Corp. or The Gap Inc.

Sending Baby to College

THEY'RE HARD to miss. In doctor's offices, hospital waiting areas and baby furniture stores, you often see brochures exhorting parents to save for their children's education.

Virtually every parent wants his or her child to go to university or college. And that's getting very expensive. After decades of being kept artificially low, tuition and other fees are now greatly outrunning the rate of inflation.

So does this mean you should sign up for a Registered Education Savings Plan while the little one is still in diapers? Let's consider the RESP and some alternatives.

The RESP

Contributions can be made over 21 years. The annual limit is $4,000 per beneficiary, with a lifetime cap of $42,000. That's the limit per beneficiary, no matter how many contributors there are. The plan can run 25 years. You can set up an individual plan with just one beneficiary, or a "family plan" with several beneficiaries related to you by blood or adoption. Godparents cannot set up family plans because there is no blood or adoption relationship.

Contributions are not tax-deductible, but there are two significant tax breaks. Compounding earnings are not taxed until the money is withdrawn. Then, the earnings are taxable for the student — not you. Students usually owe little or no tax.

The 1998 federal budget added a huge incentive, the Canada Education Savings Grant. Ottawa will pay a 20% grant on RESP contributions of up to $2,000 a year. The maximum $400 grant applies to contributions for children under 18 and will be paid directly to the plan. It's up to the RESP trustee to apply for it.

Over 18 years, the new grants can total up to $7,200 per child — plus investment income. If the $400 is invested at the start of each year and averages 8%, the grants will produce $16,179 in extra savings. If the child does not pursue post-secondary education, the grant must be repaid but the plan keeps the earnings. Grants are transferable among children in family RESPs but still face the $7,200 per child limit.

There's a carry-forward if you don't contribute $2,000. For example, you might put in $1,000 one year and catch up later by putting in $3,000. But you still face the annual contribution limit of $4,000. To get a grant for a 16- or 17-year-old, the plan must pre-date the child's 16th birthday, and there must have been contributions of at least $2,000 in total or at least $100 in each of any four years.

Why not use your RRSP tax refund for RESP contributions? Thanks to the grant, that would likely yield more than using the refund to pay down your mortgage. The monthly federal Child Tax Benefit that many families get is another source. That money can be invested in the child's name even outside an RESP, so using it for the plan provides no special tax break. But you would benefit from the federal grant.

What if the child does not pursue post-secondary education and there is no other eligible beneficiary? Before 1997, you got back your capital but forfeited all earnings. But then there was a major change. Now — if the plan is at least 10 years old and the beneficiary is at least 21 — you have two ways to get the earnings:

1   You can transfer up to $50,000 of RESP earnings to your RRSP in lieu of normal RRSP contributions. That can be spread over two years. You'll likely know by age 18 if the child or any siblings can use the RESP. You could then halt your own RRSP deposits and stockpile contribution room in anticipation of the RESP transfer during the plan's 24th and 25th years. Although you'll get the same tax-sheltered growth, you won't get full value for your RRSP deductions if the huge transfers push you into a very low marginal tax rate.

2   You can take out RESP earnings not covered by the RRSP transfer as fully taxed income, less a 20% penalty. That penalty may seem steep, but you'll still likely win, thanks to years of tax-sheltered compounding.

There are two types of RESPs: pooled plans and self-directed plans. Pooled plans date back to the 1960 launch of the Canadian Scholarship Trust Foundation. Other pooled plans include University Scholarships of Canada, Heritage Scholarship Trust and Children's Education Trust of Canada. Although advertised as non-profit funds, these plans are all tied to profit-making distributors.

Pooled plans gather money from many families — usually by automatic monthly deposit — and invest it in mortgages and deposits, both insured. Your child belongs to the pool for his or her age. The capital you put in — minus fees — is normally paid back when the child is 18, ostensibly for use for the first year of university or college. Earnings are then distributed as the child moves through school.

The traditional pools are set up to fund four years of study. Generally, children who do less forfeit earnings, which go to the others. That's a "tontine." Promoters say 75-85% do get "scholarships" but they exclude those who quit the pool early on and those who start college but then quit. The pools offer newer, flexible options based on Revenue Canada's minimal study requirements. Those options eliminate forfeiture risk, but get no tontine benefit.

You'll find the newer self-directed RESPs at mutual fund companies, financial institutions and investment dealers. The fee setups are more straightforward. You also get control over how the money is invested. Depending on your financial acumen, that can be good or bad. Timing withdrawals is up to you and your child.

Both types of plans must detail their terms and conditions in a prospectus, a booklet filed with securities regulators. Don't sign anything until you've read it — especially if considering a pooled plan with a long-term contractual commitment. These plans are complex, and unhappy clients often claim salespeople glossed over or misrepresented key points.

Remember that RESPs are long-term commitments. Here are some points to check. Have the salesperson show you the applicable section of the contract or prospectus. Get verbal answers confirmed in writing.

- Is there a setup and/or enrolment fee? Pooled plans generally draw enrolment fees from deposits during the first two years. The amount is limited by law to $200 per unit. Each child's plan normally holds several units.

- Is there a cooling-off period? For pooled plans, you get 60 days to back out at no cost. How much would it cost to cancel the plan after that? You could lose all or most of what you put in during the first two years.

- How many periodic deposits can you miss before the plan is cancelled?

- If there is an annual administration fee, can you pay it yourself, not from the plan? With annual contributions capped at $4,000, yearly fees of $25-$50 can really sap a plan's growth.

- If you buy mutual fund units and if the fund has a back-end load, how long does it take to decline to zero? Is there a fee for switching from one fund to another? If so, don't buy. Most fund companies now offer no-fee switching. Chapter 29 discusses mutual fund fees and terminology.

- What's the plan's management fee? That's the money skimmed off each year for operating expenses.

- If your child does not pursue postsecondary education, what's the last date for changing beneficiaries? That might be as early as age 10 or run right up to university or college. Must the new beneficiary be a family member?

- What earnings are lost if the child does less than four years of study? Many salespeople say Revenue Canada only requires three weeks of study, but tax officials say the recipient must also have full-time status in a program that qualifies for the education tax credit. Three weeks normally isn't enough.

- What happens if the child takes time off between high school and college, or once in a postsecondary program? There may be a grace period of just one year.

- When will the first payment be made to the student? It may not be until the second year of school. Pooled plans are set up so the first year is covered by capital return at age 18. But if you pass up monthly deposits and prefund the plan with lump-sum $1,500 payments in the first two years, the capital return at 18 would be just $3,000. Pre-funding requires far less capital than monthly deposits since more money goes to work sooner earning compound growth.

- Are payouts made in set scheduled amounts or can the student take any amount any time?

Check the assumptions if the salesperson offers a payout projection. Pooled-plan RESPs from a few years ago look very good because they enjoyed high interest rates. Also, there used to be tighter rules on beneficiary changes. Since it was harder to change beneficiaries, forfeitures left eligible children with more to share.

Some people — often grandparents — used to fund RESPs with a lump-sum payment of $30,000 or so. That's no longer allowed, but a lump sum could be used to buy a term-certain annuity that would generate money for a yearly contribution within the $4,000 limit.

Here are some RESP alternatives. Several can be combined, but none qualify for CESG grants.

In-Trust Account

An equity mutual fund (discussed in chapter 29) can tax-shelter growth, like the RESP but with less complexity.

Tax attribution rules do not apply to capital gains earned by minors, so you can give your child money through on account opened "in trust" for him or her and have its gains taxed in his or her hands. The child can earn about $8,600 in tax-free capital gains each year, thanks to the basic personal credit. You will face tax on yearly interest or dividends paid by the fund on units bought with your money, but those amounts are usually small.

Technically, under tax rules, you can't control this money or reclaim it. You and your spouse can write an agreement with one spouse named as the "settlor" who provides the money and the other as the trustee who controls it, ideally with an alternate trustee named in case of death or other mishap. The account should be labelled "Mary Doe in trust for Jane Doe." When all this is put in writing, the settlor can state how and when the child gets the money. Otherwise, the child could drain the account at age 18. The best, though costly, route is for a lawyer to draft a formal trust covering all your kids.

Gradually shift from equities to interest vehicles such as GICs as the child moves through high school. You then ensure the fund will be intact for use during university.

Strip Bonds

Strip bonds are discussed in chapter 25. It would be nice if parents of a newborn could just buy a few strips that mature as the child moves through university. You would then know today just how much there will be down the road.

You could do that with an RESP at an investment dealer. Otherwise, if you put up the cash, Revenue Canada's attribution rules hold you taxable for the yearly growth. And tax would be due each year, even though no payment is received until the bond matures.

There is, however, an opportunity for parents who have relatives outside Canada. I don't travel in wealthy circles, but from what I've seen it's not uncommon for a grandparent in the United States, Europe or Asia to send $5,000 or $10,000 for a newborn's education.

Canada's attribution rules don't apply to foreigners, so that money could be used to buy strips in the child's name. It's best if the grandparent makes out the cheque to the parent "in trust" for the child and attaches a letter directing that it be invested for the child's use. Keep that letter and a photocopy of the cheque as a paper trail. Then open a brokerage account in the child's name and buy the strips. The yearly growth would be taxable for the child, but it would take years to reach the point where any tax would actually have to be paid. The same applies to money from a family friend or distant relative in Canada, but not a Canadian grandparent.

A broker told me this is done all the time. But he warned that most investment dealers now levy fees on inactive accounts. To beat that, he suggested putting some of the money into an international mutual fund. The fund's annual distribution — which you can have reinvested automatically — should be enough to keep the account "active." Check that with your own broker.

Universal Life Insurance

Many insurance agents push universal life insurance policies (discussed in chapter 14) as an RESP alternative. These setups tie a life insurance policy on your child to an investment fund that offers the RESP's tax-sheltered growth without its restrictions.

Your agent may produce a very attractive projection. Be skeptical if it's based on high interest rates or assumes use of equity funds. Ask how long the interest rate is guaranteed. Is that rate paid on all money, or must periodic deposits build to a certain level? What interest is earned in the meantime?

Ask for the true return after the "pure insurance cost" is applied. That cost is deducted before your money is invested. It represents the cost of the insurance itself, a policy administration fee and any provincial tax.

Ask if the insurance cost will rise each year or every few years. Is that on a fixed scale or a variable one? Will you be paying for an increasing death benefit? Given that hardly any children need life insurance at all, why boost coverage each year?

Withdrawal or cancellation fees can be onerous. One plan I saw keeps 100% for the first two years. That tapers to 40% in the fifth year, after which no fee is due.

Many insurance agents urge parents to use their child tax benefit money for these plans. But as we've seen, this "baby bonus" can already grow tax-free for many years if invested in trust for the child or qualify for a federal CESG grant if put into an RESP; you don't need the cost and complications of universal life insurance.

The agent will probably show how, if left intact, the insurance savings pool can grow to $1 million by the time the child is 55 or 65. Don't confuse your objectives; you want to save for your child's education. There's no point in considering his or her retirement unless you're already funding your own and have met your other financial priorities — including becoming debt-free.

Gift to "Adult" Children

In the year your child turns 17, give him or her a fair-sized chunk of money. Put the cash into a one-year GIC. Since that deposit will mature after the child turns 18, attribution rules won't apply — if the money is given, not loaned.

Ideally, the initial amount should be high enough so the principal and earnings cover school fees through the postsecondary period. Once he or she turns 18, the child — not you — is taxed on the interest.

The big downside here is that the money becomes the property of the child, who may choose to spend it in ways you do not approve. If that's a concern, put it in a trust.

Child's Earnings

Whenever your child earns money — perhaps in a part-time high school job — strike a deal. Have the child save that money for university or college while you replace it with an allowance. That way, the money can earn interest taxable for your child, not you.

Parents with incorporated businesses have several good planning opportunities. Consult your accountant.

Pay Off Your Own Mortgage

This concept is for the disciplined. It comes from Richard Birch, financial writer and devoted father. You might find it a bit dicey.

Young families have a limited amount of spare cash. Birch feels they're best off overall when the parents first focus on their own fundamental financial needs — building an emergency fund, establishing RRSPs and paying down the mortgage.

Mortgage paydown can be very useful. When you bump up your regular payment, you reduce the payback schedule. Ideally, the house will be paid off several years before your first child finishes high school. Money that would have gone for the mortgage can then be used for schooling. Meanwhile, each paydown generates a healthy tax-free return.

The downside is that you're likely to move to a more expensive house, so there won't be freed-up cash flow when the crunch comes. Of course, you will have home equity against which you can borrow.

Establishing a pattern of full RRSP contributions now will provide more flexibility later, Birch adds. Stop contributing a bit before school-time and divert that money to school fees. Thanks to compound growth on your very early RRSP deposits, you will likely be in the same shape — or better — than someone who sacrificed early RRSP contributions to build educational savings. After the university/college crunch, the RRSP carry-forward rules let you top up your plan.

Finally, don't underestimate your children. If raised properly, they should be willing to work part-time during high school and university or college. It's hard to believe now, but demographic projections point to a labor shortage in 20 years. There are also special student loans. As a father, Birch feels every child should bear some responsibility for funding his or her own diploma. I did. I suspect you did too.

Educational RRSPs

FOR MANY years, adults who have gone back to school have tapped their RRSPs for spending money. It seemed like a good deal since students typically have low incomes and pay little or no tax.

Now, there's a better way. The 1998 federal budget contained a rule change permitting you to borrow money from your RRSP if you or your spouse are doing full-time study in a program running at least three months. Disabled students need only to pursue part-time study.

This program is similar to the RRSP Home Buyers' Plan discussed in chapter 17. You can take out as much as $20,000 over four years, with a limit of $10,000 in any one year. The loan must be repaid over no more than 10 years after you have completed the program. Like the Home Buyers' Plan, there's no interest on the loan, but you still face a cost. The longer the loan is outstanding, the more current and future growth your RRSP gives up on that money. So repay the loan as quickly as possible.

This plan is a big improvement over straightforward withdrawals because you get to use the money without facing withholding tax and you get to repay the RRSP. With a straightforward withdrawal, you lose that RRSP room forever.

TABLE 31.1: The Cost of Raising a Child

These tables were released in 1998, based on 1997 surveys.

Notes: Durables such as clothing are depreciated over their expected life.

Food: Based on Agriculture Canada's Nutritious Food Basket data. Infant figures, established by Manitoba Health nutrition consultants, assume breast-feeding for the first two months.

Clothing: Infant costs include baby furniture and equipment that would normally be one-time purchases. Costs for older children cover normal attire, not designer products.

Health care: Based on the difference between single and family coverage in the Blue Cross Medi-Blue Plan. This also includes annual dental checkups and cleaning, but not eyeglasses or other special needs.

Personal care: Covers haircuts and toiletries.

Recreation/school: Recreation covers only basic needs for toys, sports equipment, a bicycle, reading materials and lessons for one activity. Does not include costly pursuits such as private music, dance and gymnastics lessons or competitive hockey or ringette.

School needs: Covers school supplies. They do not include savings for postsecondary education.

Transport: Reflects Winnipeg public transit costs.

Child care: Based on licensed daycare.

Shelter: Reflects the difference in average rent for a one- and two-bedroom apartment in Winnipeg. There is also an estimate of wear and tear on furniture and the cost of laundry and cleaning supplies for an extra person.

The Cost of Raising a Boy

Age	Food	Clothes	Health care	Personal care	Recreation & school	Transport	Child care	Shelter	Total
Infant	1,274	1,679	206	0	0	0	4,363	1,928	9,450
1	997	459	206	87	394	0	5,963	2,006	10,112
2	1,080	467	206	87	394	0	4,988	1,975	9,197
3	1,080	467	277	87	394	0	4,988	1,943	9,236
4	1,479	475	277	87	394	0	4,988	1,943	9,643
5	1,479	475	277	87	486	44	4,988	1,943	9,779
6	1,479	594	277	87	567	44	3,626	1,943	8,617
7	1,605	594	277	83	794	44	3,626	1,943	8,966
8	1,605	594	277	83	794	44	3,626	1,943	8,966
9	1,605	632	277	83	794	44	3,626	1,943	9,004
10	1,806	632	277	83	794	44	3,626	1,943	9,205
11	1,806	632	277	83	794	44	3,626	1,943	9,205
12	1,806	1,105	291	152	811	370	0	1,943	6,478
13	1,969	1,105	291	152	811	370	0	1,943	6,641
14	1,969	1,105	291	152	918	370	0	1,943	6,748
15	1,969	1,048	291	227	1,109	370	0	1,943	6,957
16	2,302	1,048	291	227	1,109	370	0	1,943	7,290
17	2,302	1,048	291	227	1,109	370	0	1,943	7,290
18	2,302	1,048	291	227	969	370	0	1,943	7,150

TABLE 31.1: continued

The Cost of Raising a Girl

Age	Food	Clothes	Health care	Personal care	Recreation & school	Transport	Child care	Shelter	Total
Infant	1,274	1,679	206	0	0	0	4,363	1,928	9,450
1	997	515	206	87	394	0	5,963	2,006	10,168
2	1,080	497	206	87	394	0	4,988	1,975	9,227
3	1,080	497	277	87	394	0	4,988	1,943	9,266
4	1,479	505	277	87	394	0	4,988	1,943	9,673
5	1,479	505	277	87	486	44	4,988	1,943	9,809
6	1,479	681	277	83	567	44	3,626	1,943	8,700
7	1,510	681	277	83	794	44	3,626	1,943	8,958
8	1,510	681	277	83	794	44	3,626	1,943	8,958
9	1,510	706	277	83	794	44	3,626	1,943	8,983
10	1,641	706	277	83	794	44	3,626	1,943	9,114
11	1,641	706	277	83	794	44	3,626	1,943	9,114
12	1,641	1,166	291	260	811	370	0	1,943	6,482
13	1,721	1,166	291	260	811	370	0	1,943	6,562
14	1,721	1,166	291	260	918	370	0	1,943	6,669
15	1,721	1,199	291	326	1,109	370	0	1,943	6,959
16	1,721	1,199	291	326	1,109	370	0	1,943	6,959
17	1,721	1,199	291	326	1,109	370	0	1,943	6,959
18	1,721	1,199	291	326	969	370	0	1,943	6,819

Source: Manitoba Agriculture, 1998

32

Where There's a Will . . .

. . . THERE'S A WAY TO ENSURE YOUR ESTATE is wound up with a minimum of fuss after you die.

About half of all adult Canadians don't have wills, according to a 1997 survey done for the Canandian Bar Association.

If you die without a will, provincial law governs who gets what. See table 32.1 at the end of this chapter.

As you might imagine, the law's distribution may vary considerably from your own wishes. In Manitoba, for example, your spouse gets everything. Grown children could be done out. In several provinces, your spouse gets just a flat sum and splits the rest with the kids. That sum may not be enough for the spouse to live on.

If there is neither spouse nor children, the law sets a ranking among parents, siblings, nieces and nephews. If there are no relatives, everything goes to the government.

If your children are minors and there's no will, their inheritance is paid into court and administered by your province's official guardian — often a very bureaucratic institution. As the kids turn 18, they get all their money — with no controls. In a will, bequests can be put into trusts, so you get to set controls on when and how the money is paid out.

Dying without a will also means it will likely cost more to administer your estate. Since you didn't name an executor, the court must appoint an administrator and your estate must post a bond to protect the assets. That often costs $500-$1,000 a year. The administrator is normally a family member, based on a ranking set by provincial law. For example, in Ontario your spouse would be first choice, and then adult children. Your brother or sister might be ideal, but siblings fall sixth on the list.

Your estate will be tied up until the court acts, and courts can move quite slowly.

Many single people figure they don't need wills. Consider that if you die "intestate" — that's without a will — the law makes no provision for bequests to a lover, friend or anyone else not related to you.

Many couples believe they don't need wills because everything is owned together. But there are two types of common ownership. "Joint tenancy with right of survivorship" means the deceased's share automatically passes to the other owner. But ownership as "tenants in common" means it doesn't.

Relying on joint ownership — "the poor man's will" — is also a problem if both people die at the same time, perhaps in a car crash.

Enough said. Get a will.

Now let me sell you on the idea of having your will drawn up by an experienced lawyer or a trust company.

Nothing prevents you from writing your own will, but if you're not careful the will may not be valid. In Ontario, for example, a "holograph" will must be entirely handwritten. If it's typed or if you use a fill-in-the-blank form, you must meet the same witness requirements as with a formal will. Courts can be very picky about those formalities. Consider that wills are usually challenged only if there are substantial sums or deep-seated grievances. In such cases, trivial errors can have major consequences.

Provincial laws set minimum standards for bequests to spouses and children. A lawyer or trust officer who handles wills all the time should know those rules backwards and forwards. These professionals can also provide valuable tax advice. For example, if your estate is named beneficiary of your insurance, probate fees will be levied on that money. But if you name a person or charity as beneficiary, probate won't apply. If you have foreign property — perhaps a sunbelt condo — a lawyer or accountant can advise you on any foreign estate tax liabilities.

A lawyer can advise you on the critical choice of an executor. Your first pick may be a brother or sister, but if that person lives outside your province, your estate may have to post a bond.

Most importantly, a lawyer can make sure the wording of the document and the identification of beneficiaries accurately reflect your wishes and will stand up to legal challenge. Apparently, do-it-yourself wills often prove faulty because the proper names of charities were not used.

It would likely cost less than $250 to get a straightforward will professionally done. That's small change when you consider the grief a mistake can cause. Remember that if your will is challenged, the best witness — you — won't be around to testify.

Again, enough said. Have a will professionally prepared — by someone well-versed in the subject. The lawyer who handled the purchase of your home may be an expert on real estate, but know little about the current state of family and estate law. Family law, in particular, seems to change all the time.

To save money on fees and ensure all bases are covered, spend some time in preparation before meeting with a lawyer or trust officer. Ideally, your lawyer will send you a questionnaire. If not, try your local trust company branch; most have free checklists.

This should be a joint exercise with your spouse. Maybe you've squirrelled away private money and don't want your mate to know. At least tell your lawyer. The Bank of Canada is holding more than $100 million from unclaimed bank accounts. I wonder how much of that was squirrelled away. A friend of mine once reviewed the unclaimed numbered accounts at one Canadian bank's branch in a foreign tax haven. More than $30 million had been sitting idle for years — often decades. Because the accounts carried numbers only — not names — there was no way to trace the owners or their heirs. Trust officers acting as executors have found negotiable bonds hidden under floorboards, jewellery frozen in ice cube trays and cash stuffed inside furniture. Why not keep a list of your cubby holes with your will?

List all assets and their values. Then rough out who gets what. Send your lawyer the tentative division before the meeting, so he or she can check that it jibes with family and succession laws.

Your assets will fall into two categories — specific bequests and the "residue." A specific bequest goes to a named person or charity. It might be an item of value or a sum of money. That sum might be a set amount or a percentage of your estate. Think about what you want done if your investments plunge and those payouts won't leave enough for your spouse or children. Also consider that your intended beneficiaries may die before you. Some people prefer to make bequests in a letter attached to the will. The letter can then be changed without redoing the will. Be careful; while such a list could be a guide for your executors, it may not be legally binding. Consult your lawyer.

If nothing else, professional advisers are worth the money because they are trained to ask the "what if" questions do-it-yourselfers often overlook. For example, what if you and your spouse are in a serious car crash and both die? Financially speaking, the law will determine who died first and levy probate fees on that estate, and then again on the other. So the same money could be taxed twice. Lawyers routinely put in a clause stating that one spouse inherits the other's assets only if he or she lives 30 days past the first death.

More seriously, who would you want to be guardian of your children? That's really up to the court, but the wishes expressed in your will would be given consideration. Similarly, indicate if there's anyone you definitely don't want appointed.

Remarriage is also a good "what if" area. A lawyer can advise you on how to provide for your spouse while still ensuring your children are not done out if he or she remarries.

If you are about to head down the aisle, be aware that marriage normally revokes a will unless the document states it was drafted "in contemplation" of that particular marriage. Separating? If you want to disinherit your spouse, immediately draft a new will. Separation does not automatically invalidate your old will. Divorce will void bequests made to your ex-spouse unless you state otherwise. If your spouse was named executor, that's invalidated too, assuming you divorced after signing the will.

If you depend on alimony or support payments, make sure they're covered in your former partner's will. Otherwise, you could be left out in the cold. It might be a good idea to get insurance on your former partner's life.

Every will needs at least one executor (technically, the male term) or executrix (the female term). Most people select a spouse, other relative or close friend. It's usually a good idea to pick someone your age or younger.

Make sure your choice is willing to take on the job. It can be a time-consuming and frustrating task. Also arrange for an alternate in case your first choice can't or won't serve.

The executor's main responsibilities include:

- Arrange the funeral and disposal of the body.

- Locate the will and obtain probate. That's when the will is confirmed by the provincial court.

- Identify and value all assets. Prepare a statement of assets and liabilities.

- File claims for life insurance and pension payouts.

- Advertise for creditors and pay all debts.

- File final tax returns and pay taxes due. Unless a case really is straight-forward, preparing a final tax return can be complex. Consulting an accountant or lawyer is usually worthwhile.

- Close out financial and pension accounts, redirect mail, cancel memberships and subscriptions.

- As required, convert assets to cash. Distribute assets as instructed by the will.

If the estate is complex, if trusts are expected to run for a long time or if family members don't get along, consider using a trust company as executor. You could also name both a trusted person and a trust company as co-executors.

If you decide to name a trust company as executor and/or trustee for any trust, talk to your lawyer about providing a mechanism for the business to be moved elsewhere should the trust company not do a good job. Trust companies named long ago have a permanent hold on many of today's trusts, and there is virtually nothing unhappy beneficiaries can do about it.

Most provinces regulate the executor's compensation. The rule-of-thumb is 5% of the estate plus expenses. A trust company would also collect an ongoing percentage of any trusts it manages. If an individual serves as executor, consider leaving him or her a tax-free bequest in lieu of taxable fees.

If you want a trusted person and a trust company as co-executors, consult your lawyer about mandating ways to compensate them. For example, you might specify that your friend or relative should receive the standard percentage — and simply give him or her authority to hire a trust company for professional services billed on an hourly basis. Otherwise, you run the risk that both executors will claim full percentage fees. One financial planner told me about a case in which double percentage fees cost an estate $13,000 for about $2,000 worth of work.

If naming three or more executors, state whether decisions should be unanimous or by majority. You may want expert executors for special assets such as a valuable stamp collection or a sunbelt condo. Or, at least, give your general executors authority to hire them.

Ideally, your executor should live in your community. Otherwise, time and estate funds will be eaten up in commuting. As noted, if your executor lives outside your province, a performance bond may have to be posted.

Make sure your will grants your executor wide discretion in selling your assets and managing the cash. Otherwise, beneficiaries could force a sale when prices are depressed. Unless the will specifies otherwise, your executor may face legal limits on the types of investments the estate can make.

Be kind to your executor:

- Keep easily accessible files with lists of assets and liabilities. Update them periodically. Ditto for your list of advisers. Make sure your executor can find your past tax returns and RRSP contribution records. As noted in chapter 23, the executor can make top-up RRSP contributions that could save your estate thousands of dollars in tax. Be certain your will grants that authority. Do you have unused capital losses from past years? Make sure your executor can find a record of them; they will save your estate money on the deemed disposition tax.

- Attach a memo to your will giving the address and phone number of each person named. Update it periodically. Often, estates get tied up while executors track down beneficiaries.

- Review your will with your executor. The Trust Companies Association survey found only about one-third of people do that. Flesh out your wishes by attaching a letter of memorandum to the will. While it may not be legally binding, it would ease the executor's decision-making and could strengthen his or her hand in dealing with beneficiaries.

- People typically outline their funeral wishes in their wills. But the will may not be read until after the service. Your executor is held responsible for disposal of your body. Make sure he or she knows what you want. If you are an organ/body donor, be aware that provincial law may let your family override that decision. Let your family know how you feel.

- Keep the original copy of your will in a safe place, easily accessible to your executor. Many people have their lawyers keep the original and make photocopies for executors and home files. If you use a safe deposit box, consider granting your executor access now. He or she simply has to sign the signature card at your bank or trust company. Make sure the executor knows where the key is kept.

More and more, people are interested in "living wills." That's a statement in which you declare to what extent, if any, doctors should use "heroic measures" to prolong your life. This area of law is changing fast. Your lawyer can advise you on whether your province recognizes such documents. If you own a business, definitely consult a lawyer. What would happen to your business if you were kept on life support for a year or two, neither awake nor dead?

Review your will after every change in your family: birth, death, disability, marital breakup, a child reaching the age of adulthood. If you move outside your province, make sure your will is still valid. Even if no major changes happen in your life, check your will every two or three years just to make sure it's not affected by new tax laws.

Probate Fees

IN MID-1992 the cash-hungry Ontario government caused quite a stir when it nearly tripled probate fees. They were set at $5 per $1,000 of estate value for the first $50,000 and then $15 per $1,000, with no upper limit. Probate for a $500,000 estate now costs $7,000.

Several other provinces have since jacked up their rates, though not by as much.

The law does not require probate for a will, but financial institutions generally demand it before transferring assets. They want to be certain the will is valid. For small estates, a will might be accepted without probate if it's notarized and the estate puts up a guarantee for a while.

There are ways to avoid or minimize probate, but you should get professional advice. Consider the options in the context of your total estate planning; each one may raise serious income tax or family law problems. Options include:

- Couples could hold real estate and financial accounts in "joint tenancy with right of survivorship." The property then goes directly to the survivor without probate.

- Have life insurance proceeds paid to a named beneficiary so this money does not pass through your estate. The same might be true for your RRSP or RRIF, though provincial laws vary.

  For insurance policies, name an alternate beneficiary in case the main beneficiary dies before you or at the same time.

- Consider setting up an *inter vivos* trust. That's a trust created during your lifetime. While alive, you could be the beneficiary and also the trustee. On your death, or at some other date, the trust would make payments to other beneficiaries directly, not through your estate. There are significant income tax considerations; professional advice is a must.

- Instead of making an outright bequest to your spouse, consider having your will establish a testamentary trust with your children or grandchildren as beneficiaries. That's a trust that takes effect on your death. Your spouse would draw regular income and be allowed to encroach on the capital. Probate fees would apply when the trust takes effect, but they'll be avoided when your spouse dies because the remaining assets would go directly to the ultimate beneficiaries without flowing through the spouse's estate.

- If you have a very large estate, consult your adviser about probate shopping. Here, you would transfer assets to a private holding company set up in the province with the best deal. Even after a hefty increase in 1993, Alberta had the lowest fees of the common-law provinces; probate for estates of $1 million or more was capped at $6,000.

Power of Attorney

GET A power of attorney drawn up at the same time you do your will. This document should authorize someone to handle your affairs if you can't because of illness or injury. That "attorney" can be any one you trust. He or she does not have to be a lawyer.

Suppose a stroke or car crash injury leaves you incapable of making decisions. You might think your spouse could just take over, but that's not so. Unless there's a POA, your affairs will be tied up until a court or your provincial public trustee decides that your spouse is fit for the job.

Do you own your home jointly? Without a POA or official status, your spouse can't sell that property or even renew the mortgage. Everything must go through the public trustee. Do you feel diversified well-managed mutual funds are a more prudent investment than direct ownership of stocks and bonds? Outdated laws in several provinces prohibit court-appointed trustees from investing in funds. But that need not be a problem if there's a POA.

A general power of attorney lets your stand-in do almost anything you can do. Or you can restrict it.

Normally, a power of attorney would not apply if you become mentally incompetent. But the lawyer who drafts your POA can cover that with an "enduring" power of attorney. If you don't make such advance arrangements and you become mentally incompetent, your family will face the agony and expense of going to court to have you certified and someone appointed to act on your behalf. Or, your provincial public trustee may take over your affairs.

If you are concerned about Alzheimer's or another degenerative disease, a power of attorney — or POA — can gradually increase your stand-in's authority as your capacity diminishes. Without one, court findings of incompetency are all-or-nothing.

Normally, a power of attorney deals only with your property. But there has been pressure for the law to allow substitute decision-making about your personal care and medical treatment. Ontario and British Columbia allowed this in 1995. Discuss it with your lawyer.

Technically, a POA becomes effective as soon as it is signed and delivered to the person named. It's a very powerful document. In the worst case, your stand-in could immediately clear out all your financial holdings. Choose your attorney carefully and safeguard the papers.

Here are some ways to guard against abuse:

- State in advance how incapacity would be determined. For example, you might require a written opinion from one or more doctors. Lawyers differ on whether that statement should be in the POA itself or a side letter.

- Leave the POA with your lawyer along with written instructions on when to release it. Your stand-in can't act without the document.

- Name two people who must act jointly.

To revoke a power of attorney, you should inform your stand-in in writing and retrieve all original copies. It's also a good idea to notify all the institutions where you have accounts.

Be aware that your attorney will not have the legal authority to support others with your money. So support for family members could be cut off if you become incompetent. If that's a concern, consult your lawyer about setting up a "revocable trust." Though widely used in the United States, this concept is fairly new in Canada.

Under guidelines set while you're healthy, the trust would grant your trustees discretion in using your assets to support you and others. To avoid ongoing costs and complexity, you could create the trust with a small amount of money and leave it dormant until needed. Meanwhile, one of the trustees would hold a limited enduring power of attorney. That POA would simply authorize the transfer of all your property to the trust if you can no longer manage your own affairs.

Let's face it: wills and powers of attorney can be scary. They force us to prepare for the reality of death and the threat of disability. If you're reluctant, consider that you get a will and POA not for yourself, but for your loved ones. If that guilt trip doesn't work, consider this comment from an accountant: "Your will is your last — and often your best — opportunity to do tax planning. Nobody wants to pay Ottawa any more than they have to."

TABLE 32.1: How Provincial Law Divides Assets of Those Who Die Without Wills (1)

Province	Spouse only	Children only	Spouse + 1 child	Spouse + children
Newfoundland	All to spouse	All to children	Split equally	1/3 to spouse 2/3 to children
Nova Scotia	All to spouse	All to children	$50,000 to spouse; rest split equally	$50,000 to spouse 1/3 rest to spouse 2/3 rest to children
P.E.I.	All to spouse	All to children	Split equally	1/3 to spouse 2/3 to children
New Brunswick	All to spouse	All to children	Belongings to spouse; rest split equally	Belongings to spouse 1/3 rest to spouse 2/3 rest to children
Quebec	All to spouse (2)	All to children	1/3 to spouse 2/3 to child	1/3 to spouse 2/3 to children
Ontario	All to spouse	All to children	$200,000 to spouse; rest split equally	$200,000 to spouse 1/3 rest to spouse 2/3 rest to children
Manitoba	All to spouse	All to children	All to spouse (3)	All to spouse (3)
Saskatchewan	All to spouse	All to children	$100,000 to spouse; rest split equally	$100,000 to spouse 1/3 rest to spouse 2/3 rest to children
Alberta	All to spouse	All to children	$40,000 to spouse; rest split equally	$40,000 to spouse 1/3 rest to spouse 2/3 rest to children
British Columbia	All to spouse	All to children	$65,000 to spouse; rest split equally	$65,000 to spouse 1/3 rest to spouse 2/3 rest to children

(1) Based on legislation in effect in 1998

(2) If deceased is not survived by parents, siblings, nieces or nephews

(3) If children are not children of surviving spouse, spouse gets half of estate to $50,000 and splits rest with children

33

A Matter of Trust

THIS CHAPTER PROVIDES A GENERAL DIS-
cussion of formal trusts. You need a lawyer to establish one. I just want to
show a few of the things these remarkably flexible arrangements can do.

Trusts are commonly used for two purposes. They let you control
how money is used, both before and after death. They can also generate
tax savings

In certain cases, trusts can also be used to protect assets from creditors.

There are two types of trusts. An *inter vivos* trust — also called a living trust — is established while you're alive. A testamentary trust is set
up under your will after you die.

Here are some examples of how trusts are used:

- As mentioned earlier in this book, a parent can give money to a minor
  child for investment, and any capital gains are then taxable for the child,
  not the parent. But brokerage firms won't open accounts for minors. Even
  if they would, you probably wouldn't want the risk of junior blowing the
  college fund on a sports car. Setting up a trust lets you have the money
  invested for your child while you retain control.

- A trust can be used to split income with adult family members, perhaps
  aged parents who are in a low- or no-tax bracket. You can put money or
  securities into a trust for them on an irrevocable basis. The investment
  income is then taxed in their hands, not yours.

- Trusts are often set up to support disabled family members so you're
  assured the person will be provided for if you suffer serious injury or
  death. This can save tax if the disabled person is in a lower tax bracket.

The trust's deed should name other beneficiaries once the money is no longer needed to support the disabled person.

- On marital breakup, a trust can be used to provide support so the recipient spouse doesn't have to worry about late or missed payments.

- A testamentary trust can ensure an heir doesn't squander his or her bequest.

  Such a trust can also save heirs tax on the investment income generated by their bequests every year. By putting the money into a trust, you effectively create two taxpayers — the trust and the beneficiary. Ideally, the payment will be structured so together they owe less tax than if all the money were taxed in one set of hands. One accountant estimated this structure can generate tax savings of as much as $7,000 per year for each beneficiary.

  Using a trust even allows you to leave money to generations not yet born. One man created a "half skip" trust that will pay income to his grandchildren until age 27. That will help cover school fees and give them a start in life. After that point, the money will be used to help the kids' parents in their retirement.

- A "charitable remainder trust" lets you donate a cottage, artwork or other valuable property to charity but continue to use it for as long as you live. Meanwhile, you get the tax credit for the gift now.

- "Asset protection trusts" set up in Grand Cayman or one of several other offshore financial havens are increasingly used by professionals and others worried about the risk of malpractice awards, environmental judgments or other claims by future creditors.

  The idea is to transfer financial assets to a trust in a locale where it's much harder for creditors to press claims than in Canada. This only works with portable financial assets, not Canadian real estate or an RRSP. Also, you can run afoul of Canadian fraudulent conveyance laws if transfers occur within certain time periods. You really do need advance planning, excellent legal advice and enough money to make these trusts worthwhile. One rule-of-thumb calls for at least $200,000.

- A foreign trust can save you tax if you support a relative outside Canada or expect to receive a large sum from a relative outside Canada.

  If you are a foreigner planning to move to Canada, get advice on the benefits of creating an "immigrant's trust" before you arrive.

34

Professional Help

PEOPLE OFTEN ASK ME TO RECOMMEND A financial planner. I always ask why they want one. Usually they say it's because their finances are "a mess."

Sorry, a planner probably won't be much help — at least for now. If your records are in disarray, there's very little he or she can do until you gather up the stuff and put it in order.

Some people say they're tired of chronically spending more than they make and want someone to "just straighten it all out." Again, there's little a planner can do unless you're willing to reassess your lifestyle and even your psychology. A planner may be able to juggle your debts and find some tax breaks to free up cash, but how long will it be before you're in the hole again?

Most financial planning is just old-fashioned common sense:

- Spend less than you make and invest the difference to meet meaningful future goals.

- Keep records.

- Prepare for disaster.

Some people want to know how much they need for retirement and whether they're on track. Where a planner can truly be helpful is in making sure you've covered the bases. Your financial security involves a range of disciplines that must be integrated. A good financial plan should address day-to-day cash flow and debt management, insurance, estate planning, taxation and investing.

Why not do the basic plan yourself? Then have an adviser suggest improvements and handle the complex issues. You'll save money on fees and get top value because the professional's time will be spent on advanced points, not humdrum explanations and advice.

The same goes for your tax return. Unless you have complex affairs, why not do the return yourself and then pay an accountant to review it and provide planning advice for the new year? Starting a business? See an accountant now for help in tax planning and record-keeping. You'll save money in the long run.

Planners can also help you determine if your investments are tax-effective and in line with your objectives. Many use sophisticated software that can answer specific questions requiring complex analysis. Examples include whether to tap your RRSP for a home down payment, or whether to make an RRSP contribution or a mortgage prepayment.

A good planner can also be a great comfort at a time of financial distress, perhaps if you lose your job and find yourself with a large severance payment but few re-employment prospects.

Selecting a Financial Planner

UNFORTUNATELY, FINDING the right adviser can be difficult. Only Quebec directly regulates financial planners. Elsewhere, anyone can hang out a shingle — and, increasingly, every type of financial salesperson does.

Don't assume your bank manager is a financial planner. Or your accountant. Or your stockbroker. Financial planning is not part of their basic education, though they may have taken extra courses. Don't expect your business accountant to provide personal investment advice, your estate lawyer to comment on RRSP investment strategies or your bank manager to weigh the pros and cons of setting up a trust for your child. Advice-giving has become highly specialized. No one person is capable of mastering all the ins and outs of all the disciplines involved in financial planning.

An alphabet soup of designations adds to the confusion. There are Chartered Financial Planners, Certified Financial Planners, Registered Financial Planners, Chartered Financial Consultants, Certified Investment Managers, Personal Financial Planners and more. Those people have done courses and/or passed exams run by their various industry associations. These courses vary greatly in content and required commitment.

The Financial Planners Standards Council of Canada was created in 1996 to grant a Certified Financial Planner designation that cuts across industry lines by requiring a uniform exam. But the bank and brokerage industries quit in 1998, claiming the requirements were too broad for their clients' needs. They're now promoting their own designations.

Many advisers belong to the Canadian Association of Financial Planners and/or the Canadian Association of Insurance and Financial Advisors. These voluntary organizations have codes of ethics and educational requirements. Phone CAFP at 1-800-346-2237 or (416) 593-6594 in Toronto. Its web site is http://www.cafp.org. Phone CAIFA at 1-800-563-5822 or (416) 444-5251 in Toronto. Its web site is http://www.caifa.com.

There are three types of financial planners: fee-only, commission-only and mixed.

Fee-only advisers just do plans; they don't sell financial products. They can, of course, refer you to salespeople, and some fee-only firms are in fact linked with companies that market investments. They may receive finder's fees when they refer clients to salespeople. Expect to pay $100 an hour or more for the time it takes to do your plan.

Commission-only advisers do not charge for planning, but obviously expect you to place money through them. Some are tied to single companies while others represent a range of vendors. Some charge for a plan but pay refunds if you invest through them.

Mixed advisers charge for plans and receive commissions on products they sell. They might use the term "fee based."

As a journalist I've dealt with all three groups. I originally assumed fee-only planners would be the most objective and knowledgeable. Over the years, however, I've found that personal integrity, education and experience count for far more than how a person is paid. I have good and bad stories about all three camps.

Where I have found a difference is that fee-only firms tend to focus on providing more sophisticated expertise for higher-end clients while others serve the broad middle-class.

It's easy to suggest that you seek referrals from friends and colleagues. The problem is that many people are dazzled by personality or sizzle. Under no circumstances should you judge a financial adviser by his or her appearance, office or car. It doesn't take much for a mediocre performer to look like a star. Indeed, trade magazines run features on how to dress for success. Office furnishings and cars are easily leased.

If you organize your own affairs, educate yourself about the basics and do your own groundwork, you'll be in a much better position to judge a prospective planner. Ask these questions:

- What is the method of compensation? In addition to those noted above, does the planner receive any incentives for selling certain products?

- Does the planner favor his or her company's own investment or insurance products?

- What are the planner's credentials, education and level of experience? What is his or her key area of expertise?

- Does the planner belong to any professional association with a code of ethics? If not, why?

- Does the planner have liability insurance?

- Will you get a full written plan? Will it cover budgeting and debt management, insurance, estate planning, taxation and investing?

- Does the adviser prefer aggressive or conservative clients? Is he or she used to working with people at your stage of life and financial level? Can you see a sample plan done for someone in a similar situation?

- How much will the service cost? (At least a ballpark estimate.)

- Will you work with an associate? Meet him or her.

- What communication can you expect? When and how can you fairly evaluate the service?

Always ask a few technical questions to which you already know the answers. That way, you can listen for gaps in knowledge or analytical ability and also judge the person's ability to explain things.

Selecting an Investment Adviser

THE INVESTMENT industry offers a variety of arrangements.

The most traditional — and most common — is where you deal with a broker who earns a commission on everything you buy. Many people swear by their brokers. Many swear at them.

It's a very tough business. When investments work, the client's a genius. When they don't, the broker's an idiot. Make sure your objectives are realistically in line with your risk tolerance and that your broker understands what you want.

Remember that your broker is a salesperson whose success depends on matching products to your needs and wants. Some brokers prefer conservative clients. Others want aggressive ones.

Don't be impressed if the broker is a vice-president. That just means he or she generated a certain level of sales.

When opening your account, discuss with the broker how you plan to measure his or her performance. Compare that performance to a stock index or mutual fund that reflects the type of investing you plan to do. Expect above-average results, not miracles.

Understand that brokers and the analysts behind them are not infallible.

Use your judgment in assessing their advice. Don't take lightly the "know your client" form you must fill out. That will be a key document if you ever claim you were advised to make an inappropriate investment.

If an investment goes bad, first ask yourself if you acted reasonably. Did you understand the investment? Remember that big returns carry big risks.

If you tell the broker you're a conservative investor, act like one. Don't demand super-duper returns. If you decide to change your stance, tell your broker before signing on with a new one.

Traditionally, people who didn't want to, or couldn't, manage their own money hired trust companies to do that for them. Trust companies still manage personal portfolios, but face increasing competition.

Investment dealers are also in that arena, actively marketing "wrap accounts." Instead of paying commissions on each transaction, you pay one yearly fee, typically a percentage of your account balance. That covers investment advice, commissions and periodic reports on how you're doing. There are three common arrangements:

- **Broker discretionary.** The client's retail broker is given authority to manage the money without client approval for each transaction. There are also non-discretionary accounts that maintain the traditional broker-client relationship, but wrap all charges within the one account fee.

- **Mutual fund wrap.** An asset allocation plan is devised, based on the client's constraints and desired return. This may be done by computer. The money is then spread among several mutual funds. The investment dealer monitors the performance and sends periodic reports.

- **Limited consulting.** This is similar to the mutual fund wrap, but the money is spread among pools run by several private money management firms. Those firms normally serve pension funds and millionaires. Here, the investment dealer bundles money from groups of clients. The clients have no direct contact with the money managers. They continue to deal with their brokers. Unlike mutual funds, pooled funds are not required to include management fees when quoting their returns.

Clearly, before signing up you should examine the fees — including charges for opening and closing the account. How much would the advisory and "order execution" services cost if purchased separately? Will the program cost more than do-it-yourself mutual fund investing? If so, will the returns — or time saved — justify the extra cost?

Wealthy individuals can get personalized service from private investment counsellors. Some firms require $1 million. Others may go as low as $200,000. These firms tend to be small. A key concern is continuity of service if one or more of the principals leave or retire. Is the firm getting lots of new clients? Service can suffer if the staff isn't expanded.

Carefully examine sample portfolios for those with your objectives. Compare the performance of each asset category to that of a standard benchmark such as a stock or bond index. But remember that the performance should reflect the objectives; don't expect a portfolio with a conservative mandate to beat a hot stock market.

The One Constant

NO MATTER what the discipline or arrangement, every one of your advisers must be able to communicate with you. They must be able to understand what you want, and you must be able to understand their explanations.

If the adviser isn't in tune with your thinking, try someone else. People who don't understand what they're doing make mistakes. Mistakes cost money and cause anguish.

You can delegate only so much. No hired hand should be expected to care more about your money than you do. No matter how much expertise you buy, ultimately you're responsible for your own financial security. Good luck.

A

Reference Tables

THIS SECTION CONTAINS A SET OF REFERENCE tables. Here are their formulas for those with computer spreadsheets or business/scientific calculators.

i = interest/discount rate (e.g.; 5% = .05)
n = amount of time/number of payments
r = indexing rate
t = compounding frequency (e.g.; monthly = 12, daily = 365)

A-1: Future value of $1

$$(1 + i)^n$$

A-2: Present value of a future $1

$$\frac{1}{(1 + i)^n}$$

A-3: Effective annual yield #1

$$\left[\left(1 + \frac{i}{t}\right)^t\right] - 1$$

A-4: Effective annual yield #2

$$\left[\left[(1 + i)^{\left(\frac{1}{t}\right)} - 1\right]\right] \times t$$

A-5: Future value of regular annuity

$$\frac{(1 + i)^n - 1}{i}$$

A-6: Future value of an annuity due

$$(1 + i) \times \left[\frac{(1 + i)^n - 1}{i}\right]$$

A-7: Present value of regular annuity

$$\frac{1-\left[\dfrac{1}{(1+i)^n}\right]}{i}$$

A-8: Present value of annuity due

$$1+\left[\frac{1-\left[\dfrac{1}{(1+i)^{n-1}}\right]}{i}\right]$$

A-9: Present value of indexed regular annuity

This is a 2-step process

1. $k=\left[\dfrac{1+i}{1+r}\right]-1$

2. $\dfrac{1}{k}-\dfrac{1}{k\left[(1+k)^n\right]}$

A-10: Present value of indexed annuity due

This is a 2-step process

1. $k=\left[\dfrac{1+i}{1+r}\right]-1$

2. $1+\left[\dfrac{1-\left[\dfrac{1}{(1+k)^{n-1}}\right]}{k}\right]$

APPENDIX A-1: Future value of $1 compounding annually

After year	1%	2%	3%	4%	5%	6%	7%	8%	9%	10%	11%	12%	13%	14%	15%
1	1.0100	1.0200	1.0300	1.0400	1.0500	1.0600	1.0700	1.0800	1.0900	1.1000	1.1100	1.1200	1.1300	1.1400	1.1500
2	1.0201	1.0404	1.0609	1.0816	1.1025	1.1236	1.1449	1.1664	1.1881	1.2100	1.2321	1.2544	1.2769	1.2996	1.3225
3	1.0303	1.0612	1.0927	1.1249	1.1576	1.1910	1.2250	1.2597	1.2950	1.3310	1.3676	1.4049	1.4429	1.4815	1.5209
4	1.0406	1.0824	1.1255	1.1699	1.2155	1.2625	1.3108	1.3605	1.4116	1.4641	1.5181	1.5735	1.6305	1.6890	1.7490
5	1.0510	1.1041	1.1593	1.2167	1.2763	1.3382	1.4026	1.4693	1.5386	1.6105	1.6851	1.7623	1.8424	1.9254	2.0114
6	1.0615	1.1262	1.1941	1.2653	1.3401	1.4185	1.5007	1.5869	1.6771	1.7716	1.8704	1.9738	2.0820	2.1950	2.3131
7	1.0721	1.1487	1.2299	1.3159	1.4071	1.5036	1.6058	1.7138	1.8280	1.9487	2.0762	2.2107	2.3526	2.5023	2.6600
8	1.0829	1.1717	1.2668	1.3686	1.4775	1.5938	1.7182	1.8509	1.9926	2.1436	2.3045	2.4760	2.6584	2.8526	3.0590
9	1.0937	1.1951	1.3048	1.4233	1.5513	1.6895	1.8385	1.9990	2.1719	2.3579	2.5580	2.7731	3.0040	3.2519	3.5179
10	1.1046	1.2190	1.3439	1.4802	1.6289	1.7908	1.9672	2.1589	2.3674	2.5937	2.8394	3.1058	3.3946	3.7072	4.0456
11	1.1157	1.2434	1.3842	1.5395	1.7103	1.8983	2.1049	2.3316	2.5804	2.8531	3.1518	3.4785	3.8359	4.2262	4.6524
12	1.1268	1.2682	1.4258	1.6010	1.7959	2.0122	2.2522	2.5182	2.8127	3.1384	3.4985	3.8960	4.3345	4.8179	5.3503
13	1.1381	1.2936	1.4685	1.6651	1.8856	2.1329	2.4098	2.7196	3.0658	3.4523	3.8833	4.3635	4.8980	5.4924	6.1528
14	1.1495	1.3195	1.5126	1.7317	1.9799	2.2609	2.5785	2.9372	3.3417	3.7975	4.3104	4.8871	5.5348	6.2613	7.0757
15	1.1610	1.3459	1.5580	1.8009	2.0789	2.3966	2.7590	3.1722	3.6425	4.1772	4.7846	5.4736	6.2543	7.1379	8.1371
16	1.1726	1.3728	1.6047	1.8730	2.1829	2.5404	2.9522	3.4259	3.9703	4.5950	5.3109	6.1304	7.0673	8.1372	9.3576
17	1.1843	1.4002	1.6528	1.9479	2.2920	2.6928	3.1588	3.7000	4.3276	5.0545	5.8951	6.8660	7.9861	9.2765	10.7613
18	1.1961	1.4282	1.7024	2.0258	2.4066	2.8543	3.3799	3.9960	4.7171	5.5599	6.5436	7.6900	9.0243	10.5752	12.3755
19	1.2081	1.4568	1.7535	2.1068	2.5270	3.0256	3.6165	4.3157	5.1417	6.1159	7.2633	8.6128	10.1974	12.0557	14.2318
20	1.2202	1.4859	1.8061	2.1911	2.6533	3.2071	3.8697	4.6610	5.6044	6.7275	8.0623	9.6463	11.5231	13.7435	16.3665
21	1.2324	1.5157	1.8603	2.2788	2.7860	3.3996	4.1406	5.0338	6.1088	7.4002	8.9492	10.8038	13.0211	15.6676	18.8215
22	1.2447	1.5460	1.9161	2.3699	2.9253	3.6035	4.4304	5.4365	6.6586	8.1403	9.9336	12.1003	14.7138	17.8610	21.6447
23	1.2572	1.5769	1.9736	2.4647	3.0715	3.8197	4.7405	5.8715	7.2579	8.9543	11.0263	13.5523	16.6266	20.3616	24.8915
24	1.2697	1.6084	2.0328	2.5633	3.2251	4.0489	5.0724	6.3412	7.9111	9.8497	12.2392	15.1786	18.7881	23.2122	28.6252
25	1.2824	1.6406	2.0938	2.6658	3.3864	4.2919	5.4274	6.8485	8.6231	10.8347	13.5855	17.0001	21.2305	26.4619	32.9190

After year	1%	2%	3%	4%	5%	6%	Compound growth rate 7%	8%	9%	10%	11%	12%	13%	14%	15%
26	1.2953	1.6734	2.1566	2.7725	3.5557	4.5494	5.8074	7.3964	9.3992	11.9182	15.0799	19.0401	23.9905	30.1666	37.8568
27	1.3082	1.7069	2.2213	2.8834	3.7335	4.8223	6.2139	7.9881	10.2451	13.1100	16.7386	21.3249	27.1093	34.3899	43.5353
28	1.3213	1.7410	2.2879	2.9987	3.9201	5.1117	6.6488	8.6271	11.1671	14.4210	18.5799	23.8839	30.6335	39.2045	50.0656
29	1.3345	1.7758	2.3566	3.1187	4.1161	5.4184	7.1143	9.3173	12.1722	15.8631	20.6237	26.7499	34.6158	44.6931	57.5755
30	1.3478	1.8114	2.4273	3.2434	4.3219	5.7435	7.6123	10.0627	13.2677	17.4494	22.8923	29.9599	39.1159	50.9502	66.2118
31	1.3613	1.8476	2.5001	3.3731	4.5380	6.0881	8.1451	10.8677	14.4618	19.1943	25.4104	33.5551	44.2010	58.0832	76.1435
32	1.3749	1.8845	2.5751	3.5081	4.7649	6.4534	8.7153	11.7371	15.7633	21.1138	28.2056	37.5817	49.9471	66.2148	87.5651
33	1.3887	1.9222	2.6523	3.6484	5.0032	6.8406	9.3253	12.6760	17.1820	23.2252	31.3082	42.0915	56.4402	75.4849	100.6998
34	1.4026	1.9607	2.7319	3.7943	5.2533	7.2510	9.9781	13.6901	18.7284	25.5477	34.7521	47.1425	63.7774	86.0528	115.8048
35	1.4166	1.9999	2.8139	3.9461	5.5160	7.6861	10.6766	14.7853	20.4140	28.1024	38.5749	52.7996	72.0685	98.1002	133.1755
36	1.4308	2.0399	2.8983	4.1039	5.7918	8.1473	11.4239	15.9682	22.2512	30.9127	42.8181	59.1356	81.4374	111.8342	153.1519
37	1.4451	2.0807	2.9852	4.2681	6.0814	8.6361	12.2236	17.2456	24.2538	34.0039	47.5281	66.2318	92.0243	127.4910	176.1246
38	1.4595	2.1223	3.0748	4.4388	6.3855	9.1543	13.0793	18.6253	26.4367	37.4043	52.7562	74.1797	103.9874	145.3397	202.5433
39	1.4741	2.1647	3.1670	4.6164	6.7048	9.7035	13.9948	20.1153	28.8160	41.1448	58.5593	83.0812	117.5058	165.6873	232.9248
40	1.4889	2.2080	3.2620	4.8010	7.0400	10.2857	14.9745	21.7245	31.4094	45.2593	65.0009	93.0510	132.7816	188.8835	267.8635
41	1.5038	2.2522	3.3599	4.9931	7.3920	10.9029	16.0227	23.4625	34.2363	49.7852	72.1510	104.2171	150.0432	215.3272	308.0431
42	1.5188	2.2972	3.4607	5.1928	7.7616	11.5570	17.1143	25.3395	37.3175	54.7637	80.0876	116.7231	169.5488	245.4730	354.2495
43	1.5340	2.3432	3.5645	5.4005	8.1497	12.2505	18.3444	27.3666	40.6761	60.2401	88.8972	130.7299	191.5901	279.8392	407.3870
44	1.5493	2.3901	3.6715	5.6165	8.5572	12.9855	19.6285	29.5560	44.3370	66.2641	98.6759	146.4175	216.4968	319.0167	468.4950
45	1.5648	2.4379	3.7816	5.8412	8.9850	13.7646	21.0025	31.9204	48.3273	72.8905	109.5302	163.9876	244.6414	363.6791	538.7693
46	1.5805	2.4866	3.8950	6.0748	9.4343	14.5905	22.4726	34.4741	52.6767	80.1795	121.5786	183.6661	276.4448	414.5941	619.5847
47	1.5963	2.5363	4.0119	6.3178	9.9060	15.4659	24.0457	37.2320	57.4176	88.1975	134.9522	205.7061	312.3826	472.6373	712.5224
48	1.6122	2.5871	4.1323	6.5705	10.4013	16.3939	25.7289	40.2106	62.5852	97.0172	149.7970	230.3908	352.9923	538.8065	819.4007
49	1.6283	2.6388	4.2562	6.8333	10.9213	17.3775	27.5299	43.4274	68.2179	106.7190	166.2746	258.0377	398.8813	614.2395	942.3108
50	1.6446	2.6916	4.3839	7.1067	11.4674	18.4202	29.4570	46.9016	74.3575	117.3909	184.5648	289.0022	450.7359	700.2330	1083.6574

APPENDIX A-2: Present value of $1 at the end of a period after compounding

After year	1%	2%	3%	4%	5%	6%	7%	8%	9%	10%	11%	12%	13%	14%	15%
1	0.9901	0.9804	0.9709	0.9615	0.9524	0.5434	0.9346	0.9259	0.9174	0.9091	0.9009	0.8929	0.8850	0.8772	0.8696
2	0.9803	0.9612	0.9426	0.9246	0.9070	0.8900	0.8734	0.8573	0.8417	0.8264	0.8116	0.7972	0.7831	0.7695	0.7561
3	0.9706	0.9423	0.9151	0.8890	0.8638	0.8396	0.8163	0.7938	0.7722	0.7513	0.7312	0.7118	0.6931	0.6750	0.6575
4	0.9610	0.9238	0.8885	0.8548	0.8227	0.7921	0.7629	0.7350	0.7084	0.6830	0.6587	0.6355	0.6133	0.5921	0.5718
5	0.9515	0.9057	0.8626	0.8219	0.7835	0.7473	0.7130	0.6806	0.6499	0.6209	0.5935	0.5674	0.5428	0.5194	0.4972
6	0.9420	0.8880	0.8375	0.7903	0.7462	0.7050	0.6663	0.6302	0.5963	0.5645	0.5346	0.5066	0.4803	0.4556	0.4323
7	0.9327	0.8706	0.8131	0.7599	0.7107	0.6651	0.6227	0.5835	0.5470	0.5132	0.4817	0.4523	0.4251	0.3996	0.3759
8	0.9235	0.8535	0.7894	0.7307	0.6768	0.6274	0.5820	0.5403	0.5019	0.4665	0.4339	0.4039	0.3762	0.3506	0.3269
9	0.9143	0.8368	0.7664	0.7026	0.6446	0.5919	0.5439	0.5002	0.4604	0.4241	0.3909	0.3606	0.3329	0.3075	0.2843
10	0.9053	0.8203	0.7441	0.6756	0.6139	0.5584	0.5083	0.4632	0.4224	0.3855	0.3522	0.3220	0.2946	0.2697	0.2472
11	0.8963	0.8043	0.7224	0.6496	0.5847	0.5268	0.4751	0.4289	0.3875	0.3505	0.3173	0.2875	0.2607	0.2366	0.2149
12	0.8874	0.7885	0.7014	0.6246	0.5568	0.4970	0.4440	0.3971	0.3555	0.3186	0.2858	0.2567	0.2307	0.2076	0.1869
13	0.8787	0.7730	0.6810	0.6006	0.5303	0.4688	0.4150	0.3677	0.3262	0.2897	0.2575	0.2292	0.2042	0.1821	0.1625
14	0.8700	0.7579	0.6611	0.5775	0.5051	0.4423	0.3878	0.3405	0.2992	0.2633	0.2320	0.2046	0.1807	0.1597	0.1413
15	0.8613	0.7430	0.6419	0.5553	0.4810	0.4173	0.3624	0.3152	0.2745	0.2394	0.2090	0.1827	0.1599	0.1401	0.1229
16	0.8528	0.7284	0.6232	0.5339	0.4581	0.3936	0.3387	0.2919	0.2519	0.2176	0.1883	0.1631	0.1415	0.1229	0.1069
17	0.8444	0.7142	0.6050	0.5134	0.4363	0.3714	0.3166	0.2703	0.2311	0.1978	0.1696	0.1456	0.1252	0.1078	0.0929
18	0.8360	0.7002	0.5874	0.4936	0.4155	0.3503	0.2959	0.2502	0.2120	0.1799	0.1528	0.1300	0.1108	0.0946	0.0808
19	0.8277	0.6864	0.5703	0.4746	0.3957	0.3305	0.2765	0.2317	0.1945	0.1635	0.1377	0.1161	0.0981	0.0829	0.0703
20	0.8195	0.6730	0.5537	0.4564	0.3769	0.3118	0.2584	0.2145	0.1784	0.1486	0.1240	0.1037	0.0868	0.0728	0.0611
21	0.8114	0.6598	0.5375	0.4388	0.3589	0.2942	0.2415	0.1987	0.1637	0.1351	0.1117	0.0926	0.0768	0.0638	0.0531
22	0.8034	0.6468	0.5219	0.4220	0.3418	0.2775	0.2257	0.1839	0.1502	0.1228	0.1007	0.0826	0.0680	0.0560	0.0462
23	0.7954	0.6342	0.5067	0.4057	0.3256	0.2618	0.2109	0.1703	0.1378	0.1117	0.0907	0.0738	0.0601	0.0491	0.0402
24	0.7876	0.6217	0.4919	0.3901	0.3101	0.2470	0.1971	0.1577	0.1264	0.1015	0.0817	0.0659	0.0532	0.0431	0.0349
25	0.7798	0.6095	0.4776	0.3751	0.2953	0.2330	0.1842	0.1460	0.1160	0.0923	0.0736	0.0588	0.0471	0.0378	0.0304

APPENDIX A-2 CONTINUED

After year	1%	2%	3%	4%	5%	6%	Compound growth rate 7%	8%	9%	10%	11%	12%	13%	14%	15%
26	0.7720	0.5976	0.4637	0.3607	0.2812	0.2198	0.1722	0.1352	0.1064	0.0839	0.0663	0.0525	0.0417	0.0331	0.0264
27	0.7644	0.5859	0.4502	0.3468	0.2678	0.2074	0.1609	0.1252	0.0976	0.0763	0.0597	0.0469	0.0369	0.0291	0.0230
28	0.7568	0.5744	0.4371	0.3335	0.2551	0.1956	0.1504	0.1159	0.0895	0.0693	0.0538	0.0419	0.0326	0.0255	0.0200
29	0.7493	0.5631	0.4243	0.3207	0.2429	0.1846	0.1406	0.1073	0.0822	0.0630	0.0485	0.0374	0.0289	0.0224	0.0174
30	0.7419	0.5521	0.4120	0.3083	0.2314	0.1741	0.1314	0.0994	0.0754	0.0573	0.0437	0.0334	0.0256	0.0196	0.0151
31	0.7346	0.5412	0.4000	0.2965	0.2204	0.1643	0.1228	0.0920	0.0691	0.0521	0.0394	0.0298	0.0226	0.0172	0.0131
32	0.7273	0.5306	0.3883	0.2851	0.2099	0.1550	0.1147	0.0852	0.0634	0.0474	0.0355	0.0266	0.0200	0.0151	0.0114
33	0.7201	0.5202	0.3770	0.2741	0.1999	0.1462	0.1072	0.0789	0.0582	0.0431	0.0319	0.0238	0.0177	0.0132	0.0099
34	0.7130	0.5100	0.3660	0.2636	0.1904	0.1379	0.1002	0.0730	0.0534	0.0391	0.0288	0.0212	0.0157	0.0116	0.0086
35	0.7059	0.5000	0.3554	0.2534	0.1813	0.1301	0.0937	0.0676	0.0490	0.0356	0.0259	0.0189	0.0139	0.0102	0.0075
36	0.6989	0.4902	0.3450	0.2437	0.1727	0.1227	0.0875	0.0626	0.0449	0.0323	0.0234	0.0169	0.0123	0.0089	0.0065
37	0.6920	0.4806	0.3350	0.2343	0.1644	0.1158	0.0818	0.0580	0.0412	0.0294	0.0210	0.0151	0.0109	0.0078	0.0057
38	0.6852	0.4712	0.3252	0.2253	0.1566	0.1092	0.0765	0.0537	0.0378	0.0267	0.0190	0.0135	0.0096	0.0069	0.0049
39	0.6784	0.4619	0.3158	0.2166	0.1491	0.1031	0.0715	0.0497	0.0347	0.0243	0.0171	0.0120	0.0085	0.0060	0.0043
40	0.6717	0.4529	0.3066	0.2083	0.1420	0.0972	0.0668	0.0460	0.0318	0.0221	0.0154	0.0107	0.0075	0.0053	0.0037
41	0.6650	0.4440	0.2976	0.2003	0.1353	0.0917	0.0624	0.0426	0.0292	0.0201	0.0139	0.0096	0.0067	0.0046	0.0032
42	0.6584	0.4353	0.2890	0.1926	0.1288	0.0865	0.0583	0.0395	0.0268	0.0183	0.0125	0.0086	0.0059	0.0041	0.0028
43	0.6519	0.4268	0.2805	0.1852	0.1227	0.0816	0.0545	0.0365	0.0246	0.0166	0.0112	0.0076	0.0052	0.0036	0.0025
44	0.6454	0.4184	0.2724	0.1780	0.1169	0.0770	0.0509	0.0338	0.0226	0.0151	0.0101	0.0068	0.0046	0.0031	0.0021
45	0.6391	0.4102	0.2644	0.1712	0.1113	0.0727	0.0476	0.0313	0.0207	0.0137	0.0091	0.0061	0.0041	0.0027	0.0019
46	0.6327	0.4022	0.2567	0.1646	0.1060	0.0685	0.0445	0.0290	0.0190	0.0125	0.0082	0.0054	0.0036	0.0024	0.0016
47	0.6265	0.3943	0.2493	0.1583	0.1009	0.0647	0.0416	0.0269	0.0174	0.0113	0.0074	0.0049	0.0032	0.0021	0.0014
48	0.6203	0.3865	0.2420	0.1522	0.0961	0.0610	0.0389	0.0249	0.0160	0.0103	0.0067	0.0043	0.0028	0.0019	0.0012
49	0.6141	0.3790	0.2350	0.1463	0.0916	0.0575	0.0363	0.0230	0.0147	0.0094	0.0060	0.0039	0.0025	0.0016	0.0011
50	0.6080	0.3715	0.2281	0.1407	0.0872	0.0543	0.0339	0.0213	0.0134	0.0085	0.0054	0.0035	0.0022	0.0014	0.0009

APPENDIX A-3: Effective annual yield table

| | Compounded | | | | Compounded | | | | Compounded | | | | Compounded | |
| Stated rate | Semi-annually | Monthly | | Stated rate | Semi-annually | Monthly | | Stated rate | Semi-annually | Monthly | | Stated rate | Semi-annually | Monthly |
	= Annualized rate				= Annualized rate				= Annualized rate				= Annualized rate	
1.000%	1.002%	1.005%		5.000%	5.062%	5.116%		9.000%	9.203%	9.381%		13.000%	13.423%	13.803%
1.125	1.128	1.131		5.125	5.191	5.247		9.125	9.333	9.516		13.125	13.556	13.944
1.250	1.254	1.257		5.250	5.319	5.378		9.250	9.464	9.652		13.250	13.689	14.085
1.375	1.380	1.384		5.375	5.447	5.509		9.375	9.595	9.789		13.375	13.822	14.226
1.500	1.506	1.510		5.500	5.576	5.641		9.500	9.726	9.925		13.500	13.956	14.367
1.625	1.632	1.637		5.625	5.704	5.772		9.625	9.857	10.061		13.625	14.089	14.509
1.750	1.758	1.764		5.750	5.833	5.904		9.750	9.988	10.198		13.750	14.223	14.651
1.875	1.884	1.891		5.875	5.961	6.036		9.875	10.119	10.334		13.875	14.356	14.792
2.000	2.010	2.018		6.000	6.090	6.168		10.000	10.250	10.471		14.000	14.490	14.934
2.125	2.136	2.146		6.125	6.219	6.300		10.125	10.381	10.608		14.125	14.624	15.076
2.250	2.263	2.273		6.250	6.348	6.432		10.250	10.513	10.746		14.250	14.758	15.219
2.375	2.389	2.401		6.375	6.477	6.565		10.375	10.644	10.883		14.375	14.892	15.361
2.500	2.516	2.529		6.500	6.606	6.697		10.500	10.776	11.020		14.500	15.026	15.504
2.625	2.642	2.657		6.625	6.735	6.830		10.625	10.907	11.158		14.625	15.160	15.646
2.750	2.769	2.785		6.750	6.864	6.963		10.750	11.039	11.296		14.750	15.294	15.789
2.875	2.896	2.913		6.875	6.993	7.096		10.875	11.171	11.434		14.875	15.428	15.932

APPENDIX A-3: CONTINUED

Stated rate	Compounded Semi-annually = Annualized rate	Monthly
3.000%	3.022%	3.042%
3.125	3.149	3.170
3.250	3.276	3.299
3.375	3.403	3.428
3.500	3.531	3.557
3.625	3.658	3.686
3.750	3.785	3.815
3.875	3.913	3.945
4.000	4.040	4.074
4.125	4.168	4.204
4.250	4.295	4.334
4.375	4.423	4.464
4.500	4.551	4.594
4.625	4.678	4.724
4.750	4.806	4.855
4.875	4.934	4.985

Stated rate	Compounded Semi-annually = Annualized rate	Monthly
7.000%	7.123%	7.229%
7.125	7.252	7.362
7.250	7.381	7.496
7.375	7.511	7.629
7.500	7.641	7.763
7.625	7.770	7.897
7.750	7.900	8.031
7.875	8.030	8.166
8.000	8.160	8.300
8.125	8.290	8.435
8.250	8.420	8.569
8.375	8.550	8.704
8.500	8.681	8.839
8.625	8.811	8.974
8.750	8.941	9.110
8.875	9.072	9.245

Stated rate	Compounded Semi-annually = Annualized rate	Monthly
11.000%	11.302%	11.572%
11.125	11.434	11.710
11.250	11.566	11.849
11.375	11.698	11.987
11.500	11.831	12.126
11.625	11.963	12.265
11.750	12.095	12.404
11.875	12.228	12.543
12.000	12.360	12.683
12.125	12.493	12.822
12.250	12.625	12.962
12.375	12.758	13.102
12.500	12.891	13.242
12.625	13.023	13.382
12.750	13.156	13.522
12.875	13.289	13.663

Stated rate	Compounded Semi-annually = Annualized rate	Monthly
15.000%	15.562%	16.075%
15.125	15.697	16.219
15.250	15.831	16.362
15.375	15.966	16.506
15.500	16.101	16.650
15.625	16.235	16.794
15.750	16.370	16.938
15.875	16.505	17.083
16.000	16.640	17.227
16.125	16.775	17.372
16.250	16.910	17.517
16.375	17.045	17.662
16.500	17.181	17.807
16.625	17.316	17.952
16.750	17.451	18.098
16.875	17.587	18.243

APPENDIX A-4: Effective annual yield table

You need this annual rate			You need this annual rate			You need this annual rate			You need this annual rate		
To get annual rate of	compounding Semi-annually	Monthly	To get annual rate of	compounding Semi-annually	Monthly	To get annual rate of	compounding Semi-annually	Monthly	To get annual rate of	compounding Semi-annually	Monthly
1.000%	0.998%	0.995%	5.000%	4.939%	4.889%	9.000%	8.806%	8.649%	13.000%	12.603%	12.284%
1.125	1.122	1.119	5.125	5.061	5.008	9.125	8.926	8.764	13.125	12.720	12.396
1.250	1.246	1.243	5.250	5.183	5.128	9.250	9.045	8.880	13.250	12.838	12.507
1.375	1.370	1.366	5.375	5.305	5.247	9.375	9.165	8.995	13.375	12.955	12.619
1.500	1.494	1.490	5.500	5.426	5.366	9.500	9.284	9.110	13.500	13.073	12.730
1.625	1.618	1.613	5.625	5.548	5.485	9.625	9.404	9.225	13.625	13.190	12.842
1.750	1.742	1.736	5.750	5.670	5.604	9.750	9.523	9.340	13.750	13.307	12.953
1.875	1.866	1.859	5.875	5.791	5.722	9.875	9.643	9.454	13.875	13.424	13.064
2.000	1.990	1.982	6.000	5.913	5.841	10.000	9.762	9.569	14.000	13.542	13.175
2.125	2.114	2.105	6.125	6.034	5.959	10.125	9.881	9.683	14.125	13.659	13.285
2.250	2.237	2.227	6.250	6.155	6.078	10.250	10.000	9.798	14.250	13.776	13.396
2.375	2.361	2.350	6.375	6.277	6.196	10.375	10.119	9.912	14.375	13.892	13.507
2.500	2.485	2.472	6.500	6.398	6.314	10.500	10.238	10.026	14.500	14.009	13.617
2.625	2.608	2.594	6.625	6.519	6.432	10.625	10.357	10.140	14.625	14.126	13.727
2.750	2.731	2.716	6.750	6.640	6.550	10.750	10.476	10.254	14.750	14.243	13.838
2.875	2.855	2.838	6.875	6.761	6.667	10.875	10.594	10.368	14.875	14.360	13.948

APPENDIX A-4: CONTINUED

You need this annual rate			You need this annual rate			You need this annual rate			You need this annual rate		
To get annual rate of	compounding Semi-annually	Monthly	To get annual rate of	compounding Semi-annually	Monthly	To get annual rate of	compounding Semi-annually	Monthly	To get annual rate of	compounding Semi-annually	Monthly
3.000%	2.978%	2.960%	7.000%	6.882%	6.785%	11.000%	10.713%	10.482%	15.000%	14.476%	14.058%
3.125	3.101	3.081	7.125	7.002	6.902	11.125	10.832	10.595	15.125	14.593	14.168
3.250	3.224	3.203	7.250	7.123	7.020	11.250	10.950	10.708	15.250	14.709	14.278
3.375	3.347	3.324	7.375	7.244	7.137	11.375	11.069	10.822	15.375	14.826	14.387
3.500	3.470	3.445	7.500	7.364	7.254	11.500	11.187	10.935	15.500	14.942	14.497
3.625	3.593	3.566	7.625	7.485	7.371	11.625	11.305	11.048	15.625	15.058	14.606
3.750	3.715	3.687	7.750	7.605	7.488	11.750	11.424	11.161	15.750	15.174	14.716
3.875	3.838	3.808	7.875	7.726	7.604	11.875	11.542	11.274	15.875	15.291	14.825
4.000	3.961	3.928	8.000	7.846	7.721	12.000	11.660	11.387	16.000	15.407	14.934
4.125	4.083	4.049	8.125	7.966	7.837	12.125	11.778	11.499	16.125	15.523	15.043
4.250	4.206	4.169	8.250	8.087	7.954	12.250	11.896	11.612	16.250	15.639	15.152
4.375	4.328	4.290	8.375	8.207	8.070	12.375	12.014	11.724	16.375	15.754	15.261
4.500	4.450	4.410	8.500	8.327	8.186	12.500	12.132	11.836	16.500	15.870	15.370
4.625	4.573	4.530	8.625	8.447	8.302	12.625	12.250	11.948	16.625	15.986	15.478
4.750	4.695	4.650	8.750	8.567	8.418	12.750	12.368	12.060	16.750	16.102	15.587
4.875	4.817	4.769	8.875	8.686	8.533	12.875	12.485	12.172	16.875	16.217	15.695

APPENDIX A-5: Future value of a regular annuity

A regular annuity is based on equal payments made at the END of each period.

After pym't	\multicolumn{15}{c}{Discount rate}													
	1%	2%	3%	4%	5%	6%	7%	8%	9%	10%	11%	12%	13%	14%	15%
1	1.0000	1.0000	1.0000	1.0000	1.0000	1.0000	1.0000	1.0000	1.0000	1.0000	1.0000	1.0000	1.0000	1.0000	1.0000
2	2.0100	2.0200	2.0300	2.0400	2.0500	2.0600	2.0700	2.0800	2.0900	2.1000	2.1100	2.1200	2.1300	2.1400	2.1500
3	3.0301	3.0604	3.0909	3.1216	3.1525	3.1836	3.2149	3.2464	3.2781	3.3100	3.3421	3.3744	3.4069	3.4396	3.4725
4	4.0604	4.1216	4.1836	4.2465	4.3101	4.3746	4.4399	4.5061	4.5731	4.6410	4.7097	4.7793	4.8498	4.9211	4.9934
5	5.1010	5.2040	5.3091	5.4163	5.5256	5.6371	5.7507	5.8666	5.9847	6.1051	6.2278	6.3528	6.4803	6.6101	6.7424
6	6.1520	6.3081	6.4684	6.6330	6.8019	6.9753	7.1533	7.3359	7.5233	7.7156	7.9129	8.1152	8.3227	8.5355	8.7537
7	7.2135	7.4343	7.6625	7.8983	8.1420	8.3938	8.6540	8.9228	9.2004	9.4872	9.7833	10.0890	10.4047	10.7305	11.0668
8	8.2857	8.5830	8.8923	9.2142	9.5491	9.8975	10.2598	10.6366	11.0285	11.4359	11.8594	12.2997	12.7573	13.2328	13.7268
9	9.3685	9.7546	10.1591	10.5828	11.0266	11.4913	11.9780	12.4876	13.0210	13.5795	14.1640	14.7757	15.4157	16.0853	16.7858
10	10.4622	10.9497	11.4639	12.0061	12.5779	13.1808	13.8164	14.4866	15.1929	15.9374	16.7220	17.5487	18.4197	19.3373	20.3037
11	11.5668	12.1687	12.8078	13.4864	14.2068	14.9716	15.7836	16.6455	17.5603	18.5312	19.5614	20.6546	21.8143	23.0445	24.3493
12	12.6825	13.4121	14.1920	15.0258	15.9171	16.8699	17.8885	18.9771	20.1407	21.3843	22.7132	24.1331	25.6502	27.2707	29.0017
13	13.8093	14.6803	15.6178	16.6268	17.7130	18.8821	20.1406	21.4953	22.9534	24.5227	26.2116	28.0291	29.9847	32.0887	34.3519
14	14.9474	15.9739	17.0863	18.2919	19.5986	21.0151	22.5505	24.2149	26.0192	27.9750	30.0949	32.3926	34.8827	37.5811	40.5047
15	16.0969	17.2934	18.5989	20.0236	21.5786	23.2760	25.1290	27.1521	29.3609	31.7725	34.4054	37.2797	40.4175	43.8424	47.5804
16	17.2579	18.6393	20.1569	21.8245	23.6575	25.6725	27.8881	30.3243	33.0034	35.9497	39.1899	42.7533	46.6717	50.9804	55.7175
17	18.4304	20.0121	21.7616	23.6975	25.8404	28.2129	30.8402	33.7502	36.9737	40.5447	44.5008	48.8837	53.7391	59.1176	65.0751
18	19.6147	21.4123	23.4144	25.6454	28.1324	30.9057	33.9990	37.4502	41.3013	45.5992	50.3959	55.7497	61.7251	68.3941	75.8364
19	20.8109	22.8406	25.1169	27.6712	30.5390	33.7600	37.3790	41.4463	46.0185	51.1591	56.9395	63.4397	70.7494	78.9692	88.2118
20	22.0190	24.2974	26.8704	29.7781	33.0660	36.7856	40.9955	45.7620	51.1601	57.2750	64.2028	72.0524	80.9468	91.0249	102.4436
21	23.2392	25.7833	28.6765	31.9692	35.7193	39.9927	44.8652	50.4229	56.7645	64.0025	72.265	81.6987	92.4699	104.7684	118.8101
22	24.4716	27.2990	30.5368	34.2480	38.5052	43.3923	49.0057	55.4568	62.8733	71.4027	81.2143	92.5026	105.4910	120.4360	137.6316
23	25.7163	28.8450	32.4529	36.6179	41.4305	46.9958	53.4361	60.8933	69.5319	79.5430	91.1479	104.6029	120.2048	138.2970	159.2764
24	26.9735	30.4219	34.4265	39.0826	44.5020	50.8156	58.1767	66.7648	76.7898	88.4973	102.1742	118.1552	136.8315	158.6586	184.1678
25	28.2432	32.0303	36.4593	41.6459	47.7271	54.8645	63.2490	73.1059	84.7009	98.3471	114.4135	133.3339	155.6196	181.8708	212.7930

APPENDIX A-5 CONTINUED

After pym't							Discount rate								
	1%	2%	3%	4%	5%	6%	7%	8%	9%	10%	11%	12%	13%	14%	15%
26	29.5256	33.6709	38.5530	44.3117	51.1135	59.1564	68.6765	79.9544	93.3240	109.1818	127.9988	150.3339	176.8501	208.3327	245.7120
27	30.8209	35.3443	40.7096	47.0842	54.6691	63.7058	74.4838	87.3508	102.7731	121.0999	143.0786	169.3740	200.8406	238.4993	283.5688
28	32.1291	37.0512	42.9309	49.9676	58.4026	68.5281	80.6977	95.3388	112.9682	134.2099	159.8173	190.6989	227.9499	272.8892	327.1041
29	33.4504	38.7922	45.2189	52.9663	62.3227	73.6398	87.3465	103.9659	124.1354	148.6309	178.3972	214.5828	258.5834	312.0937	377.1697
30	34.7849	40.5681	47.5754	56.0849	66.4388	79.0582	94.4608	113.2832	136.3075	164.4940	199.0209	241.3327	293.1992	356.7868	434.7451
31	36.1327	42.3794	50.0027	59.3283	70.7608	84.8017	102.0730	123.3459	149.5752	181.9434	221.9132	271.2926	332.3151	407.7370	500.9569
32	37.4941	44.2270	52.5028	62.7015	75.2988	90.8898	110.2182	134.2135	164.0370	201.1378	247.3236	304.8477	376.5161	465.8202	577.1005
33	38.8690	46.1116	55.0778	66.2095	80.0638	97.3432	118.9334	145.9506	179.8003	222.2515	275.5292	342.4294	426.4632	532.0350	664.6655
34	40.2577	48.0338	57.7302	69.8579	85.0670	104.1838	128.2588	158.6267	196.9823	245.4767	306.8374	384.5210	482.9034	607.5199	765.3654
35	41.6603	49.9945	60.4621	73.6522	90.3203	111.4348	138.2369	172.3168	215.7108	271.0244	341.5896	431.6635	546.6808	693.5727	881.1702
36	43.0769	51.9944	63.2759	77.5983	95.8363	119.1209	148.9135	187.1021	236.1247	299.1268	380.1644	484.4631	618.7493	791.6729	1014.3457
37	44.5076	54.0343	66.1742	81.7022	101.6281	127.2681	160.3374	203.0703	258.3759	330.0395	422.9825	543.5987	700.1867	903.5071	1167.4975
38	45.9527	56.1149	69.1594	85.9703	107.7095	135.9042	172.5610	220.3159	282.6298	364.0434	470.5106	609.8305	792.2110	1030.9981	1343.6222
39	47.4123	58.2372	72.2342	90.4091	114.0950	145.0585	185.6403	238.9412	309.0665	401.1478	523.2667	684.0102	896.1984	1176.3378	1546.1655
40	48.8864	60.4020	75.4013	95.0255	120.7998	154.7620	199.6351	259.0565	337.8824	442.5926	581.8261	767.0914	1013.7042	1342.0251	1779.0903
41	50.3752	62.6100	78.6633	99.8265	127.8398	165.0477	214.6096	280.7810	369.2919	487.8518	646.8269	860.1424	1146.4858	1530.9086	2046.9539
42	51.8790	64.8622	82.0232	104.8196	135.2318	175.9905	230.6322	304.2435	403.5281	537.6370	718.9779	964.3595	1296.5289	1746.2358	2354.9969
43	53.3978	67.1595	85.4839	110.0124	142.9933	187.5076	247.7765	329.5830	440.8457	592.4007	799.0655	1081.0826	1466.0777	1991.7088	2709.2465
44	54.9318	69.5027	89.0484	115.4129	151.1430	199.7580	266.1209	356.9496	481.5218	652.6408	887.9627	1211.8125	1657.6678	2271.5481	3116.6334
45	56.4811	71.8927	92.7199	121.0294	159.7002	212.7435	285.7493	386.5056	525.8587	718.9048	986.6386	1358.2300	1874.1646	2590.5648	3585.1285
46	58.0459	74.3306	96.5015	126.8706	168.6852	226.5081	306.7518	418.4261	574.1860	791.7953	1096.1688	1522.2176	2118.8060	2954.2439	4123.8977
47	59.6263	76.8172	100.3965	132.9454	178.1194	241.0986	329.2244	452.9002	626.8628	871.9749	1217.7474	1705.8838	2395.2508	3368.8380	4743.4824
48	61.2226	79.3535	104.4084	139.2632	188.0254	256.5645	353.2701	490.1322	684.2804	960.1723	1352.6996	1911.5898	2707.6334	3841.4753	5456.0047
49	62.8348	81.9406	108.5406	145.8337	198.4267	272.9584	378.9990	530.3427	746.8656	1057.1896	1502.4965	2141.9806	3060.6258	4380.2819	6275.4055
50	64.4632	84.5794	112.7969	152.6671	209.3480	290.3359	406.5289	573.7702	815.0836	1163.9085	1668.7712	2400.0182	3459.5071	4994.5213	7217.7163

APPENDIX A-6: Future value of an annuity due

An annuity due is based on equal payments made at the START of each period.

After pym't	1%	2%	3%	4%	5%	6%	7%	8%	9%	10%	11%	12%	13%	14%	15%
										Discount rate					
1	1.0100	1.0200	1.0300	1.0400	1.0500	1.0600	1.0700	1.0800	1.0900	1.1000	1.1100	1.1200	1.1300	1.1400	1.1500
2	2.0301	2.0604	2.0909	2.1216	2.1525	2.1836	2.2149	2.2464	2.2781	2.3100	2.3421	2.3744	2.4069	2.4396	2.4725
3	3.0604	3.1216	3.1836	3.2465	3.3101	3.3746	3.4399	3.5061	3.5731	3.6410	3.7097	3.7793	3.8498	3.9211	3.9934
4	4.1010	4.2040	4.3091	4.4163	4.5256	4.6371	4.7507	4.8666	4.9847	5.1051	5.2278	5.3528	5.4803	5.6101	5.7424
5	5.1520	5.3081	5.4684	5.6330	5.8019	5.9753	6.1533	6.3359	6.5233	6.7156	6.9129	7.1152	7.3227	7.5355	7.7537
6	6.2135	6.4343	6.6625	6.8983	7.1420	7.3938	7.6540	7.9228	8.2004	8.4872	8.7833	9.0890	9.4047	9.7305	10.0668
7	7.2857	7.5830	7.8923	8.2142	8.5491	8.8975	9.2598	9.6366	10.0285	10.4359	10.8594	11.2997	11.7573	12.2328	12.7268
8	8.3685	8.7546	9.1591	9.5828	10.0266	10.4913	10.9780	11.4876	12.0210	12.5795	13.1640	13.7757	14.4157	15.0853	15.7858
9	9.4622	9.9497	10.4639	11.0061	11.5779	12.1808	12.8164	13.4866	14.1929	14.9374	15.7220	16.5487	17.4197	18.3373	19.3037
10	10.5668	11.1687	11.8078	12.4864	13.2068	13.9716	14.7836	15.6455	16.5603	17.5312	18.5614	19.6546	20.8143	22.0445	23.3493
11	11.6825	12.4121	13.1920	14.0258	14.9171	15.8699	16.8885	17.9771	19.1407	20.3843	21.7132	23.1331	24.6502	26.2707	28.0017
12	12.8093	13.6803	14.6178	15.6268	16.7130	17.8821	19.1406	20.4953	21.9534	23.5227	25.2115	27.0291	28.9847	31.0887	33.3519
13	13.9474	14.9739	16.0863	17.2919	18.5986	20.0151	21.5505	23.2149	25.0192	26.9750	29.0949	31.3926	33.8827	36.5811	39.5047
14	15.0969	16.2934	17.5989	19.0236	20.5786	22.2760	24.1290	26.1521	28.3609	30.7725	33.4054	36.2797	39.4175	42.8424	46.5804
15	16.2579	17.6393	19.1569	20.8245	22.6575	24.6725	26.8881	29.3243	32.0034	34.9497	38.1899	41.7533	45.6717	49.9804	54.7175
16	17.4304	19.0121	20.7616	22.6975	24.8404	27.2129	29.8402	32.7502	35.9737	39.5447	43.5003	47.8837	52.7391	58.1176	64.0751
17	18.6147	20.4123	22.4144	24.6454	27.1324	29.9057	32.9990	36.4502	40.3013	44.5992	49.3953	54.7497	60.7251	67.3941	74.8364
18	19.8109	21.8406	24.1169	26.6712	29.5390	32.7600	36.3790	40.4463	45.0185	50.1591	55.9395	62.4397	69.7494	77.9692	87.2118
19	21.0190	23.2974	25.8704	28.7781	32.0660	35.7856	39.9955	44.7620	50.1601	56.2750	63.2023	71.0524	79.9468	90.0249	101.4436
20	22.2392	24.7833	27.6765	30.9692	34.7193	38.9927	43.8652	49.4229	55.7645	63.0025	71.2651	80.6987	91.4699	103.7684	117.8101
21	23.4716	26.2990	29.5368	33.2480	37.5052	42.3923	48.0057	54.4568	61.8733	70.4027	80.2143	91.5026	104.4910	119.4360	136.6316
22	24.7163	27.8450	31.4529	35.6179	40.4305	45.9958	52.4361	59.8933	68.5319	78.5430	90.1479	103.6029	119.2048	137.2970	158.2764
23	25.9735	29.4219	33.4265	38.0826	43.5020	49.8156	57.1767	65.7648	75.7898	87.4973	101.1742	117.1552	135.8315	157.6586	183.1678
24	27.2432	31.0303	35.4593	40.6459	46.7271	53.8645	62.2490	72.1059	83.7009	97.3471	113.4133	132.3339	154.6196	180.8708	211.7930
25	28.5256	32.6709	37.5530	43.3117	50.1135	58.1564	67.6765	78.9544	92.3240	108.1818	126.9988	149.3339	175.8501	207.3327	244.7120

After pym't	1%	2%	3%	4%	5%	6%	7%	Discount rate 8%	9%	10%	11%	12%	13%	14%	15%
26	29.8209	34.3343	39.7096	46.0842	53.6691	62.7058	73.4838	86.3508	101.7231	120.0999	142.0786	168.3740	199.8406	237.4993	282.5688
27	31.1291	36.0512	41.9309	48.9676	57.4026	67.5281	79.6977	94.3388	111.9682	133.2099	158.8173	189.6989	226.9499	271.8892	326.1041
28	32.4504	37.7922	44.2189	51.9663	61.3227	72.6398	86.3465	102.9659	123.1354	147.6309	177.3972	213.5828	257.5834	311.0937	376.1697
29	33.7849	39.5681	46.5754	55.0849	65.4388	78.0582	93.4608	112.2832	135.3075	163.4940	198.0209	240.3327	292.1992	355.7868	433.7451
30	35.1327	41.3794	49.0027	58.3283	69.7608	83.8017	101.0730	122.3459	148.5752	180.9434	220.9132	270.2926	331.3151	406.7370	499.9569
31	36.4941	43.2270	51.5028	61.7015	74.2988	89.8898	109.2182	133.2135	163.0370	200.1378	246.3236	303.8477	375.5161	464.8202	576.1005
32	37.8690	45.1116	54.0778	65.2095	79.0638	96.3432	117.9334	144.9506	178.8003	221.2515	274.5292	341.4294	425.4632	531.0350	663.6655
33	39.2577	47.0338	56.7302	68.8579	84.0670	103.1838	127.2588	157.6267	195.9823	244.4767	305.8374	383.5210	481.9034	606.5199	764.3654
34	40.6603	48.8945	59.4621	72.6522	89.3203	110.4348	137.2369	171.3168	214.7108	270.0244	340.5896	430.6635	545.6808	692.5727	880.1702
35	42.0769	50.9944	62.2759	76.5983	94.8363	118.1209	147.9135	186.1021	235.1247	298.1268	379.1644	483.4631	617.7493	790.6729	1013.3457
36	43.5076	53.0343	65.1742	80.7022	100.6281	126.2681	159.3374	202.0703	257.3759	329.0395	421.9825	542.5987	699.1867	902.5071	1166.4975
37	44.9527	55.1149	68.1594	84.9703	106.7095	134.9042	171.5610	219.3159	281.6298	363.0434	469.5106	608.8305	791.2110	1029.9981	1342.6222
38	46.4123	57.2372	71.2342	89.4091	113.0950	144.0585	184.6403	237.9412	308.0665	400.4478	522.2667	683.0102	895.1984	1175.3378	1545.1655
39	47.8864	59.4020	74.4013	94.0255	119.7998	153.7620	198.6351	258.0565	336.8824	441.5926	580.8261	766.0914	1012.7042	1341.0251	1778.0903
40	49.3752	61.6100	77.6633	98.8265	126.8398	164.0477	213.6096	279.7810	368.2919	486.8518	645.8269	859.1424	1145.4858	1529.9086	2045.9539
41	50.8790	63.8622	81.0232	103.8196	134.2318	174.9505	229.6322	303.2435	402.5281	536.6370	717.9779	963.3595	1295.5289	1745.2358	2353.9969
42	52.3978	66.1595	84.4839	109.0124	141.9933	186.5076	246.7765	328.5830	439.8457	591.4007	798.0655	1080.0826	1465.0777	1990.7088	2708.2465
43	53.9318	68.5027	88.0484	114.4129	150.1430	198.7580	265.1209	355.5496	480.5218	651.6408	886.9627	1210.8125	1656.6678	2270.5481	3115.6334
44	55.4811	70.8927	91.7199	120.0294	158.7002	211.7435	284.7493	385.5056	524.8587	717.9048	985.6386	1357.2300	1873.1646	2589.5648	3584.1285
45	57.0459	73.3306	95.5015	125.8706	167.6852	225.5081	305.7518	417.4261	573.1860	790.7953	1095.1688	1521.2176	2117.8060	2953.2439	4122.8977
46	58.6263	75.8172	99.3965	131.9454	177.1194	240.0986	328.2244	451.9002	625.8628	870.9749	1216.7474	1704.8838	2394.2508	3367.8380	4742.4824
47	60.2226	78.3535	103.4084	138.2632	187.0254	255.5645	352.2701	489.1322	683.2804	959.1723	1351.6996	1910.5898	2706.6334	3840.4753	5455.0047
48	61.8348	80.9406	107.5406	144.8337	197.4267	271.9584	377.9990	529.3427	745.8656	1056.1896	1501.4965	2140.9806	3059.6258	4379.2819	6274.4055
49	63.4632	83.5794	111.7969	151.6671	208.3480	289.3359	405.5289	572.7702	814.0836	1162.9085	1667.7712	2399.0182	3458.5071	4993.5213	7216.7163
50	65.1078	86.2710	116.1808	158.7738	219.8154	307.7561	434.9860	619.6718	888.4411	1280.2994	1852.3360	2688.0204	3909.2430	5693.7543	8300.3737

APPENDIX A-7: Present value of a regular annuity

A regular annuity is based on equal payments made at the END of each period.

No. of pymt's	1%	2%	3%	4%	5%	6%	7%	8%	9%	10%	11%	12%	13%	14%	15%
								Discount rate							
1	0.9901	0.9804	0.9709	0.9615	0.9524	0.9434	0.9346	0.9259	0.9174	0.9091	0.9009	0.8929	0.8850	0.8772	0.8696
2	1.9704	1.9416	1.9135	1.8861	1.8594	1.8334	1.8080	1.7833	1.7591	1.7355	1.7125	1.6901	1.6681	1.6467	1.6257
3	2.9410	2.8839	2.8286	2.7751	2.7232	2.6730	2.6243	2.5771	2.5313	2.4869	2.4437	2.4018	2.3612	2.3216	2.2832
4	3.9020	3.8077	3.7171	3.6299	3.5460	3.4651	3.3872	3.3121	3.2397	3.1699	3.1024	3.0373	2.9745	2.9137	2.8550
5	4.8534	4.7135	4.5797	4.4518	4.3295	4.2124	4.1002	3.9927	3.8897	3.7908	3.6959	3.6048	3.5172	3.4331	3.3522
6	5.7955	5.6014	5.4172	5.2421	5.0757	4.9173	4.7665	4.6229	4.4859	4.3553	4.2305	4.1114	3.9975	3.8887	3.7845
7	6.7282	6.4720	6.2303	6.0021	5.7864	5.5824	5.3893	5.2064	5.0330	4.8684	4.7122	4.5638	4.4226	4.2883	4.1604
8	7.6517	7.3255	7.0197	6.7327	6.4632	6.2098	5.9713	5.7466	5.5348	5.3349	5.1461	4.9676	4.7988	4.6389	4.4873
9	8.5660	8.1622	7.7861	7.4353	7.1078	6.8017	6.5152	6.2469	5.9952	5.7590	5.5370	5.3282	5.1317	4.9464	4.7716
10	9.4713	8.9826	8.5302	8.1109	7.7217	7.3601	7.0236	6.7101	6.4177	6.1446	5.8892	5.6502	5.4262	5.2161	5.0188
11	10.3676	9.7868	9.2526	8.7605	8.3064	7.8869	7.4987	7.1390	6.8052	6.4951	6.2065	5.9377	5.6869	5.4527	5.2337
12	11.2551	10.5753	9.9540	9.3851	8.8633	8.3838	7.9427	7.5361	7.1607	6.8137	6.4924	6.1944	5.9176	5.6603	5.4206
13	12.1337	11.3484	10.6350	9.9856	9.3936	8.8527	8.3577	7.9038	7.4869	7.1034	6.7499	6.4235	6.1218	5.8424	5.5831
14	13.0037	12.1062	11.2961	10.5631	9.8986	9.2950	8.7455	8.2442	7.7862	7.3667	6.9819	6.6282	6.3025	6.0021	5.7245
15	13.8651	12.8493	11.9379	11.1184	10.3797	9.7122	9.1079	8.5595	8.0607	7.6061	7.1909	6.8109	6.4624	6.1422	5.8474
16	14.7179	13.5777	12.5611	11.6523	10.8378	10.1059	9.4466	8.8514	8.3126	7.8237	7.3792	6.9740	6.6039	6.2651	5.9542
17	15.5623	14.2919	13.1661	12.1657	11.2741	10.4773	9.7632	9.1216	8.5436	8.0216	7.5488	7.1196	6.7291	6.3729	6.0472
18	16.3983	14.9920	13.7535	12.6593	11.6896	10.8276	10.0591	9.3719	8.7556	8.2014	7.7016	7.2497	6.8399	6.4674	6.1280
19	17.2260	15.6785	14.3238	13.1339	12.0853	11.1581	10.3356	9.6036	8.9501	8.3649	7.8393	7.3658	6.9380	6.5504	6.1982
20	18.0456	16.3514	14.8775	13.5903	12.4622	11.4699	10.5940	9.8181	9.1285	8.5136	7.9633	7.4694	7.0248	6.6231	6.2593
21	18.8570	17.0112	15.4150	14.0292	12.8212	11.7641	10.8355	10.0168	9.2922	8.6487	8.0751	7.5620	7.1016	6.6870	6.3125
22	19.6604	17.6580	15.9369	14.4511	13.1630	12.0416	11.0612	10.2007	9.4424	8.7715	8.1757	7.6446	7.1695	6.7429	6.3587
23	20.4558	18.2922	16.4436	14.8568	13.4886	12.3034	11.2722	10.3711	9.5802	8.8832	8.2664	7.7184	7.2297	6.7921	6.3988
24	21.2434	18.9139	16.9355	15.2470	13.7986	12.5504	11.4693	10.5288	9.7066	8.9847	8.3481	7.7843	7.2829	6.8351	6.4338
25	22.0232	19.5235	17.4131	15.6221	14.0939	12.7834	11.6536	10.6748	9.8226	9.0770	8.4217	7.8431	7.3300	6.8729	6.4641

APPENDIX A-7 CONTINUED

No. of pym'ts	1%	2%	3%	4%	5%	6%	Discount rate 7%	8%	9%	10%	11%	12%	13%	14%	15%
26	22.7952	20.1210	17.8768	15.9828	14.3752	13.0032	11.8258	10.8100	9.9290	9.1609	8.4881	7.8957	7.3717	6.9061	6.4906
27	23.5596	20.7069	18.3270	16.3296	14.6430	13.2105	11.9867	10.9352	10.0266	9.2372	8.5478	7.9426	7.4086	6.9352	6.5135
28	24.3164	21.2813	18.7641	16.6631	14.8981	13.4062	12.1371	11.0511	10.1161	9.3066	8.6016	7.9844	7.4412	6.9607	6.5335
29	25.0658	21.8444	19.1885	16.9837	15.1411	13.5907	12.2777	11.1584	10.1983	9.3696	8.6501	8.0218	7.4701	6.9830	6.5509
30	25.8077	22.3965	19.6004	17.2920	15.3725	13.7648	12.4090	11.2578	10.2737	9.4269	8.6938	8.0552	7.4957	7.0027	6.5660
31	26.5423	22.9377	20.0004	17.5885	15.5928	13.9291	12.5318	11.3498	10.3428	9.4790	8.7331	8.0850	7.5183	7.0199	6.5791
32	27.2696	23.4683	20.3888	17.8736	15.8027	14.0840	12.6466	11.4350	10.4062	9.5264	8.7686	8.1116	7.5383	7.0350	6.5905
33	27.9897	23.9886	20.7658	18.1476	16.0025	14.2302	12.7538	11.5139	10.4644	9.5694	8.8005	8.1354	7.5560	7.0482	6.6005
34	28.7027	24.4986	21.1318	18.4112	16.1929	14.3681	12.8540	11.5869	10.5178	9.6086	8.8293	8.1566	7.5717	7.0599	6.6091
35	29.4086	24.9986	21.4872	18.6646	16.3742	14.4982	12.9477	11.6546	10.5668	9.6442	8.8552	8.1755	7.5856	7.0700	6.6166
36	30.1075	25.4888	21.8323	18.9083	16.5469	14.6210	13.0352	11.7172	10.6118	9.6765	8.8786	8.1924	7.5979	7.0790	6.6231
37	30.7995	25.9695	22.1672	19.1426	16.7113	14.7368	13.1170	11.7752	10.6530	9.7059	8.8996	8.2075	7.6087	7.0868	6.6288
38	31.4847	26.4406	22.4925	19.3679	16.8679	14.8460	13.1935	11.8289	10.6908	9.7327	8.9186	8.2210	7.6183	7.0937	6.6338
39	32.1630	26.9026	22.8082	19.5845	17.0170	14.9491	13.2649	11.8786	10.7255	9.7570	8.9357	8.2330	7.6268	7.0997	6.6380
40	32.8347	27.3555	23.1148	19.7928	17.1591	15.0463	13.3317	11.9246	10.7574	9.7791	8.9511	8.2438	7.6344	7.1050	6.6418
41	33.4997	27.7995	23.4124	19.9931	17.2944	15.1380	13.3941	11.9672	10.7866	9.7991	8.9649	8.2534	7.6410	7.1097	6.6450
42	34.1581	28.2348	23.7014	20.1856	17.4232	15.2245	13.4524	12.0067	10.8134	9.8174	8.9774	8.2619	7.6469	7.1138	6.6478
43	34.8100	28.6616	23.9819	20.3708	17.5459	15.3062	13.5070	12.0432	10.8380	9.8340	8.9886	8.2696	7.6522	7.1173	6.6503
44	35.4555	29.0800	24.2543	20.5488	17.6628	15.3832	13.5579	12.0771	10.8605	9.8491	8.9988	8.2764	7.6568	7.1205	6.6524
45	36.0945	29.4902	24.5187	20.7200	17.7741	15.4558	13.6055	12.1084	10.8812	9.8628	9.0079	8.2825	7.6609	7.1232	6.6543
46	36.7272	29.8923	24.7754	20.8847	17.8801	15.5244	13.6500	12.1374	10.9002	9.8753	9.0161	8.2880	7.6645	7.1256	6.6559
47	37.3537	30.2866	25.0247	21.0429	17.9810	15.5890	13.6916	12.1643	10.9176	9.8866	9.0235	8.2928	7.6677	7.1277	6.6573
48	37.9740	30.6731	25.2667	21.1951	18.0772	15.6500	13.7305	12.1891	10.9336	9.8969	9.0302	8.2972	7.6705	7.1296	6.6585
49	38.5881	31.0521	25.5017	21.3415	18.1687	15.7076	13.7668	12.2122	10.9482	9.9063	9.0362	8.3010	7.6730	7.1312	6.6596
50	39.1961	31.4236	25.7298	21.4822	18.2559	15.7619	13.8007	12.2335	10.9617	9.9148	9.0417	8.3045	7.6752	7.1327	6.6605

APPENDIX A-8: Present value of an annuity due

An annuity due is based on equal payments made at the START of each period.

No. of pym'ts	1%	2%	3%	4%	5%	6%	7%	8%	9%	10%	11%	12%	13%	14%	15%
1	1.0000	1.0000	1.0000	1.0000	1.0000	1.0000	1.0000	1.0000	1.0000	1.0000	1.0000	1.0000	1.0000	1.0000	1.0000
2	1.9901	1.9804	1.9709	1.9615	1.9524	1.9434	1.9346	1.9259	1.9174	1.9091	1.9009	1.8929	1.8850	1.8772	1.8696
3	2.9704	2.9416	2.9135	2.8861	2.8594	2.8334	2.8080	2.7833	2.7591	2.7355	2.7125	2.6901	2.6681	2.6467	2.6257
4	3.9410	3.8839	3.8286	3.7751	3.7232	3.6730	3.6243	3.5771	3.5313	3.4869	3.4437	3.4018	3.3612	3.3216	3.2832
5	4.9020	4.8077	4.7171	4.6299	4.5460	4.4651	4.3872	4.3121	4.2397	4.1699	4.1024	4.0373	3.9745	3.9137	3.8550
6	5.8534	5.7135	5.5797	5.4518	5.3295	5.2124	5.1002	4.9927	4.8897	4.7908	4.6959	4.6048	4.5172	4.4331	4.3522
7	6.7955	6.6014	6.4172	6.2421	6.0757	5.9173	5.7665	5.6229	5.4859	5.3553	5.2305	5.1114	4.9975	4.8887	4.7845
8	7.7282	7.4720	7.2303	7.0021	6.7864	6.5824	6.3893	6.2064	6.0330	5.8684	5.7122	5.5638	5.4226	5.2883	5.1604
9	8.6517	8.3255	8.0197	7.7327	7.4632	7.2098	6.9713	6.7466	6.5348	6.3349	6.1461	5.9676	5.7988	5.6389	5.4873
10	9.5660	9.1622	8.7861	8.4353	8.1078	7.8017	7.5152	7.2469	6.9952	6.7590	6.5370	6.3282	6.1317	5.9464	5.7716
11	10.4713	9.9826	9.5302	9.1109	8.7217	8.3601	8.0236	7.7101	7.4177	7.1446	6.8892	6.6502	6.4262	6.2161	6.0188
12	11.3676	10.7868	10.2526	9.7605	9.3064	8.8869	8.4987	8.1390	7.8052	7.4951	7.2065	6.9377	6.6869	6.4527	6.2337
13	12.2551	11.5753	10.9540	10.3851	9.8633	9.3838	8.9427	8.5361	8.1607	7.8137	7.4924	7.1944	6.9176	6.6603	6.4206
14	13.1337	12.3484	11.6350	10.9856	10.3936	9.8527	9.3577	8.9038	8.4869	8.1034	7.7499	7.4235	7.1218	6.8424	6.5831
15	14.0037	13.1062	12.2961	11.5631	10.8986	10.2950	9.7455	9.2442	8.7862	8.3667	7.9819	7.6282	7.3025	7.0021	6.7245
16	14.8651	13.8493	12.9379	12.1184	11.3797	10.7122	10.1079	9.5595	9.0607	8.6061	8.1909	7.8109	7.4624	7.1422	6.8474
17	15.7179	14.5777	13.5611	12.6523	11.8378	11.1059	10.4466	9.8514	9.3126	8.8237	8.3792	7.9740	7.6039	7.2651	6.9542
18	16.5623	15.2919	14.1661	13.1657	12.2741	11.4773	10.7632	10.1216	9.5436	9.0216	8.5488	8.1196	7.7291	7.3729	7.0472
19	17.3983	15.9920	14.7535	13.6593	12.6896	11.8276	11.0591	10.3719	9.7556	9.2014	8.7016	8.2497	7.8399	7.4674	7.1280
20	18.2260	16.6785	15.3238	14.1339	13.0853	12.1581	11.3356	10.6036	9.9501	9.3649	8.8393	8.3658	7.9380	7.5504	7.1982
21	19.0456	17.3514	15.8775	14.5903	13.4622	12.4699	11.5940	10.8181	10.1285	9.5136	8.9633	8.4694	8.0248	7.6231	7.2593
22	19.8570	18.0112	16.4150	15.0292	13.8212	12.7641	11.8355	11.0168	10.2922	9.6487	9.0751	8.5620	8.1016	7.6870	7.3125
23	20.6604	18.6580	16.9369	15.4511	14.1630	13.0416	12.0612	11.2007	10.4424	9.7715	9.1757	8.6446	8.1695	7.7429	7.3587
24	21.4558	19.2922	17.4436	15.8568	14.4886	13.3034	12.2772	11.3711	10.5802	9.8832	9.2664	8.7184	8.2297	7.7921	7.3988
25	22.2434	19.9139	17.9355	16.2470	14.7986	13.5504	12.4693	11.5288	10.7066	9.9847	9.3481	8.7843	8.2829	7.8351	7.4338

APPENDIX A-8 CONTINUED

No. of pym'ts	1%	2%	3%	4%	5%	6%	7%	Discount rate 8%	9%	10%	11%	12%	13%	14%	15%
26	23.0232	20.5235	18.4131	16.6221	15.0939	13.7834	12.6536	11.6748	10.8226	10.0770	9.4217	8.8431	8.3300	7.8729	7.4641
27	23.7952	21.1210	18.8768	16.9828	15.3752	14.0032	12.8258	11.8100	10.9290	10.1609	9.4881	8.8957	8.3717	7.9061	7.4906
28	24.5596	21.7069	19.3270	17.3296	15.6430	14.2105	12.9867	11.9352	11.0266	10.2372	9.5478	8.9426	8.4086	7.9352	7.5135
29	25.3164	22.2813	19.7641	17.6631	15.8981	14.4062	13.1371	12.0511	11.1161	10.3066	9.6016	8.9844	8.4412	7.9607	7.5335
30	26.0658	22.8444	20.1885	17.9837	16.1411	14.5907	13.2777	12.1584	11.1983	10.3696	9.6501	9.0218	8.4701	7.9830	7.5509
31	26.8077	23.3965	20.6004	18.2920	16.3725	14.7648	13.4090	12.2578	11.2737	10.4269	9.6938	9.0552	8.4957	8.0027	7.5660
32	27.5423	23.9377	21.0004	18.5885	16.5928	14.9291	13.5318	12.3498	11.3428	10.4790	9.7331	9.0850	8.5183	8.0199	7.5791
33	28.2696	24.4683	21.3888	18.8736	16.8027	15.0840	13.6466	12.4350	11.4062	10.5264	9.7686	9.1116	8.5383	8.0350	7.5905
34	28.9897	24.9986	21.7658	19.1476	17.0025	15.2302	13.7538	12.5139	11.4644	10.5694	9.8005	9.1354	8.5560	8.0482	7.6005
35	29.7027	25.4986	22.1318	19.4112	17.1929	15.3681	13.8540	12.5869	11.5178	10.6086	9.8293	9.1566	8.5717	8.0599	7.6091
36	30.4086	25.9986	22.4872	19.6646	17.3742	15.4982	13.9477	12.6546	11.5668	10.6442	9.8552	9.1755	8.5856	8.0700	7.6166
37	31.1075	26.4888	22.8323	19.9083	17.5469	15.6210	14.0352	12.7172	11.6118	10.6765	9.8786	9.1924	8.5979	8.0790	7.6231
38	31.7995	26.9695	23.1672	20.1426	17.7113	15.7368	14.1170	12.7752	11.6530	10.7059	9.8996	9.2075	8.6087	8.0868	7.6288
39	32.4847	27.4406	23.4925	20.3679	17.8679	15.8460	14.1935	12.8289	11.6908	10.7327	9.9186	9.2210	8.6183	8.0937	7.6338
40	33.1630	27.9026	23.8082	20.5845	18.0170	15.9491	14.2649	12.8786	11.7255	10.7570	9.9357	9.2330	8.6268	8.0997	7.6380
41	33.8347	28.3555	24.1148	20.7928	18.1591	16.0463	14.3317	12.9246	11.7574	10.7791	9.9511	9.2438	8.6344	8.1050	7.6418
42	34.4997	28.7995	24.4124	20.9931	18.2944	16.1380	14.3941	12.9672	11.7866	10.7991	9.9649	9.2534	8.6410	8.1097	7.6450
43	35.1581	29.2348	24.7014	21.1856	18.4232	16.2245	14.4524	13.0067	11.8134	10.8174	9.9774	9.2619	8.6469	8.1138	7.6478
44	35.8100	29.6616	24.9819	21.3708	18.5459	16.3062	14.5070	13.0432	11.8380	10.8340	9.9886	9.2696	8.6522	8.1173	7.6503
45	36.4555	30.0800	25.2543	21.5488	18.6628	16.3832	14.5579	13.0771	11.8605	10.8491	9.9988	9.2764	8.6568	8.1205	7.6524
46	37.0945	30.4902	25.5187	21.7200	18.7741	16.4558	14.6055	13.1084	11.8812	10.8628	10.0079	9.2825	8.6609	8.1232	7.6543
47	37.7272	30.8923	25.7754	21.8847	18.8801	16.5244	14.6500	13.1374	11.9002	10.8753	10.0161	9.2880	8.6645	8.1256	7.6559
48	38.3537	31.2866	26.0247	22.0429	18.9810	16.5890	14.6916	13.1643	11.9176	10.8866	10.0235	9.2928	8.6677	8.1277	7.6573
49	38.9740	31.6731	26.2667	22.1951	19.0772	16.6500	14.7305	13.1891	11.9336	10.8969	10.0302	9.2972	8.6705	8.1296	7.6585
50	39.5881	32.0521	26.5017	22.3415	19.1687	16.7076	14.7668	13.2122	11.9482	10.9063	10.0362	9.3010	8.6730	8.1312	7.6596

APPENDIX A-9: Present value of an indexed regular annuity

How much capital is needed to fund an indexed payment at END of each year?

If your money grows at this rate per year

And indexing is 2% — multiply desired amount by this factor

Yrs of income	5%	6%	7%	8%	9%	10%	11%	12%
5	4.5874	4.4616	4.3412	4.2259	4.1153	4.0093	3.9075	3.8099
10	8.5559	8.1427	7.7586	7.4013	7.0684	6.7578	6.4678	6.1967
15	11.9889	11.1796	10.4488	9.7873	9.1874	8.6421	8.1454	7.6920
20	14.9587	13.6852	12.5665	11.5803	10.7080	9.9336	9.2445	8.6288
25	17.5278	15.7524	14.2335	12.9275	11.7991	10.8194	9.9647	9.2156
30	19.7503	17.4579	15.5458	13.9399	12.5821	11.4265	10.4366	9.5833
35	21.6729	18.8650	16.5788	14.7006	13.1439	11.8427	10.7458	9.8137
40	23.3362	20.0259	17.3919	15.2272	13.5471	12.1280	10.9483	9.9580
45	24.7750	20.9837	18.0321	15.7017	13.8364	12.3236	11.0811	10.0484
50	26.0196	21.7739	18.5360	16.0244	14.0440	12.4577	11.1681	10.1050

And indexing is 3% — multiply desired amount by this factor

Yrs of income	5%	6%	7%	8%	9%	10%	11%	12%
5	4.7214	4.5912	4.4664	4.3470	4.2325	4.1227	4.0174	3.9163
10	9.0100	8.5684	8.1581	7.7766	7.4214	7.0903	6.7812	6.4924
15	12.9054	12.0137	11.2095	10.4826	9.8241	9.2264	8.6826	8.1870
20	16.4437	14.9984	13.7316	12.6175	11.6344	10.7640	9.9908	9.3017
25	19.6576	17.5839	15.8162	14.3020	12.9984	11.8708	10.8907	10.0349
30	22.5769	19.8237	17.5393	15.6310	14.0261	12.6675	11.5099	10.5173
35	25.2285	21.7640	18.9635	16.6795	14.8004	13.2410	11.9358	10.8345
40	27.6370	23.4448	20.1406	17.5068	15.3838	13.6538	12.2289	11.0432
45	29.8248	24.9008	21.1136	18.1595	15.8234	13.9509	12.4305	11.1805
50	31.8119	26.1622	21.9178	18.6745	16.1546	14.1648	12.5692	11.2708

If your money grows at this rate per year

And indexing is 4% — multiply desired amount by this factor

Yrs of income	5%	6%	7%	8%	9%	10%	11%	12%
5	4.8589	4.7240	4.5948	4.4711	4.3526	4.2389	4.1299	4.0253
10	9.4909	9.0188	8.5807	8.1734	7.7944	7.4412	7.1118	6.8042
15	13.9064	12.9925	12.0382	11.2390	10.5159	9.8604	9.2648	8.7227
20	18.1156	16.4735	15.0374	13.7774	12.6679	11.6879	10.8194	10.0471
25	22.1282	19.7009	17.6392	15.8792	14.3697	13.0685	11.9418	10.9614
30	25.9533	22.6352	19.8960	17.6197	15.7153	14.1115	12.7522	11.5926
35	29.5997	25.3028	21.8538	19.0608	16.7793	14.8994	13.3373	12.0284
40	33.0757	27.7282	23.5520	20.2541	17.6207	15.4946	13.7598	12.3293
45	36.3893	29.9332	25.0252	21.2422	18.2860	15.9443	14.0048	12.5369
50	39.5482	31.9379	26.3031	22.0604	18.8121	16.2840	14.2851	12.6803

And indexing is 5% — multiply desired amount by this factor

Yrs of income	5%	6%	7%	8%	9%	10%	11%	12%
5	5.0012	4.8603	4.7265	4.5984	4.4757	4.3581	4.2453	4.1371
10	10.0000	9.4955	9.0275	8.5927	8.1884	7.8118	7.4608	7.1131
15	15.0012	13.9163	12.9413	12.0622	11.2679	10.5487	9.8962	9.3028
20	20.0001	18.1324	16.5027	15.0759	13.8225	12.7177	11.7408	10.8741
25	24.9989	22.1533	19.7435	17.6936	15.9414	14.4365	13.1379	12.0121
30	30.0001	25.9881	22.6925	19.9674	17.6991	15.7986	14.1961	12.8361
35	35.0013	29.6454	25.3761	21.9424	19.1570	16.8781	14.9976	13.4329
40	40.0001	33.1335	27.8180	23.5580	20.3664	17.7335	15.6046	13.8651
45	45.0013	36.4600	30.0401	25.1482	21.3696	18.4114	16.0644	14.1781
50	50.0002	39.6326	32.0621	26.4425	22.2017	18.9486	16.4127	14.4048

APPENDIX A-10: Present value of an indexed annuity due

How much capital is needed to fund an indexed payment at START of each year?

Yrs of income	If your money grows at this rate per year							
	5%	6%	7%	8%	9%	10%	11%	12%
And indexing is 2% multiply desired amount by this factor								
5	4.7223	4.6366	4.5540	4.4745	4.3977	4.3237	4.2523	4.1834
10	8.8075	8.4620	8.1390	7.8367	7.5534	7.2878	7.0385	6.8042
15	12.3415	11.6180	10.9610	10.3631	9.8179	9.3199	8.8641	8.4461
20	15.3987	14.2219	13.1825	12.2615	11.4428	10.7129	10.0602	9.4747
25	18.0434	16.3701	14.9312	13.6880	12.6088	11.6680	10.8439	10.1191
30	20.3312	18.1425	16.3078	14.7599	13.4455	12.3227	11.3575	10.5229
35	22.3104	19.6048	17.3914	15.5653	14.0459	12.7715	11.6939	10.7758
40	24.0225	20.8112	18.2445	16.1705	14.4768	13.0792	11.9144	10.9342
45	25.5036	21.8066	18.9160	16.6253	14.7859	13.2901	12.0588	11.0335
50	26.7849	22.6278	19.4446	16.9670	15.0078	13.4347	12.1535	11.0957

Yrs of income	If your money grows at this rate per year							
	5%	6%	7%	8%	9%	10%	11%	12%
And indexing is 3% multiply desired amount by this factor								
5	4.8131	4.7249	4.6399	4.5580	4.4790	4.4029	4.3294	4.2584
10	9.1850	8.8179	8.4750	8.1541	7.8537	7.5721	7.3079	7.0597
15	13.1560	12.3637	11.6448	10.9915	10.3964	9.8534	9.3570	8.9023
20	16.7630	15.4352	14.2649	13.2300	12.3122	11.4955	10.7667	10.1144
25	20.0393	18.0961	16.4305	14.9963	13.7556	12.6775	11.7366	10.9118
30	23.0153	20.4011	18.2204	16.3898	14.8432	13.5284	12.4038	11.4362
35	25.7184	22.3979	19.6999	17.4892	15.6626	14.1408	12.8629	11.7812
40	28.1737	24.1276	20.9728	18.3567	16.2800	14.5817	13.1787	12.0082
45	30.4039	25.6261	21.9335	19.0411	16.7451	14.8990	13.3960	12.1575
50	32.4296	26.9242	22.7690	19.5810	17.0956	15.1274	13.5454	12.2557

Yrs of income	If your money grows at this rate per year							
	5%	6%	7%	8%	9%	10%	11%	12%
And indexing is 4% multiply desired amount by this factor								
5	4.9057	4.8148	4.7274	4.6431	4.5618	4.4835	4.4079	4.3349
10	9.5821	9.1923	8.8282	8.4877	8.1691	7.8705	7.5905	7.3276
15	14.0401	13.1720	12.3854	11.6712	11.0215	10.4293	9.8884	9.3936
20	18.2898	16.7903	15.4712	14.3073	13.2770	12.3622	11.5476	10.8199
25	22.3410	20.0798	18.1480	16.4900	15.0605	13.8225	12.7455	11.8046
30	26.2029	23.0705	20.4700	18.2974	16.4708	14.9256	13.6105	12.4844
35	29.8843	25.7894	22.4842	19.7939	17.5860	15.7590	14.2350	12.9537
40	33.3938	28.2614	24.2314	21.0331	18.4678	16.3886	14.6859	13.2777
45	36.7392	30.5088	25.7471	22.0592	19.1651	16.8642	15.0115	13.5013
50	39.9284	32.2521	27.0619	22.9089	19.7165	17.2235	15.2466	13.6557

Yrs of income	If your money grows at this rate per year							
	5%	6%	7%	8%	9%	10%	11%	12%
And indexing is 5% multiply desired amount by this factor								
5	5.0009	4.9065	4.8165	4.7298	4.6462	4.5657	4.4879	4.4129
10	9.9998	9.5860	9.1995	8.8382	8.5003	8.1838	7.8871	7.6086
15	15.0010	14.0488	13.1878	12.4069	11.6972	11.0511	10.4617	9.9230
20	19.9998	18.3051	16.8171	15.5066	14.3490	13.3233	12.4117	11.5991
25	24.9987	22.3643	20.0196	18.1991	16.5487	15.1240	13.8886	12.8129
30	29.9999	26.2356	23.1248	20.5379	18.3733	16.6509	15.0073	13.6919
35	35.0011	29.9278	25.8594	22.5694	19.8868	17.6818	15.8546	14.3285
40	40.0022	33.3490	28.3479	24.3339	21.1423	18.5779	16.4963	14.7895
45	45.0011	36.8073	30.6123	25.8667	22.1837	19.2881	16.9824	15.1233
50	49.9999	40.0101	32.6728	27.1980	23.0475	19.8509	17.3506	15.3651

B

Marginal Tax Rate Tables

THESE TABLES SHOW THE 1998 MARGINAL tax rates for salary, interest, dividends and capital gains in each province plus the two territories.

The calculations were done by the national tax office of chartered accountants KPMG.

Although there are just three federal tax brackets, there are far more marginal rates. That's because of variations in provincial systems which, except for Quebec, are piggy-backed on Ottawa's take. There are so many variations that we've had to double up in some cases. Where two rates appear in the same bracket, footnotes indicate when the rate changes.

The tax brackets shown are for taxable — not gross — income. Taxable income is the amount midway on page 2 of the T1 return. That's after RRSP contributions and other deductions, but before the personal credits. Factor in your own deductions before using this table.

The basic personal non-refundable tax credit was taken into account. So were credits for Canada/Quebec Pension Plan and Employment Insurance premiums. There is a slight difference between some tax rates for salary and interest because the C/QPP and EI credits don't apply to interest.

No other credits were used.

Calculations for interest, dividends and capital gains assume there is also employment income. To find the appropriate rate:

1. Determine the taxable amount. For capital gains, the inclusion rate is 75%.

Therefore, the taxable amount on a $1,000 gain would be $750.

Gross up Canadian dividends actually received by 125%. If you receive $1,000 in dividends, the taxable amount would be $1,250.

2. Add the taxable investment income to your taxable salary and locate your tax bracket.

3. Read down to the lines for your province. The appropriate rate for capital gains is applied to the entire gain, not just the taxable portion. The appropriate rate for dividends is applied to the actual amount of dividends received, not the grossed-up amount. Marginal rates for net rental income would be the same as for interest.

APPENDIX B-1: **1998 Combined federal-provincial marginal tax rates (%)**

	Taxable Income					
Salary	**$6,735 to $29,590**	**$29,591 to $36,900**	**$36,901 to $39,000**	**$39,001 to $59,180**	**$59,181 to $63,440**	**$63,441 and over**
British Columbia[1]	24.3	38.0	38.8	39.5/40.7/44.6	49.8	50.4/54.2
Alberta[2]	23.8	36.9	37.7	38.3/39.3/40.4	45.0	45.6
Saskatchewan[3]	27.1	41.1	41.9	42.6/44.8/46.0	51.0	51.6
Manitoba[4]	26.4	40.1/42.1	43.0	43.7/44.8	49.5	50.1
Ontario[5]	23.1	36.1	36.8	37.5/38.7/40.9	45.5/49.7	50.3
Quebec[6]	32.3/35.3	43.0	44.2	45.2/46.3/49.4	52.0	52.6
New Brunswick[7]	26.0	40.6	41.5	42.3/43.4	48.4	49.0/50.4
Nova Scotia[8]	25.4	39.8	40.6	41.3/42.5	47.4	48.0/49.7
Prince Edward Island[9]	25.8	40.3	41.1	41.9/43.0/44.6	49.7	50.3
Newfoundland[10]	27.3	42.6	43.6	44.3/45.5	50.8/52.8	53.3
Yukon[11]	24.2	37.9	38.7	39.4/40.6	45.2/46.0	46.6
Northwest Territories[12]	23.4	36.6	37.4	38.1/39.3	43.8	44.4

Interest	**$6,459 to $29,590**	**$29,591 to $46,520**	**$46,521 to $59,180**	**$59,181 to $62,210**	**$62,211 and over**
British Columbia[1]	25.8	39.5	40.7/44.6%	49.8	50.4/54.2
Alberta[2]	25.2	38.3/39.3	40.4	45.0	45.6
Saskatchewan[3]	28.6	42.6/44.8	46.0	51.0	51.6
Manitoba[4]	27.9	41.7/43.7	44.8	49.5	50.1
Ontario[5]	24.5	37.5	38.7/40.9	45.6/49.7	50.3
Quebec[6]	34.5/37.5	45.2	46.3/49.4	52.0	52.6
New Brunswick[7]	27.6	42.3	43.4	48.4	49.0/50.4
Nova Scotia[8]	27.0	41.3	42.5	47.4	48.0/49.7
Prince Edward Island[9]	27.4	41.9	43.0/44.6	49.7	50.3
Newfoundland[10]	29.0	44.3	45.5/47.3	52.8	53.3
Yukon[11]	25.8	39.4	40.6	45.2/46.0	46.6
Northwest Territories[12]	24.9	38.1	39.3	43.8	44.4

Capital Gains	**$6,459 to $29,590**	**$29,591 to $46,520**	**$46,521 to $59,180**	**$59,181 to $62,210**	**$62,211 and over**
British Columbia[1]	19.4	29.6	30.5/33.5	37.3	37.8/40.6
Alberta[2]	18.9	28.8/29.4	30.3	33.8	34.2
Saskatchewan[3]	21.5	32.0/33.6	34.5	38.3	38.7
Manitoba[4]	20.9	31.2/32.7	33.6	37.2	37.6
Ontario[5]	18.4	28.1	29.0/30.7	34.2/37.3	37.7
Quebec[6]	25.9/28.1	33.9	34.8/37.0	39.0	39.5
New Brunswick[7]	20.7	31.7	32.6	36.3	36.8/37.8
Nova Scotia[8]	20.3	31.0	31.9	35.6	36.0/37.3
Prince Edward Island[9]	20.5	31.4	32.3/33.4	37.3	37.7
Newfoundland[10]	21.7	33.3	34.1/35.5	39.6	40.0
Yukon[11]	19.3	29.5	30.4	33.9/34.5	34.9
Northwest Territories[12]	18.7	28.6	29.4	32.8	33.3

	Taxable Income				
Dividends	**$6,459 to $29,690**	**$29,691 to $59,180**	**$59,181 to $88,530**	**$88,531 to $115,125**	**$115,126 and over**
British Columbia[1]	7.0	24.1	29.8	30.7/33.6	34.0/36.6
Alberta[2]	7.3	23.7	29.1/29.8	30.7	31.1
Saskatchewan[3]	9.9	26.3/27.4	33.2/35.0	35.9	36.3
Manitoba[4]	9.5	26.7/29.2	34.9	35.8	36.1
Ontario[5]	6.6	22.8	28.3	29.1/30.8/33.6	34.0
Quebec[6]	17.9/21.6	31.2/34.9	38.1	39.0	39.4
New Brunswick[7]	7.5	25.7	31.8	32.7	33.1/34.1
Nova Scotia[8]	7.3	25.2	31.1	32.0	32.4/33.5
Prince Edward Island[9]	7.4	25.5	31.5	32.4/33.6	34.0
Newfoundland[10]	7.8	27.0	33.4	34.3/35.6	36.0
Yukon[11]	6.9	24.0	29.7	30.6/31.0	31.4
Northwest Territories[12]	6.7	23.2	28.7	29.6	30.0

1 Secondary rate thresholds are $47,901, $56,220 and $79,470 for salary; $54,835 and $78,230 for interest/capital gains; $102,330 and $144,800 for dividends

2 Secondary rate thresholds are $46,450 and $47,901 for salary; $45,115 for interest/capital gains; $86,115 for dividends

3 Secondary rate thresholds are $40,840 and $47,901 for salary; $39,640 for interest/capital gains; $31,600 and $69,375 for dividends

4 Secondary rate thresholds are $30,000 and $47,901 for salary; $30,000 for interest/capital gains and dividends

5 Secondary rate thresholds are $47,901, $52,360 and $62,440 for salary; $50,975 and $61,180 for interest/capital gains; $95,925 and $113,250 for dividends

6 Secondary rate thresholds are $25,000, $47,901 and $50,000 for salary; $25,000 and $50,000 for interest, capital gains and dividends

7 Secondary rate thresholds are $47,901 and $96,650 for salary; $95,410 for interest/capital gains; $176,600 for dividends

8 Secondary rate thresholds are $47,901 and $80,310 for salary; $79,060 for interest/capital gains; $146,350 for dividends

9 Secondary rate thresholds are $47,901 and $49,470 for salary; $48,080 for interest/capital gains; $91,125 for dividends

10 Secondary rate thresholds are $47,901 and $59,820 for salary; $58,505 for interest/capital gains; $108,425 for dividends

11 Secondary rate thresholds are $47,901 and $61,730 for salary; $60,475 for interest/capital gains; $111,940 for dividends

12 Secondary rate threshold is $47,901 for salary

C

Canadian Life Expectancy

A LIFE EXPECTANCY TABLE REFLECTS AVERage longevity. For example, of men now aged 40, half will likely live less than 36.77 more years and half will likely live longer. The detailed projections on the next page are Statistics Canada's latest, based on 1990-92 data.

Those planning only to the stated life expectancy run a fair-sized risk of outliving their money. Check the probabilities on the table below. For example, a woman who is now 35 has a 10% chance of living past 95.

Male life expectancy					Female life expectancy				
Age now	Percentage chance of reaching				Age now	Percentage chance of reaching			
	80	85	90	95		80	85	90	95
35	42	25	11	3	35	62	45	26	10
40	42	25	11	3	40	62	45	26	10
45	43	25	11	3	45	63	46	26	10
50	44	26	11	3	50	64	46	27	11
55	45	26	12	3	55	65	47	27	11
60	47	28	12	4	60	66	48	28	11
65	51	30	13	4	65	69	50	29	12
70	58	34	15	4	70	74	54	31	12
75	72	42	19	5	75	83	60	35	14
80	100	59	26	8	80	100	72	42	17

Age now	Years left		Age now	Years left	
	Male	Female		Male	Female
20	55.58	61.67	50	27.65	32.80
21	54.64	60.69	51	26.77	31.89
22	53.70	59.71	52	25.90	30.98
23	52.77	58.73	53	25.04	30.08
24	51.83	57.75	54	24.19	29.19
25	50.89	56.77	55	23.35	28.30
26	49.94	55.80	56	22.53	27.42
27	49.00	54.82	57	21.71	26.55
28	48.05	53.84	58	20.91	25.69
29	47.11	52.86	59	20.12	24.83
30	46.17	51.89	60	19.35	23.98
31	45.22	50.91	61	18.59	23.15
32	44.28	49.94	62	17.85	22.31
33	43.34	48.96	63	17.13	21.49
34	42.39	47.99	64	16.42	20.68
35	41.45	47.02	65	15.72	19.88
36	40.51	46.05	66	15.04	19.09
37	39.58	45.09	67	14.37	18.31
38	38.64	44.12	68	13.72	17.54
39	37.71	43.16	69	13.08	16.78
40	36.77	42.20	70	12.46	16.03
41	35.84	41.24	71	11.85	15.30
42	34.91	40.28	72	11.27	14.57
43	33.98	39.33	73	10.70	13.87
44	33.06	38.38	74	10.15	13.18
45	32.14	37.44	75	9.61	12.50
46	31.23	36.50	76	9.10	11.85
47	30.32	35.57	77	8.60	11.21
48	29.42	34.64	78	8.13	10.59
49	28.53	33.72	79	7.67	9.99
			80	7.24	9.42

D

How to Build a Mortgage Table

THIS APPENDIX EXPLAINS HOW TO CALCULATE mortgage payments. It's only for the most committed!

First, you need the interest factor. That's the periodic interest rate, in this case monthly.

There is, however, a wrinkle. The weekly and biweekly factors on that table are based on a 365-day year. That means the periodic payments for a weekly schedule would be based on 365 divided by seven days, or 52.1429 per year. A few lenders use a 364- or 360-day year. If you want to be picky, determine your own factor by using the following formula. In each case, p equals the total days divided by the number of days in the payment period — for example, seven for a weekly payment.

$$\left[\left[1 + \frac{i}{c} \right]^c \right]^{(1/p)} - 1 \right] \times 100$$

Say the interest rate — i — is 8%. We divide 0.08 by the compounding frequency — c. That's 2, because standard Canadian mortgages compound semi-annually. (Remember that variable rate mortgages compound monthly.) We add 1 to get 1.04 and raise that to the power of c, or 2. That's 1.08160. Next we divide 1 by the payment frequency. Use 12 if the payment is monthly. The answer is 0.08333. Raise 1.08160 to the power of 0.08333 and you get 1.00656. Subtract 1 and multiply by 100 to get 0.65582.

Now we can go one of two routes — calculator or spreadsheet.

If you have a business calculator, you can easily determine the payment. Key the sample $100,000 loan amount and press PV for present value. Key the factor — 0.65582 — and press I. Key the total number of periodic payments and press N. Here, that's 300 — 12 months a year for 25 years. Press COMP and then PMT. Your answer should be 763.21, perhaps with a minus sign.

If you have a computer spreadsheet, plug those numbers into this formula:

$$\dfrac{\text{Loan amount}}{\left[\dfrac{1}{f} - \dfrac{1}{f\,(1+f)^{\,n}}\right]}$$

Our factor is f, but shove two zeroes in front to make it 0.0065582. Add 1 and raise that to the power of the number of payments — 300. That's 7.10669. Multiply that by 0.0065582 to get 0.04661. Divide 1 by that to get 21.45596. Divide 1 by 0.0065582 to get 152.48086. Subtract 21.45596 to get 131.02490. Divide the loan amount — 100,000 — by the whole shebang to get the monthly payment — 763.21.

Understand that if you use this for a weekly or biweekly mortgage, you're getting the straight amortization that won't save you a ton of money. As discussed in chapter 17, the real money-saving setups simply take the normal monthly payment and divide by four for weekly payments and two for biweekly ones.

Now you know why most people just use standard reference tables — or, better yet, commercially produced amortization software.

If you're a spreadsheeter building an amortization table for your own mortgage, start with payment 1. Multiply the $100,000 outstanding balance by the factor 0.0065582 to get 655.82. That's the interest component of this payment. Subtract that from the 763.21 payment amount and you'll see you're repaying 107.39 of principal. Subtract that from 100,000 to get 99,892.61. That's the outstanding balance for the next month. Repeat that cycle until the loan is paid off.

Once the spreadsheet is done, do you want to test the impact of a $1,000 prepayment? Just increase that month's payment amount by the prepayment, so the calculation uses $1,763.21.

Your spreadsheet probably won't match your lender's precisely, but you should be within a few cents on each payment and a few dollars over the total life.

TABLE D.1: Mortgage Interest Factors

This table shows the interest factor for each periodic mortgage payment. The biweekly and weekly factors are based on a 365-day year.

Mortgage rate	Interest factor Monthly	Interest factor Biweekly	Interest factor Weekly	Mortgage rate	Interest factor Monthly	Interest factor Biweekly	Interest factor Weekly	Mortgage rate	Interest factor Monthly	Interest factor Biweekly	Interest factor Weekly
5.000	0.41239	0.18960	0.09476	8.000	0.65582	0.30132	0.15055	11.00000	0.89634	0.41157	0.20557
5.125	0.42259	0.19429	0.09710	8.125	0.66590	0.30595	0.15286	11.12500	0.90630	0.41613	0.20785
5.250	0.43279	0.19897	0.09944	8.250	0.67597	0.31057	0.15516	11.25000	0.91625	0.42069	0.21012
5.375	0.44298	0.20365	0.10177	8.375	0.68604	0.31518	0.15747	11.37500	0.92620	0.42525	0.21240
5.500	0.45317	0.20833	0.10411	8.500	0.69611	0.31980	0.15977	11.50000	0.93615	0.42980	0.21467
5.625	0.46335	0.21300	0.10644	8.625	0.70617	0.32441	0.16207	11.62500	0.94609	0.43435	0.21694
5.750	0.47353	0.21767	0.10878	8.750	0.71622	0.32902	0.16438	11.75000	0.95602	0.43890	0.21921
5.875	0.48370	0.22234	0.11111	8.875	0.72627	0.33363	0.16668	11.87500	0.96595	0.44345	0.22148
6.000	0.49386	0.22701	0.11344	9.000	0.73631	0.33823	0.16897	12.00000	0.97588	0.44799	0.22375
6.125	0.50402	0.23167	0.11577	9.125	0.74635	0.34284	0.17127	12.12500	0.98580	0.45254	0.22601
6.250	0.51418	0.23634	0.11810	9.250	0.75639	0.34744	0.17357	12.25000	0.99572	0.45708	0.22828
6.375	0.52433	0.24099	0.12042	9.375	0.76641	0.35203	0.17586	12.37500	1.00563	0.46161	0.23054
6.500	0.53447	0.24565	0.12275	9.500	0.77644	0.35663	0.17816	12.50000	1.01553	0.46615	0.23280
6.625	0.54461	0.25030	0.12507	9.625	0.78646	0.36122	0.18045	12.62500	1.02543	0.47068	0.23506
6.750	0.55475	0.25496	0.12740	9.750	0.79647	0.36581	0.18274	12.75000	1.03533	0.47521	0.23732
6.875	0.56488	0.25960	0.12972	9.875	0.80648	0.37040	0.18503	12.87500	1.04522	0.47974	0.23958
7.000	0.57500	0.26425	0.13204	10.000	0.81648	0.37498	0.18732	13.00000	1.05511	0.48426	0.24184
7.125	0.58512	0.26889	0.13436	10.125	0.82648	0.37956	0.18960	13.12500	1.06499	0.48879	0.24409
7.250	0.59524	0.27353	0.13667	10.250	0.83648	0.38414	0.19189	13.25000	1.07487	0.49331	0.24635
7.375	0.60535	0.27817	0.13899	10.375	0.84647	0.38872	0.19417	13.37500	1.08474	0.49782	0.24860
7.500	0.61545	0.28281	0.14130	10.500	0.85645	0.39330	0.19645	13.50000	1.09461	0.50234	0.25085
7.625	0.62555	0.28744	0.14362	10.625	0.86643	0.39787	0.19874	13.62500	1.10447	0.50685	0.25311
7.750	0.63565	0.29207	0.14593	10.750	0.87641	0.40244	0.20102	13.75000	1.11433	0.51136	0.25535
7.875	0.64574	0.29670	0.14824	10.875	0.88637	0.40700	0.20330	13.87500	1.12418	0.51587	0.25760

Index